Historical Archaeology

This readable introduction to historical archaeology focuses on modern history in all its fascinating regional, cultural, and ethnic diversity. Accessibly covering key methods and concepts, including fundamental theories and principles, the history of the field, and basic definitions, *Historical Archaeology* also includes a practical look at career prospects for interested readers. Orser discusses central topics of archaeological research such as time and space, survey and excavation methods, and analytical techniques, encouraging readers to consider the possible meanings of artifacts. Drawing on the author's extensive experience as an historical archaeologist, the book's perspective ranges from the local to the global in order to demonstrate the real importance of this subject to our understanding of the world in which we live today.

The third edition of this popular textbook has been significantly revised and expanded to reflect recent developments and discoveries in this exciting area of study. Each chapter includes updated case studies that demonstrate the research conducted by professional historical archaeologists. With its engaging approach to the subject, *Historical Archaeology* continues to be an ideal resource for readers who wish to be introduced to this rapidly expanding global field.

Charles E. Orser, Jr. is Research Professor of Anthropology at Vanderbilt University, USA. He is the author of over 90 professional articles and a number of books, and is the founding editor of the *International Journal of Historical Archaeology*.

Historical Archaeology

Third Edition

Charles E. Orser, Jr.

Routledge
Taylor & Francis Group

NEW YORK AND LONDON

Third edition published 2017
by Routledge
711 Third Avenue, New York, NY 10017

and by Routledge
2 Park Square, Milton Park, Abingdon, Oxon OX14 4RN

Routledge is an imprint of the Taylor & Francis Group, an informa business

First edition published by Harper Collins College Publishers 1995

Second edition published by Pearson Education Inc. 2004

British Library Cataloguing in Publication Data
A catalogue record for this book is available from the British Library

Library of Congress Cataloging-in-Publication Data
Names: Orser, Charles E., author.
Title: Historical archaeology / Charles E. Orser, Jr.
Description: Third edition. | Abingdon, Oxon : Routledge, 2016. | Includes index.
Identifiers: LCCN 2016004565 | ISBN 9781138126053 (pbk. : alk. paper) |
  ISBN 9781315647128 (ebook)
Subjects: LCSH: Archaeology and history.
Classification: LCC CC77.H5 O77 2016 | DDC 930.1—dc23
  LC record available at https://lccn.loc.gov/2016004565

ISBN: 978-1-138-12605-3 (pbk)
ISBN: 978-1-315-64712-8 (ebk)

Typeset in Frutiger and Sabon
by Apex CoVantage, LLC

To Janice

Contents

Contents

Contents

Figures

Preface

Archaeology is an odd discipline. Most people have heard of it and think they know what it is, but when questioned, they actually know very little about it. Archaeology is perhaps the most famous and yet least understood academic pursuit in existence. Movies depict archaeologists either as bold adventurers or as absentminded scholars digging in the shadows of lofty pyramids. Television programs and websites show archaeologists cutting through dense jungles, poring over clay tablets, and getting excited about ancient stone tools and faint drawings on cave walls. These images, though often quite fanciful, are not completely inaccurate. Archaeologists do get excited about what they do; they love the past and want to share their passion with all who will listen. Archaeology is both an adventure and a sophisticated discipline studying the entire spectrum of human history. Archaeologists examine the full range of human life, from our simple origins to our present-day urban landfills.

Archaeology, like most of today's academic disciplines, has a number of specializations. No one can be expected to know everything about the entire sweep of human history. As a result, some archaeologists study ancient ways of life, while others concentrate on more recent history. This book explores the archaeology that focuses on modern history in all its fascinating regional, cultural, and ethnic diversity. Its perspective ranges from the small and local to the huge and global.

Historical archaeology, the archaeological study of the past 500 years, or since about 1492 C.E. (or in some cases even slightly earlier), has expanded dramatically in recent years. This book provides an introduction to this exciting field by covering its basic methods and concepts. The text is divided into three sections. Section I, "Foundations of Historical Archaeology," addresses the basic elements of the field. The first chapter defines the field and outlines its general goals. A brief history of the field is presented in the next chapter. This information is important because students of historical archaeology must understand the field's growing pains and appreciate how archaeologists struggled to create the discipline. The next chapter presents definitions of culture, society, and cultural changes, and outlines the major site types studied by historical archaeologists. The final chapter in the section explores two central topics of archaeological research—time and space—with special reference to historical archaeology. Dating methods and the use of GIS are presented here. Section II is entitled "Doing Historical Archaeology." Its five chapters present information about archaeological surveying, non-excavation research, excavation methods, analytical techniques, and the possible meanings of artifacts. The final chapter presents information about cultural resource management, an environment in which most historical archaeologists currently find employment. Section III, "Interpretation in Historical Archaeology," explores the complex subject of archaeological interpretation in four chapters. The final chapter in the section explains some of the challenges facing historical archaeology and the directions some archaeologists are taking the field.

Major references for further study are provided at the end of the book. A glossary is also presented as an easy guide to some of the archaeologists' more technical terms.

This third edition has been significantly revised and expanded. I have corrected the mistakes from the first two editions and updated many of the examples. I have also expanded the references to include works of importance published since the second edition. At the end of each chapter, I include a brief "site visit." These are vignettes based on archeological and historical research conducted by professional historical archaeologists. They are intended to indicate the richness of today's historical archaeology. I have included sites I think are interesting or that have something especially enlightening to say. I could easily have chosen 13 other sites because the field today is so vast and varied. My hope is that these brief examples will encourage students to explore historical archaeology further.

No one book can hope to offer an exhaustive overview of today's historical archaeology. The field is simply expanding far too rapidly for that. My goal, therefore, is to offer this brief volume to give you insights into the fascinating world of historical archaeology. An exciting field of study awaits you and you are very welcome to join us!

Charles E. Orser, Jr.
Vanderbilt University

Acknowledgments

I am deeply grateful to all my colleagues who assisted me during the arduous task of writing this book. Many individuals graciously answered questions, supplied information, and provided illustrations, including: Douglas Armstrong, Uzi Baram, Kevin Barton, Mary Beaudry, Colin Breen, Stephen Brighton, Eleanor Casella, David Colin Crass, James Delle, Charles Ewen, Richard A. Fox, Pedro Funari, Barry Gaulton, John Halsey, Scott Hamilton, Donald Hardesty, Edward C. Harris, Robert Hoover, Katherine Hull, Gerald Kelso, Hanley Kruczek-Aaron, Susan Kepecs, Adria La Violette, Susan Lawrence, Kenneth Lewis, Donald Linebaugh, Barbara Little, Randall McGuire, Rochelle A. Marrinan, Allan Meyers, Stephen Mrozowski, Robert Paynter, Jacqui Pearce, Adrian and Mary Praetzellis, Jonathan Prangnell, David Ryder, Prudence Rice, Kathryn Sampeck, Elizabeth Scott, Paul Shackel, Peter Schmidt, Gregory Waselkov, Steve Wernke, Suzanne Spencer-Wood, Jonathan Thayn, Douglas Veltre, Barbara Voss, Gifford Waters, W. Haio Zimmermann, and Rebecca Yamin. Please forgive me if I have inadvertently left some-one out; my oversight was not intentional.

I would like to thank my colleagues in the Vanderbilt University Department of Anthropology for creating a scholarly and professional environment for research. Specifically, I wish to acknowledge the support and assistance of Beth Conklin, Bill Fowler, Steve Wernke, and Tom Dillehay. I would also like to thank the students in the Historical Archaeology course for their comments and suggestions. I also wish to thank Jane Landers, of the Department of History, for her encouragement and support.

I also appreciate the guidance and assistance of Matthew Gibbons, Lola Harre, Autumn Spalding, and Estalita Slivosky, and all the wonderful people who helped me prepare this text. The staff's professionalism has been an inspiration. It has been a joy working with them.

I also wish to extend my most heartfelt thanks to Janice L. Orser, who assisted with editing, reading, and many other much-appreciated tasks. This book could never have been written without her.

Foundations of Historical Archaeology

Chapter 1

What Is Historical Archaeology?

In the year 1781, Thomas Jefferson, the future president of the United States, retired to the peace of his country estate at Monticello, Virginia, where he indulged a passion for academic research (Figure 1.1). Surrounded by "his family, his farm, and his books," Jefferson sat down to compile a lengthy discourse, which he entitled *Notes on the State of Virginia*. He wrote of laws and money and of products "animal, vegetable, and mineral." He was especially interested in the native peoples of his beloved state, and like many learned men of the time, he wondered about their origins. European settlers in America asked about the builders of the silent earthen mounds that dotted the landscape of the eastern United States. In some places, the mounds were majestic and flat-topped, in others small and rounded. Were the Moundbuilders a vanished race who had migrated to the New World, perhaps from as far away as the Holy Land? Had they constructed the great mounds after battling and subjugating the Native Americans around them? Or were the mysterious earthworks built by the forebears of the Native Americans who still lived in eastern North America? Were the mounds built by someone else entirely?

Jefferson was cautious and initially decided not to take a stand on the Moundbuilders' origins. The debate raged for years among his friends, in the coffee houses of Philadelphia and Boston, and with antiquarians around the world. But unlike his contemporaries, Jefferson decided to use excavation to find conclusive information about the mysterious people.

Jefferson chose an earthwork near the Rivanna River, a small mound that was a "repository of the dead" (Figure 1.2). In 1784, his slaves dug a perpendicular trench through the earthwork so that he might "examine its internal structure." He recorded layers of human bones at different depths, many lying in complete confusion, "so as, on the whole, to give the idea of bones emptied promiscuously from a bag or basket."

The story of America's first scientific archaeological excavation, one of the earliest in the world, is well known. Jefferson was the first scientist to identify the Moundbuilders as Native Americans. He stands as the first person in the history of archaeology to make a careful and, for his day, scientific excavation of a Native American burial mound.

But even Jefferson, the great thinker that he was, would never have guessed that he and his contemporaries—the slaves who performed the digging, the carriage driver who drove him to the earthwork, and the merchant who sold him the paper on which to pen his pioneering

Figure 1.1 Thomas Jefferson, early American archaeologist
(Burstein Collection/Corbis)

Figure 1.2 Earthen mound in the eastern United States
(From *Ancient Monuments of the Mississippi Valley* by E. G. Squier and E. H. Davis, 1847.)

notes—would one day themselves become the subject of archaeological study. Little would Jefferson suspect that two centuries later, archaeologists would comb through the soils of his estate searching for the relics of bygone eras. Perhaps he would be surprised to learn that the many common, and to him, uninteresting objects he and his contemporaries used in their daily lives would be unearthed with the same care and wonder that he felt toward the smoking pipes and copper ornaments of the ancient North American Moundbuilders. Jefferson might even be delighted to discover that archaeology is now as much a part of the study of history as are historic buildings, faded documents, and government archives.

Dividing Human History

Eccentric pith-helmeted professors, ragged adventurers overcoming myriad dangers to retrieve a priceless relic, and excavations in the shadow of great pyramids are all popular images of archaeology. Most people know that archaeology deals with ancient history and with old things, but beyond that, they may know nothing more concrete about the discipline. Agatha Christie, the famed mystery writer and wife of acclaimed British archaeologist Sir Max Mallowan, reinforced the idea that archaeologists are interested in old things when she remarked that she liked being married to an archaeologist because the older she became, the more he liked her!

Many people assume that archaeology focuses only on the old and the venerated, and the older the better. Nothing could be further from the truth. Today's archaeologists study the entire range of human history, from our origins in East Africa more than 2.5 million years ago to Victorian railroad stations, nineteenth-century mining towns, and twentieth-century missile silos. Some archaeologists even spend their careers researching modern garbage dumps and landfills as a way of studying contemporary waste management. Others are studying World War II camps and fortifications, and even the remains of Cold War installations. Modern archaeology is not treasure hunting, nor is it the search for mysterious lost worlds; *archaeology is simply the systematic study of humans in the past.* This general definition covers not only ancient technology and human behavior, but also social organization, religious belief, material culture, and all aspects of human culture throughout history.

For convenience, archaeologists and historians often divide the enormous span of human existence into ancient history and modern history. These terms substitute for the once common "prehistoric" and "historic," ideas once dividing prehistoric archaeology from historical archaeology. Careful thinking about the meaning of these terms, however, has meant that the old terms are no longer acceptable.

The division of time is merely an artificial convenience because history is actually an unbroken flow of time. All past times are history. Many archaeologists have chosen not to segment time at all, preferring to envision history as it is—one long continuous stream of days, months, seasons, and years. Some archaeologists have even written about the "death of prehistory." The segmentation of time, no matter how artificial, however, merely facilitates analysis. Individual archaeologists generally do not study the entire span of human history. The past is too complex for easy interpretation, so individual archaeologists usually become specialists in one particular era of history.

Given the complexity of human history and the diversity of the world's cultural traditions, artificial divisions help archaeologists segment time into broad categories. For the sake of this text, it is useful to divide human history into three broad categories: oral cultures, textual cultures of antiquity, and textual cultures of the modern era (Figure 1.3).

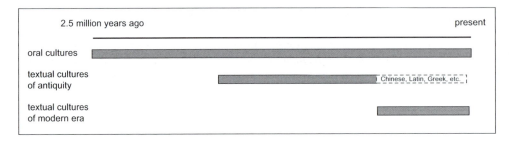

Figure 1.3 Representation of oral, ancient textual, and modern textual
cultures
(Charles E. Orser, Jr.)

About 99 percent of all human cultures have used oral communication exclusively. Archaeologists in the past once referred to ancient, non-literate times as "prehistory," and they described their field as "prehistoric archaeology." Since about the 1990s, however, this term has been used less and less because archaeologists have acknowledged that non-literate cultures can still be found in a few places. These still-living cultures are clearly not part of "prehistory" because they share the world with us. Equating existing cultures with ancient times can be viewed as a subtle form of racism because some people may read "prehistoric" as "primitive." For this reason, archaeologists must think differently about how to segment human history into convenient categories.

Archaeologists investigate how early oral societies all over the world came into being, how they differed from one another, and how they changed through time. The research constitutes the main source of information on the earliest development of cultures the world over. Cultural anthropologists still visit cultures that prefer to use oral communication over written texts. Even cultures that have adopted written language may still prefer to pass along their traditions orally.

Archaeologists know, however, that literate societies were created in antiquity. Writing appeared in Mesopotamia and in the Nile Valley about 5,000 years ago. Literate civilization developed in northwest India in about 2000 B.C.E., in northern China by about the same time, and among the Maya of Central America about the third century B.C.E.

Archaeologists have examined these textual cultures of antiquity for many years, and many of the world's most spectacular discoveries have come from the earliest civilizations. The royal library of Assyrian King Assurbanipal from Nineveh, the gold-rich tomb of Egyptian pharaoh Tutankhamun, the terra-cotta regiment buried at the tomb of Chinese emperor Xuang Ti in the second century B.C.E. are excellent examples. The investigation of these sites can be characterized as *text-aided archaeology: archaeology carried out with the aid of historical documentation.*

Many specialties exist within text-aided archaeology. Assyriologists, Egyptologists, Mayanists, and Sinologists (specialists in Chinese civilization) are just a few of the archaeologists who focus on single societies or even minute details of a single period. In addition, classical archaeologists study the civilizations of Greece and Rome, and European medieval archaeologists investigate the abbeys, ruined churches, and residential settlements of people throughout the continent. Scholars in these text-aided realms of research concentrate on architecture and changing art styles as well as on the economic and social circumstances of past life.

The archaeology of "modern" history—called "historical archaeology" and "modern-world archaeology"—is *the archaeological study of people documented in recent history* (generally conceived as the past 500 years). This includes Jefferson and his contemporaries and is the subject of this book.

Historical archaeology is the archaeology of the relatively recent past. It is a past including both the colonial and early modern history most people learn in school, as well as the well-remembered history unfolding in living people's lifetimes. The latter is of vital importance. For historical archaeologists, the history that people carry around in their heads—their own personal experiences—is often as important, and sometimes more so, than the "official" histories in books. Historical archaeology breathes life into an arid history composed only of dates and names; it animates history with the lives of real people going about their daily tasks. It treats kings and queens (the rich and famous) the same as the common folk (the anonymous makers of history). Historical archaeologists study a multicultural past composed of Europeans, African Americans, Native Americans, Chinese, immigrants, prostitutes, merchants, convicts, and entrepreneurs; in short, all the people who built the "modern" world. Too often, the writers of history's documents ignored the often-anonymous millions. Historical archaeology offers exciting opportunities to study changing social roles and the ways in which our world today was shaped by the actions and attitudes of the past.

A clear overlap exists between text-aided archaeology and historical archaeology. Historical archaeologists are text-aided archaeologists, but not all text-aided archaeologists are historical archaeologists. Both archaeologists employ the same techniques to locate historical records and the same critical methods to evaluate them. The difference is that historical archaeologists are interested in the most recent past, approximately the past 500 years or so. Text-aided archaeologists can be interested in ancient Egypt, medieval Germany, or nineteenth-century Japan.

Historical archaeology is important not only because it provides a means to examine the past, but because it also has the potential to teach us about our world. We may not be able to relate to the circumstances faced by people who lived many centuries ago—except on the most basic human level—but we can certainly achieve an understanding of the long-forgotten and often-compelling histories of once-anonymous folk from the eighteenth century. We are the descendants of these men and women.

British archaeologist Stuart Piggott once described archaeology as the "science of rubbish." He is partially right. Historical archaeologists do spend much of their time looking into old garbage heaps and abandoned dwellings, and their interest in the mundane things of the past allows them to find value in the most prosaic details of day-to-day history. These are the minute aspects of daily life left out of government reports and census records. Excavations at Red Bay, Labrador, have revealed astoundingly comprehensive information about sixteenth-century Basque whaling in the Strait of Belle Isle off the coast of northeastern Canada. The survival of traditional African beliefs is revealed through telltale artifacts excavated in the Caribbean. Sites on both sides of the Atlantic document the African Diaspora in minute detail, towns in Mexico and Peru show how indigenous Indians interacted with Spanish officials, and the towns inhabited by Christianized Indians in New England reveal a history long forgotten by most of the public. Whatever the place and time, the trowels of archaeologists add an engrossing dimension to world history over the past 500 years. Their findings are not accessible through other means. Only excavation can provide the missing information.

The archaeology of ancient history documents the emerging biologic and cultural diversity of humankind. It shows us how our earliest ancestors faced and solved the challenges of daily existence. Many of these problems, except for their antiquity, are not all that different from the dilemmas of survival faced by much of humanity today. In contrast, historical archaeology, because of its more recent focus, holds a mirror directly before the face of the contemporary world and reflects the complex roots of our own increasingly diverse societies. This unique reflection is a vital tool for achieving a better understanding of ourselves. Small wonder, then, that the rapidly growing field of historical archaeology is becoming a useful tool for social scientists and historians alike.

The Roots of Today's Historical Archaeology

Historical archaeology has deep roots in the historical preservation movement. In its earliest days, historical archaeology was a full partner in the often-herculean efforts to interpret sites of national importance to an eager public. In the United States, archaeology at places like Jamestown and Colonial Williamsburg, both in Virginia, provided many of the architectural details that made historic homes and their yards come alive for modern visitors. But architecture alone was not enough. It was clear that the lives of once-living men and women had to be included within the reconstructed buildings and landscapes. Modern historical archaeology grew out of this realization.

The new discipline borrowed much from all the other kinds of archaeology practiced before it, including many of its excavation methods and analytical techniques. But throughout its development, historical archaeology has also invented its own rich perspectives and methods. The definition of the discipline changed as the number of archaeologists engaged in the study of recent history increased. The varied interests of its rapidly growing number of practitioners have meant that the field presents an engrossing array of research opportunities and different ways of approaching history.

Historical Archaeology as the Study of a Period of History

In the beginning, many archaeologists saw historical archaeology simply as a study of a period of history. The Conference on Historic Sites Archaeology was the first professional organization dedicated to historical archaeology founded in the United States. When it was organized in 1960 at the University of Florida, its expressed purpose was to focus on the "historical" period, a time defined as "post-prehistoric" (literally meaning "after prehistory"). Soon afterward, archaeologist Robert Schuyler defined historical archaeology as "the study of the material remains from any historic period." This viewpoint is consistent with the idea that human history is like a layer cake, with the bottommost, thickest layer being prehistoric times and the thin top layer being the historical period. In between prehistory and history is a poorly defined intermediate era that is neither prehistory nor history.

Such distinctions, though easy to understand, cause problems when studying actual examples from the past. In thinking about that part of New England colonized by English settlers in the seventeenth century, we might say that the Europeans were "historic" (because they were from a literate culture) and that the Native Americans they encountered were "prehistoric" (because they had an oral culture). Upon contact, we might say the natives were "protohistoric" (because they used some European objects but conducted themselves in ways not terribly different from those of their ancestors; who we might in turn describe as "prehistoric"). The problem arises because all cultures—regardless of when they existed in time—made history, just as we do today. It is therefore logically inaccurate to refer to Native Americans as "prehistoric" when they lived alongside European immigrants. The appellation "prehistoric" makes them appear primitive and uncultured, a view that is most certainly incorrect. The terms "history," "protohistory," and "prehistory" are thus mere conventions, useful only in the broadest sense for segmenting history for analytical purposes. As terms of definition, they have little true value.

The broadly defined historical archaeology envisioned by Schuyler incorporates numerous subfields, including classical archaeology, medieval archaeology, post-medieval archaeology, historic sites archaeology, industrial archaeology, and what he calls "a series of mainly unnamed areas of research such as the study of literate civilizations in India and the Islamic world." These subfields are firmly rooted in different periods of the past. Classical archaeologists study a period beginning with the Minoans around 3000 B.C.E. and ending with the Later Roman Empire at about 527 C.E.; medieval archaeologists concentrate roughly on the 400 to 1400 C.E. period; post-medieval archaeologists focus on the period from 1450 to 1750 C.E.; historic sites archaeology considers the period from 1415 C.E. to industrialization; and industrial archaeology studies the world's complex technologies after about 1750 C.E. These subfields were originally linked with various parts of the world. Classical archaeology is associated with the Mediterranean and Europe, medieval and post-medieval archaeology with Europe, historic sites archaeology with the world colonized by the European superpowers, and industrial archaeology with Europe and the European post-colonial world. The periods of emphasis for the subfields are somewhat arbitrary—for example, the post-medieval period in Scotland is considered to extend from 1488 to 1609, while in England it is 1450 to 1750. Their usage demonstrates how historical archaeology can be seen to focus on a broadly conceived "historical period." Schuyler's "historic sites archaeology" approximately corresponds to our sense of historical archaeology.

The situation in Great Britain, as suggested by Schuyler's use of the term "post-medieval archaeology," was different from that in the United States. The archaeology practiced throughout Europe was not institutionally linked with anthropology, and as a result, post-medieval archaeology developed as an extension of medieval archaeology, a subject matter that was clearly text-aided. Early post-medieval archaeologists, like many of their contemporaries in the United States and Canada, were interested in learning more about the artifacts they were uncovering at sites occupied in relatively recent times. In 1963, K. J. Barton and John Hurst launched the Post-Medieval Ceramic Research Group in Bristol to serve as a forum for the detailed examination of glazed ceramics, a most important source for archaeologists. Barton and Hurst established 1450 as their initial date of interest and their end date as 1750.

In England, the development of post-medieval archaeology was also closely linked to "landscape history." This area of research, often completed on the local level, included the examination of house styles, rural village locations, the construction of roadways, and changes in field boundaries. These often-brilliant studies typically combined historical research with field examination. The multidisciplinary approach their practitioners promoted is a hallmark of today's historical archaeology.

Only three years after the creation of the ceramic study group, interest in the archaeology of post-medieval history had grown so large the organizers disbanded the ceramic group and started the Society for Post-Medieval Archaeology, one of today's most prestigious bodies of historical archaeologists. Much of the interest of the Society's members remains dedicated to 1450–1750 history, but most post-medieval archaeologists now extend their interests up to the present. Post-medieval archaeology in the United Kingdom, and throughout Europe, is today a vibrant and active field, and archaeologists there are making many exciting discoveries.

As a purely analytical convention, a central idea encompassed by the term the "historical period" is that it consists of those times for which written information is available. This is what ties the subfields together. In a famous definition, James Deetz stated, "the literacy of the people it studies is what sets historical archaeology apart from prehistory." The association of historical archaeology with "history"—it is more accurate now to write the "discipline of history"—brings to the fore the important point that many of the methods used by historical archaeologists are those of professional historians.

The understanding that historical archaeologists often conduct research like historians once led to the view that historical archaeology is really just a method. Thus, historical archaeology is unrestricted in time. The field is only a research method resting on the combination of historical sources and archaeological data. In the strictest sense, research in Mayan civilization, Roman Britain, and pharaohic Egyptology all constitute historical archaeology. The periods of history are different in each field of inquiry, but in each, archaeologists use a combination of so-called "nonarchaeological" materials with archaeological data. They work as both historians and archaeologists.

Definitions that focus on the methodological aspects of historical archaeology give written records precedence over chronology. Under this rubric, we may consider Heinrich Schliemann's use of Homer's texts in his excavations at Troy in 1871 as an example of historical archaeology, as were Neville Chittick's excavations at the fourteenth-century Swahili town of Kilwa on the East Africa coast in the 1960s. We could conclude that Chittock was a historical archaeologist because he combined Islamic chronicles with archaeological materials. By the same token, Robin Birley studied letters written on thin slivers of wood from the Roman frontier fort at Vindolanda on Hadrian's Wall in northern Britain. These writings provide priceless information on Roman garrison life in the first century C.E. Under this restricted sense of historical archaeology, Birley would be a practitioner of the field.

The dates of a site's occupation are not important under the broad definition of historical archaeology. What takes precedence is the presence of some form of written text—transcribed on paper, clay, stone, or whatever—that may be used by archaeologists in their efforts to interpret the past. In the late nineteenth century, British classical archaeologist David G. Hogarth distinguished between "literary documents" (that is, writings) and "material documents" (artifacts) in an effort to explain how archaeologists use "nonarchaeological" pieces of information in their research. The combined interpretation of these different kinds of "documents" defines how historical archaeology can be viewed as a methodology.

The methodological definition can be drawn even wider by including some alternate but valuable sources of historical information obtained from ethnohistory and oral history. *Ethnohistory* is *the study of the past using non-Western, indigenous historical records, including oral traditions.* Like historical archaeology, ethnohistory rests upon the combined use of different sources of information. It often focuses on peoples who are known to have existed in the past but who are recognized largely through the writings of outsiders or through orally transmitted accounts.

Ethnohistory

Ethnohistory became vitally important in the United States with the creation of the Indian Claims Commission in August 1946. Native groups and governmental agencies required the testimony of experts when the government began the process of terminating native tribal status. Anthropologists began to work as historians in archives and other documentary repositories, and historians started to work as anthropologists as they researched the histories of nonliterate peoples and used ethnological concepts.

In the case *Sac and Fox Tribe of Indians, et al. v. The United States,* filed in 1955, for example, the Native American defendants hired ethnohistorians to prepare scholarly reports about their history and culture. Defendant's Exhibit 97 is entitled "An Anthropological Report on the Indian Occupancy [of land] Ceded to the United States by the United Tribes of Sac and Fox under the Treaty of November 3, 1804." These legal documents, centrally important to the case, provide significant cultural information. For instance, Defendant's Exhibit 57, "An Account of the Manners and Customs of the Sauk Nation of Indians," begins: "The original and present name of the Sauk Indians proceeds from the compound word Saw-kie alias A-saw-we-kee literally Yellow Earth. The Fox Indians call themselves Mess-qua-a-kie alias Mess-qua-we-kie literally Red Earth." Claims Commission reports contain invaluable ethnohistorical information about Native American history and culture, ranging from games and dances to cosmology and language. The documents demonstrate the interpretive power of ethnohistorical interpretation.

When Hernán Cortés and his conquistadors entered the Aztec capital, Tenochtitlán, in 1519, they marveled at the sophisticated, cosmopolitan city. Its market was larger than Constantinople's (today's Istanbul). Cortés overthrew the Aztec rulers in 1521, bringing a vibrant civilization to an end. Fortunately, however, Dominican friar Bernardino de Sahagún developed a passion for Aztec culture and devoted his lifetime to recording their history. He assembled informants at strategic missions and recorded many details of a culture that transmitted information with picture signs and oral recitations. Sahagún's *History of the General Things of New Spain* was considered so heretical by his priestly superiors that it was not published until the nineteenth century. But his work is a mine of priceless ethnohistorical information for today's archaeologists and cultural historians. When Mexican archaeologist Eduardo Matos Moctezuma excavated the Templo Mayor (Great Temple) of the Aztec gods Huitzilopochtli and Tlaloc from beneath modern Mexico City, he found that many details of the structure and its history were corroborated by both Spanish accounts and Sahagún's informants.

Ethnohistory is a powerful tool for historical archaeologists, especially when combined with archaeological and conventional historical sources. It is a truly multidisciplinary form of research.

Oral History

Oral history is *historical tradition, often genealogies, passed down from generation to generation by word of mouth*. It is transitory history in the sense that it lives in the memory, destined to vanish if not written down or passed on to the next generation. Much oral history is understandably related to family history, for tracing ties back to ancestral kin is a major concern of many societies. Maya lords were obsessed with establishing their royal legitimacy back to divine ancestors, and many Africans think of the past in terms of links to ancestors who are intermediaries with the spiritual world. Many men and women in Western societies are equally interested in understanding their genealogies and many of them spend their vacations squinting at faded manuscripts and scrolling through microfilmed or online census rolls housed in the world's archives or posted on genealogical websites.

Oral traditions treat far more than genealogies, however. They include vivid personal memories of major events like solar eclipses, wars, floods, and famines, of nineteenth-century family migrations from east to west or west to east, and so forth. Only in recent years have we fully appreciated the value of the historical memories of elderly people. In far too many cases, these valuable repositories of personal history pass away unnoticed, and their priceless legacies of historical information is lost forever.

The study of oral history has achieved great sophistication in numerous places around the world, including sub-Saharan Africa, which is rich in eighteenth- and nineteenth-century oral tradition. Many of the accounts were recorded early in the twentieth century, when memories were still vivid. Such traditions are a historical minefield, for they require careful critical analysis before they can be accepted as accurate reflections of the past.

When archaeologist Peter Schmidt studied the ancient Buhaya kingdoms in East Africa, he combined oral traditions with data from archaeological and historical sources. Schmidt spent two to four hours with each informant as he learned the art of extracting relevant information from individuals who had acquired a lifetime's experience. He had to learn how to evaluate the Buhaya's rich mythology about the people's cultural origins and early migrations, and then he had to correlate the accounts with the archaeological sites he had discovered in the field. Schmidt used the myths to tie the sites together, and in combining archaeology with oral history, he provided a truly insightful study of Iron Age metalworking.

Oral history is a vital tool in more recent history, especially when studying the experiences of ethnic groups and working class and poor families. Beginning as a kind of local history focused on what people could remember about themselves and their times, oral researchers, working in places like urban neighborhoods, realized that much recent history was not written down. Instead, this history was almost entirely remembered. Tracking down oral traditions required archaeologists to adopt the field methods of anthropologists and folklorists, scholars who had long experience with collecting and interpreting oral information. During his time in Tanzania, for example, Schmidt heard several stories about the founding of the Buhaya kingdoms and many accounts of their royal lineages. In one tale, he learned how the king Rugomora Mahe traveled through his domains, eventually arriving at a place where some people were smelting iron, a prehistoric technology documented by Schmidt's research. "They failed to welcome Rugomora, who, then, out of pique, changed their clan name to *Bahuge,* or 'the dull ones.'" Traveling further, Rugomora saw more people making iron tools, and he became inspired to "build a tower to the heavens to see what they looked like." Schmidt's informant told him he knew the precise spot where the iron for Rugomora's tower was smelted.

Thinking of historical archaeology as a methodology brings out a critical point. Like all archaeology, historical archaeology is a multidisciplinary enterprise. Archaeologists of ancient history draw on the researches of botanists, chemists, and zoologists, as well as scholars from other fields. Historical archaeologists do the same, but they use an even greater diversity of sources, including everything from documents to oral traditions, from photographs to the minute details of the technology of making nails (Figure 1.4). Historical archaeology is truly multidisciplinary detective work, the only limit being the archaeologist's creativity and ingenuity.

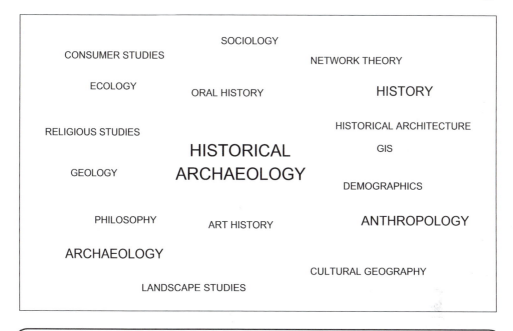

SOCIOLOGY

CONSUMER STUDIES

NETWORK THEORY

ECOLOGY

ORAL HISTORY

HISTORY

RELIGIOUS STUDIES

HISTORICAL ARCHITECTURE

GIS

HISTORICAL ARCHAEOLOGY

GEOLOGY

DEMOGRAPHICS

PHILOSOPHY

ART HISTORY

ANTHROPOLOGY

ARCHAEOLOGY

CULTURAL GEOGRAPHY

LANDSCAPE STUDIES

Figure 1.4 Historical archaeology and its many associates
(Charles E. Orser, Jr.)

Historical Archaeology Today

It is certainly true that historical archaeology is an archaeological field of inquiry that has a central methodology of combining archival research with archaeological excavation. Viewed in this way, historical archaeology may be broadly defined as a method of research. In truth, however, all archaeologists regardless of their era of interest regularly use written documents of many kinds. Even archaeologists investigating humanity's earliest ancestors read reports written by other archaeologists, geological texts, environmental records, and early traveler's accounts.

Given this reality of research, most historical archaeologists today agree they use an archaeological-historical method, but they would add that their field is defined more by what they study than simply how they study it. In a now-classic definition, James Deetz defined historical archaeology as "the archaeology of the spread of European culture throughout the world since the fifteenth century and its impact on indigenous peoples." Although Deetz's definition contains an element of time—"since the fifteenth century"—his main idea is that historical archaeology is the archaeology of a specific subject, namely the spread of Europeans and European culture and institutions throughout the world by adventurers, explorers, merchants, and traders. As these Europeans traveled outward from their homelands and into Africa, the Far East, the New World, and the Pacific, they carried with them the ideas, perceptions, and material things with which they were familiar. Scholars sometimes refer to the interconnected network of European outposts, trading ports, and towns as a "modern world system." Historical archaeology is unique as the archaeology that studies this system and the spread of ideas and people that were part of it.

This understanding assumes that historical archaeology is a combined anthropological and historical study of the modern world. By "modern world," historical archaeologists mean the world that contained the earliest elements of our own world, including large-scale urbanization, complex industrial production, mercantilism and capitalism, widespread literacy, global travel, and contacts between large numbers of people from vastly different cultures. If there is one overriding assumption behind Deetz's definition, it is the interconnectedness between different peoples.

The connections between far-flung human societies are nothing new, for they date back at least to the beginnings of early civilizations in the Near East. By 2500 B.C.E., long-distance trade networks connected Mesopotamia with the Mediterranean and the Persian Gulf with northwest India. By 200 B.C.E., coastal routes around the Indian Ocean connected the Red Sea with India, Sri Lanka with China, and East Africa with Arabia. The voyages of discovery and trade created in Asia in the fourteenth and fifteenth centuries, and the European Age of Discovery between the fifteenth and twentieth centuries expanded international trade routes to every corner of the Earth (Figure 1.5). In

Figure 1.5 Asia ca. 1600, showing major centers of European trade

(From *The World Encompassed: The First European Maritime Empires*, c. 800–1650 by G. V. Scammell. © 1981, Taylor and Francis.)

archaeological terms, these burgeoning connections are reflected in artifacts such as Ming porcelain bowls from China and majolica plates from Spain traded all over the world and found by archaeologists far from their places of manufacture. Ideas and spiritual beliefs, new ways of doing things, and different ways of seeing the world accompanied the traders on their voyages. As a result, historical archaeologists can study Portuguese colonial settlements in central Africa, Brazil, and India, or English outposts in Virginia, South Africa, and Australia, with the understanding that each nation's settlements were part of the same global "system." In this way, many objects found by archaeologists at colonial sites in Massachusetts, and in equally dated towns in South Africa and southern England, can be expected to look similar or be identical. The people who made, used, and discarded them were members of the same cultures who, for various reasons, lived in different parts of the world. Deetz termed the archaeological interest in these large-scale, modern connections the "comparative international perspective" because this approach is a conscious attempt to examine the spread of Europeans across historically changing national boundaries.

Anyone who attempts to study any global issue soon discovers what geographer Peter Haggett learned: The "problem posed by any subject which aims to be global is simple and immediate: the earth's surface is so staggeringly large," to which should be added, "and its people so diverse." The use of an overt international perspective means that historical archaeologists face a formidable task, not only because of the complexity of their data, but also because they research complex interactions between rapidly changing societies. The cultural changes that may occur can be infinite in detail.

When Portuguese explorer Bartolemeu Diaz rounded the Cape of Good Hope at the southern tip of Africa in 1488, he anchored in a bay with low hills where Khoikhoi herders grazed their cattle (Figure 1.6). Dutch colonists settled at the Cape two centuries later, and usurped lands the Khoikhoi had used for centuries. The Dutch forcibly evicted many Khoikhoi from their lands and forced them to become indentured servants. This appropriation catastrophically disrupted the herders' ancient lifeways. The disruptions continued for more than a century. As a result, an archaeologist excavating a seventeenth-century colonial Dutch settlement in southern Africa must not only achieve an understanding of European history and material culture, but also must be sensitive to the complex social dynamics that governed indigenous cattle herding in the area. The artifacts found in the region will provide unique information about those dynamics.

The anonymous servants came from a radically different physical and spiritual world than the Europeans who sought to control them. Did the Khoikhoi perpetuate their beliefs or did they adopt the alien faith of the foreigners? Did they perceive advantages in adopting a European diet? Did they maintain contacts with their people still living outside the Dutch settlements? Excavators can seek answers to these questions, but to begin their investigation they must know something about the complex history of at least two disparate peoples—the Dutch and the Khoikhoi—as well as the ever-changing nature of their cultural contacts, the material cultures used by both, and the ways in which each group exploited the natural environment (see Chapter 12).

As a result of the historical interactions of culturally distinct peoples from Europe and elsewhere, historical archaeologists see the examination of the modern world as the study of a process. The influence of the indigenous peoples on the foreigners who settled among them is what kept the various colonial villages of each European nation from being identical copies of cities at home. Non-Westerners reacted to, embraced, rejected, and fought against the Spanish, Dutch, English, Portuguese, French, and other colonizing cultures in diverse ways, depending upon their individual circumstances, cultural

Wie die Hottentotten die Elfenbeinerne Ringe machen A. Wie sie die Matten machen B. C. Wie sie ihre Stricke machen D. Wie sie ihre Töpfe verfertigen. E.

Figure 1.6 Seventeenth-century Dutch drawing of the Khoikhoi
(Private Collection / Bridgeman Images)

traditions, and outlooks (Figure 1.7). Thus, even though Deetz tended to focus on European cultures in his definition, historical archaeologists today give equal weight to the actions and reactions of the many non-Westerners who accepted and rejected European social mores, economic ideas, political organizations, and religious beliefs and traditions. Today, a historical archaeologist may study a particular settlement of native North Americans, not because they lived in the "historical period," but because they constitute part of the history of the modern world. The actions, beliefs, and attitudes of native peoples throughout the globe are as important to the telling of world history as were the actions, beliefs, and attitudes of the powerful nation-states that are the usual stuff of basic history courses.

Based on current perspectives, historical archaeology may best be summarized as *a multi-disciplinary field that shares a special relationship with the formal disciplines of anthropology and history, focuses its attention on the post-Columbian past, and seeks to understand the global nature of modern life.* Each clause in this definition is particularly important to developing a clear understanding of the nature and direction of contemporary historical archaeology. Let us dissect it a little further.

Figure 1.7 The massacre at Cholula by the Spanish, according to the Aztecs
(From Bernardino de Sahagún, Florentine Codex, 1577)

Historical Archaeology Is Multidisciplinary

All modern archaeology is multidisciplinary because all archaeologists, regardless of special-ization, routinely use information from a huge array of related fields, including anthropol-ogy, botany, geography, geology, sociology, and zoology. What makes historical archaeology unique is that it is *by nature* multidisciplinary. It is virtually impossible for a historical archaeologist to conduct any serious research without consulting information from other disciplines, most notably history and cultural anthropology. With their feet firmly planted in both history and anthropology, historical archaeologists regularly draw on the letters, maps, diaries, and governmental records that modern historians use, as well as the cultural anthro-pologist's culture histories, ethnographies, insights, and concepts. Historical archaeologists also must rely on the site maps, soil profile drawings, and artifacts that are common to all archaeological research.

Historical archaeology is text-aided archaeology because documents are a primary source of information. Documents and texts of all kinds support and supplement archaeological information to such an extent that historical archaeologists must be as adroit at archival research and documentary interpretation as they are at site research and artifact analysis. Like historians, they must be adept at locating and dissecting textual sources, but they must also be able to relate these sources to their archaeological evidence. They must decide whether a group of documents is an independent source of information on their site or region or whether it only supplements the archaeological evidence. If their assessment is that the sources are entirely independent, then the two sources—one archaeological, one documentary—will shed light on the same problems, with each possibly having equal weight. If the documentary sources are supplementary, however, then the archaeological and the historical information may cast light on the same issue in slightly different ways. In such cases, the archaeological evidence is often the most revealing of the two. Disagreement will sometimes occur between the archaeological data and the historical information, and only meticulous analysis can resolve the issue.

Take, for example, the excavation of a plantation cabin inhabited by an enslaved family in the American South dating to about the year 1800. Excavation reveals the cabin's limestone foundation measures 12 by 16 feet (3.7 by 4.8 m), and that it contains numerous artifacts including glass bottle fragments, sherds of ceramic dishes, brass buttons, clay pipes, and other objects. A series of letters written by the plantation's owner are also available in a nearby archive. In one or two of these letters, the owner describes the cabins and mentions some of the articles the occupants used in their daily lives. Depending on the data at hand, the letters may supplement what is learned from the archaeological remains or the excavated artifacts may amplify what is learned from the documents. In either case, the two sources of information work to complement one another. The letters describe the material condition of the excavated cabin at one point in time as the writer perceived them, and the physical remains provide tangible amplification of the owner's comments.

Imagine for a moment that the archaeological data and the letters are completely independent sources, with each providing a different perspective on the historical reality of the enslaved experience. Without doubt, the cabin's residents created the archaeological deposits found at the cabin site. This creative process was probably not always consciously performed. When a dish was broken, a button lost, or a hog bone discarded, the individuals were only living their daily lives, not seeking to leave a material record of their lives for future generations to examine. The artifacts became part of the archaeological record almost by accident. But the plantation owner, a descendant of a different culture than the cabin's inhabitants, *was* consciously attempting to create a record of life at his plantation. He may have misrepresented the lives of his enslaved laborers, either purposefully or through his own misunderstanding of them. He may simply have written down his plans for how they might live according to his future designs for his estate. In this case, the archaeological and the documentary sources of information are not supplementary but are actually distinct. Each source was created by a different sort of person for a unique reason, and each reflects the past in a disparate way.

The interpretive controversy noted above is important for historical archaeology because it forces archaeologists to continue exploring various ways of using "nonarchaeological" research materials. That most of the nonarchaeological sources used by historical archaeologists derive from the formal discipline of history means that text-aided archaeology has a special relationship with history, a relationship whose boundaries must be continually tested by new ideas and innovative approaches. This part of our definition draws on the idea that historical archaeology provides a useful method for examining the past, a method that combines "historical" and "archaeological" sources of information. The basic assumption is that historical archaeologists have many sources of information available to them and the failure to use them is simply poorly conducted historical archaeology.

Historical Archaeology Focuses on the Post-Columbian Past

This element of our definition assumes that historical archaeology focuses on a relatively recent era rather than ancient times. Most historical archaeology described in this book concentrates on the "modern age"—the age some historians say began in 1415 C.E. with Portugal's successful capture of Ceuta in North Africa. This event was the catalyst for Prince Henry the Navigator's African explorations and the Age of Discovery that took Portuguese and other Western navigators across the globe. The date 1415 is, however, arbitrary, because many institutions of the "modern age" actually began to develop much earlier. For instance, some elements of modern mercantilism may be found in the ways Europe's Knights Templars—the powerful religious-military organization of the Middle Ages—trafficked in fabrics, wool, spices, dyes, porcelain, and glass. The link between these medieval entrepreneurs and modern industrial capitalists may be weak, but historical archaeologists understand that the practices of modern peoples can constitute tenacious traditions that extend backward in time beyond 1415. In this sense, then, we may expect some overlap between historical archaeology and European medieval archaeology based not solely on a similarity of method—both make extensive use of written records—but on a similarity of subject matter. By the same token, the researches of historical archaeologists may overlap with investigations into the Chinese explorations of the early fifteenth century. In general, however, the vast majority of research in contemporary historical archaeology focuses on the post-Columbian past, an era that extends from about 1500 C.E. to the present. Historical archaeology finds much of its subject matter in places that explorers and settlers visited in the "modern age," however it may be defined. By "modern" we only mean to suggest that the world was a different place after the intercontinental spread of cultural institutions beginning sometime around 1500 and expanding dramatically after that date.

We accept the special place of literacy in helping to transform the modern world, but we do not give it a primary role in shaping recent history. Without question, the adoption in the West of a movable type printing press in 1451, after centuries of use in China, made written knowledge available to more people than just society's elites. The effects of printed books and increasing literacy eventually did change the world, but many of the individual Europeans who traveled into the non-Western world were illiterate. The actions of these explorers, missionaries, traders, and settlers and the ideals of the nations that drove them forward were more important than whether they could read and write. We must also remember that most of the cultures these colonialists encountered lived in oral cultures. Such cultures did not need writing, and so the concept of literacy, as we commonly use it today, is not always relevant.

Historical Archaeology Seeks to Understand the Global Nature of Modern Life

Perhaps the most important facet of historical archaeology is its focus on modern life. No matter where we choose to set the beginning of "the modern world," the fundamental point is that the world of today was shaped in considerable part by compelling historical forces.

The exploration of the New World, the African slave trade, the Industrial Revolution, the invention of the steamship and the railroad—these are only some of the developments that have created our world. Many of these events and inventions affected hundreds of diverse human societies throughout the world. The invention of the steamship alone sparked human migration on a hitherto unheard of scale in the nineteenth century. Mass cultural migration is one reason historical archaeology is a global field that shuns often-arbitrary political boundaries in favor of large-scale events and broad processes that cemented together people and groups by their involvement in a common enterprise (such as colonial settlement, economic trade, or diaspora) or by common, historical circumstances (such as slavery or membership in a social class).

Despite the increasingly globalized world, historical archaeologists also work on a small scale, investigating in detail military forts, mining towns, colonial taverns, isolated shipwrecks, villages, hunting camps, and cabins. They focus on the minute and the particular, on the humblest of artifacts, and on the often-anonymous men, women, and children who made, used, and lost them. From these small-scale researches come new insights into the larger issues of world history.

The nations of the modern world were neither isolated nor necessarily inward looking. Europe, for instance, was not a monolithic empire during its Age of Discovery. It was an ever-changing mosaic of competing nation-states, each with its own goals, histories, and traditions. Each had its own agenda, its own ambitions, and its special values, and each was affected by the actions and technological achievements of societies across the world. The technological innovations that helped make it possible for Portugal to become a major world power in the sixteenth century included the astrolabe from the Near East and the magnetic compass from China. Thus, in using the term multinational, historical archaeologists generally refer both to a rising internationalism within the modern era, and to a globalization that took men and women into diverse and often remote parts of the world. This openly extranational focus means that historical archaeologists frequently study issues of vital concern today: multiculturalism, gender roles, the effects of exploration and settlement on native peoples and environments, racism, ethnicity, social inequality, consumerism, and the rise of the global mass market.

The prominence of these contemporary issues means that historical archaeologists constantly negotiate between the past and the present. Many archaeologists now acknowledge that archaeology, although it studies the past, is part of the contemporary world. Interpretations of the past are always bound within and constrained by contemporary perceptions and attitudes. The connection between present and past is the subject of much debate among all archaeologists. Some argue that archaeologists with a Western cultural perspective, however well trained, cannot legitimately interpret indigenous history. In historical archaeology specifically, many current perceptions on the recent past are shaped by personal histories, ideas, and experience. For example, the history of mass consumerism that many historical archaeologists are working diligently to document is still being played out, and we are all actors in this continuing drama. Because much of the past studied by historical archaeology is still unfolding, its practitioners find it difficult to argue that the past they study is too remote to be relevant to the present.

The conscious internationalism of historical archaeology means that the field studies a vast array of people. Rather than focusing on an archaeological record that is essentially anonymous—as so often is the case for archaeologists of very ancient history—historical archaeology often has the ability to concentrate on identifiable people from the past. For example, a great deal of archaeological research has been conducted at Monticello, Virginia, Jefferson's stately mansion, as well as on the properties of other people well known in history. More importantly, historical archaeology also has the ability to document the lives of people whose general histories may be known, but whose daily lives remain a mystery. We can explore the daily lives of factory workers, the enslaved, native villagers, farm laborers, colonists, and fur traders by excavating their humble abodes and workplaces. Archaeology writes histories not only of the rich and famous, but also of the common folk. Historical archaeology thus makes a priceless contribution to the human past (Figure 1.8).

Douglas Armstrong's excavations at Drax Hall, Jamaica, provide a perfect case in point. Drax Hall was built on St. Ann's Bay, on the north coast of the island. Columbus and his crew were marooned in this bay for a year and five days after his ship became infested with wood-borers during his fourth voyage to the New World. During his survey of the plantation estate, Armstrong found some 60 possible house locations lying behind the mansion. These dwellings were the residences of the enslaved (1760–1810), transitional laborers (1810–1840), and fully freed men and women (1840–1925) (Figure 1.9). Rather than focus only on the mansion, as some earlier historical archaeologists might have done, Armstrong sought to give voice to the laborers, the people who actually provided the wealth for the William Drax family. Armstrong examined both sides of the social fence, the rich and the poor, the literate and the nonliterate.

The focus of historical archaeology means, too, that archaeologists can have a vital role to play in helping to foster group identity and ethnic pride. In the United States alone, archaeologists have uncovered African American cemeteries under the streets of New York and

SCENE ON A COTTON PLANTATION. GATHERING COTTON.

Figure 1.8 African-American slaves at work on a plantation in the eighteenth century
(AS400 DB / Corbis)

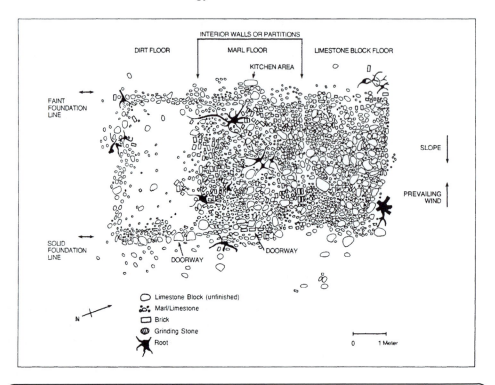

Figure 1.9 House remains at Drax Hall, Jamaica

(From *The Old Village and the Great House: An Archaeological and Historical Examination of Drax Hall Plantation, St. Ann's Bay, Jamaica* by Douglas V. Armstrong. Copyright 1990 Board of Trustees. Used with permission from the University of Illinois Press.)

Philadelphia, they have documented the survival of traditional African beliefs in their plantation and free communities, they have chronicled daily life at Catholic missions throughout the Southwest, and they have illustrated the changing nature of Native American life in the Northeast. Humble, day-to-day artifacts, food remains, house ruins, and myriad other seemingly insignificant finds combine into complicated jigsaw puzzles of history as compelling as any document or faded nineteenth-century photograph. It is from such finds that historical archaeologists infuse into history a human element that has too-often been ignored, pushed aside, or just plain forgotten.

Historical archaeology shines a searchlight into the recent past, clothing the deeds of common people with historical and cultural perspective, examining changing gender roles, and investigating ethnic communities and technological innovations. The archaeology of the recent past is more than a fascinating curiosity; it provides a truly multifaceted view of history during those centuries when everyone on earth became part of an ever-widening web of interconnectedness. Historical archaeology offers unrivaled opportunities for understanding the complex and often-subtle forces that shaped our own evermore-diverse world. Historical archaeology is changing the way we perceive our ancestors and ourselves.

The Goals of Historical Archaeology

Historical archaeology in the twenty-first century is a multifaceted field of study with diverse topics and various theoretical approaches. Despite this complexity, three major goals of the discipline can be identified:

- to provide information useful for historic preservation and site interpretation;
- to document the lifeways of past peoples; and
- to study the complex process of modernization and all the cultural and social changes, adaptations, and non-adaptations that accompanied it.

Historical archaeologists can meet these goals at a single site or at many sites, depending upon their plan of research.

Preservation and Site Interpretation

Historical archaeology has a large role to play in documenting how buildings looked in the past. In fact, providing evidence about past buildings was one of the first uses of historical archaeology.

Excavation can provide unique information about building size, when room additions were constructed or removed, and where fence lines and outbuildings were located. Homeowners of the past often made reference in their letters and diaries to room additions or to the construction of new buildings on their properties, and in many cases they may have even kept sketches or plans of them. Many people may have made the effort to document the buildings in which they lived, but most homeowners did not. Some people wrote about how they *hoped* to improve their property, but this does not necessarily mean they realized their plans. Few people recorded where they located their privy or how often they moved it, thinking perhaps that the subject was too delicate or perhaps too unimportant to be mentioned in writing. Sometimes a past meaning may be difficult to decipher. For example, while in London, Benjamin Franklin wrote his wife, Deborah, in 1765, "I cannot but complain in my mind of Mr. Smith that the house is so long unfit for you to get into, the fences not put up, nor the other necessary articles got ready." What he meant by "necessary articles" cannot be known, but he may have been referring to the privy behind the house. People at the time called them by the polite term "necessaries" or "necessary houses." In 1953, archaeologist Paul Schumacher found one of these "necessaries" near the back of the very house to which Franklin referred.

Living history museums—old houses and settlements where history is actively interpreted for the public, often with guides wearing period costumes—and historical organizations that try to preserve or restore old buildings are usually interested in knowing "where things were" and "what they looked like" (see Chapter 13). Site interpreters can use this detailed information to enrich the stories they tell visitors. Historical archaeology, even in cases where abundant historical records exist, is often the only way to document the full history of a building, from the day it was built to the day it was abandoned to when it was torn down. Archaeological excavation can provide exacting details permitting the better interpretation and understanding of a site by tourists, thereby promoting the study of history by putting a human face on it.

In addition to providing basic details about when structures were built, how they were built, their size and design, and the location of their associated outbuildings, historical archaeologists also provide unique information about the furnishings inside homes and other buildings. When archaeologists compare these kinds of archaeological findings with *probate inventories*—lists of a person's possessions at the time of death—a more complete picture of a property emerges (see Chapter 8).

Undocumented Lifeways

Since the 1960s historical archaeologists have maintained a strong interest in providing information about people not well represented in historical records. Research into how people actually lived in the recent past is an effective way to shed light on the disfranchised or forgotten men and women of history—the enslaved, factory workers, miners, farmers, and so forth.

The search for information about past lifeways can be expanded to include people well known in history as well. Historians have told us a great deal about the large industrialists, financiers, and international merchants who used their wealth to help build today's economic superpowers. Almost every public library and bookstore has more than one biography of men like Henry Ford and J.P. Morgan. These books relate where such individuals attended school, where they lived, or on what boards of directors they served, but what do they really say about their day-to-day lives?

Henry Ford's assembly line production methods and his vision to provide affordable automobiles to the public forever changed the modern world. Concerned in the 1920s about preserving the nineteenth-century world his automobiles were helping to transform, Ford built a living monument to mythic America called Greenfield Village, in Dearborn, Michigan. His plan was to identify and purchase buildings he deemed either important to American history or associated with famous American citizens. Once acquired, Ford had the buildings disassembled and moved to Michigan, where his workers carefully and accurately reconstructed them. When the invented village was completed, Ford proudly declared: "We have no Egyptian mummies here, nor any relics of the Battle of Waterloo nor do we have any curios from Pompeii, for everything we have is strictly American."

The research conducted by Ford's team was not systematic or consistent with today's professional standards. Ford's workmen did not use archaeological methods to compile architectural histories of the individual buildings. He was concerned only with the bricks, the clapboard siding, and the floorboards of places like the Armington and Sims Machine Shop, the Logan County Courthouse where Abraham Lincoln practiced law, Edison's Menlo Park laboratory (Figure 1.10), and the other two dozen buildings he ordered reconstructed. Ford was definitely not interested in documenting anyone's lifeways. An archaeologist *could* have excavated around Ford's birthplace (the first home Ford restored, but the last he had moved to Greenfield Village). They could have collected valuable information about the daily life of the Ford family during Henry's formative years, but this was not done. If historical archaeology had been conducted at Ford's birthplace, it would have underscored the discipline's ability to answer questions about all past peoples, regardless of wealth and social position.

Consumption and Globalization

One of the greatest challenges faced by historical archaeologists is in the area of studying globalization, the worldwide spread of material objects, people, cultures, and ideas. Globalization includes such complex topics as the rise of consumer consumption, the spread of urbanization, industrialization, capitalist economics, and the expansion of nations and their institutions to all parts of the world. Archaeologists can study these processes using a diverse

Figure 1.10 The reconstruction of Thomas Edison's laboratory complex at Greenfield Village, Michigan, in January 1929
(From the Collections of Henry Ford Museum and Greenfield Village.)

storehouse of information, including artifacts, architecture, food remains, personal letters, governmental records, and travelers' accounts.

The European Age of Discovery brought peoples of diverse cultures in contact for the first time. The interactions that developed were complex and bidirectional in their impact, meaning that culture change occurred between both parties. As both sides borrowed from one another, they created the modern world. To understand, one only has to mention the American potato, which became a staple of European peasants, or tobacco. At the same time, various European nations built forts, missions, and small colonies in distant lands, transplanted settlements that were altered versions of communities at home.

Portugal became a global superpower in the sixteenth and seventeenth centuries by virtue of its international trade in gold, spices, sugar, and human beings. Its agents planted colonies along the coasts of Africa, in India, throughout Asia, and across the Atlantic in Brazil. In each place, the colonists erected buildings that were copies of prototypes back home. For example, they constructed their late fifteenth-century fort at Elmina on the Ghanian coast in West Africa according to the latest European ideas on fortification, with no concession to local conditions. Even entire town plans were imported to foreign lands. The eighteenth-century town of Ouro Prêto in Brazil looks as if it were mail-ordered from Portugal. The streets are narrow and cobblestoned, the houses are small and have red-tiled roofs, and the language heard in the shops is Portuguese. Minute details of architecture and material culture often disclose telling differences between colonial towns and their homeland's prototypes, details that are seldom if ever mentioned in the documents of the day.

Site Visit: La Isabella, Hispaniola, 1493–1498

In 1493, the Spanish built a medieval town in the New World. Columbus's second voyage across the Western Sea had been harrowing, and he, his crew, and his animals were feeling the effects of sickness and exhaustion. The weather had been harsh and unforgiving, and the crew of over one thousand was growing restless and rebellious. Columbus's goal was to build a Spanish city in the New World, a place that would serve as a central outpost of what would become the powerful Spanish empire. Knowing he had to decide on a location for his town before his crew revolted, he chose a rocky promontory on the north shore of Hispaniola, in today's Haiti. He named his ill-fated town La Isabella, after the Spanish queen.

Hispaniola, like most places in what the Europeans called the New World, was neither new nor uninhabited. The islands of the Caribbean were home to the Taínos, a people who had lived in the region for generations. Inhabiting both small hamlets and large towns (with as many as 1,000 houses), the Taínos had a vibrant culture, a rich religious tradition, and leaders who could be either male or female.

Columbus and his European crew did not know what to think of the non-Christian Taínos, but they knew they would have to rely on them, at least during the first few months, for food if for nothing else. The Taínos grew maize and manioc, and caught and ate fish, mammals, birds, rodents, and snakes. The Spanish, however, had not gone to the New World to meet strange peoples and to learn their ways. Their goals were mostly imperialistic and economic: They wanted gold and, to a lesser extent, souls for God. Given the cultural gap between the Taínos and the Spanish invaders, it was not long before open hostilities erupted.

The design of La Isabella reflected the Spaniards' European mindset and their plans for Hispaniola. Even though he and his men were feeling the effects of sickness—either influenza or syphilis—Columbus immediately ordered the construction of a walled town. The wall, which the Spaniards made of packed earth (called *tapia*), was clearly a defensive feature. Inside the wall they placed five structures: a customs house/storehouse, a church, a powder magazine, Columbus's house, and a circular, stone watchtower (Figure 1.11). Built of stone rather than the wood and grass of the Taínos's houses, these buildings implied that the Spaniards intended to stay for a long time. They also oriented the buildings to command the cliff and the beach. The church was the only building they had not defensively oriented; it conformed to the higher principles of Christianity and was sited east to west.

Figure 1.11 Aerial photograph of La Isabella, Hispaniola
(Courtesy of the Florida Museum of Natural History.)

The Spanish situated Columbus's house to give it spectacular views of the area and to make it open to the fresh, ocean breezes that could temper the island's intense, tropical heat. The house served as the southwest corner of the town's defenses, and it incorporated a small watchtower on its northeast corner. The main room of the house measured over 18 by 39 feet (5.5 by 12 m) and had a plaster floor. The house had four doors, all of which gave access to a patio or courtyard enclosed by a surrounding wall.

The Spanish residents of La Isabella, though far from home, lived in many ways like their countrymen and women in Spain. They surrounded themselves with plates and bowls in forms that were familiar to them, they wore finger rings and other ornaments, and they practiced Christianity in the settlement's church. They wore chain mail and spurs, and they armed themselves with crossbows, swords, and firearms. When their fellows died, they buried them in a manner that was consistent with Spanish practice. They lived a Spanish life in the Caribbean, making only a few concessions to local circumstances.

By 1497, the troubles in the colony—mostly over the scarcity of food and their deteriorating relations with the Taínos—came to a head, and a Spanish settler revolted. This man, named Roldán, questioned the authority of Columbus's administration and made alliances with groups of Taínos and disaffected Spaniards. By this time, however, the Spanish crown had largely given up on La Isabella, choosing to set their eyes on other parts of the New World. By 1498, Columbus's dreams for his colonial outpost were dashed, and this town was quickly forgotten by the Spanish crown.

Source: Kathleen Deagan and José María Cruxent, *Columbus's Outpost Among the Taínos: Spain and America at La Isabella, 1493–1498.*
(New Haven: Yale University Press, 2002).

Chapter 2

A Brief History of Historical Archaeology

In 1855 a Jesuit father named Félix Martin traveled westward from Montreal, Canada, to the eastern edge of Georgian Bay in what is today Ontario. Carrying with him an official commission from the Canadian government, Father Martin planned to explore and excavate the site known as Sainte Marie I, a location as important as any in nineteenth-century Canadian history (Figure 2.1). The Jesuit fathers had built this tiny mission deep in the country of the Hurons, in 1639, with the hope of bringing these powerful people to the altar of Christianity. The Jesuits had established their mission with promise and hope, but only a decade later they abandoned it and burned it to the ground. Devastating smallpox epidemics and constant attacks by the more powerful Iroquois, who lived to the southeast, decimated the Huron and forced the missionaries to evacuate Sainte Marie. Instead of going there to save souls, however, Father Martin went to record history. He drew a map of the famous mission's remains and documented the presence of the Jesuits at Georgian Bay.

The following year, similar activities were underway further south in the United States. James Hall decided to excavate the home of his famous ancestor, Miles Standish, the renowned leader of the *Mayflower* Pilgrims. Hall, a trained civil engineer, made careful excavations of Standish's home, faithfully recording the soil layers he found. He also mapped the stone foundation and even plotted the locations of several artifacts he uncovered during his dig.

These nineteenth-century investigations are early examples of historical archaeology in North America. This chapter describes the early history of historical archaeology and some of the general trends of the field as it developed in the United States and Canada. Our focus on North America is simply one of convenience. The broad trends outlined here have generally been played out (or are being played out) in other countries where historical archaeology has developed.

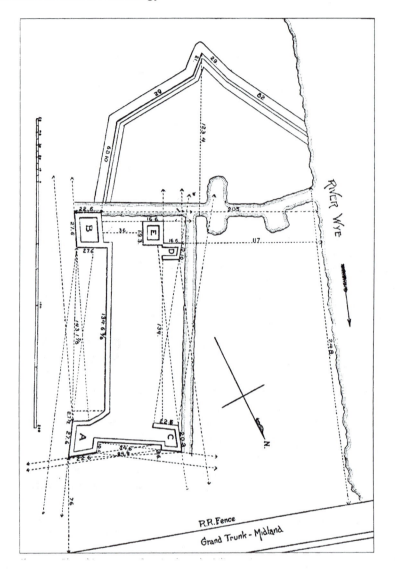

Figure 2.1 Plan of Ste. Marie I, Ontario
(Drawn by Félix Martin, from *The Excavation of Ste Marie I* by Kenneth Kidd © University of Toronto Press 1949.)

The Important and the Famous
(1855 to the 1960s)

Martin's excavations in Canada and Hall's in the United States more than a century ago would not meet the rigorous standards of today's scientific archaeology. Each man paid little attention to the minute details that often disclose startlingly new information to today's archaeologists. Their excavations are nonetheless significant, not simply because they represent examples of early historical archaeology, but also because they neatly define the scope of much historical archaeology conducted before the mid-twentieth century.

The earliest excavators tended to investigate sites associated with famous people or with events important in American or Canadian national history. In the United States, this kind of historical archaeology was sanctioned by the Historic Sites Act of 1935, which declared it national policy "to preserve for public use historic sites, buildings, and objects of national significance for the preservation and benefit of the people of the United States." This act came five years after the Canadian National Parks Act, which stipulated the same protection for historical landmarks and objects having "national importance."

The authors of the acts may have been aware that archaeology was already underway at sites having national significance. For example, Jamestown, Virginia, was the first permanent English settlement in America (1607), the seat of the country's first legislative assembly (1619), and the site of Bacon's Rebellion (1676–1677). President Herbert Hoover proclaimed Jamestown a Colonial National Monument in 1930. The first systematic excavations began there only four years later. Before the Second World War, excavations were conducted with the support of two governmental public works agencies active during the Great Depression: the Emergency Conservation Work group and the Civilian Conservation Corps. In 1938, the government built an archaeological field laboratory and a storage building at Jamestown. Excavations resumed in 1954, as part of a larger plan to celebrate the town's 350th anniversary in 1957.

The initial archaeology at Jamestown was dedicated to interpreting and presenting the site to tourists. Archaeologists used the excavated iron hinges and door locks, the white ceramics etched with delicate blue lines, and the foundations of the settlement's glasshouse to help interpret the history and the daily life of the town's residents. The reconstructed buildings, furnished with excavated remains or reproductions from the appropriate period, enabled visitors to experience something of what it meant to live in the seventeenth century. Jamestown's archaeologists focused on all the men and women who built and lived in the settlement, even though John Smith, Pocahontas, and John Rolfe are most famous. Jamestown is renowned because these individuals lived there, but the archaeology was about the *entire* Jamestown community. The site was valued because of its place as the first permanent English colony in North America.

During this period, a number of historical archaeologists specifically focused their attention on sites associated with famous people. When archaeologist Richard Hagen first thought of excavating Abraham Lincoln's two-story frame house in Springfield, Illinois, he went immediately to a reliable historical source: Lincoln's insurance policy, written by the Hartford Insurance Company on February 8, 1861. This policy protected "Abraham Lincoln of Springfield Illinois against loss or damage by fire to the amount of . . . Three Thousand and Two Hundred Dollars." Three thousand dollars protected the house, with the remainder covering the carriage house and privy. The policy carefully described Lincoln's home just in case the company had to replace it. Hagen began his excavation armed with this valuable document. He hoped to discover objects he could directly associate with Lincoln himself, but he was disappointed. When he unearthed an 1857 penny and a large brass key, he could imagine that the penny had fallen from Lincoln's pocket and that some careless member of the family had lost the key. He could even envision "the Lincolns' temporary distress at being locked out!" but his research could not provide evidence for Lincoln's exact behavior. The best contribution he could make was to provide architectural details about the size, shape, and location of Lincoln's carriage house and woodshed. He also provided information about the kinds of objects used by the Lincoln family, as represented by artifacts recovered from the two excavated privies.

During this period of historical archaeology's development, several archaeologists interested in Canadian history investigated an important early industry—the fur trade. Starting in 1938, archaeologist Emerson Greenman studied the trade that existed between French settlers and Native Americans who lived in Ontario's Georgian Bay region. The Ottawa River served as a convenient highway for canoes traveling west from Montreal to Lake Huron, and the route passed close to Old Birch Island, a tiny island in Georgian Bay. Greenman used written records to document the presence of both European fur traders and Native Americans in this area. The *Jesuit Relations*—letters and reports Jesuit fathers sent home to Rome to explain their missionary activities—related much of the history of the region between 1608 and 1760. Using these documents as a guide, Greenman conducted a field survey of the island. He found a Native American cemetery containing the remains of 16 individuals in 12 graves. His discovery of brass pails, iron butcher knives, and brightly colored glass beads in the graves told him that this group of Native Americans had conducted commerce with French traders from Montreal. The objects also told him that the native traders had adopted at least some European artifacts and technology into their traditional way of life.

Further west in North America, the Flood Control Act of 1944 mandated the construction of a series of dams along the Missouri River in North and South Dakota. These projects spurred the archaeological investigation of several locales important in the history of the American West. For instance, agents of the powerful Columbia Fur Trading Company built "Kipp's Post"—sometimes called "Fort Kipp"—on the Missouri River in the fall and winter of 1826–1827. The post, about 50 miles (80 km) east of present-day Williston, North Dakota, was named for its builder, James Kipp, a Canadian fur trader of German descent who traded with the Assiniboines at this site. Traders abandoned Kipp's Post around 1828, when the larger Fort Union was constructed nearby. Historians of the fur trade knew Kipp's Post had existed, but they knew little else about it. European American traders only occupied the post for a short time, and they left painfully few records about their activities there. As a result, the archaeology conducted at the site provided a rare opportunity to learn about life at a frontier outpost.

Archaeologists Alan Woolworth and Raymond Wood excavated Kipp's Post in July and August 1954 (Figure 2.2). They documented that the stockade around the post was 96 feet (29.3 m) on a side, with a rectangular bastion extending 5 feet (1.5 m) beyond the northeastern corner of the enclosure. The wall posts were badly rotted, but the dark postholes that remained in the ground showed they were about 6 inches (15.2 cm) in diameter. The entrance to the post was on the south side and measured 9.5 feet (2.9 m) across. The fort's builders had placed four structures of various sizes along the back of the stockade, facing the gate. The traders must have had a cannon, but it was apparently of questionable use. The discovery of several cannon fragments around the fort suggested it had exploded when fired!

Excavations at Kipp's Post also documented the commodities imported to the post. The traders ate from plain, white plates and drank from glass tumblers and white cups. Their stores, however, contained a far wider range of artifacts. These were things they bartered in exchange for furs—white clay smoking pipes, pieces of gold braid, small brass bells, and brass arrowheads. They also traded tiny, glass beads in green, amber, blue, black, and white, as well as spherical brass beads and delicate, conical-shaped, silver ear bangles.

Woolworth and Wood used their extensive archaeological and historical research to present a detailed picture of this one small trading post on the Missouri River. Kipp's Post is but a footnote in the larger story of the North American fur trade. The pioneering archaeological research, however, added remarkable details to the history of the region.

Even though much of the historical archaeology conducted during the field's formative years was directed toward sites of national importance, some archaeologists did turn to the

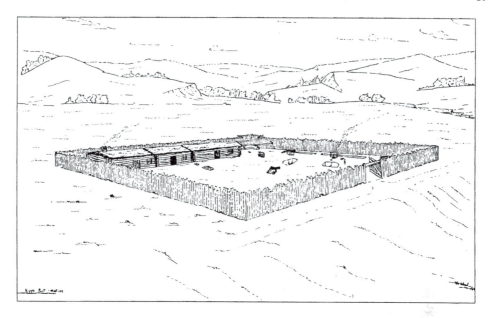

Figure 2.2 Artist's reconstruction of Kipp's Post, North Dakota

(From *The Archaeology of a Small Trading Post, River Basin Survey Papers* by Alan Woolworth and Raymond Wood. Bulletin 176, Washington, D.C. Government Printing Service, 1960.)

study of sites associated with less prominent people. For example, in 1943, Adelaide and Ripley Bullen excavated the home of Lucy Foster, an African American freedwoman who lived in Andover, Massachusetts. The Bullens published a short statement of their research in 1945, but in 1978 a larger report was presented under the authorship of archaeologist Vernon Baker.

As is true of most people who are neither prominent in a community nor wealthy, little documentary information exists about Lucy Foster. Baptismal records on file at the Andover South Parish Congregational Church include the following brief note: "July 14, 1771, Sarah, a child given to Job Foster and Lucy, a Negro. Child was baptized." These few words place Lucy Foster in Massachusetts in the 1770s. Lucy was apparently freed sometime in the early 1800s, and lived for 30 years in her cabin. She survived her later years in desperate poverty until her death of asthma in November 1845.

When the Bullens excavated Foster's home, they discovered that the house had burned and that someone had apparently rummaged through the rubble looking for something, perhaps useful building materials. The archaeology of the cellar foundation, made of dry-laid fieldstone, showed that the house was small, only 10.5–11.5 feet (3.2–3.5 m) on a side (Figure 2.3). This size of building may represent African American tradition because folklorists have demonstrated that the narrow, long houses built in West Africa, Haiti, and in the American South—called "shotgun" houses—generally have twelve-foot dimensions. The Bullens also excavated a shallow well, an oval pit about 3.6 feet (1.1 m) deep, and a trash dump, located just west of the cellar. When Baker compared the ceramic vessels from these archaeological features with those from a cabin inhabited by the enslaved at Cannon's Point Plantation, Georgia (see

Figure 2.3 Artist's reconstruction of Lucy Foster's Home in Massachusetts
(From *Historical Archaeology at Black Lucy's Garden: Ceramics from the Site of a Nineteenth Century Afro-American* by Vernon G. Baker. © Robert S. Peabody Museum of Archaeology, Phillips Academy, Andover, Massachusetts. All Rights Reserved.)

Chapter 11), he made a startling discovery. The percentages of vessel forms from the cabin matched those from Lucy Foster's house. Excavations yielded 44 percent serving bowls at Cannon's Point and 41 percent at Foster's home. The plantation cabin had 49 percent serving flatware (plates, platters), and Foster's home had 51 percent. Both sites also had a low percentage of other shapes.

Baker's analysis could not reveal whether the similarity between the ceramic collections was an element of the African American heritage of the residents of both sites, or whether it resulted from a condition of extreme poverty (see Chapter 11). In any case, the Bullens' pioneering research, like that at Kipp's Post, showed archaeology's ability to investigate basic historical questions such as the relationship between material culture and social position.

Theoretical Foundations

A number of archaeologists provided the theoretical foundation for much of the historical archaeology of the early period by arguing that historical archaeology was a historical pursuit. As early as 1910, archaeologist Carl Russell Fish, in a paper presented before the Wisconsin Archaeological Society, observed that "Nearly every historian should be something of an archaeologist, and every archaeologist should be something of an historian." Fish knew about the archaeological discoveries in Egypt and Assyria, and he was impressed by recent research on the Roman colonization of Britain. Viewing these excavations as historical archaeology—because the archaeologists had combined historical sources of information with excavated remains—he reasoned that the same attention could be given to American history: "We have monuments which are worthy of preservation, and which can add to our knowledge of our American ancestors."

Forty years later, J. C. Harrington, famous for his excavations at Jamestown, defined historical archaeology as an "auxiliary science to American history." He vigorously argued that the archaeology of the historical period was an "important historical tool" that should be developed and used by historians. In the early 1960s, Ivor Noël Hume, the famed excavator of Colonial Williamsburg, referred to historical archaeology as "the handmaiden of history." These authorities all viewed historical archaeology as a way to contribute unique, tangible information to the study of history.

The idea that archaeology could provide information for historians rather than for anthropologists made historical archaeology unique but not truly unusual. In fact, the view that historical archaeology is about "history" was generally consistent with the way other archaeologists conducted their research on pre-Columbian history during this period. They thought of themselves as a "special kind of anthropologist," directing most of their efforts toward the construction of cultural chronologies. These chronologies were broad-brush histories of non-literate peoples based on artifacts—stone axes, clay pots, and the like—and other archaeological evidence, rather than on written documents. Under this "culture historical approach," past cultures were defined on the basis of the artifacts collected from a certain number of key sites of the same approximate age. For instance, one archaeological culture might be defined on the basis of pottery incised with an S pattern, crescent-shaped copper ornaments, and the use of small, conical burial mounds. A separate archaeological culture might be identified by its undecorated pottery, round shell ornaments, and the use of large, flat-topped burial mounds. To this day, archaeologists still somewhat rely on culture histories of pre-Columbian societies, created by reference to the artifacts the peoples left behind.

The creation of cultural chronologies forms the foundation of much archaeological research, whether post- or pre-Columbian, but the situation for historical archaeology is slightly different. The societies studied by historical archaeologists usually do not require construction by means of stratified artifacts because their histories are generally known from documentary sources. Father Martin knew Jesuit fathers had traveled to the country of the Hurons, they had built Ste. Marie Mission in 1639, and in 1649 they had burned it to the ground. Martin did not need to establish these historical facts because they were well documented in the Jesuit records. His archaeological research was important, however, because he used it to substantiate and flesh out the historical facts. How large was the mission? How did the Jesuits actually build it? Did they place the chapel in the center or near the gate? What kinds of religious objects did the Jesuits give to the Huron men, women, and children who visited the mission? The authors of historical accounts often ignore such mundane matters when they write their narratives. What is left out is precisely what archaeologists find most interesting.

Two short case studies demonstrate how historical archaeology was conceived before the mid-1960s. J. C. Harrington's research at Fort Necessity, Pennsylvania, and Edward B. Jelks's excavations at Signal Hill, Newfoundland, are well known in the annals of early historical archaeology.

Fort Necessity, Pennsylvania

The history of Fort Necessity began in 1754 when George Washington, then a lieutenant colonel in the Virginia militia, took about 160 poorly trained men to what is today south-western Pennsylvania. Washington was sent to the area because of French encroachments on land "notoriously known to be the property of the Crown of Great Britain." The French paid no heed to the warnings of the British because they, too, had established forts at strategic locations in North America. They were as eager as the British were to control this territory. Washington's orders were to reinforce the English detachment at today's Pittsburgh and to improve the trail to the British stronghold. He did not originally plan to construct a fort, but after his troops attacked a small French force in the vicinity of Great Meadow, south of today's Pittsburgh, and killed their leader, he decided a small fortification was a wise idea. He and his men thus built the aptly named Fort Necessity, and so began the French and British contest for North America.

The fort's location had never been forgotten, but its exact shape was a mystery. In 1816, a professional surveyor drew the fort as triangular, but a local historian in 1830 described it as shaped like a diamond or flattened square (Figure 2.4). The fort's precise design became important when the U.S. National Park Service decided to reconstruct it in 1932. Since documents could not settle the question of the fort's shape, the Park Service found it necessary to use excavation in conjunction with the incomplete documentary record. When excavations finally got underway in 1952—after the Great Depression and World War II had considerably

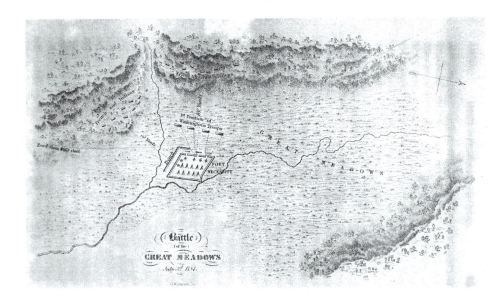

Figure 2.4 Map of Fort Necessity, Pennsylvania, published in 1837
(Shirley Small Special Collections Library, University of Virginia)

slowed the historic preservation movement—two objectives were "to settle, once and for all, the 'triangle versus square' controversy," and "to secure additional objects for museum display."

J.C. Harrington's excavations proved that the fort actually consisted of two design elements: a diamond-shaped earthwork with a circular stockade inside it. The charred posts of the stockade were still visible in the soil of the old fortification trench. Harrington combined his archaeological findings with a deposition by John Shaw, a member of Washington's regiment, which explains the way the fort was built. Historians did not take this document seriously until the archaeological findings confirmed its accuracy. In this way, then, Harrington used a combination of archaeological findings and historical documents to establish the size and shape of Washington's strategic frontier fort. Only historical archaeology could provide the required level of detail.

Signal Hill, Newfoundland

Like Fort Necessity, Signal Hill figured in the history of the French and British campaigns for control of North America. Situated on a strategic point overlooking the Atlantic Ocean and the harbor leading to St. John's and Fort William (established shortly before 1700), settlers used the promontory from 1750 to the mid-nineteenth century as a signal station to identify arriving ships. The British lost the area to the French in 1762 but then quickly regained it. Signal Hill, for all its strategic importance, did not have any fortifications built on it until 1795. The British had made numerous plans to construct fortifications on the hill, but many of these efforts were never carried out. During its greatest period of activity—from 1795 until the mid-nineteenth century—three batteries, or cannon stations, and several other buildings were built on the hill. Signal Hill also had other uses. On December 12, 1901, wireless pioneer Guglielmo Marconi used it as the base from which to make his first transatlantic Morse code transmission. His message, simply the letter S, sent all the way from Cornwall, England, proved that ships could communicate with one another and with the shore for at least 2,000 miles (3,200 km).

The number and locations of buildings on the hill became extremely important when the Canadian government decided to build an interpretive center for the new Signal Hill National Historic Park. When archaeologist Edward Jelks was commissioned to conduct the excavations in 1958, his objective was to dig in the area of the interpretive center to ensure that no archaeological remains would be destroyed by construction. He also wanted to determine the development potential of the park for future visitors, and to recover artifacts and other information valuable to the archaeological investigation of British colonialism in North America.

Jelks's excavations documented the complex construction history at Signal Hill and unearthed buttons, bottles, coins, and other objects used by the soldiers there. The story of what happened at Signal Hill would be much less well known had these excavations not occurred.

Historical Archaeology of People and Communities (1960s to Today)

Archaeologists have long used their excavations to construct the broad culture histories of past peoples, but not every archaeologist accepted this was all archaeology had to offer. In the 1960s, American archaeologists, having been trained mostly in departments of anthropology, began to think their discipline could be more like cultural anthropology, in the sense that it could provide information about people's daily lives. As a result, archaeologists trained since the mid-1960s often envision themselves as historical anthropologists working to reconstruct past people's ways of life instead of simply adding to their cultural histories.

In 1962, archaeologist Lewis Binford presented one vision of anthropological archaeology in his essay "Archaeology as Anthropology." He proposed that archaeologists—instead of simply following paths leading only to large-scale cultural histories based on the identification of "archaeological cultures"—could be pathfinders who could lead the way to understanding the cultural processes of the past. Rather than viewing culture as statically represented in a collection of artifacts, Binford adopted the anthropologist's perspective that culture is active, that it represents adaptations to changing social and physical environments. From this point of view, archaeologists could work like anthropologists and provide information about economics, kinship, religion, social interaction, and almost all other elements of past daily life. Archaeologists would study cultural processes rather than history perceived as a fixed series of stages represented by a few key artifacts.

Binford used an archaeological expression called the ancient Old Copper Culture in Wisconsin (3000–500 B.C.E.) to illustrate his argument, but he also believed that an anthropological approach would serve historical archaeology well. Unlike many of his contemporaries, he had obtained personal experience in historical archaeology by serving in 1959 as a field assistant for excavations at Fort Michilimackinac, an eighteenth-century French and British military post in Michigan (Figure 2.5).

Figure 2.5 Restored Fort Michilimackinac, Michigan
(Svetlana Foote / Shutterstock)

Theoretical Foundations

The impact of Binford's article was immense. Paul Martin proclaimed that Binford had created a "revolution" in archaeology by proposing an entirely new theoretical paradigm for studying the past. Before long, archaeologists were referring to anthropological archaeology as the "New Archaeology" because it represented an attempt to introduce greater scientific and theoretical rigor into field and laboratory research.

The furor over the study of cultural process instead of strict chronological history indeed spilled over into historical archaeology. A year after the publication of Binford's essay, a number of archaeologists held a symposium entitled "The Meaning of Historic Sites Archaeology" at the annual meeting of the Society for American Archaeology in Boulder, Colorado. Binford was a panelist at this symposium, but the chair was Bernard Fontana. Fontana, an anthropologist who had conducted historical archaeology in Arizona, was inspired by the session and wrote an essay entitled "On the Meaning of Historic Sites Archaeology," which appeared in 1965.

As an anthropologist, Fontana understood the important role non-Europeans had played in creating the modern world. In line with this thinking, he designed a classification of archaeological sites stressing their degree of Native American influence. His scale extended from "protohistoric" (a site occupied after 1492 containing some European artifacts, but predating actual face-to-face contact between Native Americans and Europeans) to "nonaboriginal" (a site with little or no Native American influence).

Robert Schuyler reinforced Fontana's anthropological message in his paper "Historical and Historic Sites Archaeology as Anthropology: Basic Definitions and Relationships," published in 1970. Schuyler proposed that historical archaeology had much to offer anthropology and that historical archaeology was not simply a way to reinforce or to substantiate historical facts.

By the early 1970s, then, many historical archaeologists had realized that their main theoretical foundation should be anthropological. Even so, the question of whether anthropologists or historians should conduct historical archaeology remained a topic of considerable debate. The controversy revolved around two central issues: first, whether the subject matter of historical archaeology was "history"—the realm of historians—or "culture"—the realm of anthropologists, and second, whether artifacts were historical documents—because they "told" about the past—or whether documents were really artifacts—because they were made and modified by conscious human effort. Traditional wisdom held that historians study written documents and that archaeologists study artifacts, but this neat distinction was not at all clear for historical archaeology.

Proponents of both sides of the argument tended to caricature the other. Some portrayed historians as narrow-minded scholars who wore tweed jackets while blissfully rummaging through stacks of dusty documents oblivious to the outside world. Others described archaeologists as brash adventurers who knew nothing about written records and who would go to any lengths to obtain rare artifacts. In 1962, Bernard Cohn published an article entitled "An Anthropologist among the Historians: A Field Study." In this seemingly tongue-in-cheek study, Cohn said that "Historians are older than anthropologists." He also said that "A historian is usually regular in his work habits. The archives are open only certain hours," but that "An anthropologist often works in great bursts." Cohn also contrasted the relevance of each discipline's work: "A historian usually studies a topic which, even if somewhat obscure, is intrinsically important," but "An anthropologist may study intrinsically insignificant things"!

In hindsight, the history-or-anthropology debate raised a false issue by attempting to draw too fine a line between two closely related fields. Some of the debate's participants continued to promote stereotyped characterizations of historians and anthropologists while misunderstanding the theoretical bases of both history and anthropology. The debate was important, however, because it forced historical archaeologists to consider seriously the theoretical foundations of their field and to help them define its boundaries.

At about the same time historical archaeologists were debating history versus anthropology, many professional historians "discovered" anthropology (largely as ethnohistory; see Chapter 1) and began to employ concepts and ideas from ethnography in their historical interpretations. Rhys Isaac, for example, won a Pulitzer Prize in history for his highly anthropological *The Transformation of Virginia, 1740–1790*. Isaac's first word in this "historical" book is "Anthropologists." He was specifically interested in explaining how society in Tidewater, Virginia, had changed from 1740 to 1790, or before and after the American Revolution. Virginia's social hierarchy had become more rigid during this half century for reasons that were hard to discern. Hoping to understand this change, Isaac stayed away from politics and economics, choosing instead to examine such "anthropological" topics as architecture, interior design, furniture, silverware, dance, dress, manners, and the use of space (Figure 2.6). Isaac drew two important conclusions from these lines of evidence. First, that rich planters had made common cause with poorer farmers to claim independence from England and to forge a new government. This conclusion was not entirely new, but his second, related conclusion was pathbreaking. He concluded that planters became increasingly threatened with the rise of American independence and liberty during the course of the eighteenth century. To

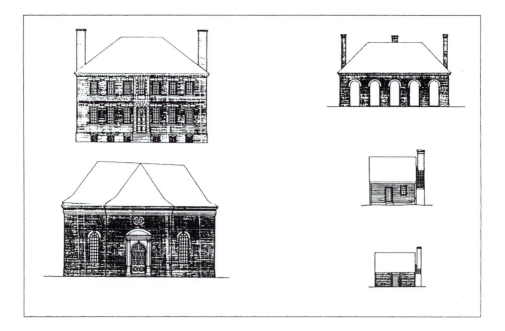

Figure 2.6 Hierarchy of buildings in eighteenth-century Virginia, ranging from mansion to slave cabin

(Drawn by Cary Carson and Benjamin Hellier. From *The Transformation of Virginia, 1740–1790*, by Rhys Isaac © 1982 by the University of North Carolina Press. Published for the Omohundro Institute of Early American History and Culture. Used by permission.)

maintain their elite positions in the social order, planters tightened their control over society. One way they expressed this control was the so-called "Georgian Order," a perspective that had significant relevance to material culture. House styles became more symmetrical and neat; dining and dance became more structured and orderly (see Chapter 10). Isaac had to look to the material expressions of daily life to find evidence of these changes. He had to examine them as an anthropologist would investigate a foreign culture.

As some historians were turning toward anthropology, some archaeologists were leaning more toward history. In 1986, Ian Hodder wrote that "archaeology should recapture its traditional links with history." Hodder apparently had not thought too much about "history" until the writings of Australian-born archaeologist V. Gordon Childe had again become popular in archaeological circles in the early 1980s. Childe considered archaeology to be a form of history, and in the 1930s and 1940s he wrote tremendously popular books about Europe's remote past, using archaeological objects to explain his main points. Hodder sought to reemphasize Childe's view that archaeologists were adding to historical knowledge by their research into the past.

Historical archaeologists have explored the connections between history and anthropology in numerous ways. Their inquiries have forced them to acknowledge and appreciate the multidisciplinary foundation of their field. In 1982, Kathleen Deagan, renowned for her research on colonial New Spain and Columbus's settlement on Hispaniola (see Chapter 1), noted that the "debate over the proper orientation of historical archaeology has not altogether been resolved." Deagan has repeatedly demonstrated, through her many important projects, the power of using historical records in archaeological research to study such topics as domestic architecture and changing gender roles. As was the case during her study of Fort Mose, Florida—the earliest free African American settlement in North America—she often closely collaborates with professional historians in a further attempt to link anthropology and history.

One of the most forceful statements for the adoption of an overt anthropological and scientific perspective in historical archaeology was Stanley South's *Method and Theory in Historical Archaeology,* published in 1977. South had been a graduate student with Lewis Binford at the University of North Carolina in the 1950s. He was a confirmed believer in the theory of cultural evolution as explained by anthropologist Leslie White. Following White, South believed that cultural progress could be measured by the amount of energy a culture harnessed. The captured energy could be evaluated in terms of technological achievement, extending from the controlled use of fire to atomic power.

South agreed with Binford's ideas about archaeological reasoning, and argued that historical archaeologists should think scientifically and make regular use of hypotheses, laws, and scientific testing procedures. South proposed that historical archaeology could be quantifiable, meaning that the artifacts found at different sites could be counted, grouped into categories, and then compared in a scientific manner with the artifact groups from other sites. The comparisons would reveal cultural information about the people who once lived at the different sites. Although archaeologists have been conducting comparative analysis for years, South's "pattern" concept was unique because of its strong anthropological and scientific basis (see Chapter 4).

People "Without History"

Historical archaeology truly came of age in the late 1960s and 1970s, when archaeologists and historians both realized the potential of the humblest of artifacts for studying people whose daily lives are not well documented in historical sources. These "undocumented" people came from diverse ethnic groups, including African American enslaved workers, Chinese railroad laborers, Métis fur trappers, Welsh miners, and Irish canal diggers.

The realization that historical archaeology provides a unique way to study the men and women of history who seldom left detailed, written commentaries on their lives probably stemmed from two different yet related directions. First, by the late 1960s and early 1970s, it had become clear that most historical archaeologists would be trained by anthropologists rather than strictly by historians. Most of the freshly minted archaeologists would have formal training in, or at least experience with, archival research methods, but they also would have extensive knowledge of the ethnography of nonliterate peoples. These archaeologists realized they could successfully combine their anthropological perspectives with their knowledge of archival materials. Historical documents, for all the information they contain about the construction of railroads through the American West, relate virtually nothing about the daily lives of the Chinese immigrants who actually performed the hard labor. Without archaeology, almost nothing would be known about their daily living conditions and material culture. Basic questions would remain unanswered, including: What kind of housing did the workers inhabit? What kind of ceramic dishes did they use? What did they eat? Did they retain elements of Chinese culture in North America? And which elements did they keep and which did they surrender? Historical archaeology is the only discipline that can address such basic questions in minute and exacting detail.

The growth in ethnic pride throughout the world in the 1960s and 1970s was a second factor convincing many historical archaeologists that their discipline was relevant to society at large, and that their specialized knowledge was meaningful well beyond the narrow confines of professional archaeology. It became clear that historical archaeology, seeking to document the undocumented, could be invaluable for providing abundant details about the daily lives of peoples whose contributions to history might otherwise be forgotten. Two examples will illustrate this important point.

Yaughan and Curriboo Plantations, South Carolina

Yaughan and Curriboo were two eighteenth-century plantations in coastal South Carolina, a part of the southern United States that was home to thousands of enslaved Africans. Historical records make it possible to reconstruct the basic histories of ownership and family association within Yaughan and Curriboo. But even for all their usefulness, these records only tell the "official" history of the plantations and provide no information about the men, women, and children who actually performed the manual labor that helped to amass the riches of the plantation-owning families.

Thomas Wheaton and Patrick Garrow excavated 29 dwellings on the plantation and added an entirely new dimension to the history of the region. They showed that between the 1740s and 1770s, the enslaved lived in rectangular, mud-walled buildings possibly resembling their traditional houses in Africa or the Caribbean (Figure 2.7). From the 1780s to the 1820s they lived in smaller, square buildings placed on brick piers. Wheaton and Garrow believed the change meant that, as a result of constant interaction, enslaved Africans slowly learned the customs of their enslavers. To put this another way, the enslaved men and women slowly replaced their African traditions with those of their owners. This interpretation is controversial today because it can be just as easily argued that the enslaved moved into European houses because they were forced to do so. They may have had no choice in the matter. Nonetheless, the view presented by Wheaton and Garrow caused archaeologists to think about the meaning of the housing change, rather than simply to accept it as merely two elements of a disconnected history.

Figure 2.7 Artist's reconstruction of slave cabins at Curriboo Plantation, South Carolina

(From *The Archaeology of Slavery and Plantation Life* by Theresa Singleton. Orlando: Academic Press © 1985 Elsevier.)

Yaughan and Curriboo yielded a wealth of information on the nutrition of the enslaved. The men, women, and children housed there lived on corn, rice, beef, and pork, supplemented with some wild plants and game. Musket parts found at several dwellings indicate they used firearms to kill game. In addition to using a variety of European objects in their daily lives, the enslaved people also made their own pottery and probably also used some pots made by local Native Americans. (Archaeologists currently think that the coarse, low-fired pottery found at many slave plantations, including Yaughan and Curriboo, were produced by mixing African, Native American, and European pottery traditions.)

Historical archaeology adds an incredible richness to our knowledge of plantation life and gives the largely undocumented people who lived there a chance to be heard. The lives of wealthy owners tend to be revealed by a combination of archaeological and written sources, but only archaeology can document the daily conditions experienced by the enslaved.

Gold Bar Camp, Nevada

Gold Bar Camp in Nevada was a classic western mining settlement inhabited between 1905 and 1909. Only about 100 gold and silver miners and their families lived there. The camp is largely invisible in official documents because it was settled after the 1900 federal census and abandoned before the 1910 count. Only a few newspaper articles refer to the place. These limited accounts mention the presence of boarding houses, bunkhouses, and a superintendent's bungalow (Figure 2.8). The homes of the miners' families must also have existed in the camp because the records state that 18 school-aged children lived there in 1908. Photographs of the camp present general views of it, but like contemporary writings, they reveal little about daily life.

Historical archaeologist Donald Hardesty used excavation and survey to add an entirely new dimension to life at the Gold Bar Camp. He showed that the miners lived in houses measuring from 400 to over 1,000 square feet (37.1 to 92.9 sq. m), that many of these residences

Figure 2.8 The Gold Bar Camp, Nevada, as it looked in 1908
(Nevada Historical Society)

seemed to have special functions, and that the people at the camp used a huge variety of artifacts, including tin cans. These lowly cans, considered merely trash by nonarchaeologists, indicate that the residents of the mining community imported fruits and vegetables, meats, coffee, and milk for their meals. Glass bottles and lamp chimneys document the drinking of whiskey, wine, and beer, and the lighting of homes with kerosene lamps.

The people of Gold Bar maintained regular contact with the outside world. They wrote and received letters and were visited by traveling merchants and salespeople, and thus lived much like other people throughout the United States. Their difference, of course, was that they worked as hardrock miners, toughened laborers whose daily lives have been largely forgotten in written history. Without historical archaeology, their lives, though merely a footnote in the broad sweep of world history, would be forever shrouded in mystery, and our understanding of the past would be much less complete.

Contemporary Historical Archaeology

Historical archaeologists' interest in the rich and famous, as well as in the poor and undocumented, helps define the history of the discipline. Their interests reflect a growing awareness of the importance of cultural interactions after about 1500 C.E. The changing attitude is easy to identify in the literature. For instance, whereas before the early 1960s archaeologists' focus was almost exclusively on a plantation owner's mansion, by the late 1960s the emphasis had largely shifted to the cabins of the enslaved. This change in orientation, though not absolute, is nonetheless striking.

As the number of historical archaeologists continues to grow, historical archaeology is quickly becoming an international discipline. Once confined largely to North America and Great Britain, historical archaeology today flourishes on all continents, from South America to the South Pacific, from Cape Town to the Arctic Circle, from China to the Baltics.

Theoretical Foundations

Historical archaeology continues to mature. A number of archaeologists are playing a major role in this intellectual growth by experimenting with diverse ideas and theoretical points of view at a large variety of sites. This explosive growth makes it virtually impossible to provide a single theoretical theme to describe the field after the mid-1980s (see Chapter 10). Today's historical archaeologists use ideas and concepts from numerous disciplines, including but not limited to anthropology, sociology, philosophy, material culture studies, geographic information systems, social history, political economics, feminist and gender studies, and cultural and historical geography. Most archaeologists are no longer content with simply describing collections of artifacts or preparing archaeological reports that document the undocumented. Most contemporary historical archaeologists are examining the deeper meanings of artifacts and the complex relationships existing between people and the things around them, including buildings and landscapes. These concerns are taking the field in fascinating directions. Examples of a few well-known studies from the United States and the Caribbean demonstrate the roots of twenty-first-century historical archaeology.

The Paca Mansion, Annapolis, Maryland

Annapolis, Maryland, has a rich history, and the city has been the subject of intense archaeological investigation for more than two decades. Mark Leone has investigated the eighteenth-century residences of the city, including a large mansion built by William Paca, a wealthy lawyer and signer of the Declaration of Independence. As part of his research at Paca's house, Leone has provided an innovative interpretation of Paca's magnificent garden.

Many wealthy elites in Europe and European America built luxurious pleasure gardens behind their spacious homes. Like many of his contemporaries, Paca commissioned a large and rigidly structured formal green space to stretch behind his mansion in four distinct terraces, or platforms (Figure 2.9). The garden's designers symmetrically planted the first three platforms with trees and shrubs to give the garden a neat, manicured appearance. At the back of the property, however, they designed a "wilderness," an area they allowed to grow wildly. In among the wilderness, the designers placed a fish-shaped pond.

Most researchers have viewed such formal gardens as an architectural feature designed simply to enhance the appearance of the house itself. Scholars have tended to consider these gardens to have had a purely aesthetic function. In a departure from this view, Leone proposed that Paca had used his garden in a symbolic manner to reinforce the existing social order of early America. The garden, though indeed aesthetically pleasing, had a much more serious meaning. Leone interpreted the difference between the manicured garden and the unkempt wilderness as representing the increased chaos as one moved further away from (and physically below) the order and symmetry of the mansion. In addition to the manicured trees and shrubs, the designers had also incorporated a number of optical illusions into the plan that altered the visitor's perspective of space and distance. Leone believed the garden's designers wished to use these illusions to hide, in a symbolic sense, both the contradictions in Paca's own life—as a passionate defender of liberty and an owner of enslaved laborers—and in American society at large, contradictions that could assign inalienable rights to some and demand lifelong bondage from others.

Leone could easily have used his archaeological research simply to define the limits of the garden and to document the exact locations of trees and shrubs. Paca was an important historical figure, and architectural information about his mansion and its garden would interest many people, just as does Abraham Lincoln's house in Illinois. Leone chose, however, to offer an innovative interpretation by using the archaeological information in a new way.

45

Figure 2.9 Paca House and Restored Garden
(Kevin Fleming / Corbis)

The importance of Leone's article, whether or not one accepts his interpretation—and it has been much discussed—is that it demonstrates historical archaeologists are deeply engaged in important anthropological and historical debates about the past.

Boott Mill, Lowell, Massachusetts

In 1835, when a group of Boston entrepreneurs decided to build a mill to produce cotton and woolen goods, they settled on a location in Lowell, Massachusetts, near the New Hampshire state line. They called their industrial complex the Boott Cotton Mills, after Kirk Boott, the first mill agent. The mill site, now a museum, operates as part of the Lowell National Historical Park. In the 1980s, the U.S. National Park Service sponsored an extensive archaeological study of the mill. Written records indicated that most of the "mill girls" were New England farm girls and immigrants' daughters, but little else was known about them. In an effort to learn something about these mill workers, the team of archaeologists turned their attention to their boardinghouses (Figure 2.10).

As a way to understand the meaning of the artifacts collected from the mill's boarding-houses, archaeologists Mary Beaudry, Lauren Cook, and Stephen Mrozowski decided to envision the artifacts as a language—a complex discourse incorporating a huge number of diverse and often subtle meanings. They proposed that undocumented people such as mill workers, though uncounted in many historical records, communicated through their artifacts. Such

Figure 2.10 Lauren J. Cook excavating at Boott Mills boardinghouses, Lowell, Massachusetts, 1985

(Photograph by Mary C. Beaudry.)

individuals only remain undocumented if historical archaeologists fail to study the ways in which they documented themselves. One objective of the Boott Mills research was to study the mill workers from the "inside out" (meaning from the place in society where they document themselves) rather than from the "top down" (from the perspective of their social "betters") or from the "bottom up" (from the people's own viewpoint). One enlightening way to learn about the undocumented is to discover how they created their own worlds on their own terms.

The artifacts found during excavation point to the ways ordinary men and women used the things around them to express themselves. The archaeological discovery of liquor, wine, and beer bottles—along with beer mugs and wine glasses—demonstrate the boardinghouse residents' flagrant violation of the corporation's strict sobriety rules. Flowerpot fragments show how workers attempted to brighten their often-dreary lives by reclaiming a small bit of beauty in their otherwise monotonous, regulated work routines. The presence of marbles and doll parts suggest children also breathed life into the daily grind.

The men and women of Boott Mills, as consumers much like us today, were forced to purchase the objects they used. Like us, they had neither the technology nor the knowledge to make their own ceramic plates and glass bottles. The mill workers had to enter into relationships with merchants and grocers to obtain their possessions. These relationships, just like those they maintained with the mill's agents and owners, were a dialogue between people occupying different class positions within New England society. The social power of the owners far outweighed that of the workers, but the workers were not entirely powerless.

The Chesapeake

Some historical archaeologists use information from individual sites to provide new insights about whole regions (see Chapter 12). The Chesapeake region, which centers upon Chesapeake Bay and includes parts of Maryland and northern Virginia, is just such a place (Figure 2.11). This environmentally rich region was home to numerous Native Americans for generations, and a lush environment sought after by European settlers. The region contains some of the most well-studied historical archaeological sites in North America, including Annapolis, Mt. Vernon, Williamsburg, and St. Mary's City, to name only a few.

In one study, archaeologist Anne Yentsch used ceramics and animal bones in conjunction with written records from 16 sites in the region to identify small-scale social changes in the period from about 1680 to 1740. By adopting a regional and long-term perspective, Yentsch was able to observe a marked shift from wooden and pewter plates to ceramic dishes, an increase in the number of plates used, a greater variation in plate sizes in individual households, and a trend away from communal servings to individualized portions. The cultural issues involving changes in food preferences are complicated, but Yentsch's focus on them allowed her to think like an anthropologist interested in cultural continuity and social change, instead of thinking like an antiquarian concerned only with the appearance and date of the artifacts. Yentsch provided an interesting way for historical archaeologists to examine the transition from a pre-modern to a modern way of life through an analysis of mundane artifacts.

In another study in the Chesapeake region, archaeologist L. Daniel Mouer investigated the creation of colonial culture. He adopted a view of culture resting on the idea of "creolization." A creolized culture is one in which several strands from two or more cultures are consciously blended into a new expression, one that bears resemblance to the ancestral cultures but is itself new. Mouer was specifically interested in documenting how the men and women of the seventeenth-century Chesapeake created a way of life that contained elements

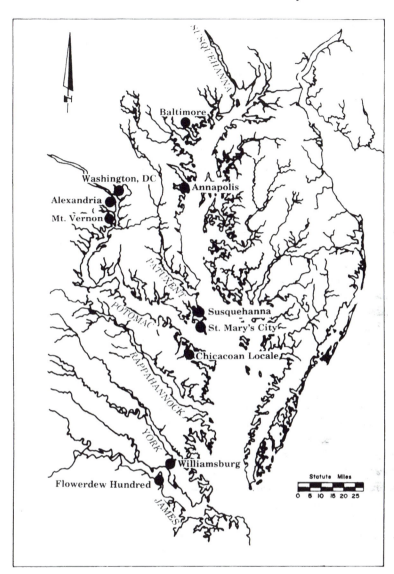

Figure 2.11 Chesapeake Region of the eastern United States, showing key sites

(From *Historical Archaeology of the Chesapeake*, edited by Paul A. Shackel and Barbara J. Little, Percheron Press, 2014.)

of English, Native American, and African American cultures. To illustrate his idea, he examined dietary habits, methods of food preparation, the use of tobacco, the manufacture of pottery, and the decoration of European-made smoking pipes. He learned that the residents of villages throughout the Chesapeake selected various cultural elements to create a folk culture unlike anything that had previously existed.

The Blue Mountains, Jamaica

In addition to examining specific regions, historical archaeologists also tackle special topics that have broad and often international significance. New World slavery and its aftermath clearly fit the bill as subjects of analysis that have intercontinental meaning and which are guaranteed to provide archaeological remains that can be studied in detail.

In an investigation of New World enslavement and freedom, historical archaeologist James Delle examined the changes occurring on the coffee plantations of Jamaica between 1790 and 1865. These years bracketed a time of great social upheaval on the island. The emancipation of thousands of enslaved men, women, and children, and the resultant transition from bondage to wage labor spelled the end of the old regime. The change from enslavement to freedom is complicated because diverse social, economic, and political variables may have played different roles in the process. Archaeologists do not know beforehand how best to study these complex features of history. One of the ways Delle sought to examine the monumental transformation of Jamaican plantation society was through the use of space.

Archaeologists know that space is profoundly significant to all cultures because houses, roads, schools, and other features built on the landscape are not randomly placed. Any real estate agent will tell you that location is everything, and the situation was not much different in the past. Knowing this, Delle set out to learn how the buildings and other features of Jamaica's coffee estates were situated. One thing he learned, for example, was that planters' houses were constructed to be considerably more durable and larger than the cabins of the enslaved—and later, the freed. The owners had ordered that the houses of plantation overseers (later foremen) were placed to increase surveillance over the workforce. Numerous maps commissioned by plantation owners provided mute testimony to the ways plantation owners sought to manage and control the physical space of their plantations. The maps also substantiated how the owners struggled to use space as a measure of social position. Without question, the use of space on Jamaican coffee plantations was not mere happenstance; it was well planned and executed.

In-depth studies of past settlements allow historical archaeologists to examine cultural complexity with everyday objects. Such investigation requires the careful construction of the people's context—the cultural, social, and natural environments within which they lived. As shown in the projects mentioned above, historical archaeologists now view artifacts—which also include buildings and roads—as active objects helping to create, structure, and maintain life rather than merely as passive, inanimate objects yielding information only about the date they were made (see Chapter 8).

Indigenous Connections

One of the most significant advances made in historical archaeology since the late 1980s has been the growth of collaborative projects between professional archaeologists and nonarchaeological members of descendant communities. The impetus for these projects came from many sources, but primary among them was the recognition by archaeologists that indigenous peoples have significant, legitimate interests in the results of archaeological research. Once archaeologists acknowledge their research has meaning to people living outside the archaeological community, it becomes clear that descendants and other interested individuals should be collaborators in research. Numerous archaeologists thus began to work alongside nonarchaeological "stakeholders" as full partners. Gone were the days when archaeologists arrived in a region to explain local history to its residents. With collaboration, research developed as a true dialogue.

The first realization about the need to consider sensibilities and cultural traditions involved the excavation of human remains. In the 1970s, the American Indian Movement and other groups had made it clear they were opposed to both the excavation of Native American remains and to their removal to archaeological laboratories where they would remain in boxes. Native American activists demanded an end to excavation and the return of excavated remains.

The realization that living people had concerns about the nature of archaeological research was initially contested within archaeology. Some thought as professionals they should be left alone to do the research for which they had been trained. Others believed archaeology was best served when it became a source of widespread education and when nonarchaeologists appreciated the value of historical knowledge. With time, most archaeologists came to accept the anthropological wisdom of showing respect to the wishes of others, and collaborative efforts were one result.

One outcome of inclusive thinking led archaeologists to appreciate that their field of study is not simply "about the past." Rather, with collaboration came the view that archaeological knowledge has a significant role to play in the contemporary world. Archaeologists may study history but they also belong to today's world. For some, this realization has led to the idea that archeology is a true social science, a discipline investigating the past as one route toward understanding the present.

Examples of community engagement now abound in historical archaeology. One goal of this research, as explained by archaeologist Barbara Little—a leader in this area—is to use archaeological research to empower communities to partner with academic researchers with the eventual goal of using archaeological and historical knowledge to create a better future (see Chapter 13). The realization of this goal is admirable, but it will take years to realize. It is especially pertinent in historical archaeology because the discipline's subject is not far removed from our own time. We face many of the challenges faced by our ancestors not so long ago.

In the next chapter we take up some of the basic elements of today's historical archaeology. These include the fields of anthropology and history, the two disciplines forever linked in historical archaeology. We then present an overview of the major site types historical archaeologists examine.

Site Visit: Smith's Fort, Bermuda, 1613

The more than 300 islands of Bermuda lie about 670 miles (1,080 km) southeast of New York City, in the Atlantic Ocean. The islands are named for a Spaniard named Juan de Bermúdez, a seafarer who may have sailed with Columbus on his first voyage. The European superpowers would dispute ownership of the Caribbean and its islands for many years, and by the middle of the sixteenth century, the British had staked their empire-building claim on the Bermuda islands. They sought to control the islands, believing they could serve as a sanctuary, a convenient and much-needed respite for ocean-weary colonists on their way to Virginia. Because other European powers might see the islands the same way and attempt to possess them, between 1612 and 1957 (when the British garrison

Figure 2.12 Smith's Fort, Bermuda
(Excavated by Norman Barka; courtesy of Edward Harris.)

finally withdrew), 90 forts had been raised on the islands. One of the earliest was called Smith's Fort (Figure 2.12).

British colonists at Bermuda feared attacks from their Spanish enemies, whose ships regularly patrolled the Caribbean seeking new conquests. The British, seeking to stress their seriousness in holding Bermuda, built a fortification on a tiny island on the eastern end of the archipelago. The spot, called Governor's Island, provided excellent defensive terrain because it guarded the harbor of the English town of St. George. The idea for the fort had begun with Governor Richard Moore, and he worked feverishly to defend the islands and transform them into a viable British colony. The fortification soon became known as Smith's Fort, a name it retains today. Captain John Smith, indefatigable self-promoter and friend to Pocahontas, published a map of Bermuda that depicted its forts in 1624, including the one he had modestly named for himself.

Smith pictured the tiny fort as triangular in shape with two circular towers facing seaward. A small house, possibly a power magazine, is shown inside the walls, and five soldiers, with swords and early seventeenth-century firearms, patrol around it. A neat row of defensive loopholes appear along the wall facing the viewer and in the nearest tower. Smith drew the fort's back wall as straight with a large doorway at its mid-point. In overall appearance, then, the drawing shows the fort as a truncated triangle; one point is sliced off and the other two have circular towers on them. Outside the fort's front wall, and between it and the shore, are arranged a row of five cannon pointing outward in a semi-circle. A three-masted ship (friend or foe?) approaches from the lower right.

Military engineers always understood the defensive importance of Governor's Island. In the eighteenth century, long after Smith's Fort was abandoned, Captain Andrew Durnford, of the Royal Engineers, arrived to construct a new installation on the island. The new fort, called Durnford's Redoubt, was in place before 1811. Henry Lauzan, one of Durnford's surveyors, drew a plan of Smith's Fort as it looked to him in 1790. His plan, since confirmed by archaeology, depicts a fort more square than triangular, with a back wall bowing out into a semi-circle rather than flat as Smith had shown it. Lauzan also drew a D-shaped "sea battery" extending outward from the front wall of the fort, with the curved part of the D pointing toward the sea.

The maximum dimension of Smith's Fort was only about 56 by 82 feet (17 by 25 m). The two circular towers were located where both Smith and Lauzan had drawn them. They were made of cut limestone, and each had an interior diameter of only about 6.5 feet (2 m). The distance from the midpoint of each tower was only 24 feet (7.5 m). The builders of the fort had chiseled a flat surface into the bedrock between the towers, along the fort's outer wall, and had hewn steps into the east side of the western tower to allow access from the sea battery.

Smith's Fort is one of the few examples of early English forts built in the New World still visible above ground. Most forts, being made of timber, have long since deteriorated and disappeared. As a historical monument, part of the significance of Smith's Fort derives from its being one of the last truly defensive "castles" to be constructed anywhere in the world. Its designers worked during a time of transition in the technology of warfare from medieval to modern. Castles were mostly abandoned with the development of cannons because castle walls could not withstand bombardment. Castles came from an age of crossbows and rudimentary firearms. The towers of Smith's Fort were too small for cannons; they had been designed for archers and men with muskets. The small cannons depicted by Smith on the shore could possibly have defended against lightly armed ships, but the fort's defensive might could have easily been tested. The coastal defensive fortification, first designed by Romans in Britain, received one of its final expressions at Smith's Fort.

Sources: Edward Cecil Harris, *Bermuda Forts, 1612–1957*. (Bermuda: Bermuda Maritime Museum Press, 1997); Norman F. Barka and Edward C. Harris, *Archaeology of Smith's Fort and Durnford's Redoubt, Governor's Island, Bermuda: Final Season, 2001*. (Williamsburg, Virginia: Department of Anthropology, College of William and Mary, 2002).

Chapter 3

Culture, History, and Archaeological Sites

Most people have an interest in what archaeologists do. When they meet them in the field, perhaps at a place they have driven by day after day without noticing or at a nearby historic site, they usually have a number of questions to ask: How do you know where to dig? What is so special about this place? How do you know what to look for? How deep do you dig, and how do you know when to stop? Archaeology seems so scientific and meticulous that it holds a mystery all its own. Even the most casual onlooker is fascinated by how archaeologists carefully strip away the layers of dirt and sand to reveal the objects made and used by people long dead.

One question frequently asked of historical archaeologists is seldom posed to archaeologists who study the ancient past: Why excavate history? Why should archaeologists spend scarce grant funds, endure long, tiring days in the hot sun—often in unsafe or even dangerous environments—and teach students to excavate a period of history that is documented in written records? Wouldn't it be less expensive and safer to go to an archive to learn about the more recent past? People can readily understand why archaeologists may be drawn to the study of the ancient Egyptians or the Mayas of Central America, but they may find it more difficult to understand why archaeologists would wish to excavate the home of an early twentieth-century coal miner. Surely historical records provide us with enough information about coal mining to make archaeology unnecessary.

We could provide many philosophical reasons why all archaeology is important in helping to construct knowledge about the past, and we have presented some ideas about this subject in Chapter 1. The value of excavating history was neatly summarized by prominent historian and the librarian of the U.S. Congress, Daniel Boorstin: "We know more about some aspects of daily life in the ancient Babylon of 3000 B.C.E. than we do about daily life in parts of Europe or America a hundred years ago." Boorstin's comment is perceptive. In Chapter 2, we touched upon some of the values of excavating the recent past. In this chapter, we explain more fully that an interest in historical cultures and societies makes the excavation of recent history important. Archaeological information about historical cultures and societies helps explain why today's world is the way it is.

Culture and Society

The word *culture*, though seemingly straightforward, has many meanings. We may describe someone who goes to the opera as "cultured," and someone who makes rude noises while eating soup in a restaurant as "uncultured." Used in this popular way, the word "culture" often says more about the individual using the term than about the person or group to which the person is referring. In a popular sense, "culture" only means what one person (or perhaps one group of people) views as appropriate behavior in a certain setting. Some behaviors reflect "culture"; others reflect a lack of it. The popular use of the term may be widespread, but it is not anthropological.

Another popular sense of the word *culture* is closer to its anthropological meaning. Everyone knows that other cultures exist. Their unfamiliar dress and odd customs may be seen in television documentaries and on the web, and museums present exhibits of other cultures' decorative ornaments, pieces of art, and musical instruments. Eating dishes from other countries and meeting people from other cultures in the world's largest cities and on university campuses reinforces the idea that culture is variable. The word "foreigner" indicates that people unlike "us" come from somewhere else. They may speak odd-sounding languages, prefer different foods, and dress in unfamiliar ways. Such differences allow one culture's members to sense that "foreign" people are indeed different. But how are the differences identified? What do individuals sense when meeting "foreign" peoples? What they sense is a different culture.

The concept of culture is at the core of anthropology and all anthropologists seek to contribute something to its understanding. The diversity of the world's cultures and the multitude of ways that culture can be studied have meant that anthropologists have formulated numerous definitions for this one important concept. One might reasonably expect all anthropologists to agree on the definition of a concept that is so central to their field, but this is not the case. In 1952, Alfred Kroeber and Clyde Kluckhohn, two renowned American anthropologists, collected all the definitions of culture used by their colleagues. We might expect they only found a handful of different definitions, but they gathered more than 160 of them!

In the face of such overwhelming disagreement, the best definition is perhaps the first one ever proposed. In his book *Primitive Culture*, published in 1871, Edward Tylor (Figure 3.1) defined culture as "the complex whole which includes knowledge, belief, art, morals, law, custom, and any other capabilities and habits acquired by man [humans] as a member of society." Tylor's definition captures three important elements of culture: first, that culture is composed of many diverse elements—from the shape of clay pots to beliefs about the afterlife—that are brought together in unity; second, that culture is not instinctual, but must be learned; and third, that people learn culture in societies, groups of people who are bound together by a shared way of life and who engage in social interaction. From the members of culture, individuals learn how to sit at a table to eat, how to arrange the place setting in the "correct" way, what is acceptable to serve at a meal, how to interpret what is served, and how to consume it in acceptable ways. Culture is internalized during the enculturation process, the often-unconscious way of learning "right" from "wrong." The rules of culture also can be purposefully taught. Formal schooling provides a good example. During the first years of attendance, pupils learn many cultural rules in a fairly structured way. Students learn how to sit, how to address figures of authority, and when to speak. Other rules are learned on the playground during recess in nonstructured, informal ways. Both processes of cultural instruction are equally important for teaching individuals what is expected of them within a particular cultural context.

Figure 3.1 Edward B. Tylor
(The LIFE Picture Collection / Getty Images)

Humans use culture to help them adapt to their environment. In this sense, human culture is unique. People use their intelligence, traditions, and experience to feed themselves, to shelter themselves from high and low temperatures, and to protect themselves from predatory animals and human enemies. All of these ways of surviving in the environment are determined by culture.

Anthropologists have learned they cannot really understand culture without also comprehending society. Men and women do not simply practice their cultures unaware of the other individuals around them. In fact, the enactment of culture always involves many people. All human cultures have men, women, and children who engage with one another. Anthropologists and sociologists refer to the linkages between individuals as *social relations*. Emile Durkheim, the great French sociologist whom students of anthropology and sociology continue to study today, wrote in 1915 that "There is no people and no state which is not part of another society, more or less unlimited, which embraces all the peoples and all the states with which it first comes in contact, either directly or indirectly." Durkheim is saying that cultures

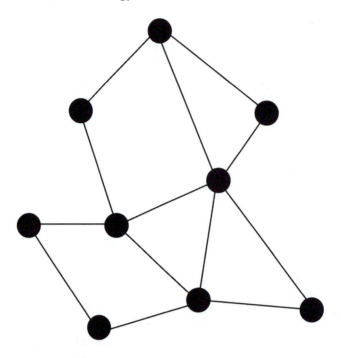

Figure 3.2 Graphic representation of a simple social network
(Charles E. Orser, Jr.)

involve real people and that these real people must regularly interact with one another to live in society.

The social relations of any society create a *social network*. We may think of a social network as a web of connections between the individuals in a specific culture (Figure 3.2). Individuals who live in today's large, highly complex, industrialized states are enmeshed in many complicated social networks. In addition, individuals who have formed themselves into groups—age grades, secret societies, clubs, classes, and so forth—also maintain social relations with other groups. Social groups usually associate themselves with material objects that archaeologists can excavate and analyze (see Chapter 10).

Culture must not be confused with behavior because not everyone in a culture acts exactly alike. Individuals act differently based on many factors, including their social relations within various social networks. Ants and wolves have societies—because they engage in social interaction and have a shared way of life—but they do not have culture. Culture structures the rules and standards that are deemed acceptable, but it provides for variability within the limits of acceptability. If culture were not variable, then everyone would act exactly the same.

Cultural Systems

Tylor's idea that culture is a "complex whole" makes the point that culture is composed of many elements. These elements are both tangible (erasers, chairs, and notebooks) and intangible (religious beliefs, economic attitudes, and folklore). They work together as a system, or interconnected network, in which the various spheres of life are related. The cultural system allows individuals to adapt to another system, the natural environment (the ecosystem).

An important feature of any system is the idea that when one of its elements changes, other elements change as well. This sort of change is easy to understand in an ecosystem. Deforestation allows rain to strike the ground directly, causing erosion and increased sedimentation in nearby rivers and streams. The change in one part of the ecosystem—in this case, the decrease in the number of trees—has brought about changes in another—the soil and the nearby watercourses. These changes can in turn affect human life, particularly if the rainfall destroys houses and agricultural fields.

The idea that change in one part of a system causes changes in others is easy to envision in small, relatively simple cultures where little social stratification exists. A change in the leadership rules of a small culture may affect a people's way of life. If the leader, who was traditionally selected by heredity alone, is now chosen on the basis of material wealth, some changes may be expected to occur in the people's economic practices. Individuals may begin to compete against one another in their effort to amass greater amounts of material things so that they, too, might one day be chosen as leader.

Systemic change is more difficult to envision in highly complex, hierarchical cultures, such as those usually studied by historical archaeologists. Neat one-to-one correlations between changes in one sphere and changes in another are often extremely difficult to make in complex cultures because too many interacting factors exist.

Consider the case of Henry the Navigator, Prince of Portugal (Figure 3.3). Born in 1394, Henry was a studious young man with a strong interest in mathematics and astronomy. He and his two older brothers, to prove themselves worthy of knighthood, raised an army in 1415 and captured Ceuta, an Islamic commercial town across the Straits of Gibraltar in Morocco. Ceuta was a major center of the Saharan gold trade. Once he had a foothold in North Africa, Henry aimed to control the gold trade and thus obtain more African wealth. He sponsored several naval expeditions southward along the African coast, with the long-term objective of outflanking the Saharan trade routes controlled by his Islamic enemies. In 1441, one of his captains, Antão Gonçalves, returned to Portugal with two black African captives, one male, the other female. These individuals were the first African slaves taken to Europe. As Portuguese ships navigated southward, they found Madeira and the Cape Verde Islands. On these tiny islands, they developed labor-intensive sugar plantations worked by enslaved laborers. These plantation outposts were also relatively close to a seemingly unlimited supply of African captives. The Portuguese soon became obsessed with the economic potential of the African slave trade, not only for human cargoes to work the fields at home, but eventually for export to sugar plantations in Brazil, the Caribbean, and elsewhere. The African men and women taken to Portugal caused Portuguese citizens to think differently about their world. Instead of seeing the world composed simply of "Christians" and "non-Christians," as before, Portuguese men and women began to envision the world as divided between "enslaved" and "free," "black" and "white," "our culture" and "their culture."

The presence of Africans on the cobbled streets of Lisbon forced the Portuguese to think about new categories of people, to contemplate the men and women among them who were from completely different, non-Portuguese cultural systems. Did the influx of Africans affect *every* part of Portuguese life? Did the presence of Africans in Portugal change the Portuguese system of government? Portuguese strategies and plans for their empire changed over time, but to conclude these changes were the sole result of African enslavement denies the complexity of Portuguese culture. The Portuguese were undoubtedly changed forever because of their involvement with African slavery, but the true extent of this change to

Figure 3.3 Prince Henry of Portugal, the Navigator
(AF Fotografie / Alamy)

their cultural system and to their many social networks must be studied for years to be understood.

All cultural systems are complex, no matter how large the population. At first glance, the Tiwi hunter-gatherers of northern Australia appear to be a "simple" culture. Living on two islands off the northern coast of Australia, they maintained minimal contact with the outside world before 1890. Early European visitors to the islands found them living in small bands, armed only with boomerangs and stone-tipped spears. The Tiwi are by our standards a "simple" people. Their "simplicity," however, is highly misleading.

The complexity of Tiwi culture is amply demonstrated by something we take for granted: our names. Personal names among the Tiwi are bestowed on a child by its father or the man currently married to the child's mother. Whenever a husband dies and the widow remarries, the child receives a new name. In fact, all names given by the dead man are taboo; they are never spoken again. Women can marry several times in their lives, so their children may have several different names during their lifetimes. A person would not typically receive a permanent name until his or her mother was dead and could no longer remarry. The Tiwi solved this problem by adopting the name taboo for only a short time. After what was judged a decent period had passed, most people slipped back into calling the person by their most familiar name. For men, this generally meant the one they had received in their twenties and thirties, and for women the most familiar name was the one they had in early adolescence. Studies of material culture prove that cultural complexity cannot be measured by artifacts and food remains alone, because many societies, like the Tiwi, enjoyed elaborate and highly sophisticated belief systems and ceremonial lives that may seem more "advanced" than their material possessions.

The archaeologist's job of interpreting past cultural systems is made especially difficult because most of the archaeologist's information about cultural complexity comes from material remains—artifacts, food remains, building ruins, and so forth. Even in the case of exceptional preservation, the intangible aspects of human culture, such as language and religious beliefs, have vanished with their users. Historical archaeologists often have an advantage over archaeologists studying ancient, unrecorded history because of the availability of written texts and other "nonarchaeological" materials, such as photographs and maps. The addition of more information, however, can also be a complicating factor, especially when the sources conflict.

Cultural Change

All cultures and societies constantly change regardless of their size and complexity. Transformations occur in all spheres of culture because people are active beings who invent new ways of doing things, who find new ideas more acceptable than old ones, and who come into contact with other peoples. Change can be endogenous (originating within the culture) or exogenous (originating outside the culture).

Archaeologists view change primarily through the material remains people left behind. One advantage of archaeology is that it allows for the study of change over long periods of time. Archaeologists excavating ancient sites occupied for centuries may observe a change in pottery decoration from red-painted to black-and-white-painted. The archaeologist's task is to seek a plausible interpretation of this process of change. Was the change caused by a switch from male to female potters? Was a religious ban on red-painted pottery enforced by powerful priests? Did red pigment sources become depleted? Did foreigners who made black-and-white pottery acquire more influence in the society? Or did a combination of several factors account for the change in pottery decoration? The search for solutions to such questions makes archaeology an exciting but challenging discipline.

Historical archaeologists face similar problems in understanding cultural change, even though they seldom study sites inhabited for several centuries. Cultural change in the modern era was often truly exogenous and far beyond the control of most peoples who experienced it. For example, as we discuss in more detail in Chapter 4, changes in ceramic usage may be mandated by the factory's owner. In the early 1760s, famous English potter Josiah Wedgwood introduced a ceramic he called "cream-colored ware." This ware, with its soft, creamy appearance, enjoyed quick and widespread popularity. Even today, collectors scour dusty showrooms and out-of-the-way antique shops hoping to find the odd example. Not every late-eighteenth-century English consumer may have liked the creamware, but many of them may have felt forced to buy it at a time when choices were far more limited than they are today. Nonetheless, the precise motivation of each purchasing consumer may have been quite distinct.

The origin of some cultural changes can originate thousands of miles from an archaeological site. For instance, the changing fashions in beaver felt hats in seventeenth- and eighteenth-century Europe had a profound impact on both the Native American cultures who lived in Canada's rich, fur-bearing landscape and the European settlers who had established settlements nearby. Archaeologists can see the pressure exerted by the fur trade at countless native village sites throughout northern North America. Tiny glass beads, copper kettles, and brass buttons provide mute clues to the impact of the European fur-based economy on the native communities. The consumption of native foods, the use of native material culture, and the adoption of native methods of building (as well as other cultural traits) by transplanted Europeans demonstrate that cultural change occurs in both directions.

A family's preference for blue-banded or red-banded plates would, of course, have little effect on culture change outside the narrow confines of a single household. But many changes have lasting significance. A shift from communal planting of crops using horse-drawn plows to the use of diesel-powered planting machines by individual farmers would ripple through even a complex culture and affect everything from threshing technology to crop yields. The change would affect the operation of social networks through the discontinuance of relations between once-cooperating individuals and groups.

One strength of historical archaeology lies in its ability to assess the impact of what may appear at first to be a minor cultural change. It may be that Wedgwood's cream-colored plates were rejected by some people who chose instead to build their own kilns to continue producing earlier styles. Such action is difficult to document unless one happens to discover a kiln site. In New Hampshire, for instance, archaeologists David Starbuck and Mary Dupré used archaeological specimens to show how the potters of Millville, an area on the western edge of Concord, produced traditional redware ceramics (somewhat resembling terra-cotta flower-pots in material) from 1790 until about 1900. This pottery tradition was virtually unchanged during this 110-year period.

Changes in ceramic style and color may be so subtle or unrecognized for their importance that authors of historical records may have completely ignored them. Starbuck and Dupré pointed out that even though 250 potters operated in New England before 1800, and more than 500 after 1850, few were mentioned in written documents. The conscious, combined use of archaeological and nonarchaeological sources of information makes it possible for historical archaeologists to study both large (regional, transnational, global) and small (local) cultural changes.

Using Anthropology and History in Historical Archaeology

The concepts of culture and society help archaeologists explain what they find at abandoned sites. The material objects and the other remains archaeologists find, however, do not represent culture as such, but rather the results of behaviors of people acting within culture and society. Archaeologists cannot directly observe past behavior, so they must infer actions and even ideas from what they find during excavation. Two ways archaeologists can infer the past are by using ethnographic analogy and the direct historical approach.

Ethnographic analogy refers to the archaeological use of a past observer's comments about a living people as added support for an inference about past behavior. A cultural anthropologist's ethnography and an account recorded by a non-professional direct observer (such as a missionary or casual traveler) can be the source for analogies. In a famous example, when archaeologist Lewis Binford found shallow, basin-shaped pits filled with charred corncobs at the pre-Columbian Toothsome Site in southern Illinois, he used ethnographies of Native Americans to infer that the pits were used during the process of tanning hides. In this scenario, tanners placed the hides over the pits and the smoke from the smoldering corncobs made the hides pliable and more easily worked. Binford was willing to make the connection between what he read in the ethnographies about the use of shallow pits and the archaeological pits he discovered by excavation. He was unable to interpret the function of the pits without relying on the ethnographic material. Archaeologist Patrick Munson later questioned Binford's conclusion, stating that the shallow pits may have been used to put a blackened surface on clay pottery. Munson also used ethnographic analogy to make his claim, but he used a different set of Native American cultures for the analogy. The correctness of one interpretation over the other is irrelevant here (they may both be correct). What is important is the use of nonarchaeological, written sources for interpreting the past using analogical reasoning. If something observed and written about in the past is similar in form to something found archaeologically, an archaeologist may have reason to suspect a similarity in function between the two objects. From this similarity may be inferred further aspects of cultural practice.

The *direct historical approach* is similar to ethnographic analogy except that here a direct link exists between the ethnographic and the archaeological cultures. In this approach, the archaeologist uses a culture that still inhabits the region in which the archaeological site is found to show the connections between the two cultures. The direct historical approach is as old as the European invasion of the New World. Spanish explorers in Middle America and Peru used it to connect the stone monuments they saw with the native cultures around them. A classic example in modern archaeology is A. V. Kidder's use of the approach in the 1910s and 1920s. Excavating at Pecos Pueblo in northern New Mexico, Kidder correlated the stratified layers of pre-Columbian occupation (containing painted potsherds) with artifacts used by modern Pueblo Indians living in the region (Figure 3.4). Kidder's methodology was a blueprint for all subsequent research in the Southwest and much farther afield as well.

Direct historical research is based on the establishment of a cultural link between past and present. Once this link is made, archaeologists can use information from the present-day or historically described culture to infer the past with greater confidence than is possible with ethnographic analogy. If a Southwestern archaeologist finds smooth, flat stones at an archaeological site and native people living 60 miles (96 km) away grind corn using flat stones, then, using the direct historical approach, one may reasonably conclude that the ancient flat stones were also used for grinding corn. From this material evidence, the archaeologist can infer the behaviors of growing, grinding, and eating corn in the past.

Historical archaeologists regularly use both ethnographic analogy and the direct historical approach. The analogies used in historical archaeology often derive from historical documents or from other materials dating to the exact time a site was inhabited. Historical archaeologists know from their own archival research and from the studies of historians that plantation owners expected certain behaviors from their enslaved work force—deference, ignorance, a willingness to work—and that the enslaved, for their part, cherished other images—bravery in the face of bondage and cruelty, the ability to trick the master, the skill to leave the plantation surreptitiously at night, and even the power to harm the planter's family with charms, spells, and more serious measures. For example, in the 1760s, the *Charleston*

Figure 3.4 Ruins of Pecos Pueblo and Mission Church
(North Wind Picture Archives / Alamy)

(South Carolina) *Gazette* complained that "The negroes have again begun the hellish practice of poisoning."

Where documents or historical studies exist, historical archaeologists need not rely on ethnographic analogies or the direct historical approach to help them devise interpretations. Rather than referring to these kinds of analogies as ethnographic, we may think of them as direct analogies, because exact agreement exists between the archaeological site and the text-based material. When used in combination, these two sources can significantly aid the development of a plausible interpretation. Historical archaeologists can make direct analogies because the people being written about and the people who lived at the archaeological site being excavated are often one and the same. Archaeologists who do not have recourse to texts cannot make direct analogies because the people they study did not write about themselves or the times in which they lived. They were also usually not written about by anyone else.

Microhistory

The close relationship between the disciplines of historical archaeology and history have been explained in previous chapters. Within the broad practice of history, however, historical archaeology shares a special association with microhistory.

Microhistory is the study of the minute and unique in exacting detail to help shed light on wider social and cultural contexts in the past. Using historical records to study the life of a single person or community, microhistorians seek to discover broader historical trends.

In two famous studies, Carlo Ginzburg wrote about the life of an obscure sixteenth-century miller named Domenico Scandella in an environment monitored by the Italian Inquisition, and Donna Merwick reconstructed the life of a notary named Adriaen Janse van Ilpendam, the only person known to have committed suicide in seventeenth-century Dutch New Netherland. Both studies, though focused on the lives of two otherwise unknown men, provided abundant information about the cultural contexts of their times.

The practices of microhistorians and historical archaeologists are similar because both start from the small (the site, the individual) with the goal of learning about a larger context of daily life (the culture, the historical contexts). A number of microhistorians have even compared their research methods to those of archaeologists by mentioning how they sift through documents like excavators, unearthing the relics of everyday life. The microhistorian's monograph is thus analogous to the archaeologist's site report.

In 1959, an American historian named George R. Stewart may have been the first historian to use the word "microhistory." He examined one event, Pickett's Charge at the Battle of Gettysburg during the American Civil War. The charge occurred on one day, July 3, and lasted only 15 hours. Stewart studied this single event in minute detail to discover how it affected national and even international history. Most historians ignored Stewart's analysis, but since the 1980s microhistory has been practiced around the world by growing numbers of historians. Many microhistories are extremely popular with the public because they present intimate details of everyday life in the past. Similarities between life in the past and in the present illustrate common features of the human experience, whenever it was lived.

One of the similarities between microhistory and historical archaeology rests on the interest of both in "the lower orders," men and women too easily ignored or misrepresented in official records. Both scholars have a commitment to documenting the lives of the poor and the forgotten by presenting unique information, whether in the form of obscure documents or artifacts. Like historical archaeologists, microhistorians use lessons learned from the careful investigation of commoners to unravel the intricacies of large-scale history.

One of the microhistorian's goals is to correct the traditional historian's emphasis on legal and political history by focusing on social networks and cultural variables. Microhistorians seek to uncover and investigate social interactions that occurred between historical actors as real men and women. The narratives they create from documents illuminate social networks that operated in history, much as do archaeologists' analyses. Understanding social relations is indispensable because historical actors must interact with others in any historical narrative. This same idea is prominent in most contemporary historical archaeology.

Without question, the small worlds of everyday life maintain connections with the larger worlds dominated by socioeconomic and political practices, ideologies, and trends. Microhistory and historical archaeology share an incredible potential to unearth heretofore unknown information about the conditions faced by individuals, families, and communities in the past.

The Major Site Types of Historical Archaeology

Historical archaeology, like all archaeology, is based on the recovery of information from sites (Figure 3.5). A *site* is any place that contains traces of past human activity. The site constitutes the archaeologists' basic source of information, the place where they get a glimpse of past culture and society. Many different kinds of sites exist, ranging from those occupied for a few hours to those inhabited for hundreds of years. Archaeologists often classify sites in terms of their past function, frequently referring to them broadly as "site types." Historical archaeology has several key site types.

Figure 3.5 Excavated foundation of an adobe house that once stood at El Polín Springs, Presidio of San Francisco. The house was likely occupied by Juana Briones and her family, a *mulata* colonial woman who developed a prosperous business as a rancher, farmer, and *curandera*.

(Courtesy of Barbara L. Voss.)

Domestic Sites

Domestic sites are places where people lived. These sites can include an array of habitations ranging from the smallest, simplest structures to the grandest mansions. Archaeologists are interested in domestic structures because they provide personal information about how past peoples lived on a daily basis. Domestic sites tell archaeologists about the kinds of objects people used, the varieties of foods they ate, whether they traded with other peoples, the nature of their religious beliefs and ceremonies, and how they chose to discard their broken and unwanted articles.

Archaeologists can study one domestic site or many. Numerous individual sites can be clustered in cities and towns, and in such cases the archaeologist may consider the entire city to be a single site.

When archaeologists from a private consulting firm excavated a small Chinese immigrant village at Rincon Point, California, they learned a great deal about mid-nineteenth-century Chinese life in one part of the American West. The village was inhabited from about 1850 until only about 1865, but today it lies beneath the western approach to the San Francisco Bay Bridge. The archaeology at the village site filled many blank spots in our knowledge about Chinese domestic life in America. The discovery of bones and shells indicated that these immigrants had been California's first commercial fishermen. Being the first to recognize the commercial potential of abalone, they used the sea as a way of adapting to American life. They ate the meat from the abalone and sold the colorful shells to craftsmen, who soon made popular jewelry for northern California's shoppers. The archaeologists also discovered that the Chinese who lived at the Rincon Point village used equal proportions of American and Chinese objects, ranging from brown stoneware jars used to store traditional Chinese foods to American beer bottles and tooth powder. Rising real estate prices and increased taxes (imposed only on the Chinese) soon drove them away from their town, and by 1870, the area had become part of the booming San Francisco waterfront. Only archaeology could provide the details of Chinese immigrant life at Rincon Point.

Long before the creation of public landfills, most families threw their trash into their yards, tossed things under their houses, or swept their refuse against the back fence. Many people also used privies as places to discard objects they did not want others to know about, such as alcohol bottles.

A privy excavated by Kenneth Lewis provided a unique perspective on the consumption habits of the planters who lived on a late seventeenth- and early eighteenth-century sugar plantation near Charleston, South Carolina. Henry Middleton founded Middleton Place Plantation in 1675 upstream from the city. He owned no less than 800 bonds men and women and 20 individual plantations. Middleton Place prospered for nearly two centuries. It had two beautifully landscaped formal gardens, a springhouse, and a long drive leading to the mansion. General Sherman's troops destroyed all the main buildings at the plantation when they cut their scorched path through the South in 1865 (Figure 3.6). The privy was the

Figure 3.6 Ruins of the main house at Middleton Place Plantation, South Carolina

(From sterescopic by B. W. Kilburn before 1886. Courtesy of the Middleton Place Foundation, Charleston, South Carolina.)

only building they left unharmed. Over 100 years later, archaeologists carefully removed the accumulated rubbish in the privy and recovered priceless information about its users. They learned, for example, that the plantation residents had eaten from blue and white porcelain dishes from China as well as other dishes with a pattern of delicate flowers, called French Bourbon Sprig, a style popular before the French Revolution. They drank from finely cut glass decanters and stemware. A jumble of broken medicine bottles in the privy revealed that the plantation's residents suffered a variety of ailments, ranging from upset stomachs to night sweats associated with consumption (tuberculosis).

The Middleton Place privy, like all such facilities, provides an imperfect picture of past life because it encapsulates only the things people threw down the open hole or dropped accidentally. Nonetheless, long-sealed privies can be a revealing source of information about every level of society.

Historical archaeologists often use their techniques to reconstruct the architectural history of standing buildings, in a more scientific way than did Henry Ford's workmen (see Chapter 1). When archaeologist Theodore Reinhart took a crew of students from the College of William and Mary to Shirley Plantation, Virginia, one of his objectives was to reconstruct the mansion's history. Many historians thought this stately brick mansion, overlooking the James River about 35 miles (56 km) west of Williamsburg, was built in the seventeenth century, probably after 1660. Because no one knew for certain, Reinhart decided to dig next to the mansion's wall to look for a builder's trench.

Construction workers building brick walls excavated linear trenches along the walls' paths to allow them space to install the lowest courses. They often lost coins or dropped broken bottles and other objects inside the trench as they worked. The trenches, which would be forever covered over with earth, were also convenient places to throw trash. Archaeologists can use the objects buried in builder's trenches to help determine the date of a building's construction (Figure 3.7).

The known manufacturing dates of the English ceramics found by Reinhart's team inside the Shirley mansion's builder's trench convinced him the mansion "was built by John Carter, sometime before his death in 1742 and possibly in the years 1738 and 1739." It was not a seventeenth-century structure at all. In this case, archaeology was the only way to answer a seemingly straightforward historical question.

Industrial Sites

Places once used for manufacturing or production are known as industrial sites. The study of industrial sites is a subfield of historical archaeology, known as industrial archaeology. Industrial archaeologists study a variety of sites including mills, factories, kilns, mines, bridges, and canals. Such sites can range in date from the earliest days of manufacturing to the present. Industrial sites are often complex and require full documentation using photographs and accurately scaled architectural renderings (see Chapter 6).

Industrial archaeology does not always involve excavation. Many individuals who are not archaeologists—but are trained as industrial architects, engineers, or in a related field—often refer to themselves as industrial archaeologists. These researchers, though not archaeologists, can be storehouses of information. For example, as documented by archaeologist Donald Linebaugh, the amateur archaeologist Roland W. Robbins was an authority on seventeenth- and eighteenth-century industrial sites in New England. From 1948 to 1984 he investigated ironworks throughout the northeastern United States and became an expert on the topic. Professional archaeologists did not always approve his methods of excavation, but his knowledge of the region's industrialization was vast.

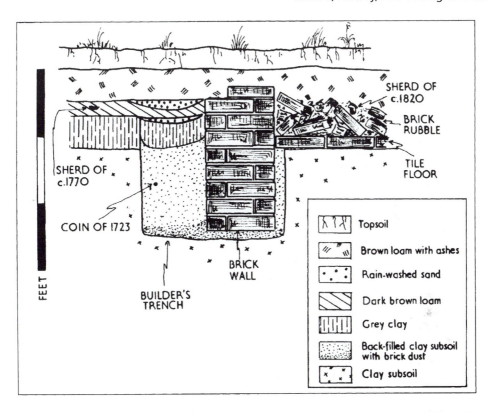

SHERD OF c.1820

BRICK RUBBLE

TILE FLOOR

SHERD OF c.1770

COIN OF 1723

FEET

BRICK WALL

BUILDER'S TRENCH

ㅅㅅㅅ	Topsoil
/// ш	Brown loam with ashes
·.·.	Rain-washed sand
▨	Dark brown loam
▥	Grey clay
▦	Back-filled clay subsoil with brick dust
⌑	Clay subsoil

Figure 3.7 Builder's trench

(From *Historical Archaeology* by Ivor Noël Hume. Alfred A. Knopf, 1972 © W. W. Norton & Company, Inc.)

Researchers sometimes only wish to document the remains at the site without disturbing the soil. At large, standing industrial sites—such as the Silver King Ore-Loading Station in Park City, Utah (Figure 3.8)—archaeologists may be asked to excavate one or two small areas to search for specific details about construction techniques or to determine dates of construction and disuse. Such research often involves collaboration with industrial architects and historians of technology.

Archaeological research sometimes provides an important way to learn about small-scale technologies. A prime example is the arrastra found in the western United States. Arrastras were circular, stone-lined depressions ranging in size from 8 to 20 feet (2.4–6.1 m) in diameter. Prospectors used arrastras to crush stones in their search for gold and silver. The arrastras' heavy grinding stones, turned by horses, steam engines, and water wheels, revolved about ten times per minute.

Archaeologists Roger Kelly and Marsha Kelly studied an arrastra site in northwest Arizona. Built sometime in the early twentieth century, this site consisted of the arrastra itself, a long, narrow trough made of flat stones extending outward from the arrastra, a stone wall, an ore pile, and a possible camp area. Laborers at the site had scratched dates of between 1910 and 1916 on the stones, and someone had etched "Hello Bill" on one of them. The

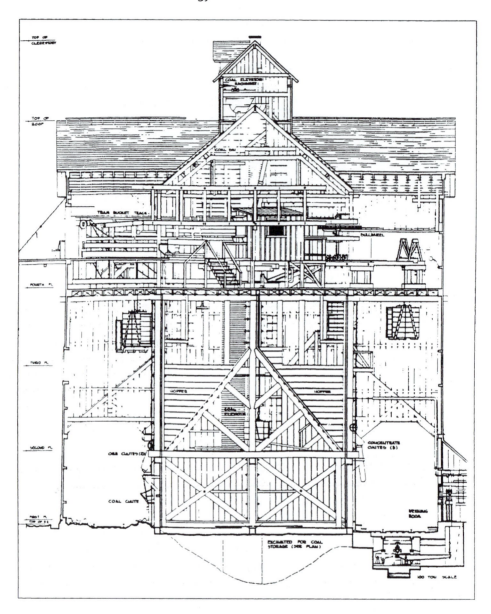

Figure 3.8 Measured drawing of the Silver King Ore-Loading Station, Park City, Utah, built in 1901

(Courtesy of the Library of Congress.)

study of this one arrastra will not change the way we think about the large sweep of world history. But as the Kellys correctly point out, arrastras challenge archaeologists to think about industrial sites, regardless of size, as storehouses of information about technological development and the people who made industry possible.

Archaeologists sometimes research industrial sites to learn about the production of artifacts. As one important example, Edward Heite studied the Collins, Geddes cannery site in

Lebanon, Delaware. The site of the cannery is largely forgotten by today's local residents, but more than a hundred years earlier it was an important industry. A local reporter wrote in 1873 that "The large fruit canning establishment of Collins & Co. at Lebanon, near Camden, is now running day and night in manufacturing sixty thousand gallons of catsup for parties in Philadelphia and New York, at one dollar per gallon." Cans, such as those that once contained catsup, are common finds at late-nineteenth-century archaeological sites (Figure 3.9). As an archaeologist, Heite was concerned not with the production of catsup but with the manufacture of the tin cans themselves.

Heite was called in to study the cannery because the site was slated to be destroyed by construction. The site was overgrown with trees and brush and stood in the path of a much-needed new bridge over the Tidbury Branch of the St. Jones River in central Delaware. Heite examined the site using a combination of surface survey and small test pits (see Chapters 5 and 7). He also used a backhoe to help him expose the cannery's brick foundations. During the fieldwork he found the wall foundations (learning someone had robbed much of the brick for use elsewhere), the brick foundations for two boilers, the building's cellar, and a dump.

Many of the most interesting artifacts from the site were small scraps of tin. Most people might consider these fragments to be junk, but they told the story of tin can production at the Lebanon cannery. Heite learned by examining the scraps that workers used two methods to make the ends of the cans. In one process, the metalworker cut the circular top from a sheet of tin with a stamping die. The die also cut the "fill hole," the spot through which the can's contents were later added. In the second method, a die cut the top and the fill hole was punched through in a separate process. Heite discovered the second method by observing that fill holes were not placed on the lids in a standardized manner. He also learned that the tin can producers had cut their cans from sheets of tin

Figure 3.9 Three tin cans produced at Collins, Geddes cannery of Lebanon, Delaware
(Heite Consulting)

averaging about 16 inches (40.6 cm) square, though they sometimes used sheets half this size. The size of the sheets was significant because tin can producers made cans based on the size of the sheets. The ideal was to cut four can bodies from one sheet. Tin can producers still make cans in the same sizes as those found in Delaware, but the tin now comes in rolls instead of sheets.

Heite's research on tin cans may strike many as trivial. After all, he only studied a few cans produced at a single cannery in one U.S. state. But it is through such detailed research that historical archaeologists expand knowledge about all aspects of history. Even the lowly tin can is part of history. Heite was correct when he wrote that his research provided "a laboratory in which to study the changes in canneries over the past century." The same can be said for industrial sites of all kinds wherever discovered.

Industrial sites may be individual large factories or even a complex of closely spaced buildings dedicated to the production of a specific product, like tin cans. But in addition to studying individual sites, industrial archaeologists also examine regions where the inhabitants were engaged in a multitude of industrial activities. In his study of the Bassar, an iron-working society living in the tiny nation of Togo, West Africa, archaeologist Philip Lynton De Barros investigated a region that contained villages inhabited by numerous industrial specialists. Archaeological research indicates that West Africans started working iron during the 900–800 B.C.E. period. The people of the Bassar region had adopted iron production sometime after 500 C.E., and they continued it until the early years of the twentieth century. During the seventeenth century, the people built specialized villages dedicated to iron smelting, iron smithing, charcoal making, and pottery manufacture. De Barros's research showed that slave raids into the area during the late eighteenth and nineteenth centuries had a significant impact on the region's people, because they had to invent new political institutions to adapt to the changing circumstances of the times. The new organizations in turn caused a change in the location of population centers in the region as people sought safety in numbers.

In her study of the manufacture of wine in Moquegua, southern Peru, from 1533 to 1823, Prudence Rice used an archaeological framework to address a multitude of complex issues extending from aspects of viniculture in one region to the global expression of emerging capitalism and the rise of early modern industry. In her effort to understand this one industry in the colonial Spanish world, Rice investigated social organization, settlement patterns, commodification, and the symbolism of alcohol consumption. She drew on information from over 130 individual wineries, conducted interviews and excavations, and examined historical documents.

Like Rice, other archaeologists interested in industrialization have turned their attention somewhat away from the industrial buildings themselves and toward the social lives of workers. This direction in industrial archaeology seeks to align the field with social history. As an example, Eleanor Conlin Casella conducted an innovative project called the Alderley Sandhills Project. This effort was designed to investigate the personal and social impacts of industrialization and de-industrialization on the workers of rural northern England from the eighteenth to the twentieth centuries. Using a combination of archaeological and historical research—combined with interviews of past residents—Casella learned about the relationships between community and work life and what it was like to live in this one industrial community.

A socially conscious industrial archaeology provides another important focus for historical archaeology. When linked with the more traditional approaches, the study of community-based industrialism has the potential to make significant advances to archaeological knowledge.

Military Sites

Military sites are places associated with armed conflict or with military occupation. Forts, blockhouses, trenches, earthworks, and fields where battles were fought are all classified as military sites.

Traditional historians have always used military actions as a way to explain international politics and world events, and so it is perhaps not surprising that military sites were some of the first places to attract both amateur and professional historical archaeologists. From 1918 until 1940, the New-York Historical Society sponsored a field exploration committee who investigated military sites dating from colonial times until the War of 1812. The committee was the brainchild of military historian William Calver. Working in collaboration with civil engineer and amateur historian Reginald Bolton, Calver wrote a series of articles on his findings for the *New-York Historical Society Quarterly Bulletin*. These articles were later collected together and republished in 1950 as *History Written with Pick and Shovel*. The publication of Calver and Bolton's study was an inspiring event for many amateur historical archaeologists. As one example, in the early 1950s Stanley Gifford began to excavate at Fort William Henry, the military installation made famous by the 1992 epic film *The Last of the Mohicans*.

In 1959, the State of Michigan began archaeological excavations at Fort Michilimackinac. These excavations have been conducted every year since (see Figure 2.5). Archaeologists have examined much of the fort's interior, unearthing over one million artifacts, including glass bottles, religious medals, brass kettle fragments, glass trade beads, ceramic dish fragments, and iron keys. Professional excavations, like those at Fort Michilimackinac, help provide significant information about how fortifications were built, how certain environments affected fortification design, and how forts were enlarged and rebuilt to adapt to changing circumstances, including housing armies from different nations. In addition, site managers and restorationists use the archaeological evidence to help interpret the site to tourists.

Historical archaeology can illuminate how individual companies of soldiers lived. The soldiers' unit may be well known, but their actual everyday lives may remain a mystery. In North America, the Royal Canadian Mounted Police—the redoubtable Mounties—is one of the world's most famous law enforcement services. The Canadian government created the North-West Mounted Police in 1874 to protect Canada's sovereignty over its most-western territories, and to keep the peace between the region's European and Native American inhabitants. The Mounties built several outposts along the frontier, including Fort Walsh, which they erected in 1875 in today's southwestern Saskatchewan. They dismantled the post in 1883, selling its logs to ranchers who were just moving into the region.

Excavations of the hospital at Fort Walsh showed that the Mounties had constructed it to be 16.4 by 44.5 feet (5 by 13.6 m) in size, including a wing measuring 12.5 by 13.5 feet (3.8 by 4.1 m). They divided the hospital into three equal-sized rooms. The rooms on both ends were used as sick wards; the post's doctors used the central room as an office and examination room. The excavations yielded 150,000 artifacts, including numerous medicine bottles.

Historical records indicate that the Mounties were often beset with sickness, including a malady they called "mountain fever." This illness is today known as Rocky Mountain spotted fever. Many of the townspeople who lived near the fort died of the fever, but during its eight years of operation, only one Mountie died at Fort Walsh. The excavated medicine bottles hold the key to the different mortality rates. The presence of 2.5-gallon (9.5-liter) bottle fragments in the hospital's remains prove the fort's doctors had bulk medicines shipped to the post. Specimens of smaller medicine bottles suggest they dispersed their own prepared remedies to the Mounties. The excavators did not unearth a single patent medicine bottle from inside the hospital. The absence of these commercial—though highly questionable—remedies is noteworthy because patent medicines were considered the wonder drugs of the nineteenth century. Government agencies did not regulate the patent medicine industry, so its practitioners were free to infuse their "medicines" with high quantities of cocaine, alcohol, codeine, and even arsenic. The archaeologists did discover numerous patent medicine bottles outside the hospital, however. These bottles imply that the fort's residents consumed great quantities of self-prescribed drugs, but only out of sight of the post's doctors. The doctors, for their part, may have refused to use patent medicines, recognizing them for what they were: long on advertising and short on efficacy.

Archaeological research can even document how battles were fought. By recording and examining patterns of bullets and matériel found in the ground, archaeologists can provide important information about military tactics and can even document what weapons were used in a battle.

A dramatic example comes from just south of Fort Walsh, in the fields of Montana where George Custer fought his famous battle with the Sioux (Dakotas) and Cheyenne in 1876. By examining the distribution of cavalry equipment and Native American artifacts on the battlefield, archaeologist Douglas Scott was able to reconstruct the sequence of the battle (Figure 3.10). The distribution of spent cartridge cases prove that Custer, or someone in

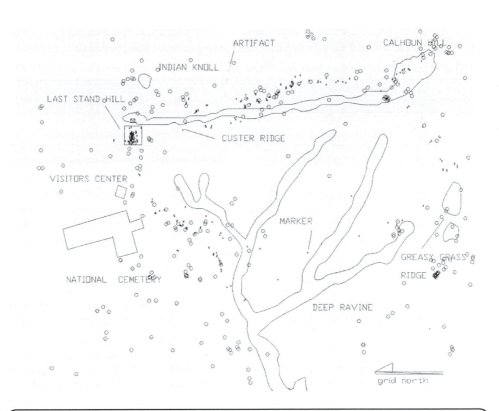

Figure 3.10 The distribution of army-related artifacts on the Custer Battlefield
(Courtesy of the National Park Service)

command, deployed a line of men facing south from Custer Ridge to meet the onrush of Cheyenne from the west and of the Sioux from the south. At the same time, another group of Sioux attacked from the east against the end of the soldier's line. Scott's team of archaeologists found at least 15 Springfield carbines and two Colt pistols in this part of the field. In the course of the battle, the solders formed themselves into a broad V, with Last Stand Hill to the north. When the soldiers' position on the east gave way, the Sioux on the east began a two-pronged attack toward the main body of soldiers, who, as the cartridges demonstrate, were already under intense attack from the west and south. The physical evidence also proved that several Native Americans used captured arms to return fire to the soldiers. At the end, the remaining soldiers were on the west end of the ridge and were completely surrounded by the hostile force.

In a related study, archaeologist Richard Fox used artifact finds and Native American testimony to shatter the Custer myth. Fox showed that the Seventh Cavalry entered the battle in a disciplined manner, in full accordance with their training. When they met the stiff resistance of the overwhelming enemy, however, the soldiers' order broke down. The famed "Last Stand," far from being a heroic battle-to-the-death, was characterized by chaos and panic. The soldiers, in complete disarray, seem to have engaged in little determined fighting.

The research archaeologists have conducted on warfare has led to the development of an entire subfield called "combat" or "conflict archaeology." Conflict archaeologists conduct research on all eras, extending to the far distant past. Their topics include the nature of warfare, the objects used, and the impact of war on communities and nations. One of the important developments for historical archaeology has been an interest in World Wars I and II, and archaeologists have completed some important studies of these conflicts.

Historical archaeologists have begun to investigate the battlefields of twentieth-century conflicts by locating and mapping trenches, earthworks, and installations. Such works illustrate how armies alter landscapes to suit their needs. As with the Battle of Little Bighorn, these examinations also document how armies arranged themselves to fight battles.

In addition to identifying and documenting battle sites, historical archaeologists also investigate how people commemorate and remember battles and wars. How societies perceive warfare can change over time as can the meaning of monuments. War monuments have several distinct meanings. Some viewers may see them as merely works of art, whereas others may perceive them as points of remembrance and even symbols of aggression and terror. Monuments to war can also serve as heritage sites attracting international tourists. In studying the Broken Hill Memorial in New South Wales, Australia, Paul Rainbird learned that a statue of a soldier in the process of throwing a hand grenade—titled "The Bomber"—was controversial when installed in 1925. Many local residents found the figure's aggressive posture an unfortunate glorification of war, though today most residents consider the statue to be part of the community's heritage.

In her investigation of the Nazi occupation of the British Channel Islands from 1940 to 1945, Gillian Carr studied the prevalence and use of the V-for-victory sign by the islands' residents. The islanders used the V sign in various secretive ways as a subtle resistance to the occupation and as a way to bolster local morale. The Germans viewed the painting of V-signs on walls as sabotage and responded by establishing fines and requiring a civilian guard to ensure that no more V's appeared. When it seemed early in the war that the Germans might be victorious, they appropriated the V for themselves. Channel Islanders responded by putting an E before the V to symbolize an English victory. Inventive people also inscribed the V sign on rings, cups, badges, and other pieces of material culture. Studies such as Carr's demonstrate the subtle meanings that can be attached to material culture and how certain meanings can change over time.

The research by conflict archaeologists does more than simply fill in the gaps in knowledge about specific military engagements. Their archaeological research challenges us to think about how archaeology can be used to study warfare, tactics, strategy, commemoration, and memory.

Burial Sites

Places where the dead are buried are understandably some of the most controversial sites archaeologists can study. Excavating a skeleton necessarily means disturbing the gravesite, and many would consider excavation a form of desecration. Studies of modern-era burial sites may generate considerable controversy because many descendants of the deceased may still be living. They may not be enthusiastic about archaeologists excavating their ancestors' remains and subjecting their bones to study in a university laboratory. Archaeologists thus have learned to be sensitive to the desires of descendants when they seek to unearth the remains of the dead.

The investigation of historic burials is often expressly forbidden or highly regulated by law. Regulations have not been universally applied, and only in recent years have laws been enacted in many countries to control the archaeological investigation of burials.

For example, in 1990, the United States government enacted the Native American Graves Protection and Repatriation Act (NAGPRA). The law describes the rights of Native American descendants, federally recognized Indian tribes, and Native Hawaiian organizations as they pertain to the treatment, disposition, and repatriation of Native American human remains and objects of cultural patrimony. The law is intended to give the nation's original inhabitants a voice in how their ancestor's remains and objects are handled and housed. It also gives recognized native groups the right to demand the return of remains and objects if they can establish their connections to them. The law also states that criminal penalties may apply if an individual is found guilty of illegally trafficking in human burial remains or in artifacts having cultural affiliation with Native Americans.

Other nations are struggling with ways to ensure that their native peoples have a voice in the disposition of human remains and burial areas. The problems are difficult to resolve because, for one reason, inherent conflicts may exist between a traditional belief system and the requirements of scientific research.

Archaeologists know that graves can provide a mine of unique information about past societies. Archaeologists who study gravesites and cemeteries usually work closely with bio-cultural anthropologists because such specialists can provide information about diets, growth rates of children and adults, the prevalence of dental cavities, disease rates, and the effects of devastating afflictions.

Historical anthropologist Jerome Handler used a collection of excavated African skeletons from a plantation in Barbados (dating from about 1660–1820) to study the effects of lead poisoning on the enslaved laborers' health and wellbeing. Handler discovered that the ailment, dry bellyache—of which the enslaved constantly complained—was actually a symptom of ingesting lead. When teetotalers proclaimed rum to have a demon inside, they did not know how right they were. As it turns out, the apparatus used for making rum was constructed with lead seams. Lead would leach into the rum during the fermentation process and those imbibing would unknowingly ingest it. The rate of lead poisoning was accordingly high among Caribbean populations relying heavily on rum for entertainment and refreshment.

Non-African skeletons are not available from Barbados to compare with those of the enslaved. Another dramatic example, however, demonstrates that no one in the historic

period was immune to lead poisoning. When Sir John Franklin left England in 1845 with 129 crewmen and officers to find the elusive Northwest Passage through the Canadian Arctic, people widely considered his expedition one of the most exciting of the day. England was thus stunned when Franklin and "his gallant crew" (as they were immortalized in song) vanished without a trace. What had happened to them? The answer to the Franklin mystery was not known until the 1980s, when the bodies of several crewmen were discovered, in an almost perfect state of preservation, in far northern Canada. Upon examining the bodies, Owen Beattie discovered that the expedition's massive supply of canned foods had in fact killed them. High-tech atomic absorption analysis of soft tissue from the buried crewmen showed they had suffered from acute lead intoxication. The heavy solder seams on their food cans had leached into the food, causing lead poisoning. The chance that the Franklin crew would be poisoned was high because each man had 248 pounds (111.6 kg) of canned meats, stews, soups, and vegetables allocated to him. Arctic explorers and historians who had studied the Franklin expedition since the mid-nineteenth century had always been puzzled by the crew's apparent aimless wanderings as evidenced by the rock cairns they built and by their irregular scatters of abandoned supplies. Neither hostile natives, the Arctic deep freeze, nor bad leadership was the cause of the crew's demise; mundane tin cans killed Franklin and his men.

As noted above, the excavation of burial sites is not always without controversy. A noteworthy dispute surrounded the study of an eighteenth-century cemetery in lower Manhattan, near Wall Street. The cemetery, known as the "African Burial Ground," came to light during the construction of a 34-story federal office building. Archaeologists discovered the remains of more than 400 individuals located from 16 to 28 feet (4.9–8.5 m) below the current street level. The human remains were those of New York's enslaved men, women, and children of African descent. The discovery of this rare archaeological find caused a broad outcry from members of the African American community. Whereas some people favored the academic study of the remains, others viewed examination unnecessary. Activists argued for more African American participation in the excavation. In September 1993, an African religious ceremony was held to commemorate the transfer of the remains from Lehman College in New York City to Howard University in Washington, D.C. In October, a second ceremony marked the final "homecoming" of the remains, as the last skeletons were transferred to Howard University. The Howard team's research is providing important new information about the daily lives of hundreds of eighteenth-century men, women, and children of African descent who once resided in New York City.

The study of burial sites often reveals completely unknown elements of history or pieces of the past covered over with silence. James Davidson analyzed the Freedman's Cemetery in Dallas, Texas, the burial place of African Americans from 1869 to 1907. His archaeological study included the remains of more than 1,100 individuals.

During analysis, the skeletal remains revealed that a number of the burials had been illegally exhumed by grave robbers. These robbers, so-called "resurrection men," dug up the remains and sold them to medical colleges as cadavers. Many of the skeletons were missing arms, legs, and heads, and some of the caskets were empty. Davidson's research showed that city and county officials had made secret agreements with Dallas medical schools, in a pattern revealing a bias toward African American remains.

In a thorough examination of death and burial in Britain and Ireland from the sixteenth to the late nineteenth centuries, archaeologists have documented that people who could afford it could purchase a "mortsafe" and have it constructed over their graves. This object was an iron cage embedded deep into the ground and surrounding the gravesite so that grave robbers would bypass it and move on to an easier target.

Special-Purpose Sites

Places where people once performed tasks unrelated to industrial production, military activities, or domestic life are termed special-purpose sites. Churches, stores, mental hospitals, and other places used for specific purposes give archaeologists the opportunity to interpret often-overlooked chapters of the past. Given the range of activities humans can undertake, the types of special-purpose sites are immense. Historical archaeologists have excavated several special-purpose sites and the numbers are certain to increase as research continues.

One intriguing example is William C. Hoff's store in San Francisco, California. William Hoff, from New York, was one of thousands of "forty-niners" who traveled west during the great California Gold Rush. Hoff's dreams of wealth lay not in prospecting but in merchandizing, and less than a year after his arrival in the West he had established a general store and ship supply house on the bustling San Francisco waterfront. Unfortunately for Hoff, however, about a year later, on May 3–4, 1851, the "Fifth Great Fire" completely engulfed his store, destroying it along with hundreds of homes, hotels, and other businesses.

After almost a full year of excavation at the store, archaeologists retrieved thousands of artifacts from the remains, encapsulated 15 feet (4.6 m) beneath the streets of San Francisco. These artifacts offer a rare glimpse of the merchandise purchased by optimistic forty-niners: leather shoes, brass military buttons, books of matches, ceramic crocks, patent medicine, silver forks, brass spoons, and ceramic crucibles used for melting gold. The archaeologists even found a charred wooden bowling pin. They also discovered numerous foodstuffs in the store deposits, including pork bones, perfectly preserved olives still in tightly closed jars, coffee beans, walnuts, peach pits, and even cakes, breads, and crackers.

Another interesting example comes from the King's Arms tavern site in England (Figure 3.11). The inn was located in Uxbridge, Middlesex, and during the height of the inn's operation in the 1780s and 1790s, the town was the first major coach stop between London and Oxford. As reported by Jacqueline Pearce, archaeological research at the King's Arms was important for two major reasons. In the first place, few tavern sites have been excavated, either in Great Britain or elsewhere. As a result, even the briefest analysis significantly

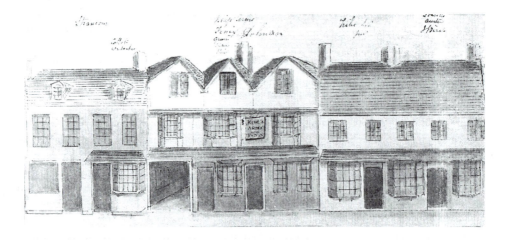

Figure 3.11 The King's Arms Inn, around 1790
(Produced by Hillingdon Borough Council.)

increases our knowledge of one kind of site important in the lives of past people. Second, because the excavated remains had been deposited as a single "clearing operation," they offer a rare, snapshot view of the objects patrons used while at the inn. Finds of encapsulated archaeological deposits are unique and archaeologists are always delighted to find them.

Pearce concentrated her analysis on the ceramics, glassware, and clay smoking pipes from the inn. The ceramics alone showed the variety of objects purchased by the innkeepers. The collection includes at least 30 dinner plates (with five different raised patterns along the rims), two oval serving plates, four sauceboats, and at least seven mugs, all of English manufacture. Also included are bowls and plates made of English and Chinese porcelain, heavy stoneware mugs, teapot lids, and punch bowls. As might be expected at an inn, the collection also contains fragments of numerous glass bottles, goblets, tumblers, and other bottles, as well as at least 75 clay smoking pipes. At that time in history, it was common for individuals to purchase a pipe of tobacco along with their spirits.

Historical archaeologists have shown great interest in the study and excavation of religious mission sites, beginning perhaps with Father Martin's mid-nineteenth-century investigation of Sainte Marie (see Chapter 2). Archaeologists in Florida, California, and in various places in Central and South America have excavated missions associated with the Spanish Empire, and archaeologists elsewhere have conducted similar research. Missions provide unique glimpses of daily interaction between European religious orders and indigenous peoples. Archaeological studies of such sites have significantly improved our understanding of culture contact and the role of religion in colonialism.

Archaeologists working in Australasia have also been investigating mission sites. For example, in New Zealand, archaeologists Ian Smith and Angela Middleton excavated at the Hohi Mission Station. This mission, the first permanent European settlement in New Zealand established in 1814, was home to around 30 Europeans and numerous Maori. The reason for doing the archaeology at the site was twofold. First, in anticipation of the 200th anniversary of the mission's founding, the government was planning a series of activities at the site, some of which may disturb fragile archaeological remains. As a result, officials deemed it necessary to know where remains were located in order to avoid them. Secondly, though a thorough body of written information exists about the early era of missionary activity, little concrete knowledge exists about the daily lives of Europeans and Maoris who lived at places like Hohi. The archaeological research revealed specific information about the first mission school. The children who attended the school—both Maori and European—decorated some of the slate pencils with X marks and scratches, and presumably Maori at the school made tools from chert, obsidian, and bottle glass.

Multipurpose Sites

Multipurpose sites are complex places where the occupants carried out several often equally important tasks. Multipurpose sites cannot be classified simply as domestic, industrial, or special purpose because their former inhabitants performed all of those tasks there. Some missions may be considered multipurpose sites because so many different activities occurred there. As is true of special-purpose sites, historical archaeologists encounter a wide range of multipurpose sites.

The plantations of the New World provide an excellent example. Richard Beavers discovered that Destrehan Plantation in Louisiana was the perfect example of a multipurpose site. The estate's owners built Destrehan in 1787 as an indigo plantation, but three-quarters of a century later, they converted it into a more profitable sugar-producing property. An inventory

made in 1792 lists the following buildings on the plantation's grounds: a mansion, a detached kitchen, a storehouse, two hospitals for the enslaved, a pigeon house, a coach house, three cabins, a "Negro camp" of 19 cabins, a blacksmith shop, a drying house for indigo, a hay shed, a pump house, a series of sheds for churning indigo during fermentation, and an engine house for the indigo grinder. With the conversion to sugar cultivation, the plantation's owners built a sugar-boiling house and a mill. Archaeologists investigated several different domestic buildings, numerous special-use structures, and many buildings associated with production. Plantations, because they housed so many different kinds of people doing diverse tasks, are perfect examples of multipurpose sites.

Sites associated with tourism represent a unique kind of multipurpose site. These sites can include fairs, manufactured "ancient" sites, inns, and tourist destinations. One of the most famous fairs in history is the 1893 World's Columbian Exposition held in Chicago. Somewhere between 11 and 16 million tourists visited the fair during the six months it was open. Complex sites like expositions present archaeologists with an array of subjects for investigation, ranging from the methods of construction to the ways in which such places are remembered today.

In her archaeological study of the Chicago fair, Rebecca Graff paid particular attention to the Ohio Building. Unlike most of the buildings at the fair, the Ohio Building was not intended to display exhibits. Instead, the building was more of a domestic space. It included parlors, a smoking room, bathrooms, and bedrooms. The unique function of the building led Graff to designate the Ohio Building, and all smaller buildings at the exposition, "pseudo-domestic" spaces because tourists used them as clubhouses and meeting places rather than as places to see exhibits.

Maritime and Underwater Sites

The archaeology of maritime sites is a highly specialized field of archaeology not restricted to modern-era sites. Underwater archaeology did not exist as a scientifically conducted kind of archaeology until 1960. Despite its relatively young age, archaeologists have successfully documented past ship designs, routes of trade, and many aspects of technology among Phoenicians, Romans, and other ancient, seagoing cultures.

Maritime archaeology is sometimes referred to as underwater archaeology to indicate that archaeological excavations frequently take place on the floors of rivers, lakes, and seas. The change in designation from "underwater" to "maritime" has developed because many archaeologists interested in seaborne history are as interested in coastal sites, like docks and shipping villages, as they are in the ships that transported goods. Like their colleagues exploring sites from ancient history, historical archaeologists also regularly conduct excavations underwater and along coastal areas with maritime connections.

An example of underwater archaeology of note is the excavation of ships used in the transatlantic slave trade. Archaeologists have found and excavated only a handful of these vessels, the most famous being the *Henrietta Marie*. Though first discovered by treasure salvors in 1972, the ship remains have since been excavated by professional archaeologists under the direction of David Moore.

Divers found the wreck site just off the Florida Keys at New Ground Reef. The scatter of artifacts on the seabed—English pewter vessels, trade beads, and elephant tusks—helped to substantiate its seventeenth-century date, but the discovery of manacles and shackles identified it as a slaver. This wreck site was deemed so important that it was included in the Florida Keys National Maritime Sanctuary created in 1990 and administered by the National Oceanic and Atmospheric Administration. Efforts by African American and other divers were

successful in having a memorial plaque placed at the wreck site in commemoration of the "courage, pain, and suffering of enslaved African people."

The wrecks of pirate ships are another kind of site that attracts attention. One of the most famous is the *Queen Anne's Revenge*, discovered off the coast of North Carolina in 1996. The ship was under the captaincy of renowned pirate Edward Teach, more widely known as Blackbeard. The ship, a 200-ton vessel with a crew of around 75, had begun its career as a French slaver named *La Concorde*. In this role, the ship sailed the triangular route from the west coast of Africa to the Caribbean and then to Europe. In the fall of 1717, Teach captured it off the coast of Martinique and rechristened it the *Queen Anne's Revenge*. He had served as a privateer during Queen Anne's War (1701–1714), but after the war, privateers—newly deemed pirates—were considered outlaws. In 1718, Teach ran the ship aground, and shortly thereafter a combined force of Royal Navy sailors and Virginia militia attacked Teach's remaining ship. He was killed, and his severed head was taken back to Virginia in triumph.

The remains of the ship now lie off Beaufort, North Carolina. The underwater archaeology branch of the North Carolina Department of Cultural Resources began studying the remains in 1996, and in 2006 began a full recovery effort. The archaeologists have excavated around 300,000 artifacts from the wreck. The catalogue of objects includes lead shot, brass musket hardware, white clay smoking pipes, glass beads, fishing weights, surveying instruments, ceramic storage vessels, glass bottles, ballast stones, and many other artifacts. Around 40 cannons may have once been aboard the ship and archaeologists have brought over half that number to the surface. The cast iron cannons each weigh around 2,000 pounds (907 kg). Conservators are stabilizing the artifacts at the Queen Anne's Revenge lab at East Carolina University in Greenville, where they are also being carefully catalogued, documented, and analyzed.

Island nations are especially likely to have large inventories of shipwrecks available for archaeological investigation and analysis. Ireland is such a case. Perhaps the most renowned wrecks are those of the Spanish Armada, which lie off the west coast of the island. Many other wrecks lie on the bottom of the sea. For example, archaeologists Colin Breen and Wes Forsythe documented the wreck *La Surveillante*, a French frigate sunk in 1797 in Bantry Bay, County Cork. Like many shipwrecks, the Bantry Bay wreck was found in the course of other undersea operations—this one to investigate the explosion of an oil tanker. The discovery of the ship allowed archaeologists to compare its construction with historical and published documents describing 12-pounder French frigates. The archaeological investigation also made it possible to understand the precise details of how the ship sank. Once on the floor of the bay, the ship's remains were susceptible to a number of destructive processes, including apparently having anchors dragged across it several times (see Chapter 6).

Archaeologists excavating in China, the Philippines, and elsewhere in the region are documenting the forms and construction of Chinese ships from the Ming Dynasty (1368–1644) and earlier eras. This research is shedding much needed new light on the ocean-going activities of Asian traders and explorers, individuals who were in contact with Islamic and Indian communities long before European ever reached these places.

A superb example of the connection between land and sea comes from Labrador. In the mid-sixteenth century, Basque whalers from northern Spain pursued their giant prey in the Strait of Belle Isle off southern Labrador. They hunted and processed whales with great efficiency from a shore base in a sheltered anchorage at Red Bay. A true understanding of the work of the Basque whalers could only come from linking their activities on land with those at sea. James Tuck examined their near-industrial whaling operation on land, while Robert Grenier searched the bay floor for the wreck for the whaling ship *San Juan*. Basque archives indicate that this vessel sank off the whaling station in late 1565, just as she was about to leave for home with a full cargo.

After eight years' work, Grenier's team located the wrecks of three whaling ships, one of them almost certainly the *San Juan*, a mid-sized sailing vessel, and several small boats. All were well preserved by the area's cold water and fine silt. After months of diving on the *San Juan*, the archaeologists recovered more than 200 whale oil barrels, parts of the ship's rigging, some navigational instruments, and details of the 250-ton (227 mt) ship. The team drew and photographed every timber, joint, tool mark, and hole before the wood was returned to the favorable preservation conditions on the sea floor. The result of their labors was a detailed reconstruction of a sixteenth-century whaling vessel.

Meanwhile on land, the terrestrial archaeologists exposed the remains of 20 "tryworks," or refineries where the whalers processed the blubber into marketable oil. They also found the cooperages, where barrel makers had constructed the casks used to transport the oil to market. In among the remains were also many personal possessions the whalers used in their daily lives in the Far North.

An intriguing kind of maritime site associated with shipwrecks are shipwreck survivor camps. These are places where survivors from wrecks have been saved from drowning, crawled ashore, and lived while awaiting rescue. Literature and popular culture are filled with examples. For archaeologists, the discovery of these campsites provides an opportunity to link life at sea with life on land. Anthropological topics such as the creation of systems of authority and social organization, methods of subsistence, and the use and adaptation of material culture can be combined with specific historical information about the camps themselves. These studies present the opportunity to understand the full historical culture of life on the sea and an appreciation for some of its perils.

The above overview of the major site types examined by historical archaeologists is by no means exhaustive. The study of post-1500 archaeological sites has expanded so rapidly and has covered the globe so completely that any overview is necessarily inadequate. The site-types presented here, however, indicate the range of places historical archaeologists conduct research. Its breadth alone indicates the complexity of the world's peoples and places.

Regardless of what sort of site is being investigated, all archaeologists must concern themselves with two questions related to time and space: when did the site exist, and where was it located? The answers to these two seemingly simple questions are the subject of the next chapter.

Site Visit: Palmares, Brazil, ca. 1650

Resistance will exist wherever men and women are kept in forced bondage. The plantations of the New World were certainly no exception. Thousands of enslaved men and women ran away from their captors, and in their flight, sought lives elsewhere on their own terms. Communities of escaped fugitives appear throughout the slave-holding world, including the Caribbean, the southern United States, and Central and South America. One of the largest runaway communities in the New World was Palmares, in northeastern Brazil. Like all maroon communities (or, in Portuguese, *quilombos*), Palmares was created as a direct response to the horrors of human bondage and the harsh treatment

received by enslaved men and women who cultivated cash crops for someone else's benefit.

Portuguese colonists had established a number of sugar plantations along Brazil's lush Atlantic coast by 1570, or about 70 years after they had first encountered the continent. They built their plantations between the white, sandy beaches of the coast and the dense green forests inland. A row of mountains created a natural barrier to the spread of colonial plantations. At the time of the Portuguese arrival, Native South Americans either lived throughout the forests or along the coast. Those on the coast were pushed inland by the clearance of land and the harsh practices of European settlers.

When the enslaved ran away from the coastal estates, they inevitably headed inland toward the mountains. By 1605, several fugitives had established Palmares, about 50 miles (80 km) from the coast. The Portuguese called it Palmares because of the palm groves that grew in the area, but the inhabitants may have called it "Angola Janga" (or Little Angola), after the African homeland of most of its people. The area encompassed by Palmares may have been as large as 10,400 square miles (27,000 sq km).

Plantation owners regarded the unwelcome departure of the enslaved from their estates as a serious affront to their power and finances. As a result, they did everything they could to destroy maroon communities when they sprang up. Their goal was to recapture their former slaves as fast as possible and return them to their plantation labors. Both Dutch explorers trying to acquire Brazil and Portuguese planters trying to keep it perceived Palmares as a substantial threat to their authority and safety. Thus, in 1612 they began almost annual attacks on the community's villages. These assaults had little effect, and Palmares continued to prosper. At the height of its development (1650–1670), the community was reported to be composed of ten separate villages and a population as high as 20,000.

The people of Palmares succeeded in creating a new culture in Brazil. It was a complex mixture of diverse strands from Africa, Europe, and South America. Their religion was a combination of African and Roman Catholic beliefs and rituals, but they had a political organization with a king at its head. He lived in a capital city and was supported by a number of lords, or sub-rulers, who lived in smaller hamlets. The material culture of Palmares also blended together various traditions. Their pottery, for instance, portrayed a mixture of Ovimbundu (African) and Tupinamba (Native South American) traits.

The houses of Palmares resembled the local Native South American homes because the fugitives had used the same materials from the forest to build them. Because they were under frequent attack, they erected wooden stockades with high watchtowers around their towns.

Even with all their attention to defense, the men and women of Palmares had to maintain a number of alliances to survive. They traded with the local Native South Americans for food, clay pottery, and other materials, and also with the

Portuguese settlers who lived on the frontier. From these Portuguese colonists, they received wheel-thrown, glazed ceramics, possibly both locally made and imported from Europe.

The Portuguese finally succeeded in destroying Palmares in 1694. They captured the community's king, a popular leader named Zumbi, took him to the Portuguese-controlled coast, and beheaded him. His memory is still very much alive in Brazil, and he is widely revered for his bravery, leadership skills, and defiance.

Source: Charles E. Orser, Jr. and Pedro P. A. Funari. Archaeology and Slave Resistance and Rebellion. *World Archaeology* 33 (2001):61–72.

Chapter 4

Time and Space

Time and space are essential aspects of archaeological research. Archaeological information would be useless without concrete knowledge of where and when. One reason looting is so damaging to archaeological remains is because the vandal has destroyed the dimensions of time and space by thoughtlessly removing artifacts without documentation (see Chapter 13). Professional archaeologists are extremely mindful of time and space during their research.

Time in Historical Archaeology

Humans are obsessed with time—with its passage, with using it wisely, and with the evils of "wasting" it. We "spend" time like money and find, like money, that there's never enough of it. Men and women have measured time for thousands of years, first using the rising and setting of the sun and the passage of the seasons to regulate their lives. The invention of the clock, standardized time, and around 1500, Peter Henlein's creation of the first spring-wound, portable clock made it possible for us to carry time around with us on our wrists and in our pockets. Today, many people use smart phones as their main timepieces. We take time zones for granted, but they were not invented until 1883 to satisfy railroad companies in the United States concerned with standardizing their schedules. Today's train, bus, and airplane schedules owe their invention to our modern desire to depart and arrive "on time." Airline companies in particular pride themselves on their percentage of "on time" departures and arrivals.

Unlike many societies, Westerners have always thought of time in linear terms, extending far back into the beginning of human history. Many cultures, however, conceive of time in cyclical terms, as an endlessly repeating passage of seasons, years, and longer periods of time. The Aztecs of central Mexico measured time in 52-year cycles, and many peoples, such as the pueblo dwellers of the American Southwest and European peasants, used the movements of heavenly bodies to mark planting and harvesting seasons.

Linear time forms the foundation of all archaeological research, with history being represented as the passage of time through centuries and millennia. The celebrated Roman orator

Marcus Cicero put it well when he wrote that "History is the witness that testifies to the passing of time; it illuminates reality, vitalizes memory, provides guidance in daily life, and brings us tidings of antiquity." Cultural achievements and events act as signposts to the passage of time. Excavations in East Africa indicate that early humans roamed the tropical savannas more than two million years ago. A combination of archaeological and historical sources sets the unification of Egypt and the beginnings of ancient Egyptian civilization at about 2900 B.C.E. More recent events are accurate to the day. Columbus landed on the island of San Salvador on October 12, 1492. On April 9, 1865, Confederate General Robert E. Lee strode up the steps of Appomattox Courthouse and surrendered to the Union army.

The more recent the event, the more accurate is its recorded date. For instance, the exact time of every rocket launch in Florida is chronicled to the second by advanced computers and atomic clocks. Columbus's movements in the Indies are known to within the day and sometimes to the time of day. Roman history is accurate for the most part to within a year or a decade, and the reigns of the ancient Egyptian pharaohs are accurate to within a quarter century or so. Rudimentary documents extend back some 5,000 years in the Near East. Archaeologists investigating ancient history are forced to measure cultural developments in centuries and often in millennia. Text-aided archaeologists can use shorter scales of time, and the history they study is often further advanced with the collection of artifacts of known age (see Chapter 8). Historical archaeologists generally satisfy their obsession with time by using four dating techniques—relative dating, dating with objects of known age, formula dating, and dendrochronology. The pace of advances in technology suggest new techniques may be available in the future as well.

Relative Dating

All objects in the world have a different relationship in time with every other object. Even every mass-produced object—bottles being filled with catsup on a mechanized assembly line, for instance—individually can be said to have a different "date." The dates may differ only by nanoseconds, but they are different nonetheless. The differences in dates between the individual bottles may not be obvious until the bottles are boxed for shipment. As factory workers stack boxes in the warehouse, common sense dictates that boxes on the bottom of the stack are older than those on top. The lower the boxes in the pile, the earlier their date of manufacture.

We all experience the same thing every day. A street in bad condition may expose four layers visible inside a pothole. The top layer may have a new, brilliantly black, smooth surface. Beneath this asphalt, a gray, weathered surface of old, worn blacktop may appear, and under this a layer of red paving bricks may be visible. At the very bottom may be a layer of grayish-white gravel. Common sense dictates that the uppermost, black surface is more recent in date than the paving bricks. Precisely how much older cannot be immediately determined. An observer could only conclude that the uppermost surface is *relatively more recent* than the bricks.

Archaeologists refer to these kinds of time differences as "relative chronology." As with the imaginary street, archaeologists can discern the basic relationships of time existing between soil layers, but they may not know exactly how much time is represented. Was the placement of the bricks and the black pavement separated by months, years, or even decades? How much time elapsed between the laying of the gravel and the bricks?

Relative chronology is based on a classic principle from geology, called the *Law of Superposition*. This law holds that under normal circumstances, deep layers of soil, sediment, or rock are older than those above them. Relative chronology is thus devised from *stratification*, the sequence of layered deposits. The deposits found at an archaeological site resemble the exposed face of a cliff that contains numerous rock strata; the difference is that at an archeological site, the deposits are usually layers of soil rather than layers of rock. Another important difference is that many of the archaeological layers encountered at an archaeological site will have been created from conscious and unconscious activities conducted by the site's past inhabitants rather than strictly through natural processes. Some soil layers may show the natural action of wind and rain, as well as disturbances caused by various animals.

Archaeologist Michael Schiffer has referred to the creation of archaeological strata—through the action of both human and natural forces—as "formation processes." These processes work together to "make" an archaeological site. Once the residents of a site leave that particular place and move somewhere else, nature's effects on the site do not cease. In fact, they continue, modifying the site and its remains for as long as the site exists. Suppose a small society lived at a village from 1550 to 1650. After 1650, nature constantly acts upon the site. The chemicals in the soil, droughts and floods, burrowing animals, and earthworms all alter the site's remains in some way. An archaeologist arriving at the site in the year 2010 will have discovered these activities at the site since its abandonment, even though no one has lived there for over 350 years.

Nature exercises a powerful effect on every archaeological site. When you walk through a neighborhood, take a close look at a neglected yard and notice how nature is slowly reclaiming it. After a few months, unkempt grass slowly creeps over the edges of the sidewalk and the front path. The grass, and even a thin layer of soil, will eventually cover the concrete, causing them to disappear from view. This same process is repeated at thousands of archaeological sites throughout the world. Strong winds blow fine sand over collapsed adobe walls, and powerful floods deposit thick layers of soft mud over house floors. Complete devastation is even possible.

A famous example from the annals of history is the destruction of the Roman towns of Herculaneum and Pompeii on August 25, 79 C.E., by the eruption of Mount Vesuvius in Italy. Mountains of fine ash covered the towns, leaving dozens of dead lying as archaeologists later found them, some still clutching rings with precious stones and bracelets of gold with embedded glass beads.

An example pertinent to historical archaeology is the destruction of Port Royal, Jamaica. At the time, the city was the largest and wealthiest English city in the New World. An important strategic naval outpost in the expanding British Empire, the streets of the city even shared names with some in London. An earthquake on June 7, 1692, changed all that, reducing the seaside half of the city to ruins. Because part of the city had been constructed on the sandy shore, the tremors caused the ground to liquefy. The ground slip that resulted caused half of the city to slide into the ocean where it remains today. When archaeologists began to excavate the underwater remains, they discovered the streets, parts of the buildings, and sunken ships that had also gone under the water. Given the nature of the destruction, archaeologists were able to document the remains in detail and to recover a large collection of ceramics, glassware, and other materials dating to the late seventeenth century. The earthquake produced a marker useful for determining relative chronology. Everything dating before June 7 was "pre-earthquake" and everything dating after June 8 was "post-earthquake."

Nature's fury thus has the power to obliterate archaeological sites. It can work quickly and dramatically or slowly and barely noticeably. In any case, its effects on archaeological deposits are very real.

Humans can equal nature as powerful, destructive agents. Major cities like London, Boston, and New York have undergone massive development in recent decades. Such large-scale construction projects slice deeply into underlying strata and disturb the archaeological deposits that lie underneath. Newly excavated foundation trenches often reveal layer upon layer of earlier occupation, buried in the haste of urban renewal.

The remains of London's venerable Rose Theatre unexpectedly came to light in 1989 in the foundations of a new high-rise office building on the south bank of the Thames River. It was in this modest, circular theater that Elizabethan actors first presented William Shakespeare's *Henry VI* in the 1590s (Figure 4.1). Four hundred years later, worldwide public outcry greeted the news that the remaining wooden foundations were to be bulldozed away. Teams of archaeologists worked day and night to record details of the theater before its remains were lost forever. The discovery of the remains of the Rose Theatre, lying beneath so much of modern-day London, provides a dramatic example of stratification and relative chronology.

Archaeologists who research ancient sites are likely to find them buried under several thick deposits of soil, even if the sites have never been affected by the destructive forces of nature. For example, the Koster site in south-central Illinois reflects more than 9,000 years of pre-European human activity. It contained no fewer than 12 separate layers of occupation, dating from modern times to about 7000 B.C.E. and extending to a depth of 34 feet (10.4 m). The Koster site provides a perfect example of how superposition works in archaeology. Archaeologists at the site knew that the sixth layer of human occupation, located about 7 feet (2.1 m) below ground, was more recent than the eleventh living surface, located almost 30 feet (9.1 m) down. Simple common sense and a knowledge of superposition told them this even before they found the first artifact.

The stratified layers of soil that cover sites occupied thousands of years ago usually extend to a greater depth than at the vast number of historic-period sites. Historical archaeologists

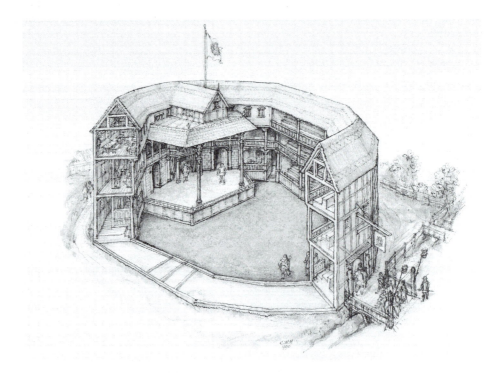

Figure 4.1 Reconstruction of the Rose Theatre, London
(Courtesy of the Museum of London.)

often excavate sites inhabited for years rather than centuries. As a result, historical archaeologists often spend a great deal of time excavating *micro-strata*. *Microstratigraphy* refers to the sum of the extremely thin soil layers that accrue on many historic-period sites.

When historical archaeologist Ivor Noël Hume excavated Martin's Hundred, a seventeenth-century settlement in colonial Virginia associated with Jamestown, he found the remains of the town almost directly beneath the present ground surface. The three and a half centuries that had passed since Martin's Hundred was abandoned was only time for a thin layer of soil to accumulate over the remains of the settlement. Koster's stratigraphy was well defined, with the occupation zones separated by natural layers accumulated during periods of abandonment that often lasted many centuries. In contrast, Martin's Hundred had thin strata. The presence of these delicate layers required meticulous observation and recording.

Noël Hume and his archaeologists found microstrata inside the remains of a subterranean "cellar" dwelling. Excavation revealed this house once had a steeply pitched, A-frame style roof supported by large, upright, interior posts (Figure 4.2). During the life of the dwelling, its inhabitants deposited a thin layer of gray clay on the floor. Subsequent to its abandonment, additional clay and earth washed into the building, creating about 4 feet (1.2 m) of gently sloping soil. Archaeologists worked for several months to understand the chronology of the soil layers.

The stratification of soil at archaeological sites, both human-made and natural, can be complex and confusing. Field archaeologists may be able to understand the most basic relative chronology through a quick appraisal of the soil layers, but they may need assistance in unraveling all the relationships that may exist between the various soil layers, zones, and deposits. In some cases, archaeologists may call on soil scientists and archaeological specialists to help them interpret the chemistry and depositional history of soils. Archaeologists generally hold it as a rule of thumb that the more soil strata at a site, the more confusing and difficult it is to interpret.

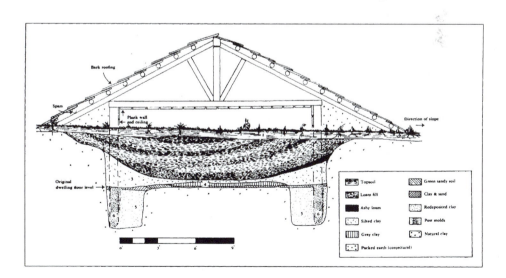

Figure 4.2 Seventeenth-century A-frame house at Martin's Hundred, Virginia

(Colonial Williamsburg Foundation, Williamsburg, VA)

To help archaeologists better envision the relationships between the various soil strata they might encounter, archaeologist Edward Harris invented the ingenious *Harris Matrix*. Working at a complex site in England, Harris was given the post-excavation task of interpreting the relative chronology of the site's many excavated soil layers. This monumental task led him to create a visual way of understanding the relationships between the strata and the human-built features at the site.

Harris's method has many important elements, but its foundation rests on the idea that units of archaeological stratification may have three relationships. They may be unrelated, meaning they do not touch one another, they may exhibit superposition or be layered on top of one another, or they may be correlated but no longer associated (such as when a ditch cuts through a soil layer and creates two pieces of the once-whole layer; the two pieces are the same layer but they are dissected and separated by the ditch).

Harris's breakthrough was to envision a way archaeologists could display the three relationships through the use of a diagram (Figure 4.3). In the diagram, boxes represent the

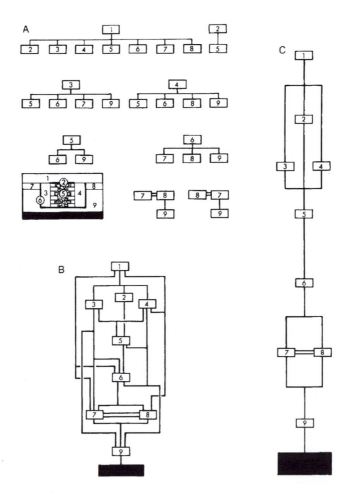

Figure 4.3 Construction of a Harris Matrix
(Edward C. Harris, *Principles of Archaeological Stratigraphy*, p. 87 © 1979 Elsevier.)

various archaeological units (soil strata, brick walls, pits, and so forth), and vertical and horizontal lines represent their relationships.

Archaeologists around the world immediately recognized the Harris Matrix as a significant tool, and Harris's method is now part of every archaeologist's set of skills. He revolutionized the way archaeologists understand stratification.

Historical archaeologists can also determine relative chronology by examining the ceramics found at sites dating from the last half of the eighteenth century to the early twentieth centuries. One of the types of ceramics studied by historical archaeologists is called "fine" or "refined earthenware." This ceramic is made with common clays, fired to a point that it becomes hard and dense, and glazed to make it impervious to liquids. They are identified by their white or whitish bodies. Potters first made fine earthenware in the middle of the eighteenth century with the goal of producing a white-bodied ware to compete with imported pieces of porcelain from Asia (and often called "China"). Importation was expensive, and most consumers could not afford the ware. English potters saw an opportunity to create a huge mass market by producing somewhat identical pieces at affordable prices.

Historical archaeologists recognize three types of fine earthenware as creamware, pearlware, and whiteware. Creamware, also called CC ware for common-cream or Queen's Ware, was first perfected by Josiah Wedgwood around 1762. It lost popularity and died out around 1820. Wedgwood introduced another ware, pearlware, around 1775. This ware was popular until the 1840s, and many potters copied it. Pearlware was replaced with whiteware first made around 1820. Ceramic factories around the world still produce whiteware dishes today.

The idea of the English potters was to produce a ceramic ware with a consistently white body, like porcelain. Creamware had a creamy body, and pieces are recognizable today by a creamy, off-white body and by green puddling or pooling in a vessel's crevices (such as around a pitcher's handle or on the base around the "foot ring," the bead of ceramic that supports the base on the bottom). For pearlware, potters added cobalt to the formula to produce a body whiter than creamware. Pearlware ceramics may be recognized by their whiteness and by the blue puddling in the crevices. Whiteware was the whitest of the all three; it has no pooling in the crevices.

In general, then, historical archaeologists can create a quick relative chronology by understanding that creamware ceramics are older in date than whiteware ceramics. They can make rapid assessments during fieldwork using the simple characteristics of the three ceramic types. This chronology, however, is only useful in a broad way. It cannot be used to construct fine-grained chronologies. Why? The problem is that individual potters constantly experimented with their ceramic formulas seeking to make their products as white as possible. Each formula was a closely guarded trade secret, something they would never share with competitors. The number of formulas could be staggering, as each factory owner struggled to make his ceramics the whitest on the market. As a result, distinguishing between the different formulas for pearlware, for example, is extremely difficult and perhaps impossible because of the likely presence of transitional pieces. Nonetheless, many historical archaeologists do regularly employ the relative chronology using refined earthenware sherds and vessels.

Dating with Objects of Known Age

Historical archaeologists are fortunate because they often excavate sites where objects of known age can provide accurate calendar dates for buildings, graves, stratified layers, and other features. Such items include common, everyday artifacts like dated coins, domestic tableware, and objects bearing telltale manufacturers' marks.

Ivor Noël Hume's Martin's Hundred excavation provides a superb example of such dating, using depictions of objects, rather than the specimens themselves, as chronological markers. After carefully digging through the silted clay that had washed into the foundation of the abandoned A-frame house (see Figure 4.2), the excavators reached the building's original floor, which appeared as a thin, fairly even layer of gray clay. The artifacts within the clay included tiny pieces of blue and white fireplace or wall tile, probably imported from the Netherlands, and known to date after the 1630s. Noël Hume's research revealed that Pieter de Hooch depicted similar tiles in a painting completed in 1660. In another painting, Dutch artist Jan Olis (1644) illustrated a pair of fireplace tongs exactly like those found on the floor of the A-frame house. Other objects—such as a green-and-yellow-glazed pot intended for kitchen use—can be seen in paintings from the mid-1660s. Noël Hume used these pictures to help him establish the occupation period of the house as the mid-seventeenth century.

Objects of known age were equally useful in the investigation of Millwood Plantation, a nineteenth- and early twentieth-century cotton plantation in the South Carolina upcountry. Archaeologists documented 21 stone building foundations among the dense underbrush that had grown up at the site since its abandonment in the 1920s. Census rolls, court records, and personal papers written by the historic plantation's owner, James Edward Calhoun (see Chapter 8), established the occupation dates of these buildings from 1832 until about 1925.

One foundation appeared as a roughly rectangular pile of red bricks and granite stones set in the middle of a large depression. The depression seemed to represent the limits of a former building with the rubble pile being what was left of the central chimney support. Upon excavation, archaeologists discovered it was indeed a stone chimney support faced with brick. Because the floor of the cabin had been raised off the ground, the brick facing must have been visible under the house. The archaeologists decided to excavate inside the brick-lined support in an attempt to establish its construction date, because it could have dated to the plantation's period of enslavement (1832–1865) or to its postwar era (1865–1925). The excavators found three layers of stones inside the chimney support. These strata were undoubtedly used to reinforce and strengthen the foundation (Figure 4.4). A layer of small cobbles appeared first, followed by a slightly thinner layer of small pebbles mixed with red clay. On the bottom was a layer of large, tightly packed stones. Pressed within a tiny space in the deepest stone layer, archaeologists found a Seated Liberty quarter dollar, dated 1876. This coin could not have fallen into the chimney support after construction because the two stone layers on top were so tightly sealed. The coin was either lost or purposely placed among the stones sometime after 1876, during the construction of the chimney support. The archaeologists could not determine exactly when the support and the house were built, but they did know it dated between 1876 (the date of the coin) and 1925 (the date of the site's abandonment).

The use of artifacts to date sites, human-built features, and soil layers at Martin's Hundred and Millwood Plantation involved only one or two key artifacts. The use of artifacts to refine relative chronologies more often includes the interpretation of several soil layers and possibly thousands of artifacts. The additional data increases the complexity of determining a date, but it may also increase its reliability.

When they excavated part of a city block in Sacramento, California, archaeologists Mary and Adrian Praetzellis used the artifacts they found to construct the block's chronology. As is typical of most urban settings, a mix of people had lived and worked on the lots during the block's existence. A careful search of historical records told the Praetzellises that members of four individual households had lived there: the Reeber family of German bakers; an unknown

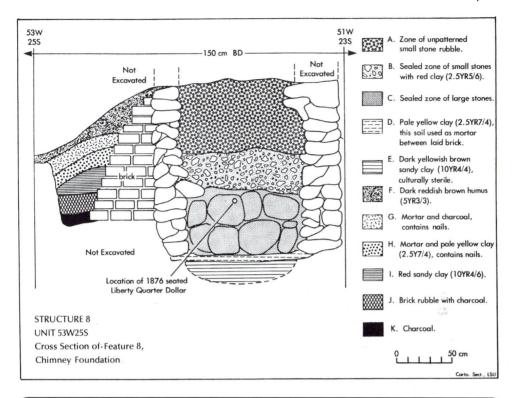

53W
25S

← 150 cm BD →

51W
23S

Not Excavated

Not Excavated

brick

Not Excavated

Location of 1876 seated
Liberty Quarter Dollar

STRUCTURE 8
UNIT 53W25S
Cross Section of·Feature 8,
Chimney Foundation

A. Zone of unpatterned small stone rubble.

B. Sealed zone of small stones with red clay (2.5YR5/6).

C. Sealed zone of large stones.

D. Pale yellow clay (2.5YR7/4), this soil used as mortar between laid brick.

E. Dark yellowish brown sandy clay (10YR4/4), culturally sterile.

F. Dark reddish brown humus (5YR3/3).

G. Mortar and charcoal, contains nails.

H. Mortar and pale yellow clay (2.5Y7/4), contains nails.

I. Red sandy clay (10YR4/6).

J. Brick rubble with charcoal.

K. Charcoal.

0   50 cm

Carto. Sect., LSU

Figure 4.4 Position of 1876 quarter at building support, Millwood Plantation, South Carolina

(Charles E. Orser, Jr.)

Gold Rush–era trader; James Meeker, a carriage lumber merchant; and the Goepel family from Germany. The Praetzellises assumed that each family contributed to the artifacts they discovered.

In an excavation 18 feet long and 3 feet wide (5.5 by 0.9 m) called Trench 3 West, the Praetzellises found at least 11 different soil layers that could be dated by their artifacts (Figure 4.5). Based on the presence of 18 coins, they dated the deepest layer to about 1852. Some of the coins were earlier in date: a ten pence Irish coin, dated 1806; a five lire Italian coin dated 1811; and an Indian rupee, dated 1840. Using common sense, however, they dated the layer on the basis of the *latest* coin, an 1852 ten-dollar gold piece issued in San Francisco. All the coins could have been used any time in 1852. Coins dated 1852 or 1840 could not have been used in 1811. They dated the next highest soil layer to the late 1850s, based on a bottle of "Mrs. Winslow's Soothing Syrup," a well-known elixir bottled in New York City starting in 1849. The Praetzellises dated a small soil lens above this layer to about 1862, based on the "Davenport" registry mark (see Chapter 8) of November 14, 1856, they found on the bottom of a white saucer. They assumed it would have taken a few years for the syrup and the English plate to have reached Sacramento. They assumed that the Davenport plate, registered in late November, probably did not reach the city before December. They assigned a date of 1861–1863 to the next highest soil layer based on the dates of the glass and ceramics within it. One difficulty with this

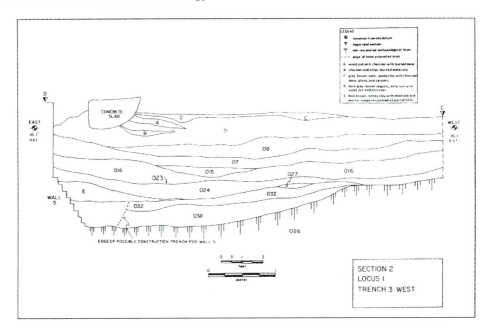

Figure 4.5 Soil layers in Trench 3, Sacramento, California

(Graphic by Adrian Praetzellis and Nelson Thompson. From *For a Good Boy: Victorians on Sacramento's J. Street* by Mary and Adrian Praetzellis © Anthropological Studies Center, Sonoma State University, 1990.)

interpretation, however, was the presence of a bottle marked *ELLENVILLE GLASS WORKS* in the same deposit. This company used this mark only between 1866 and the 1880s. Rather than causing them to rethink their relative dating, they concluded the bottle must be an *intrusion*, something not part of the original deposit but deposited later, into an already-existing deposit. This find indicated that people continued to toss broken and unwanted objects into the area until at least the late 1860s. The archaeologists dated a thin transition zone and the soil layer above it to 1863–1868 using the embossed "Corn and Oats" pattern they found on pieces of white ceramics. The Wedgwood factory in England produced this pattern during the mid-1860s. These pieces also carried a registry mark of October 31, 1863. The Praetzellises dated the soil lens directly above the last layer to 1868 using the same "Corn and Oats" ceramics. The next highest soil layer they dated to about 1875, based on a small piece of brown bottle marked "Dickey Chemist." This bottle originated in San Francisco and dates to the 1873–1920 period. The soil layers above the 1875 layer consisted of urban debris and artifacts dating from the mid-1870s to the present.

This example from Sacramento, California, demonstrates the value of having artifacts available with known dates of manufacture, sale, and use. Even in this instance, though, the plausibility of the interpretation rests on the archaeologists' research skills, ability to identify artifacts, and wide knowledge of artifact dates. In some cases, archaeologists may find thousands of artifacts that by themselves can be assigned no particular date. In such instances, they can turn to two methods of formula dating, analytical methods that are unique to historical archaeology.

Formula Dating

Many historical archaeologists have turned to formula dating to help them provide dates for large collections of white clay smoking pipes and glazed ceramics. Formula dating is based on two suppositions. First, artifacts change over time, and secondly, these changes, no matter how imperceptible they may be, are sometimes amenable to measurement in years. The steady changes in the attributes of long-stemmed smoking pipes and mass-produced ceramics can be represented in mathematical formulas.

In the past, the white clay smoking pipe was what the disposable razor is today—used for a few days or weeks (or perhaps only once) then thrown away. White clay pipes date from the mid-sixteenth century to the early twentieth century. (A few are still made today as replicas for tourists and historical reenactors.) Pipemakers operated throughout Europe, notably in the Netherlands and the British Isles, but other locales, including European settler communities, also eventually had working pipemakers.

Historical archaeologists often unearth hundreds, even thousands, of pipe bowls and stems. Excavations at the eighteenth-century Fort Michilimackinac in Michigan yielded no fewer than 5,328 pipe fragments from between 1959 and 1966 alone. Excavators at the seventeenth- and eighteenth-century Ferryland site in Newfoundland found tens of thousands of pipe fragments in only seven years! As is the case at Ferryland, many of the pipes contain identifiable maker's marks (see Chapter 8), but in the vast majority of cases, the pipes exhibit no identifiable decorations.

A white clay smoking pipe consists of two parts: a bowl and a stem (Figure 4.6). Fortunately for historical archaeologists, pipemakers altered the bowls of the white, long-stemmed

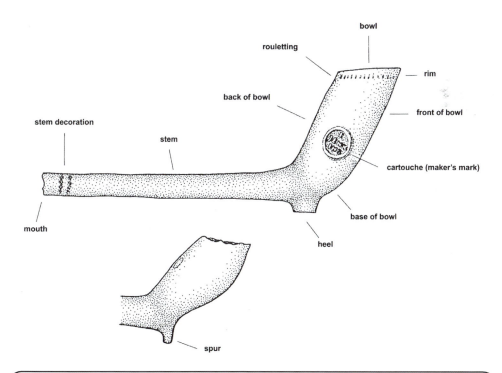

Figure 4.6 Parts of a clay smoking pipe
(Georgia L. Fox)

pipes over the decades, beginning with the late 1500s. Pipe experts have charted these changes, demonstrating when each style was popular. Sixteenth-century pipemakers typically produced undecorated and simple bowls with a sharp angle between the stem and the bowl. They straightened the sides of the bowls over time and made the angle with the stem smoother. By the early eighteenth century, pipes had straight, smooth bowls. Also in the early eighteenth century, pipemakers began to put intricate symbols and decorations on their bowls. By the late eighteenth century, even short-stemmed pipes had become popular. These pipes were smoked by inserting a reed or stem into the short, stubby bowl (Figure 4.7)

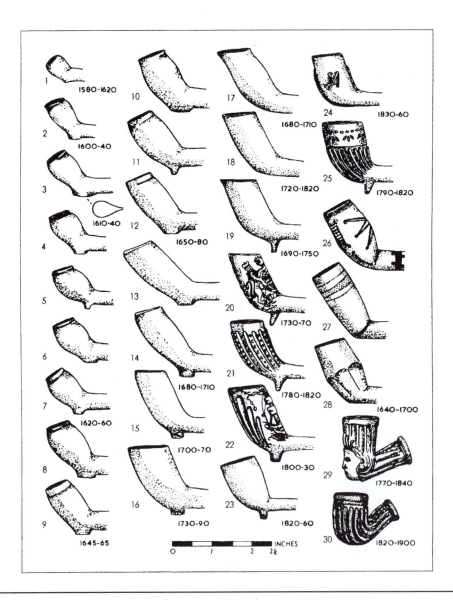

Figure 4.7 The evolution of the pipe bowl 1580–1900

(From *Historical Archaeology* by Ivor Noël Hume. Alfred A. Knopf, 1972 © W.W. Norton & Company, Inc.)

The fine, white clay pipes were fragile and easily broke into small pieces when dropped or tapped to remove the old tobacco plug. Whereas the bowls might break into only two or three pieces, the stems generally fractured into several sections, each measuring about 1 inch (2.5 cm) long. Of the pipes found at Fort Michilimackinac between 1959 and 1966, 4,347, or almost 82 percent, were pipe stems.

On the face of it, pipe stems are hardly promising dating material. In the 1950s, however, pioneer historical archaeologist J. C. Harrington, in a monumental display of patience and dedication, examined more than 50,000 pipe stems he had excavated from colonial Jamestown, Virginia. After examining the stems, he noticed that the size of the hole, or bore, appeared to get smaller through time. Harrington concluded that "if this represented a definite and consistent trend, then it might possibly be useful as a dating criterion." So inspired, he measured 330 stems from colonial sites in Virginia, and discovered that between 1620 and 1650, most of the bores measured 8/64ths of an inch (31.7 mm), whereas between 1750 and 1800, they were only 4/64ths of an inch (15.9 mm) (Figure 4.8). Harrington used

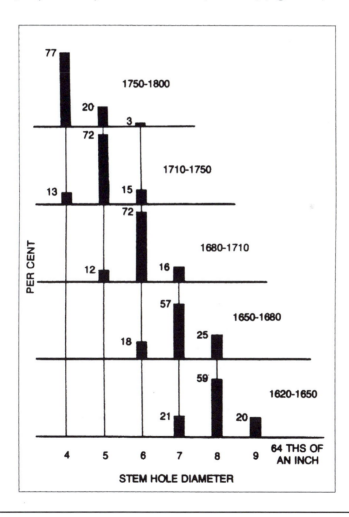

Figure 4.8 Harrington's pipe stem measurements
(Courtesy of the Archaeological Society of Virginia Press.)

64ths of an inch as his scale because he measured the pipe stem bores with a set of drill bits. These tools were available in several accurate sizes and were small enough to fit into the pipe stem bores.

Seven years after Harrington's breakthrough, Lewis Binford made the first strides in what is now called formula dating. He believed Harrington's observations could be converted into what mathematicians call a regression formula. A regression formula is a mathematical way of representing the relationship between two variables, in this case, bore diameter and date. With bore diameter plotted on the X axis of a graph and date on the Y axis, the regression formula will show the precise relationship between the two variables. According to Binford, the formula $Y = 1931.85 - 38.26X$ could be used to date collections of broken pipe stems, with Y being the mean date to be calculated, 1931.85 being the statistical date that pipe stem bores would theoretically disappear. The number of years it takes for a pipe stem bore to be reduced by 1/64 of an inch (1.6 mm) was calculated to be 38.26. (Of course, the bore in a pipe stem could never actually disappear, or else the pipe would be worthless. The calculation is based purely on statistics.)

Historical archaeologists immediately recognized they could use Binford's creative formula to determine the date of any collection of pipe stems. X is calculated by multiplying the number of pipe stems by the number of 64ths of an inch in their measurement (7 stems measuring 6/64 = 42; 35 stems measuring 7/64 = 245), and then adding the products together and dividing by the total number of pipe stems.

Many enthusiastic archaeologists began to experiment with Binford's formula. Robert Heighton and Kathleen Deagan discovered that the regression line was not straight as Binford thought, but curved. They reasoned that pipe stem bores reached a minimum diameter and then stayed constant after about 1800. Ivor Noël Hume also discovered that the formula works best with samples of more than 900 stems deposited between 1680 and 1760. These refinements have strengthened Binford's original pipe stem formula.

Encouraged by the promise formula dating held for historical archaeology, Stanley South devised a mean ceramic dating formula (or MCD) for use with eighteenth-century British ceramics. He reasoned that if English ceramic types have recognizable dates of manufacture, then it should be easy to add together all the ceramic date ranges present at a site and calculate a single midpoint for all of them.

South's formula is easy to compute (Table 4.1), and it has the advantage of yielding an actual calendar year. The year calculated represents the mean date of the combined ceramics in the sample.

To present a simple example, suppose a ceramic collection from a site only contains ten sherds. Information on British ceramics indicates seven of them were manufactured from 1800–1850, giving a mean date of 1825. Suppose the other three sherds were produced from 1830–1860, for a mean date of 1845. This means the entire manufacturing range of the ten sherds is 1800–1860. The computation of the mean ceramic date yields 1831, just about what we would expect. The formula works by weighting the collection by the number of sherds of different manufacturing dates. The sample of ten sherds would produce an MCD of 1839 if we had three sherds with a mean manufacturing date of 1825 and seven with a mean manufacturing date of 1845. The date is weighted in the direction of 1845 because more sherds of that date are present. To get a better idea of how this formula works, use the ten sherds and South's formula from Table 4.1.

Many archaeologists who calculate the mean ceramic date also calculate the standard deviation of the sample. Simplistically, the standard deviation (symbolically represented as σ, S, or SD) represents the way the individual ceramic date ranges cluster around the mean. The SD will be small if the date ranges in the sample of sherds are all about the same. Conversely,

> ## Table 4.1 Calculating a mean ceramic date using South's method

Ceramic Type	Type Median (X$_i$)	Sherd Count (f$_i$)	Product
22	1791	483	865,053
33	1767	25	44,175
34	1760	32	56,320
36	1755	55	96,525
37	1733	40	69,320
43	1758	327	574,866
49	1750	583	1,020,250
44	1738	40	69,520
47	1748	28	48,944
53, 54	1733	52	90,116
56	1733	286	495,638
29	1760	9	15,840
		1960	3,446,567

The mean ceramic date formula

$$Y = \frac{\sum_{i=1}^{n} x_i \cdot f_i}{\sum_{i=1}^{n} f_i}$$

$$Y = \frac{3,446.567}{1960} = 1758.4$$

Source: Stanley South, *Method and Theory in Historical Archaeology.* (New York: Academic Press, 1977), p. 220.

if the ranges vary, then the SD will be large. Once the SD is calculated, the MCD can be presented as Y ± 1SD. In statistical terms, it means analysts can have 68 percent confidence in a ± 1SD result and 95 percent confidence when using ± 2SD. An MCD of 1730 ± 10 indicates that the sample probably dates from 1720–1740 (with ± 1SD). The small SD means that the ceramic sample represents a short time span. An MCD of 1730 ± 60 means that the sample most likely dates from 1670–1790 (with ± 1SD). In this case, the ceramic sample may have intrusions that affect the date. One nineteenth-century sherd may skew the sample. In such cases, archaeologists can calculate a "trimmed standard deviation," meaning that the outliers (the nineteenth-century sherds) are removed and the MCD recalculated, a method that will reduce the size of the SD.

The ceramic mean dating method works best with large collections, just as does pipestem formula dating. Even so, South's dating formula has found a wider audience than the pipe stem dating, but only because mass-produced ceramics of all kinds are common finds even when pipe stems are absent. When tested against historically documented dates of occupation, the mean ceramic dates generally have been found to be in agreement. The formula is especially useful at sites with undocumented historical dates.

All formula dates should be checked against other dates—preferably documentary ones. Something is amiss if a site with a historically documented date range of 1690–1740 yields a ceramic date of 1770. Either someone has misidentified the ceramics or the historical sources are wrong or incomplete. Sometimes the mean ceramic date can provide unexpected information.

Archaeologists from the University of Delaware excavated the Williams Site in Glasgow, Delaware, a residence once occupied by an African American farm laborer named Sidney Stump. Legal records established the mean historic date of the site at 1887, but the mean ceramic date yielded 1844. How can such a discrepancy be explained? One possible answer is that Stump may have used second-hand or hand-me-down ceramics. This interpretation is plausible because he was a farm laborer for the entire time he lived at the Williams Site. The truth behind the date discrepancy may never be known with certainty, but the calculation of the mean ceramic date allowed the archaeologists to suggest an interpretation they may never have otherwise imagined.

Dendrochronology

An astronomer named A.E. Douglass invented dendrochronology, or tree-ring dating, in 1904 while studying ancient sun spot activity in the American Southwest. He soon extended his method to the ancient beams he saw preserved in ancient pueblos, and in so doing provided archaeologists with an elegant and extremely accurate dating method.

Trees grow seasonally, and the effects of rainfall and the number of frost-free days means that the trees' seasonal growth varies from year to year. The different rates of growth, especially in environments with well-defined wet and dry seasons, leaves a series of concentric growth rings of various thickness in the trunk. Dendrochronologists extract core samples from logs and match their rings to databases compiled for the region. A number of reliable databases have been created, with one of the foremost being the International Tree-Ring Data Bank operated by the National Oceanic and Atmospheric Administration (NOAA).

The master sequences are based on ring counts from living trees, and they provide an extremely accurate chronology, in some places extending back thousands of years. Even a small log from a site can be matched with the master sequence. Archaeologists in Europe have linked living trees to church beams and farmhouse timbers, as well as to ancient logs found in bogs. In Ireland, for instance, the tree-ring chronology extends back to before 5200 B.C.E.

Tree-ring analysis usually requires collaboration with an expert in the field. Inaccurate dates can be produced by simply counting the rings because some of rings may be absent in a particular specimen. Others may have false rings (or bands) that must be identified at the cellular level. In such cases, simple ring counting will not produce an accurate date. To remedy the problem, dendrochronologists use a method called crossdating. Crossdating involves examining a number of samples from the same region (or a place with similar environmental conditions) and then matching the rings against one another to determine the years of growth.

Historical archaeologists find dendrochronology to be a powerful dating tool when they can use it. Archaeologists used the method to date the historic Pueblo of Acoma, the famous "Sky City" in New Mexico, the oldest continuously inhabited city in the United States (Figure 4.9). Spanish explorers first visited the pueblo in 1540 during Coronado's efforts to locate the legendary golden Seven Lost Cities of Cibola. In 1599 the Spaniards destroyed Acoma as part of their plan to control the pueblo dwellers of the region, but the residents soon rebuilt it. Modern Acoma is a tapestry of building and rebuilding going back many centuries. In 1987 the people of Acoma invited the Laboratory of Tree-Ring Dating at the University of Arizona to date the oldest part of the village. The laboratory's core samples from well-preserved beams enabled them to date 50 rooms. They found the pueblo was begun in 1646, achieving

Figure 4.9 Acoma Pueblo, New Mexico
(Kevin Fleming / Corbis)

its current form by 1652. In 1934 the Historic American Buildings Survey (see Chapter 6) had completed accurate architectural drawings of the pueblo. When the archaeologists compared the buildings on this detailed map with their tree-ring dates, they were surprised to discover that the pueblo had changed little between 1652 and 1934, a span of 282 years.

In their investigation of a homesite located in the El Malpais National Conservation Area in New Mexico, archaeologists were able to use dendrochronology to establish that most of the wood used in the construction of the wooden structures still standing clustered in the years 1934–1940. The wood samples also told them that the people who lived at the site had built the structures in single episodes using newly cut pieces of timber. Thus, in addition to providing useful dating information, the analysis of wood samples can also reveal patterns of how people used wood in the past. Such information, when linked with archaeological and historical information, provides new insights into past activities.

Absolute (Radiometric) Dating

Absolute dating, while often significant, has little use in historical archaeology. Radiometric dating methods have greatest use at very ancient sites, so they find little application in the post-1500 era. Potassium-argon dating, for example, is used to measure the ages of rocks from the earliest history of the Earth (about 4.3 billion years ago) to about 100,000 years ago. Historical archaeologists researching the past 500 years have no use for this method except under unique circumstances.

By far the most well-known radiometric dating method is radiocarbon dating, also called C14 (or 14C) dating. This method, developed in the 1940s, revolutionized the study of ancient history. Before it was known and widely used, archaeologists mostly relied on artifact chronologies to determine their sites' dates. Radiocarbon dating allowed them to date sites and their features with much more precision.

Radiocarbon dating works by measuring the deterioration rate of carbon within once living things. The analysis, which has gotten increasingly sophisticated over time, produces a date with a ± (plus/minus) factor. A wood sample from a fire pit may yield a date of 1200±50, meaning that the sample dates to the 1150–1250 period. This date spread can be relatively insignificant when dealing with ancient settlements. If the site yielding the wood sample was inhabited from 1000 to 1500, the 100-year spread of the sample does not present a major problem. The date simply indicates the sample derives from the early history of the site's occupation, which is useful knowledge.

The date range can be a problem in historical archaeology, however, because many sites are occupied for short periods. In addition, historical archaeologists usually have access to written records or maps that may already suggest dates for the site. In most cases, the available documentary evidence will establish the likely dates of the archaeological remains. The historically documented occupation date range can be compared with the dates obtained from the other relative dating methods. Radiocarbon dating would yield little usable information.

The application of radiometric dating in historical archaeology may change as new techniques are developed and as existing methods are refined. An interesting example comes from the dating of coral using thermal ionization mass spectrometry U-series techniques. In a study of temples called *marae* in Polynesia, Warren Sharp and his colleagues were able to provide seventeenth- and eighteenth-century dates using this technique. The acquired dates, though occurring before European contact with most of the islands, certainly falls within the purview of post-1500 historical archaeology. In any case, this technique offers promise for use at other archaeological research projects in the region, a place where increasing research in historical archaeology is taking place.

Space in Historical Archaeology

Space in archaeological terms usually refers to the locations of finds, structures, and sites, and the relationships between them. One way to understand the archaeological use of space is to think of the words "position" or "place." The relative position of things in three-dimensional space is a key element in understanding how things were related in the past.

Many people envision archaeology as a kind of detective work, and a concern for the placement of things in space is a normal element of detective stories. The position of weapons, fingerprints, and blood spatter in relation to one another constitutes key crime-solving clues.

Though fictional, Sherlock Holmes solves many of his most challenging mysteries through his observations of where things are located in relation to one another. In "The Adventure of the Priory School," he ponders the disappearance of Lord Saltire, the ten-year-old son and heir of the Duke of Holdernesse. The young lord had disappeared one night, along with Heidegger the German master. Holmes is called in because, in characteristic fashion, the police had already thrown up their hands in despair. Appreciating the significance of space, Holmes draws a sketch of the landscape to help him solve the baffling mystery. With this map in hand he is able to reconstruct the route taken by the abductors, is led to the body of Heidegger, and deduces—from the bicycle tracks, also on the map—that young Saltire is being held at the Fighting Cock Inn on the top of the map near Holdernesse Hall.

Archaeologists are not scientific versions of Sherlock Holmes, but Holmes's methods are instructive. He works like an archaeologist when he demonstrates his intense interest in where things are located, and he could even have been speaking as an archaeologist when he tells Watson, "I want you to realize those geographical features which may have a good deal to do with our investigation." Archaeologists refer to the analysis of location—from the placement of artifacts at a site to the placement of the features on a landscape—as *spatial analysis*. Archaeologists have adopted many of their methods and perspectives on spatial analysis from geographers. This borrowing represents another important instance where archaeologists, including historical archaeologists, have relied on scholars from other disciplines.

Spatial analysis proceeds on many levels, or scales. Archaeologists can examine the location of artifacts and features within an individual house. Intra-site analysis can focus on the spatial associations of artifacts, houses, and other features present at a site (see Chapter 11). Archaeologists can concentrate inter-site analysis on the presence of artifacts within many sites, and so may discover important insights about broad aspects of past life, such as the extent of trade relations. They can also conduct larger-scale macro analyses of entire regions (see Chapter 12).

All spatial relationships have the potential to yield valuable cultural and historical information. The placement of sites in relation to natural resources—fertile soils, stands of good timber, streams and rivers that run the year around, and sun-drenched hillsides—also provide abundant information about the natural features people in the past chose for settlement, hunting, and other activities. Equally important are the placement of sites in relation to objects of human construction—mills, bridges, major settlements, and routes of transportation. Railroads provide an excellent example.

Railroads were an important, and indeed central, determinant of settlement in the flat, fertile prairies and plains of North America. On the plains of Saskatchewan, for instance, the Canadian Pacific Railroad gobbled up the best land and then convinced immigrants to settle on it. Author James Minifie recalls the irresistible pull this land had on his father in 1909: "The last, best West was filling up fast; my father determined to get in while he could. He closed down his business and decided to go as far west as his money would take him." Old maps of Saskatchewan show the network of railroads in the southern half of this province with settlements appearing as beads on a necklace, strung out along the rail lines. In some cases, when bypassed by an important new railroad, a town's residents may have picked up their buildings and moved them to the side of the railroad. Isolated towns could die because settlers and commerce generally moved only along the major routes of transportation, including the railroads.

The scale, or level, of a spatial analysis is determined by an archaeologist's research questions. The transportation of commodities from one place to another is essentially a problem in spatial analysis, with a scale extending between entire continents. When archaeologist Peter Danks studied the distribution of late-eighteenth-century ceramics made by the Lowestoft factory on the east coast of England, his region of interest was the entire British Isles. No written records or pattern books survived, so Danks was forced to rely strictly on artifacts to establish the spatial distribution of the Lowestoft wares. The only way he could perform this kind of study was by examining the ceramic collections from several sites. Once he had identified Lowestoft pieces in various collections, he could be reasonably certain that some sort of linkage had operated between the factory and the sites.

Most spatial analysis occurs on a far smaller scale than the continental level. When Stanley South became interested in the spatial placement of pins and beads at the eighteenth-century Public House and Tailor Shop in Brunswick Town, North Carolina, he focused only on this one 3,600 square foot (324 sq. m) building. His careful analysis of the artifacts' locations indicated all the beads and pins occurred in five of the six rooms (Figure 4.10). These tiny

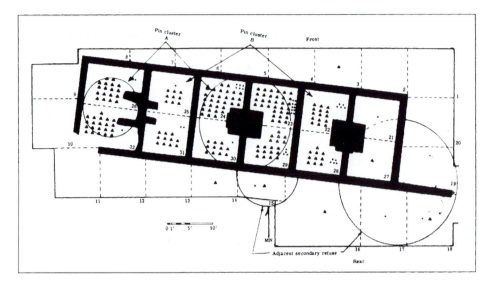

Figure 4.10 Plan of the Public House and Tailor Shop showing the location of pins and beads

(From Stanley South, *Method and Theory in Historical Archaeology*, New York: Academic Press, 1977, p. 136)

objects had fallen through the cracks in the floorboards during the building's use, where they remained until archaeologists found them. The unequal distribution of beads and pins led South to conclude the room without these objects "must have been used for merchandising the objects sewn together in the five other rooms."

Space at Archaeological Sites

The study of space is based on another fundamental principle of archaeology, the *Law of Association*. This principle holds that an artifact or other find is contemporary with the other objects found along with it in the same soil layer or human-built feature.

We mentioned above how Mary and Adrian Praetzellis dated the different soil layers in one city block in Sacramento, California, using one or two datable artifacts. The Law of Association holds that all finds within the layers were contemporaneous with the datable artifacts. This conclusion is particularly reasonable when the deposits are sealed or closed to intrusions, like the chimney support at Millwood Plantation.

Burials accompanied with grave goods provide an excellent example of the Law of Association. Interment is a single event taking place at a particular moment in time. Given the nature of burial, an archaeologist can be certain—in the absence of intrusions—that the artifacts deposited with the deceased were used in the society at the time of the person's death. Once the grave is filled over, nothing more can be put inside it.

In Barbados, Jerome Handler and Frederick Lange excavated the skeletal remains of several seventeenth-century enslaved individuals who had lived, toiled, and died at Newton Plantation. Careful excavation demonstrated that the artifacts placed alongside the dead—glass bottles, white clay smoking pipes, brass buttons, glass beads, and glazed ceramics—had been used together when these individuals were alive.

Tightly enclosed collections of artifacts help archaeologists construct the contexts of past daily life. The Law of Association allows archaeologists to develop a sense of the range of artifacts used in a culture or society for commemoration or veneration.

Beyond burials and individual soil layers, the Law of Association permits archaeologists to perceive the sites they routinely study as being arranged within a spatial hierarchy. The hierarchy extends from small spaces to extremely large ones. In historical archaeology, the range extends from activity areas to global networks. The idea behind levels of analysis is that people use space in regular ways because it is culturally determined. We can discern something of a culture's patterns of spatial use by studying the spatial distribution of artifacts, features, and whole sites on a landscape.

An appreciation for the significance of space can be gained by thinking about personal space. Anthropologists have established that different cultures have various ideas about the amount of empty space an individual should have around them. Americans have a different idea than some European and Asian cultures and, when speaking with individuals from these places, we may feel uncomfortable when our concept of personal space is violated. We may keep stepping backward, only to have the other person move forward. The study of space is called *proxemics*. Only archaeologists engaged in ethnographic fieldwork can observe the active use of personal space. Other archaeologists must develop ideas about a past culture's spatial usage from the remains left behind.

Activity Areas

An activity area is the smallest spatial unit studied by archaeologists. These zones are places within a site where people conducted specific activities. Archaeologists usually identify them as clusters of artifacts or disturbances in the soil. Artifacts and other evidence typically indicate the range of activities once carried out at that spot.

As part of her investigation into the archaeology of activity areas, Susan Kent examined a number of site locations in the American Southwest. She identified five archaeological sites associated with the Navajo. One site had an occupation date from about 1890 to around 1930. Littered across the site, she found coffee can lids, porcelain doll parts, glass bottle fragments, sheep and cow bones, and a 1927 New Mexico automobile license plate. She identified several activity areas through dense concentrations of wood chips and ash (Figure 4.11). These spots were places where people had performed activities such as chipping wood and building fires. The presence of at least three traditional Navajo dwellings, or hogans, suggested to Kent that three related families, perhaps members of the same extended family, had created the activity areas.

Information in historical records, as well as similarities to activities performed today, often allow historical archaeologists to use site labels that are more descriptive than the generic "activity area." For example, while excavating at Jamestown, Virginia, in the 1950s, John Cotter found a cluster of three kilns used by the settlers to make pottery. His crew unearthed two other archaeological features nearby: the foundation of a seventeenth-century workshop or brewhouse, and a shallow pit probably dug for clay to use in the construction of the kilns and later filled with refuse. The workshop/brewhouse was located only 20 feet (6.1 m) to the east of the kilns; the pit was only 10 feet (3.1 m) to the south. The excavators located three additional features within 160 feet (48.8 m) of the three kilns—a large dwelling, a small outbuilding, and a smaller house. At this one spot in colonial Jamestown, Cotter found what may be described as eight separate activity areas: a large house, a small building associated with it, a small house, a workshop or brewhouse, three kilns, and one pit. Each area represents the remains of activities producing archaeological evidence. Cotter was able to use his knowledge of colonial history to assign functional terms to the activity areas.

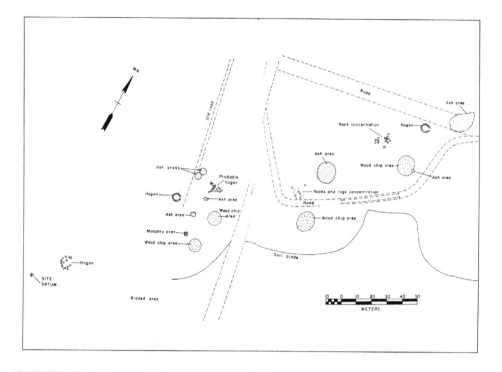

Figure 4.11 Activity areas at a Navajo site, 1890–1930
(Drawn by Eric Blinman. From *Analyzing Activity Areas: An Ethnoarchaeological Study of the Use of Space* by Susan Kent. Albuquerque: UNM, 1984.)

Kent's identification of the three Navajo hogans in the American Southwest and Cotter's discovery of the two house sites at Jamestown illustrate an important point: In historical archaeology, the word "site" often equates with "household." Much historical archaeology is focused on such residential units.

Households

Ideas about what constitutes a household vary among cultures. A useful definition in the United States comes from the Bureau of the Census. This government agency defines a household as "all the persons who occupy a housing unit." Houses, apartments, groups of rooms, and even a single room all qualify as housing units. Many of us may think of a household as being composed of a husband, a wife, and their children, individuals related by marriage and birth. Thus, we may equate "household" with "nuclear family." Within the past several years, however, Westerners have witnessed dramatic changes in the composition of the traditional male-centered family. The once so-called "nontraditional" family is becoming increasingly commonplace. As early as 1900, however, the U.S. Census Bureau defined the "family" in broad terms as "a group of individuals who occupy jointly a dwelling place or part of a dwelling place." They further noted that "All the occupants and employees of a hotel, if they regularly sleep there, make up a single family." This definition, coupled with recent changes in family structure, means the best way to think about households is to view them simply as groups of people who live together.

Households are particularly important to historical archaeologists because household residents were the consumers who bought, used, and discarded the artifacts and food remains found at domestic archaeological sites. The spatial distributions of these finds have the potential to reveal a great deal about the activities of the household.

In their archaeological history of Philadelphia, John Cotter, Daniel Roberts, and Michael Parrington describe excavations at 8 South Front Street. Located about one-and-a-half blocks from the Delaware River and not far from Independence Hall, this address was home to three different households from 1683–1833. Historic plats indicate the resident was Letitia Penn, of the prominent Penn family, from 1683 to 1713 (Figure 4.12). From 1713 to 1736, a bricklayer named Joseph Yard lived on the property with his family, but in 1736, Joseph's son, John, sold the property to Andrew Bradford. Bradford's son, Thomas, would later become a lieutenant colonel in the American militia. He spent most of his later life in the house. The Bradfords sold the property in 1833 to John Moss, a prominent shipping merchant, who never actually lived there.

The preliminary analysis of the archaeological remains discovered at 8 South Front Street indicates the occupants of the house dug three deep pits on the property. Near the end of their residence, the Yards dug an eight-foot-deep (2.4 m) privy pit near the back of the house. They later filled this pit with trash. It contained only one datable artifact, a gray stoneware chamber pot bearing the mark "A.D." These letters indicate the pot had been made at the shop of Anthony Duché sometime in the 1720–1730 period.

When the Bradfords purchased the residence from the Yards, they did not bother to have the privy cleaned. They simply dug a second one, 15 feet (4.6 m) deep, directly adjacent to the old one. Excavation of the second privy yielded a 1734 British coin. Sometime between 1736

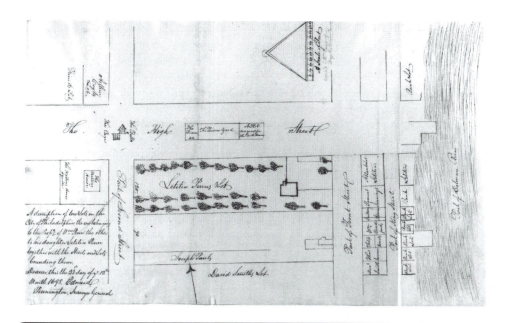

Figure 4.12 Section of a 1698 survey map of Philadelphia showing the location of Letitia Penn's lot and those of her neighbors
(Historical Society of Pennsylvania)

and 1756, the Bradfords added a kitchen to the house. Space considerations forced them to build this addition over the privy. As a replacement privy, they used an old brick-lined, 26-foot-deep (7.9 m) well, also in the backyard. While the greater depth of the well-turned-privy would have served the family longer than the shallower pits, the wells in the vicinity may have been compromised, causing health problems among the neighbors.

Households formed the basic economic unit for Letitia Penn, the Yards, and the Bradfords at 8 South Front Street, just as they have for millions of people around the world for centuries. But households, no matter how tightly knit, did not exist in a vacuum. Individual households were part of a larger unit, called a neighborhood.

Neighborhoods

Neighborhoods are simply collections of households. The U.S. Bureau of the Census considers neighborhoods to be composed of several "housing units": single-household dwellings, apartment buildings, and hotels. Neighborhoods in cities can be tightly compacted spaces, with people virtually living on top of one another in apartments and tenements. Neighborhoods in more rural settings may cover much larger areas, with individual dwellings being widely dispersed.

The families who once called 8 South Front Street home were members of a larger neighborhood. When Thomas Holme, William Penn's general surveyor, drew the lots on Front Street, he listed not only Letitia Penn, but also the names of Daniel Smith, Charles Pickering, Thomas Harriet, and other landowners who were her neighbors. All of these people were both members of households and residents of the neighborhood. They probably nodded to one another on the street, perhaps they took tea in one another's houses, and perhaps they even knew some of their neighbors' personal problems.

Historical archaeologists can often use historical documents and maps to understand neighborhoods. They link this textual information with their archaeological findings to provide a rich picture of neighborhood life. Such sources often prove invaluable for discovering details about a neighborhood's ethnic composition and physical conditions.

In large American cities, invaluable neighborhood maps were once published by the D. A. Sanborn National Insurance Diagram Bureau, later called the Sanborn Map and Publishing Company. The Aetna Insurance Company hired Sanborn in 1867 to make maps of several cities in Tennessee to show their appearance after the devastation of the Civil War. Sanborn saw the potential for a profitable business and soon created a company to specialize in producing these so-called "fire insurance maps." By the time the company stopped producing them 100 years later, they had published 700,000 maps of 12,000 cities and towns in the United States. In Great Britain, similar maps were produced by Charles E. Goad Ltd., and in Australia, newspapers sometimes published panoramic views of cities, often showing selected houses in detail around the image's border.

Memories of the highly devastating fires, like those in London in 1666, Lisbon in 1755, and Chicago in 1871, convinced city- and town-dwellers of the wisdom of knowing where buildings were located, their materials of construction, and their owners' fire precautions. Maps like those produced by the Sanborn Company depicted the spaces between buildings and noted whether the buildings were constructed of brick, stone, or wood. They distinguish between residences, stores, stables, and special-use buildings, such as glasshouses. The maps also indicate the locations of porches, outbuildings, and lot lines. The cartographers also included information about chimney design to assist firefighters called upon to distinguish chimney fires. In short, where they are available, urban insurance maps are priceless archives of the spatial relationships of late-nineteenth- and early twentieth-century neighborhoods.

Historical archaeologists also find the aptly named "bird's-eye views" of cities and towns to be as valuable as maps. Such views are really "artistic maps" because they provide three-dimensional perspectives on urban areas. Buildings appear as actual structures with windows, doors, and roofs. They also depict trees and flowerbeds, boats sailing on rivers, and horse-drawn buggies on busy thoroughfares. These images may at first appear more realistic than simple maps, but they also display far more artistic license than the sober diagrams of the insurance plats. Many artists of the bird's-eye views made their drawings look better than the towns they portrayed, so archaeologists use them with caution.

When combined, maps and bird's-eye views provide historical archaeologists with a compelling picture of old neighborhoods. These sources allow archaeologists to construct images of a neighborhood before their excavations begin, with the understanding, of course, that some of the information may be inaccurate or fanciful.

When Mary and Adrian Praetzellis investigated the Sacramento city block mentioned earlier, they excavated the household of a woman named Mary Collins, who once lived at 808 I Street. The first family to live at this address was the Leonard Kellogg family, who were there by 1858. The family of Mary Collins, a widowed Irish woman, lived there until sometime before 1910. The 1900 census indicates that Mary had three children living with her at the time. The Praetzellises used both the 1869 bird's-eye view (Figure 4.13) and the 1895

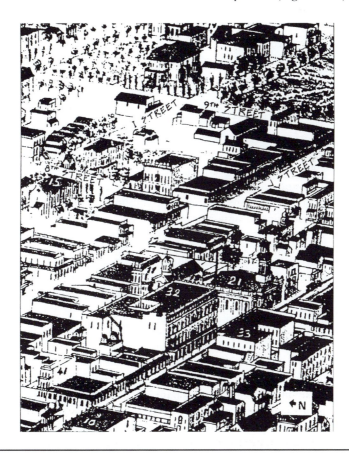

Figure 4.13 Bird's-eye view of Sacramento, California, in 1869
(Courtesy of the Bancroft Library, University of California, Berkeley.)

J Street

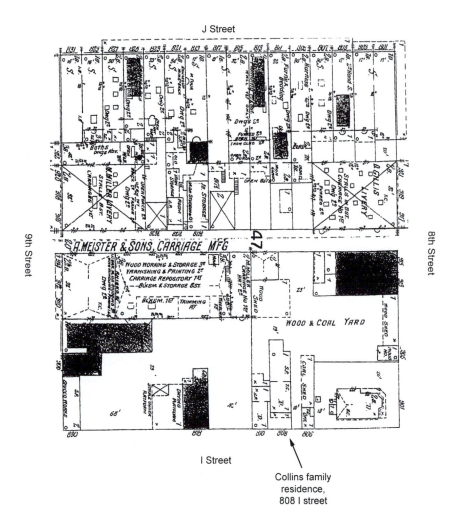

9th Street

8th Street

I Street

Collins family
residence,
808 I street

Figure 4.14 1895 Sanborn map showing the location of Mary Collins's
home at 808 I Street, Sacramento, California

(From *The Mary Collins Assemblage: Mass Marketing and the Archaeology of Sacramento Family* by Mary and Adrian Praetzellis, p. 143 © Anthropological Studies
Center, Sonoma State University, 1990.)

Sanborn map of the block (Figure 4.14) to reconstruct the history of the Collins' neighborhood. They learned a small dwelling had been built adjacent to the Collins's yard on the right
(at 810 I Street), and a narrow alleyway was located on the left. Next to the alley were two
small buildings, behind which was a large house on the corner (at 901 8th Street). A large
"Wood & Coal Yard" was directly behind the Collins home. Next to the coal yard was the
"A. Meister & Sons Carriage Mfg." company. Further behind the house, fronting J Street,
were one or two other dwellings. All of these properties—the dwellings, the coal yard, the
manufacturing company—were part of the Collins's neighborhood in 1895.

This one block in Sacramento, California, shows the many different kinds of buildings that can exist in a neighborhood. Historical archaeologists can study each of them: domestic, commercial, and manufacturing sites. The 1869 bird's-eye view also proves that the Collins neighborhood did not exist in a vacuum. It was one element of a much larger, vibrant community.

Communities

Historical archaeologists have learned that communities are more than simply a collection of people and buildings. Residents of communities can develop feelings of belonging and group identity through the creation and continuance of common traditions. Archaeologist Heather Burke illustrated this process in her examination of Armidale, Australia. By examining the 1840–1930 period, Burke learned the working class men and women who moved into the more upscale part of town created a sense of shared community among themselves as a strategy for cohesion. Their sense of togetherness fostered group identity (see Chapter 11) and made them feel a shared social rank with their neighbors even though they themselves were not at the top of the social order. The creation of the ideological community also helped to level, or at least to downplay, the internal differences that existed *within* the community, between individual households with varying amounts of income and social connections.

Communities, though larger than neighborhoods, are not the largest spatial unit historical archaeologists study. Settlement patterns link together communities.

Settlement Patterns

The study of *settlement patterns* involves analyzing how archaeological sites are distributed across a landscape. The examination of settlement distribution is often called *settlement archaeology.*

The archaeology of settlement patterns is based on two assumptions: People with free choice make informed decisions about where they choose to live, and they live in specific locales because they seek to satisfy some want or need. Ancient Egyptian farmers built their villages on high ground or just outside the Nile floodplain so their homes would not be inundated by unusually high floods. Some people lived on the edge of the desert because fertile land was so important that none of it should be wasted on village sites.

More recent historic peoples tended to locate their sites with careful regard for such factors as the availability of water, the slope of hillsides, protection against hostile attack, and access to transportation routes. In Silcott, Washington, in the late 1890s, Richard Ireland situated his homestead on the banks of the Snake River to take advantage of the ferry. Archaeologist Scott Hamilton has demonstrated how Canadian fur traders were forced to move their posts after depleting the fur-bearing mammals in the surrounding environmental zone. The miners who built the Dolly's Creek settlement in southern Australia situated their town where they hoped to find gold.

Settlement decisions can be complex, involving many buildings and properties. When the American Civil War ended in 1865, most of the enslaved families on James Edward Calhoun's Millwood Plantation decided to remain on the 15,000-acre (6,073 ha) estate as semi-autonomous tenant farmers. This had been their home for decades, and most of them wanted to stay there. As a result, the site offered a rare opportunity to study the settlement pattern of emancipated men and women who could no longer be told where to live on the property. As tenant farmers they were free to establish their homes anywhere they wished. Understandably, they did not wish to live in the cabins of their enslavement. In light of the conscious decisions made, there was an important archaeological question: What criteria did the tenant farmers use when deciding where on the plantation they should live? Old maps identified 66 tenant home sites within the plantation's boundary (Figure 4.15), each of which could

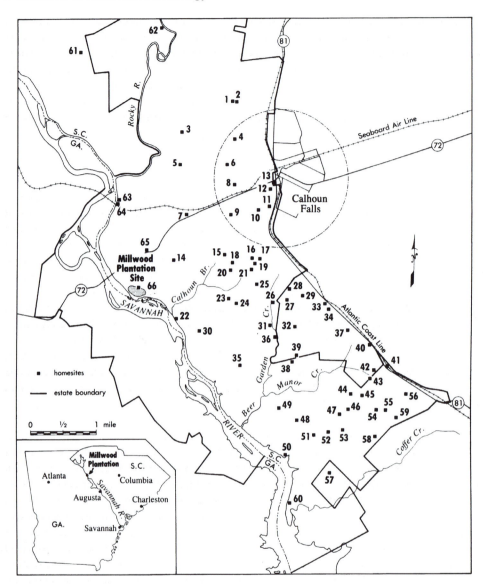

Figure 4.15 Settlement pattern at Millwood Plantation, South Carolina, after 1865

(Charles E. Orser, Jr.)

be assessed in terms of a number of factors, including agricultural potential, distance above mean sea level, degree and direction of land slope, and the distances to nearest stream, road, railroad, neighbor, and town, Calhoun Falls.

Analysis showed that most of the tenant farmers had located their homes 475 feet (148 m) above sea level, and oriented them to the southwest, west, or southeast, 0.3 miles (0.5 km) from the nearest stream, and 1.5 miles (2.4 km) from the Savannah River, which bordered the plantation. The typical farmer was located less than 0.5 miles (0.8 km) from his closest neighbor, less than 1.5 miles (2.4 km) from both the nearest road and the nearest railroad, and more than 1.5 miles (2.4 km) from the town. The Millwood tenant farmers thus established their homes on high ground close to a neighbor and a road, but not too near town. Through the placement of their farms, the tenants appear to have been saying that their community was designed to look inward, toward one another, rather than outward, to the wider world around them. Oral recollections collected from former tenants confirmed this interpretation, for the people preserved a strong sense of community on the old plantation land.

GIS in Historical Archaeology

Since about 2000, growing numbers of historical archaeologists are employing geographic information systems in their research. GIS is such a rapidly changing field that a full catalog of its applications in historical archaeology cannot be presented or even anticipated. The potential use of GIS is immense because historical archaeologists are so deeply concerned about time and space, two dimensions amenable to GIS analysis. Historians are also making use of GIS in their research, and historical archaeologists will undoubtedly collaborate with them in the future, in addition to making their own contributions independently.

GIS is a way to link spatial information with databases and images. The information about where things are situated on a landscape (called geospatial data) may derive from field surveys (called primary data in GIS as in historical analysis), maps (secondary data), or combinations of both. GIS offers a way to investigate the intersection of time and space, and though GIS is possible without the aid of computers, computation power has made GIS analysis faster, easier, and more dynamic. Flexibility is made possible by the complexity of computer programs. As a result, the applications of GIS in historical archaeology are practically limitless.

One of the major strengths of GIS is that it has layers that contain different information. For an archaeological site, individual layers may contain information about features (the location of fireplaces, walls, foundations, pits), topography (ridges and depressions), and the locations of different artifact classes (ceramics, glass, ferrous objects). For an entire landscape, the layers may provide the locations of archaeological sites, watercourses, nearest neighbors, towns, roads, and paths. Analysts can turn individual layers on and off as desired.

GIS presents complicated ways to manipulate spatial and temporal information with infinite applications being possible. Two examples will demonstrate some of what may be done with GIS in historical archaeology. The first demonstrates the use of GIS in at the micro level, within one village, and the second shows how GIS can be used at the macro level, across an entire landscape.

Steven Wernke used GIS to investigate how people moved through the space of an urban settlement in highland Peru occupied by the Inkas in prehispanic (1450–1532 C.E.) and early colonial times (about 1540–1570 C.E.). Specifically, he employed Spatial Network Analysis to model the foot traffic through the archaeological settlements. He did this because during the Spanish occupation, the main residents were Franciscan friars. After the initial rush of conducting mass baptisms and destroying the Inka's "pagan" religious symbols and rituals, the friars began a course of social engineering in which urbanism could be used as a route to a Christianized social order. One of the key questions, then, was: What was the relationship between the social order and the built environment? The hope was to discern how physical movement through the village changed as the town itself was transformed from Inka outpost to Franciscan religious center. GIS made it possible for Wernke to collect, manipulate, and analyze the geospatial data for the two periods of history.

When the Spanish arrived in the village, they began to remodel it to fit their cultural ideal of how a village should look. They constructed a church, an atrium (a plaza in front of the church), a village plaza, a cross platform, and a civic building. They also enlarged the village's residential area. Their newly built rectangular dwellings were distinguished from the older, circular houses of the Inka occupation. The new houses outnumbered the old ones by two to one.

The information Wernke collected from the village derived from the standing architectural features and the horizontal stratification of the walls and wall joints. This information allowed him to model the chronology of how the town developed and to delineate how people would have moved through it. For example, during the Hispanic era the plaza and the chapel were the main focal points of the village. Residents could only enter these areas through a single entrance on the east side of the plaza, and they could only reach the entrance by a single path along the northern edge of the eastern residential area. In addition, when a person entered the colonial plaza, he or she would immediately see the cross, the steps to the atrium, and the chapel doorway. The people also would have been forced, because of the placement of paths, to walk directly in front of all the elite dwellings. It also appeared that the new rectangular buildings had more direct access to the colonial plaza than did the older, Inka-period houses.

The reorganization of space in the town physically reinforced the colonial power structure of the Spanish Empire and the religious intent of the Franciscan friars. Because the town already existed as an Inkan space, the Spanish were not able to create it from the ground up. Rather, they had to shape it to fit their needs, in essence to place a Spanish overlay on top of the pre-existing Inka one.

In another study of the Spanish Empire, this time in the southeastern United States, Kathryn Sampeck, Jonathan Thayn, and Howard Earnest use GIS to address an old question in history: What routes did Hernando de Soto and Juan Pardo take when they traveled through the region in 1540 and 1567 respectively? To address this question, Sampeck and her colleagues used path modelling to evaluate the favorability of different routes. Key variables are the size of the parties and the slope of the paths. Small parties could take different routes than large groups, and some landforms were too steep to be practicable for an army to traverse. The GIS modelled data from landform information derived from data collected by the U.S. Space Shuttle *Endeavor* in 2000. Another important variable is distance traveled. Studies indicate that an army traveling on foot can cover around 12–20 miles (11–19 km) per day.

Using these variables, Sampeck, Thayn, and Earnest adopted a least-cost perspective to model the distance between two points in three-dimensional space. This means that when considering routes, the best ones were those requiring the least amount of effort. Obviously, de Soto's party, being composed of hundreds of individuals, an abundance of equipment, and a large herd of livestock, would have expended a great deal of energy and time walking through a narrow ravine. Common sense dictates they would have taken an easier route if available. Walking through a ravine also would make the army much more vulnerable to attack because the front would be hours ahead of the end of the line. Coordination would have been difficult under these circumstances as well.

The analysis indicated the presence of two likely routes, one narrow and southern, the other wide and northern. The northern path was longer than the southern, but it required less cost because it traversed more gradual slopes than the southern route (Figure 4.16).

With the GIS analysis in hand, Sampeck and her colleagues could re-examine the archaeological and historical information in the region. Reports filed at the time of the trips correlate well with the realities of the northern route. In fact, it is possible to follow the Spaniards' route along the northern pathway and to identify various archaeological sites with information

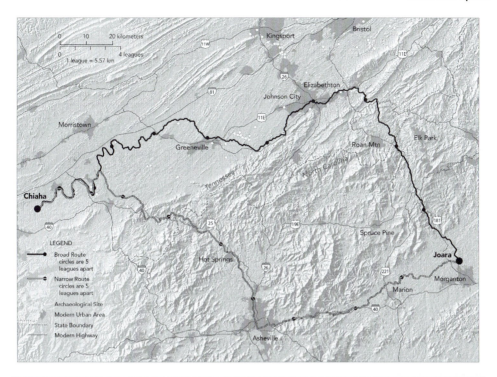

Figure 4.16 Routes of Spanish expeditions in the American Southeast
(Courtesy of Kathryn Sampeck and Jonathan Thayn.)

recorded by members of the expeditions. The description of the cold early summer night at high altitude only matches the northern route. On the southern route, the army would have been in the valley on the day of that journal entry. Artifact finds reinforce the conclusion that the northern route was most likely the one selected by Spanish explorers in the American Southeast.

Historical archaeology is of immense value in understanding past settlement patterns. Telltale house foundations, scatters of distinctive artifacts, and food remains provide unique information about settlement patterns and the cultural values that shaped them. Again and again, archaeological remains amplify impressionistic, often superficial accounts of life in the past.

People actively create space, and once created, they give it meaning. People invent networks of physical things—rooms, sites, houses, towns—with a logic that is consistent with their cultural beliefs and attitudes. Their way of situating things makes sense to them.

The Link between Time and Space

Archaeologists, no matter what period of history they investigate, are always mindful of the connection between time and space, because the two are irreversibly interlinked. Nothing in history has ever occurred outside the confines of some place. Everything has a *context*—an association with people and things linked in space and time. Without concern about where things and places belong in time and space, archaeology would lack the rigor and validity of a serious intellectual pursuit. As a result, archaeologists spend a great deal of time developing a sense of the cultural, social, and historical contexts of the sites they investigate.

The concept of context is complicated because history unfolds in a series of different-sized levels. For historical archaeology, the levels can extend from the minutely local to the broadly global (see Chapters 11 and 12). This means that an archaeologist excavating a fur trader's cabin in northern Canada must acknowledge that one context is local and refers to the way in which the cabin was built and organized. Another, broader context may refer to the local indigenous people, the connections between them and foreign fur traders, and the nature of the local environment. On the broadest level, the archaeologist must recognize that the fur trader was in the countryside to acquire furs for the European market. Such multiscalar thinking is an important element of historical archaeology because of the complicated nature of the world that began around 1492 and continues to the present day.

The linkage between time and space means as a practical matter that archaeologists must think in three dimensions when excavating a site. They must acquire the ability to imagine the archaeological site, not only as it appears on the ground surface, but also how it looks beneath the surface. They must have enough imagination to think about where the glass bottles and ceramic sherds, the stone fireplace, and the brick walls are located in relation to one another within the various soil layers. We discuss some of the practical matters faced by historical archaeologists in the next section of this book.

Site Visit: Limehouse Porcelain Manufactory, London, 1745–1748

On the north bank of the fabled Thames River, just east of London's city center, is an area of wharfs not unlike those found at the water's edge throughout the world. In the early years of the eighteenth century, the area was becoming industrialized, with picturesque, though descriptive names of nearby places: Rope Makers Field Road, Lime-Kiln Dock, Limehouse Bridge. The waterfront was alive with ships of all sorts, from oceangoing, three-masted sloops to small rowboats.

The bank of the Thames was an obvious place to develop new industries, and as early as 1363, a man named John Dik had operated a limekiln on the spot that would later house a porcelain factory. Local builders probably used lime from Dik's kilns in the plaster and mortar they needed for their nearby construction projects. Lime continued to be important in this part of town, and in fact the last limekiln at this location did not close until 1935. From 1745 to 1748, the site of Dik's kilns housed Joseph Wilson's porcelain factory.

The manufacture of porcelain was something of a mystery to Europeans during the early eighteenth century. Chinese potters had perfected their beautiful blue-and-white, hard-paste porcelains during the fifth and sixth centuries, and once Asia and Europe developed lasting trade relations, the fine porcelains became all the rage for consumers who could afford to purchase them. Eager

Europeans coveting the exquisite porcelains were so desperate to obtain them they even accepted poor-quality imports.

Merchants soon realized the importation of porcelains from Asia would not satisfy the European market. Being delicate and produced far away, porcelain was often difficult and expensive to ship. In addition, as greater numbers of Europeans began to enjoy the second great Asian import—tea—it was clear that more porcelain would have to be made available. The thick-bodied, tin-glazed earthenware traditionally made in Europe could not withstand the high boiling temperatures needed for brewing a good pot of tea. The obvious solution was for Europeans to invent their own porcelains.

Italian potters in the 1570s had begun the task of trying to manufacture thin-bodied, hard-paste porcelains, but success was elusive. Several others worked feverishly to find the secret combination of clay, glaze, and firing temperature, but it was not until the first decade of the eighteenth century that a brilliant German chemist named Johann Friedrich Böttger cracked the porcelain code. His discovery meant that German porcelains quickly became world famous for their quality and beautiful decoration, a reputation they still enjoy. England lagged woefully behind in its commitment to porcelain manufacture, and in the 1740s only two porcelain manufactories existed there: one in Chelsea, the other Joseph Wilson's Limehouse kiln. Chelsea thrived where the Limehouse factory failed, and by the 1770s at least 13 other factories rivaled the Chelsea works.

The centerpiece of any pottery manufactory was the kiln. The Limehouse kiln was circular in shape with an interior diameter of 11.8 feet (3.6 m). Its walls were made of brick, and its floor limestone flags. Its chimney was probably bottle-shaped like most kilns of the day. Charred areas on the floor indicated it probably had six fireboxes, the places where potters added fuel to maintain the kiln's internal temperature. Control of the heat was a key element of making a successful batch of ceramics, and porcelain was no exception.

Like all potters, the Limehouse artisans used a number of saggers, special kiln furniture intended to keep the individual vessels from fusing together during the firing process. The saggers were made of fine, hard white clay tempered with coal and fine particles of grit. The smooth, fine-grained surfaces of the saggers were designed to keep them from fusing to the vessels, but many of them became glazed during firing. The lack of other pieces of kiln furniture at the Limehouse kiln—pieces potters know as stands, pipes, bobs, and stilts—indicates the potters were not engaged in the production of small, decorative items (like flowers and leaves) to be applied to the most expensive wares.

The potters at the Limehouse kiln produced a number of different kinds of vessels during the short time of their factory's operation. They made polychrome (many-colored) sauceboats with enameled floral designs and pastoral scenes, white octagonal platters with blue decorations, and white cat figurines with blue eyes, whiskers, and claws. The potters were also fond of making blue-and-white pickle dishes molded in the shape of scallop shells. They also made boxes, butter boats, jars, teapots and lids, mugs, various-sized plates, and many other vessels. Some of the craftsmen in the factory even wrote their initials on the bottom of their vessels.

Wilson undoubtedly understood the consumerist desires of his English customers, because many of his products were decorated with Asian motifs. Some of his favorite Asian designs showed Chinese fishermen with fishing rods in hand, men sitting on square divans being attended to by servants, and men hunting with their dogs. To add to their non-European character, these designs had Asian-looking trees and other foliage in their backgrounds. Leaf-shaped pickle dishes, complete with molded veins, were decorated with blue butterflies or with vases holding exotic-looking plants. Skilled artisans painted all the designs.

Source: Kieron Tyler, Roy Stephenson, J. Victor Owen, and Christopher Phillpotts, *The Limehouse Porcelain Manufactory: Excavations at 108–110 Narrow Street, London, 1990.* (London: Museum of London Archaeology Service, 2000).

Section II

Doing Historical Archaeology

Chapter 5

Site Survey and Location in Historical Archaeology

Some historic sites are easily recognizable by ruins and even standing buildings. The Mission St. Xavier del Bac near Tucson, Arizona, a deserted shrimp factory in Eyri, Iceland, and walled landlord villages in rural Iran—these are all conspicuous archaeological sites because they still contain standing structures surviving into modern times. Many archaeological sites, however, even those inhabited during the recent past, can be hidden from view, silently lying beneath the earth's surface. It took years for archaeologists to locate L'Anse-aux-Meadows, a Norse settlement dating to about 1000 C.E. in northern Newfoundland. Many archaeological sites, such as the Elizabethan Rose Theatre mentioned in Chapter 4, come to light by accident during the course of construction. Archaeologists often locate sites using a combination of common sense, a well-designed research plan, and sophisticated techniques and equipment.

How do archaeologists know where to look for historic sites? Does training in archaeology give field workers special knowledge about site location? Special knowledge, often based on experience, does play a part in archaeological site location, but archaeologists most often rely on sophisticated techniques they have either developed on their own or else borrowed from scientists in related fields. This chapter presents some of the ways archaeologists find sites of all kinds.

Archaeologists understand some sites will be well known and visible on the surface and others will be mentioned in historical documents but not be visible on the surface. Still other sites may be undocumented but visible. Some may be completely underground and only discovered accidentally. As a result, archaeologists, even historical archaeologists with access to textual sources of information, adopt methods and procedures to locate and identify sites of past occupation and use.

Known Sites

Historical sites are often conspicuous features on the landscape. Many places—missions, mansions, and mills—have been continuously inhabited or otherwise maintained since their construction. Historical archaeologists have studied these kinds of known sites since the earliest days of their profession (see Chapter 2). Colonial Williamsburg, Virginia, provides a perfect example.

Henry Wetherburn built his tavern in 1743 on Duke of Gloucester Street just about midway between the Capitol of Virginia on the east and the colonial courthouse on the west. Wetherburn enlarged the tavern in the early 1750s as his business thrived and expanded. Over the next two centuries, the owners of this eighteenth-century building used the old tavern as a store, a dwelling, a boarding house, and a girls' school. But in its prime, Wetherburn's Tavern was most famously the site of numerous public meetings and scientific lectures. When the Colonial Williamsburg Foundation decided to renovate this notable landmark in the 1960s, they called on a team of architects, historians, and historical archaeologists to help them. Their chief archaeologist, Ivor Noël Hume, dug along one wall of the tavern to answer specific questions about the design of the entrance porches. He also excavated in the tavern's backyard in the attempt to find outbuildings (Figure 5.1). His efforts revealed the foundations of two kitchens, a dairy, and two buildings of unknown use, as well as evidence for several old porches. Noël Hume's field crew collected more than 200,000 artifacts, including tiny pieces of brass from the bases of small chafing dishes and pieces of the "white flowered China" listed in Henry Wetherburn's inventory of 1760. They also discovered the stems of

Figure 5.1 Archaeology in progress behind Wetherburn's Tavern, Williamsburg, Virginia, in the mid-1960s; a dairy foundation appears on the left; that of a kitchen on the right

(Courtesy of the Colonial Williamsburg Foundation, Williamsburg, VA.)

delicate wine glasses and plates reading around their edges "SUCCESS TO THE KING OF PRUSSIA AND HIS FORCES" in raised letters. These plates, popular from 1757–1763, commemorated King Frederick the Great's victory in 1757 at Rossbach against the combined armies of Austria, France, and Russia.

Known sites can be famous in the annals of history. The Battle of the Little Bighorn is one such place (see Chapter 3). Even at a place like the Little Bighorn Battlefield, archaeological research has yielded vital new information about a seemingly well-known historical event. Without archaeological research, much about the battle would remain shrouded in mystery.

The Berlin Wall is another extremely well-known site. Constructed in 1961 and standing until 1989, the wall separated East from West Berlin and was the most iconic structure of the Cold War. Stretching for 96 miles (155 km), it cut through neighborhoods and divided families. The wall itself was only reachable from its western side, where it could be viewed without obstruction. On the east, however, a series of obstacles—barbed wire fences, floodlights, and watchtowers—had been designed in such a way to keep East Berliners away from even getting close to the wall. The design of the wall and its features on the eastern side were intended to be standardized, but in actuality, the physical layout seldom matched the ideal.

News of the fall of the wall in November 1989 quickly traveled around the world. Many people thought they would never see such a momentous occasion in their lifetimes. Given the press, many people may believe that the Berlin Wall has been erased from the landscape along with the paranoia causing it to be built in the first place. On the contrary, however, evidence of the wall remains. Still-standing sections, houses situated too far from the street, and linear gaps in vegetation provide abundant proof of the wall's former presence.

The Berlin Wall may not be subject to the same kind of archaeological research as the Battle of the Little Bighorn, but this well-known site can be investigated with the archaeologist's eye, nonetheless. It represents the impact material culture can have on the people and landscape around it, and it challenges archaeologists to examine various perspectives that still remain about this monumental feature.

Accidental Discoveries

Historical archaeology at such well-known places as Colonial Williamsburg and the Little Bighorn Battlefield National Monument demonstrates the field's interpretive power. But not all sites are so famous, and accidental discoveries constitute a significant proportion of the world's archaeological finds. This is especially true in urban settings where construction, demolition, and rebuilding is almost constant.

One of the most spectacular, accidental discoveries made in recent years occurred in New York City in 1991. The General Services Administration planned to build a 34-story office building to house a number of federal offices in lower Manhattan. When the archaeologists hired to examine the building site examined old city maps, they found an area then called the "Negro Burial Ground" had existed at this location in the mid-eighteenth century. As many as 20,000 individuals could have been buried in this 5–6-acre (2 to 2.4 ha) lot. Archaeologists had assumed before the discovery that the digging of several deep basements in the nineteenth century had destroyed any burials that may have remained in the cemetery. Their report could not have been more explicit: "The construction of deep sub-basements would have obliterated any remains within the lots that fall within the historic bounds of the cemetery." Six weeks before construction was scheduled to begin, the General Services Administration hired archaeologists to check the lot just in case one or two odd burials still remained. Officials at the General Services Administration were stunned when the archaeologists found dozens of undisturbed graves over the next two months. The government had spent $104 million on the property, and the offices they planned to build were slated to cost another $276 million. By law, the GSA had to remove the burials (or leave them undisturbed), arrange for their scientific study, and make arrangements either for their reburial or permanent safe storage. In the end, archaeologists removed 420 skeletons from the cemetery.

The African Burial Ground stands today as one of the most important archaeological discoveries in the United States. In addition to providing priceless information about the health and welfare of a significant portion of New York City's historical population, it has helped people realize that the enslavement of people of African heritage occurred in the northern United States as well as in the South. Without its accidental discovery, the site would have remained merely a notation on an old map and important knowledge about the past would have remained out of reach.

Even well-known historic sites can yield unexpected discoveries. The Spanish Presidio in Santa Barbara, California, was founded in 1782 and remained in use for 17 years. Over the next two centuries, the fort and its buildings fell into disrepair, and much of it vanished beneath the nineteenth-century Chinatown. In 1967 archaeologists and local volunteers under the direction of Richard Humphrey excavated the foundations of the Presidio Chapel to provide architectural and historical information for future reconstruction. During their otherwise routine excavation to trace the building's foundations, the excavators found three burials under the church floor. When archaeologist Julia Costello and biocultural anthropologist Phillip Walker studied the bones, they discovered Humphrey had actually found the remains of four people. They compared the physical remains with Presidio records and tried to associate the graves with actual individuals. Costello and Walker were not able to identify each skeleton precisely, but they could suggest one or two candidates. Burial 1 was a middle-aged adult of unknown sex whose teeth suggested either Native American or Asian ancestry. The chapel's registry showed that Domingo Carrillo died in 1845 at the age of 45, and that José Antonio Ortega also died that year, but at an unknown age. Records show that Ortega was called "El Chino," or "The Chinaman," so the teeth suggest he is the best candidate for Burial 1. A newborn baby and a young child were interred in Burial 2. The records indicate that four infants, between the ages of three and 25 days, were buried in the chapel after 1797, so the identities of the remains are unknown. The older child, however, was probably María Dominga Carrillo, who died in 1840 at age two years six months. Burial 3 was that of a young woman between the ages of 16 and 20. The Presidio records suggested to Costello and Walker that the remains could be those of one of two unmarried young women: Soledad Carrillo (who died in 1837 at age 17) or María Antonia Carrillo (who died in 1844 at age 16 years nine months). The woman in Burial 3—Soledad Carrillo or María Carrillo—had been placed in a redwood coffin wearing a long cape ornamented with sequins, glass beads, and flower bundles. Parts of her cape were preserved. The identification of individuals in unmarked graves using historical records demonstrates the power of historical archaeology to combine archaeological and textual sources of information.

Finding Sites in Historical Archaeology

Not all archaeological sites are above ground and visible or discovered accidentally. In such cases, archaeologists must adopt certain methods for locating sites. Archaeologists investigating all periods of history use the same methods, but historical archaeologists use some methods more than others. Historical archaeologists use three main techniques for locating sites—historical maps, textual sources, and aerial images; formal archaeological survey methods; and on-site, sophisticated subsurface surveying techniques. Archaeologists decide which method is most appropriate based on numerous criteria including site history, the topography of the area, and limitations of time and funding.

Using Maps and Aerial Images to Find Modern-Era Sites

In Chapter 4, we made reference to the use of Sanborn and other maps for developing ideas about past urban neighborhoods. These sources are but the tip of a rewarding historical iceberg, for maps can be a mine of information on potential archaeological sites of all kinds. Like maps, written records can also be useful for locating sites inhabited during the past 500 years.

Where do historical archaeologists find useful maps and other sources? Many of them come from well-known reference works and repositories (see Chapter 6), but others appear in the most obscure and unsuspected places. The records kept by city governments, military bodies, land management agencies, and other groups can be remarkable sources of information. Detailed plat books (individual maps showing land ownership) and property titles can also contain invaluable information about site locations. But anyone serious about using historical maps and records to locate archaeological sites has a great deal of patient detective work in front of them. Two examples are illustrative.

The U.S. National Park Service created the Minute Man National Historical Park in Massachusetts in 1959 to commemorate "the significant events, structures, and sites of the opening day of the War of the American Revolution" in 1775. This park protects the famous sites of Lexington and Concord, where "the shot heard round the world" rang out, but it also includes a number of other, less-well-known sites, such as the Brooks "tanyard." The Brooks family operated a tannery on the Concord road west of Lexington from about 1700–1829. The business, though locally important, had little regional significance. After its demise, the buildings fell into disrepair and the old tannery was quickly forgotten. In 1984, the National Park Service decided to conduct a full archaeological survey of the sites within the boundaries of the Minute Man park.

When the historian of the archaeological team, led by Alan Synenki, combed through old newspaper accounts, notes and maps of boundary surveys, tax rolls, and census lists, she found three maps of the area that included the Brooks property. One, drawn in 1749, provides a sketch of the Brooks property and shows the "Tan House" located next to the "High way." The map depicts the tanyard as a simple, small square with a cross in the middle, like a window with four panes. An earlier document, dated 1745, notes that the tannery included "a Tann House and Tann pits." These buildings may be what the cartographer meant to show in the 1749 map. A second map, made nearly a century later, in 1830, shows no sign of the tannery whatsoever. Twelve years later, and two years before he published *Walden,* nearby resident Henry David Thoreau drew a third map. He showed only an empty "Meadow" where the tannery once stood (Figure 5.2). As often happens, the archaeologists were unable to match the old maps with the current landscape, and their limited excavations did not yield clear evidence of the tannery. They found instead the remains of a house, probably demolished in the nineteenth century, sometime before 1875. The archaeologists' failure to locate the tannery does not negate the importance of the historical maps. Quite the contrary, these maps are useful because they help document the history of the area and show how the Brooks property was used throughout the late eighteenth and early nineteenth centuries.

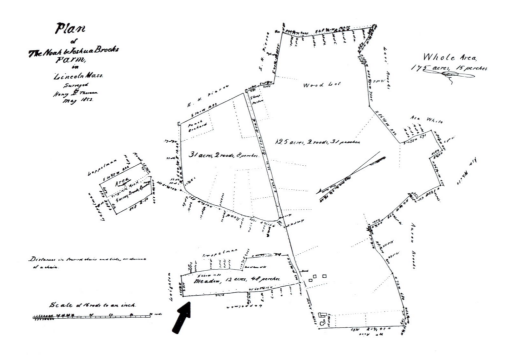

Figure 5.2 Thoreau map, 1852, of the Brooks Tannery area
(Minute Man National Historic Park, National Parks Service)

When conducting research on French colonial stations in Vietnam, Lawrence Fife relied on a map drawn in 1943 to guide him to likely locations. His goal was to record all sites associated with the colonial and post-colonial eras, including the Vietnam War period. Unsurprisingly, the map was not always accurate, but it served well as a useful locational device.

Archaeologists never know whether a particular map will help them, and not all maps are useful for site location. Many early colonial maps, for example, often show forts, missions, trading posts, and the villages of native inhabitants as simple dots or squares. This information may indicate that settlements once existed in the area, but the maps do not yield information about their precise locations. By tracking a series of maps through time, a historical archaeologist may be able to establish the dates of construction, abandonment, or destruction of buildings or settlements. In most cases, however, only excavation will answer questions about a map's accuracy and whether settlements were ever built where the mapmaker indicated.

Fort de Chartres was an important colonial French outpost located near the present town of Prairie du Rocher in southern Illinois. During the eighteenth century, the French established a number of towns along the Mississippi River in today's Illinois and Missouri as a means of connecting their Canadian settlements to the north with those around New Orleans to the south. They named one of their strongholds Fort de Chartres. The first fort was a simple wooden stockade, but its French inhabitants later replaced it with a more elaborate structure. In the mid-1750s, they replaced the second wooden fort with an impressive stonewalled fortress. The first map to show Fort de Chartres was drawn by Francois-Benjamin Dumont de Montigny in the 1720s. He depicted the fort with four bastions in a form typical of the period. He showed only one small section of the Mississippi River Valley, and his map is not accurate enough to permit archaeologists to locate the first fort. A later map, drawn in 1755 by Jacques Nicolas Bellin, provides even less information. He showed the stone-built "Nouveau Fort de Chartres" as sandwiched between the town of Prairie du Rocher and a Native American village (Figure 5.3). Luckily for archaeologists, some of the stone fort stood the test of time and the site was easily located as a series of ruins. Without this physical evidence, archaeologists would have had a difficult time finding it.

Archaeologists can also use images taken above the ground in their search for long-lost human settlements. Aerial images may indicate features on a landscape, such as roads, trackways, agricultural field systems, woods, and watercourses.

Archaeologists have used aerial photography since World War I, when excavators-turned-military-observers realized the bird's-eye view was an unrivaled way to identify inconspicuous earthworks, forts, and other such locations. One strength of aerial photography is that pictures taken from the sky can reveal hidden sites from all periods of history, many of which may not be recognizable from the ground. For example, aerial photography was essential at Fort de Chartres. In 1981 a U.S. Army Corps of Engineers archaeologist found an aerial photograph of the fort's general area taken in 1928 (Figure 5.4). This picture just happened to show a rectangular stain that upon excavation turned out to be the foundations of the first fort, a small, wooden stockade that would have been difficult to locate in the absence of the old photograph.

Advances in camera technology—in both size and image quality—as well as the lowering of costs, has provided new opportunities for archaeologists. Archaeologists are increasingly using radio-controlled aircraft, called Unmanned Aerial Vehicles (or UAVs), to locate sites.

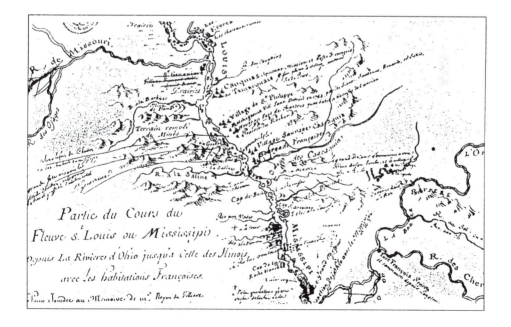

Figure 5.3 Section of a map drawn in 1755 by Jacques Nicolas Bellin, showing the area around Fort de Chartres
(Bibliotheque Service Hydrographic)

Figure 5.4 Aerial photograph, taken in 1928, showing the rectangular
stain of the first Fort de Chartres, Illinois
(Illinois Historic Preservation Agency)

The aircraft are the small planes and helicopters hobbyists have used for years. When a tiny camera is strapped to the bottom of one of these aircraft a UAV can be an efficient way to locate and photograph sites from above. In such cases, archaeologists may collaborate with a skilled hobbyist who has experience flying the aircraft with precision.

In places where it may be difficult to obtain a model aircraft, archeologists can rely on other methods to obtain aerial photographs. Some archaeologists have used tall frames to hoist a camera in the air. These structures, often made by the archaeologists themselves with telescoping tubing, can be highly effective. At the Nazi death camp Sobibor, Poland, archaeologists used a helium weather balloon with attached camera to obtain a view of the camp. The images showed the extent of the killing field and made it possible to estimate the size of the mass burial area.

Archaeologists also use aerial and satellite images produced with the latest, cutting-edge technology. Aerial photography is limited to a number of atmospheric conditions, including cloud cover, but more sophisticated equipment can be used when aerial photography fails to obtain the necessary results. Color infrared film can detect minor variations in vegetation that may hide an archaeological site. Other high-tech tools include thermal scanners and various kinds of radar. Unlike straightforward aerial photography, the more complex remote sensing techniques require an expert to analyze the data. These telltale clues may either be an archaeological site or may lead to one. Nicholas Clapp collaborated with NASA's Jet Propulsion Laboratory to locate the ancient city of Ubar on the Arabian Peninsula. He used Landsat imagery to find the otherwise invisible old roads that led to the ancient city.

Archaeologists are also using many of the opportunities available on the internet. Some archaeologists are using satellite images taken between 1959 and 1972 by the United States intelligence services. Almost one million images from this first space imaging program, called CORONA, were declassified in 1995. No longer useful for intelligence purposes, the images have tremendous potential for archaeological research because they provide aerial pictures of the earth's surface during the 1960s, before many large-scale landscape altering projects were undertaken. Other archaeologists, such as those in the previous chapter, are examining images taken from U.S. space shuttles.

As of this writing, Google Earth provides a particularly useful set of satellite images. One of the advantages Google Earth offers is that its images can be easily accessed through numerous hand-held devices. Archaeologists working in India report a few hours' research on Google Earth can identify possible site locations that can then be checked on the ground. This laboratory-based research can save archaeologists a great deal of time and money and can significantly accelerate the speed of the research.

Archaeological Survey

Documents, maps, and satellite images, no matter how informative, provide only one method for finding archaeological sites. Like all archaeologists, historical archaeologists also rely on formal archaeological survey techniques. The methods themselves are not glamorous because they simply involve the systematic, on-the-ground search for settlements within a circumscribed area—whether a small urban lot, a neighborhood, a plantation, or even an entire geographic region.

Archaeologists usually begin survey work in the library and laboratory where they examine archival sources, old maps, local histories, geological information, and search the web for useful information. This work provides the background for the fieldwork that follows. A survey of an empty lot might initially involve a title search to establish the sequence of ownership (the "chain of title") and the use of the land before being purchased by the current owner. Such preliminary investigations are vital because they provide clues to the possible character of the archaeological record. Did previous owners erect houses on the property or did they dig wells and privies? Did they corral cattle there or did they dig a cellar? The historical archaeologists' rule of thumb about background information is this: The more they gather before entering the field, the less likely they are to be surprised by what they find. Surprises are always possible—and often enlightening when they occur—but no substitute exists for being well prepared upon entering the field.

Pedestrian Survey

Some of the most effective archaeological surveys are those carried out on foot. These surveys, usually referred to as "visual inspection," a "walk-over survey," or a "pedestrian survey," involve walking slowly over the ground while looking for telltale signs of human occupation. Such traces of human activity come in many forms—surface scatters of ceramics and glass, telltale black privy soil spilling from a gopher hole, piles of bricks or stones, old walls and fences, grassed-over cellar depressions, and capped wells. In the once-active logging areas of America's Upper Midwest, archaeologists can identify the remains of camp sites by the presence of small mounds of earth, the occasional small depression, and a loose scatter of broken whiskey bottles and bent, corroded enameled tin plates and cups (Figure 5.5). The same

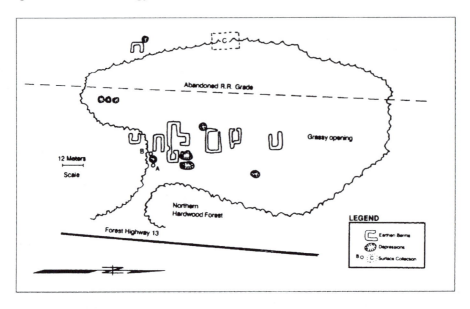

Figure 5.5 Archaeologist's map of hardwood-era logging camp in Michigan

(Northern Michigan Logging Camps: Material Culture and Worker Adaptation on the Industrial Frontier by John G. Franzen in *Historical Archaeology* 26, 2 [1992]:77, reprinted by permission of The Society for Historical Archaeology.)

evidence may reveal an abandoned mining community, such as those found in Australia, New Zealand, throughout the American West, and everywhere people sought to extract precious metals from the earth.

Historical archaeologists can also use botanical clues to identify archaeological sites. The presence of large shade trees and domestic flowers, still blooming after years of neglect, may reveal the location of a house. Archaeologists conducting field surveys often identify old house sites by the presence of lines of trees once planted as protection from the wind or by stands of stately elms and oaks. Even the presence of blooming perennials can indicate a house site.

Historical archaeologists, like all archaeologists, must learn to "read the landscape" as part of their field education. Useful information can be gleaned from books published by local historical societies and public history organizations. Great Britain has long been a leader in the concept of learning the history of a place by studying its landforms. Guidebooks and regional studies by folk-life specialists may provide information about what to look for in an area, but direct knowledge generally develops through personal experience with the landscape. Knowing the history of the land and its inhabitants can allow field surveyors to recognize faint wagon wheel ruts on a disused trail, an old fence line from a line of trees (growth from seeds deposited by birds that once sat on the fence posts), and the isolated pilings of a long-forgotten dock. Linear indentations across a field may be the remnants of an old roadbed and a square depression visible only when the sun is at the proper angle may reveal a disused cellar.

Historical archaeologists can also use oral interviews to tease out information about site location (Chapter 6). Many people, particularly in rural areas, will be familiar with the local topography. Farmers and local amateur archaeologists are often especially knowledgeable about the locations of sites and their histories. In her research in the lowland region of Soconusco in Chiapas, Mexico, for example, Janine Gasco learned that the information provided by local residents can help locate colonial-period sites. She also discovered, however, that local residents often did not know where sites could be found. As a result, she had to combine local information with conventional survey methods to sample the region. This situation is common in archaeological field research.

Sampling

In archaeology, sampling refers to the concept that not everything can be collected during any field project. Archaeologists are usually constrained by time and funding, so they must accept that they will only be able to "sample" an archaeological site or area. Archaeologists seldom have the opportunity to acquire a 100 percent sample. As a result, they must obtain enough of a sample to have confidence in their results. In some cases, a 5 percent sample will be adequate but generally a 10 percent sample or better is optimal. Archaeologists like to obtain the largest samples possible.

Surveying a city lot may simply consist of intently combing over a small area of level terrain. Such surveys are easy to perform and may take only a day or less to complete. Archaeologists understandably find it much more difficult to locate all the sites in a much larger area. One hundred percent survey coverage is rare in anything but the smallest areas, and even a complete survey may not reveal everything. Archaeological history is full of cases where surveyors have returned to a well-trodden area only to find more sites. Heavy rain, erosion, mudslides, and violent storms can uncover sites once completely buried.

A field survey of anything but the smallest plot involves the use of formal sampling methods. The realities of fieldwork—financial constraints, a lack of time, possibly dangerous conditions—make complete survey coverage rare for most archaeological projects.

An enormous literature surrounds archaeological sampling methods and some methods are controversial and difficult to apply. Effective sampling depends upon the formal strategy adopted. A proper survey is intended to provide statistically valid, and hopefully representative, samples of sites within the survey units selected for detailed examination. Common strategies involve the use of transects (straight corridors), geometrical units (squares, hexagons), and nongeometrical units (polygons). Depending upon the project goals, an archaeologist might introduce variation into these strategies as well. Transects, for instance, can consist of parallel lines (where surveyors walk abreast of one another a predefined distance), intersecting (where the surveyors may make two passes of a survey unit, one at 45 degrees of the other), and undulating or wavy (where the surveyors do not walk in straight lines) (Figure 5.6). Regardless of their exact design, archaeologists employ all sampling strategies with an eye toward examining as much ground surface as possible with maximum efficiency.

As an example, in the late 1980s, a team of archaeologists conducted a systematic survey in the Big Sioux River valley in northwestern Iowa. They devised a careful sampling strategy to investigate the 8,000 acres (3,239 ha) of their project area. Dividing the area into eight different sections, they used systematic criteria based on the topographic features in the region (floodplain, river terrace, and upland). By the end of the survey, the crew had discovered 109 pre-contact Native American sites and 20 European sites. The sites ranged from small, temporary camps of indigenous hunters to the town of Beloit, whose first European-American settlers arrived in 1868. In between were large Native American mound sites and European-American log cabins.

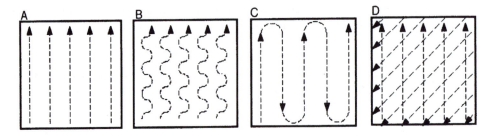

Figure 5.6 Different survey transects

(E.B. Banning, *Archaeological Survey*. New York: Kluwer Academic/Plenum, 2002, p. 91 © Springer Science.)

This survey illustrates an important point: Sampling designs are especially useful in situations where large numbers of inconspicuous sites may exist. Such sites may be stone-walled cattle enclosures on the grasslands of southeast Africa, early modern field systems in England, colonial-era settlements in the Mexican lowlands, or early nineteenth-century farmsteads in Minnesota. Many landscapes dating after about 1500—and increasingly as we move closer to our own time—consist of large, human-built features that can dictate the distribution of all kinds of sites large and small. Builders of roads, bridges, and mills knew exactly why they placed such structures where they did. When J. A. Carpenter built the Beloit Mill in 1871 he knew exactly what he was doing. He erected it on the banks of the Big Sioux River because he understood he could harness the water's energy to grind flour. He followed conventional wisdom and built a dam to control the river's flow past the mill. Carpenter was obviously successful because the 1880 industrial census reveals that his mill had three water wheels with a daily grinding capacity of 250 bushels (8,810 l) of grain.

Pedestrian survey is often not the best approach for locating sites, and archaeologists must adopt more sophisticated survey methods. These methods can involve high-tech equipment that requires extensive knowledge and experience to operate. Historical archaeologists who are not specialists in these methods, but know their potential, must collaborate with specialists in "subsurface surveying" who can both operate the equipment and interpret the results.

Subsurface Surveying

Subsurface detection methods are of critical importance to archaeologists because they allow them to acquire information about what lies underground before they begin to excavate. The noninvasive (or nondestructive) character of these methods of site assessment means that archaeologists need not disturb sites to gain an idea of their nature. They are able to use these techniques to protect precious archaeological remains from unnecessary disturbance.

The historical archaeologists' subsurface surveying methods include techniques from geophysics (using high-tech equipment to survey the ground surface) and geochemistry (using chemicals to test soil and other non-artifactual samples). These methods extend in complexity from relatively simple to extremely sophisticated. In many cases, archaeologists will collaborate with specialists, individuals who know the intricacies of the equipment, the best tests for the situation at hand, and the local environmental conditions.

Metal Detectors

Metal detectors are electromagnetic instruments that can be used to locate metal objects beneath the earth's surface. These tools, originally developed as landmine detectors, can be sophisticated and expensive. The most expensive models can be set to distinguish between different metals and can penetrate further into the ground than less expensive models.

Metal detectors usually issue a "beep" or electronic hum when they pass over a disturbance in the earth's magnetic field. Many detectors come equipped with a sensitive meter and headphones. Metal detecting is today a popular hobby, and many metal-detecting enthusiasts are skilled operators. Most hobbyists use their detectors to locate missing coins, rings, old beer cans, and other collectables. Historical archaeologists occasionally will call on a skilled operator to provide assistance because they offer an inexpensive and easy way to learn something about a site's subsurface character.

Archaeologists can use metal detectors in conjunction with site surveying, employing the detector during their visual inspection of the ground surface (see Chapter 13). The archaeologists who investigated the Little Bighorn Battlefield successfully used metal detectors in their field survey.

Archaeologists working in "forensic" or "crime-scene archaeology" can also use metal detectors to gather legal information. Archaeologist Robert Sonderman collaborated with the U.S. Federal Bureau of Investigation to survey Fort Marcy Park, Virginia, during the investigation into the 1993 death of Deputy White House Counsel Vincent W. Foster, Jr. After running a series of parallel string lines across the area of interest, the metal detector operator walked along the lines, swinging the instrument back and forth as he went. This string-line surveying technique provided for 100 percent coverage of the area's surface and provided important clues to the FBI.

In addition to the simple metal detectors used by hobbyists, a few companies are making more advanced models geared to a professional audience. For example, the German Lorenz Company makes a series of models called Deepmax. These high-tech machines use a technology called Pulse GBS, or Pulse Ground Balancing System. This system is sophisticated enough to cancel out interference from the ground, something important in places where rock layers may contain deposits of iron or other metals. These detectors are also unaffected by salt water, making them especially useful to maritime archaeology. One strength of the Deepmax series is the options of different coil sizes. The larger the coil size, the deeper the instrument can measure. The Deepnax comes with four coil options: a 35-centimeter (14 in) circle, a 45-centimeter (18 in) circle, a 1 × 1 meter (3.3 ft.) frame, and a 1.5 × 1.5 meter (5.0 ft.) frame. The frames are made of plastic pipe, meaning they are easy to carry and maneuver. The 35-centimeter coil can detect a brass plate 100 centimeters (3.3 ft.) deep and the 1.5-meter frame 170 centimeters (5.6 ft.) deep. A second advantage of the Deepmax detector is the presence of a data logger. Information collected during a survey is transmitted directly to the logger, which has an LCD (liquid crystal display). Using software, the data can be sent to a computer to produce colorful maps showing the anomalies.

Proton Magnetometers

Like its cousin the metal detector, the more sophisticated proton magnetometer locates "anomalies," or disturbances, in the earth's natural magnetic field. They give readings as quickly as metal detectors but usually with more accuracy. Historical archaeologists might use a metal detector to gain an initial understanding of the subsurface remains at a site, but then employ a more systematic method using a proton magnetometer.

A proton magnetometer survey begins by laying out a grid of equal-sized squares over the site area. Next, the magnetometer operator measures the normal magnetization of the site's ground surface. Once the magnetic background readings are known, the surveyors take one reading from each point where the grid lines intersect. This procedure creates a database of magnetic readings at the interval of the grid size. For example, a site area measuring 100 square feet (30 sq. m) with a one-foot interval will yield 100 readings. A map based on the magnetic readings can then be produced. The high magnetic readings are anomalies or "hot spots," areas of high magnetism likely to contain buried archaeological deposits.

Magnetometer surveys have proven effective at archaeological sites containing large amounts of ferrous artifacts. At the eighteenth-century French Fort Ouiatenon in Indiana, for example, the map of magnetic anomalies helped guide archaeologists to a number of subsurface features, including a cache of iron trade objects deposited outside one of the fort's buildings. The magnetic survey also helped locate four eighteenth-century burials, proving that, like metal detectors, magnetometers can be used by forensic archaeologists.

Proton magnetometer surveys can be conducted underwater to locate anchors, chains, spikes, cannons, and other ferrous objects associated with shipwrecks. Marine archaeologist J. Barto Arnold successfully used a proton magnetometer in a survey off the coast of Galveston, Texas. Historic records and maps revealed 327 known shipwrecks in Galveston Bay, many dating to the American Civil War (1861–1865). One of the most interesting wrecks was that of the ill-fated USS *Selma*, built of reinforced concrete by the U.S. Navy during World War I. She sank on her maiden voyage after ramming jetties off the coast of Mexico, and after retrieving her, the navy abandoned her a couple of years later in Galveston Bay. The wreck's general location had been known for years, but Arnold's magnetometer survey confirmed its precise placement on the Gulf floor.

Magnetic Susceptibility

Proton magnetometers, though still useful, have largely been replaced by more sophisticated instruments. One of the most useful subsurface surveying tools finding extensive application in historical archaeology is magnetic susceptibility. Like magnetometers, magnetic susceptibility meters measure the amount of magnetism in features existing beneath the ground surface. Anomalies are identified as having higher or lower amounts of magnetism than the surrounding background environment. Like all good archaeological surveying methods, magnetic susceptibility testing is conducted systematically inside grids composed of regularly sized squares.

Archaeologists under the direction of William R. Fowler used magnetic susceptibility in their examination of Ciudad Vieja in El Salvador. The town, founded in 1525, was an outpost of the expanding Spanish Empire then pushing south from Mexico. The colonial residents abandoned the site soon after developing it (being chased away by the rebelling indigenous Pipils), but returned in 1528. They stayed for the next 17 years, finally leaving the town for good in 1545. Ciudad Vieja, the first San Salvador, is an important Spanish colonial urban site.

Magnetic susceptibility surveying occurred over the site of the old city in 20 x 20 meter (66 x 66 ft) sections. The results revealed a series of linear and rectilinear anomalies under the ground surface (Figure 5.7). When excavated, this portion of the town site

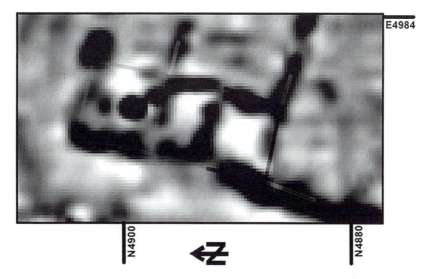

Figure 5.7 Magnetic susceptibility data and excavation from Ciudad Vieja, El Salvador

(Courtesy of William R. Fowler.)

revealed the foundation of a blacksmith's shop, also perfectly preserved (Figure 5.8). Also present were a food-preparation area, a charcoal manufacturing zone, and part of a street. Highly magnetized chunks of iron slag thrown along one of the walls produced strong readings in the susceptibility data. The excavations, in addition to providing important archaeological information, were used to "ground truth" the results of the magnetic susceptibility testing.

Research such as that conducted at Ciudad Vieja, producing such remarkable results, demonstrates the value of conducting geophysical research at historical archaeological sites. The Ciudad Vieja foundations were not deeply buried and may have been found without using magnetic susceptibility testing. Such an approach, however, would have been wasteful and shortsighted. Magnetic susceptibility surveying helped Fowler and his team identify precisely where to excavate, thus saving valuable excavation time and limiting the amount of site destruction.

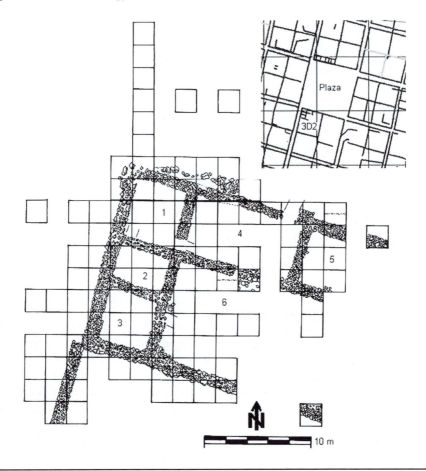

Figure 5.8 Drawing of excavation of magnetic susceptibility testing area at Ciudad Vieja

(Courtesy of Douglas W. Veltre.) William R. Fowler

Soil Resistivity Surveying

All rocks and soils, being porous, absorb different amounts of moisture, and as a result conduct varying degrees of electricity. Archaeologists can use a soil resistivity meter to measure the amount of resistance encountered by an electrical current passing through these objects. A trash pit with many open spaces will hold more moisture than the dense clay surrounding it, just as a brick wall will retain more water than the surrounding sandy soil. An electrical current introduced into the ground will encounter greater resistance when trying to pass through the wall than through the soil.

Resistivity surveys involve inserting a grid of metal probes, or electrodes, into the ground. An electrical current is passed into the ground by the electrodes and the resistivity meter measures the resistance it encounters. The analyst plots the different resistance measures across the site. As with the proton magnetometer, the finished map has the appearance of a topographic map. Instead of showing differences in the elevation of the ground surface—and the hot spots indicated by the magnetometer—the soil resistivity map illustrates the differences

in the amount of soil moisture beneath the ground. Anomalies may represent buried archaeological features.

Soil resistivity is useful in circumstances where excavation is impracticable. Archaeologists from the University of Texas used a soil resistivity survey to locate a series of lost graves in an early nineteenth-century Anglo-Texan cemetery in south Dallas. They established a grid over the site and after conducting a resistivity survey were able to distinguish eight anomalies. Given the context, the anomalies were probably graves. Being Christians, Anglo-Texans buried their dead with an east–west orientation, so any anomaly pointing north–south was probably not a burial. In this particular case, the archaeologists were allowed to test their findings by excavating the anomalies. Excavation revealed the bones of four children in three anomalies (one contained two skeletons). The burials were about 6 feet (2 m) beneath the ground surface, with the last 1.5 feet (0.5 m) chipped into the natural limestone underlying the cemetery. This research shows that soil resistivity surveying, like all nonintrusive survey methods, is particularly useful at cemeteries, locales people usually do not want disturbed by full-scale excavation. Archaeologists can also employ such methods at historic house museums where tourism would make excavation intrusive.

Ground-Penetrating Radar

Ground-penetrating radar (GPR), one of the most well-known subsurface surveying methods, works by transmitting a low-frequency electromagnetic signal into the ground by way of a radar system pulled along the ground. The path of the radar may be a series of transecting grid lines or parallel straight lines depending on the archaeologists' needs. When the radar signal encounters an anomaly beneath the ground it sends a second signal back to the receiver. This reflected signal indicates it has struck something different from the surrounding soil. Specialists can interpret the signal "profiles" to determine the locations of buried features.

Ground-penetrating radar was used effectively by a survey team led by geoarchaeologist Bruce Bevan in Virginia. Working in association with the U.S. National Park Service, Bevan and his researchers were attempting to find "Spring Garden," the home of a Mr. William Taylor in Petersburg. Taylor, a person of no particular historical note, was simply a victim of circumstance. His house was destroyed by the Union Army in their unsuccessful attempt to capture Petersburg in 1864. In 1978 the National Park Service wanted to establish the precise location of the home so they could include it in their interpretive program. Limited excavations, however, yielded little useful information. The archaeologists discovered one or two outbuildings but failed to find the Taylor home. At that point, Bevan was called in.

Bevan ran the radar along the ground in a series of parallel rows across the suspected location of the home, in a spot where the outbuildings had been discovered. The radar beam could detect anomalies three feet (1 m) to the right and to the left of the path at a depth of three feet (1 m). He surveyed an area of about 2.2 acres (slightly less than 1 ha) in four days. Using the radar, he was able to delineate a buried feature measuring about 20–25 feet by 50–55 feet (6–8 by 15–17 m). The anomaly was rectangular and was exactly parallel to a standing outbuilding. Two years later, when the National Park Service sponsored excavations over Bevan's anomaly, archaeologists found the northeast and southwest corners of a brick-lined cellar. Remarkably, the cellar measured 19 by 55 feet (6 by 17 m), exactly the dimensions indicated by the radar. The archaeologists could date the ceramics they found in the cellar to the last years of the eighteenth and the first half of the nineteenth centuries. The cellar was undeniably the foundation of Taylor's house.

In another study, William Whittaker tested the effectiveness of GPR at three fort sites in the American Midwest. The forts, called dragoon forts, were created to help remove Native Americans from in front of the wave of American settlers moving into the region. The forts date to the 1830s–1850s. At Fort Atkinson in northeastern Iowa, the GPR survey located several underground features—latrines, trenches, foundations—all later found by excavation. At the Second Fort Crawford in southwestern Wisconsin, the GPR survey identified foundations that corresponded with an 1831 map of the fort. The GPR survey at the third site, Fort Des Moines No. 2 in central Iowa, was less effective for two reasons: the depth of overlying fill layers and the ephemeral nature of the archaeological deposits. These results led Whittaker to conclude that GPR is a good way to locate substantial military fortifications but less effective when the site has been disturbed or covered over later with several layers of fill.

Whittaker's findings are important because they demonstrate two things. First, archaeologists must be aware that not every subsurface surveying method will be effective in every instance. Archaeologists must be knowledgeable about all the possible methods available to understand which may be most useful. Second, GPR testing, like all the methods, can provide specific information about a site's post-occupation history. In the case of Fort Des Moines No. 2, the effectiveness of the GPR was compromised by activities occurring after the fort was abandoned.

Sonar

Marine archaeologists use a technique related to ground-penetrating radar, called sonar, to locate lost shipwrecks. Sonar, whose name derives from SOund Navigation And Ranging, is a complex detection device that emits a sharp pulse of sound producing an echo when the sound waves strike an object. A submerged submarine or a lost ship would produce a pulse indicating their presence.

Sonar was invaluable for studying the wreck of the USS *Monitor*. The *Monitor,* once referred to as a "tin can on a shingle," is famous for engaging her Confederate counterpart, the *Merrimack,* on March 9, 1862, off the coast of Maryland. The *Merrimack* was actually a rebuilt Union frigate. Union forces had scuttled her at the Navy yard at Portsmouth, Virginia, when they evacuated the town in 1861. The Confederacy raised the vessel, encased her in iron plates, and renamed her *Virginia.* Most people today, however, continue to use her original name. The inconclusive engagement between the two ships became the stuff of legend, even though the battle did no serious harm to either vessel. But nature succeeded where the *Merrimack* had failed. The *Monitor's* ignominious end came as the ship filled with water during a violent storm as she was being towed to safety by a more buoyant vessel. The *Monitor* lay on the floor of the Atlantic Ocean until 1973, when divers found it off the coast of Cape Hatteras, North Carolina. It was promptly declared a National Marine Sanctuary and a National Historic Landmark under the administration of the National Oceanic and Atmospheric Administration. NOAA scientists conducted extensive remote sensing at the wreck site in 1985 and 1987. The 1987 project used state-of-the-art surveying equipment, including high-resolution sector-scanning sonar imaging that produced a computer-generated, three-dimensional view of the entire wreck.

Historical archaeologists use ground-penetrating radar, soil resistivity, and magnetometer surveys whenever and wherever possible. These methods can be expensive and usually require the collaboration of a highly skilled operator who fully understands how to interpret the readings. Still, when they can be employed, their results can be invaluable in helping archaeologists decide where to dig.

Soil Phosphate Analysis

Soil phosphate analysis is a geochemical subsurface surveying technique used to locate old habitation sites. Chemical changes occur in the soil of past settlements simply through human occupation. Chemicals such as calcium, nitrogen, carbon, and phosphorus are added to soils through human activity, but only phosphorus is stable over time. Phosphorus plays a role in the composition of fluids in the digestive tract, is fixed with calcium in bones and teeth, and occurs in significant amounts in animal and human excreta. The presence of humans and even domesticated animals can increase the amount of phosphorus in the soil. Because phosphorus moves so little once deposited, archaeologists can even use phosphate testing to identify stratified habitation levels.

Like all the systematic methods archaeologists use, soil phosphate analysis begins with laying out a site grid. A soil coring tool or auger is then used to collect samples below the topsoil at the grid points. A rigorous quantitative analysis can reveal precisely how much phosphorus is contained in each soil sample, but a less accurate spot test is generally adequate for most archaeological research. In the spot test method, a small amount of soil from each stratum is tested for the presence of phosphorus, using first, a solution of distilled water, ammonium molybdate, and dilute hydrochloric acid, and second, a solution of distilled water and ascorbic acid (vitamin C). After applying the two solutions to a soil sample, the analyst checks for a blue color produced by the reaction of the phosphorous and the chemicals. Depending upon the intensity of the color and the length of the blue rays emanating outward from it, the analyst assigns a number from 1 to 6 to the test. When all of the soil samples are similarly tested, the values are placed on a map at the proper coordinates, making a contour map of phosphorus concentration. The locations of high phosphorus concentrations (also called "hot spots") are likely to contain the remains of houses, yards, animal pens, fence lines, and privies.

Soil phosphate expert William Woods used a quantitative test to help locate the first Fort de Chartres in southern Illinois mentioned above. The reconstructed stone fort is today a visible landmark, but the two earlier forts were buried under the featureless topography of agricultural fields. Their locations were unknown until the 1928 aerial photograph revealed a large soil discoloration near the stone fort. The precise location of the first fort, however, was not known for certain until Woods's phosphate testing program located areas of high phosphorus concentrations (Figure 5.9). Excavations confirmed the reliability of the tests by discovering the ditches that once held the fort's palisaded walls.

Geophysicists, working in conjunction with archaeologists, also have other testing methods they can employ. In most cases, they will use a number of different methods to increase their view of what lies beneath the ground surface before excavation. Based on the goals of the research and the type of site under investigation, an archaeologist may wish to use three or four tests. Historical archaeologists often rely heavily on methods designed to identify metals, because of the introduction of European metal trade goods to indigenous peoples.

The Paranormal?

Before concluding this chapter, we should mention dowsing, a distinctly low-tech detection method most people have heard about. Some people claim they can find underground water using a forked stick or even two bent, metal coat hangers called "angle rods." Renowned historical archaeologist Ivor Noël Hume introduced dowsing to the field in the 1950s and mentioned it in his book *Historical Archaeology*. He noted having success with the method at Colonial Williamsburg and, though he did not elaborate, he said he felt "a little idiotic walking across a field intently watching two pieces of coat hanger." His most curious discovery was that 80 percent of men can make dowsing rods work, but only 30 percent of women.

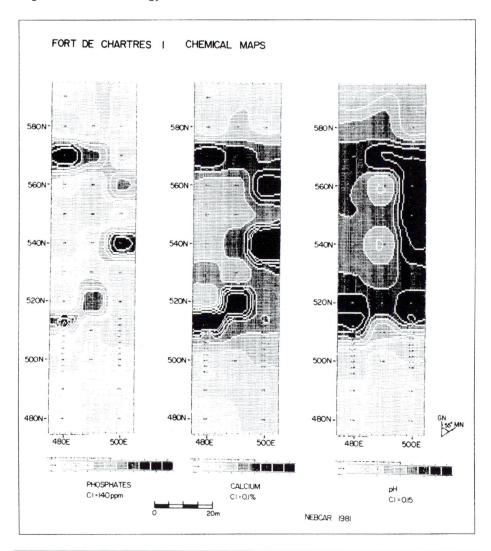

Figure 5.9 Chemical map made at the first Fort de Chartres, Illinois

(From Combined Magnetic & Chemical Surveys of Forts Kaskaskia & de Chartres #1, Illinois by J. W. Weymouth and W. I. Woods in *Historical Archaeology*, 18, 2 [1984]:22–37.)

Perhaps these figures say more about which sex is willing to walk around archaeological sites looking idiotic than anything else!

Dowsing is more widely used in Britain, and Noël Hume, a British national, mentions the existence of a British Society of Dowsers. The book *Dowsing and Church Archaeology* describes the apparent successes dowsers have had on medieval sites in England. St. Mary's Church at Woodhorn in northern England dates to at least the Norman period (post-1066 C.E.), and exhibits thirteenth- and early nineteenth-century design elements. In 1973, when the building was no longer needed as a house of worship, it was converted into a museum and cultural center. In 1982 two dowsers, Eric Cambridge and Richard Bailey, were given the opportunity to conduct a survey of the church. They found what they took to be possible

foundation walls beneath the existing chancel. The location of these walls suggested that the chancel had once been smaller, probably having been enlarged in the nineteenth century. Given the opportunity to test their findings, Cambridge and Bailey set about excavating where their angle rods indicated the presence of a foundation wall. They quickly discovered a mortared, stone wall precisely where they said it would be! The wall was 8 inches (20 cm) below the paved surface of the chancel, and was approximately 39 inches (100 cm) wide. They were not able to provide an exact date for the wall, having found both medieval floor tiles and a much more recent white clay pipe bowl (dating 1650–1680).

Dowsers complain that professional archaeologists have bitterly attacked them as occultists because their technique has no theoretical explanation. These British dowsers swear their method of subsurface surveying works, and they offer serious arguments for its use.

It is admittedly easy to be tricked by dowsing because it actually does appear to work in some cases. But can it really provide archaeological clues to buried sites? James Randi, famed professional magician and debunker of the paranormal, reported that all dowsing fails when tested using scientific methods. In fact, no dowser has ever passed a scientifically valid test. So why do dowsers continue to believe in their method? The reason is a powerful psychological phenomenon called "the ideomotor effect." This is an involuntary bodily movement evoked by an idea or thought process. In other words, the angle rods will move when the user thinks they should. Most dowsers are not aware they are causing the angle rods to move. In the case of British churches, dowsers are familiar with church architecture and they undoubtedly evoke the rods to move where they expect to find buried walls and other well-documented features.

All paranormal methods claimed to be useful in archaeological site location are best left in the hands of mediums and other characters. Serious historical archaeologists seeking to locate buried sites would do infinitely better to employ one of the methods outlined in this chapter and leave dowsers to their own devices.

Site Visit: Pribilof Islands, Alaska, 1780s

The Aleut people had lived on the Aleutian Islands, stretching into the Bering Sea west of the Alaska Peninsula, for at least four thousand years before Europeans encountered them in 1741. They lived as peoples in the far north had always lived, hunting seals and walruses in the sea and on land and, when available, collecting wild berries and other edible plants. The Europeans who made contact with the Aleuts were Russians who had come to the region also for its animals. Their interest, however, was in precious furs and skins rather than subsistence. In the decades following contact, the Russians made several dozen expeditions to the land of the Aleuts and developed a substantial fur-trading empire.

The Pribilof Islands are composed of five tiny islands located north of the main Aleutian archipelago. The two largest islands are named St. Paul and St. George. The land is rocky, windswept, and only a light covering of hearty plants can survive there. But marine mammals were well adapted to the islands, with whales and fur seals predominating (Figure 5.10). In fact, at the time of Russian contact, as many as 3–4 million fur seals may have been in the Pribilof Islands.

Figure 5.10 Northern fur seals dot the beach in front of St. Paul village in the Pribilof Islands, Alaska, a community of some 600 residents. Several hundred thousand fur seals come to the island each summer to breed and give birth.
(Courtesy of Douglas W. Veltre.)

Russian fur traders promptly viewed the islands as a source of great wealth, and they quickly began to harvest the valuable seals with enthusiasm.

The impact of the foreigners on the Aleuts was devastating. Diseases ravaged them, and as many as 80 percent of them may have died as a direct result of contact. As may be expected, profound social changes accompanied the steep demographic drop, and by the early 1700s, the Aleuts were no longer in control of their lives. Their population was devastated, their traditional social networks were disrupted, and their food supply was in danger of being destroyed by over-hunting. Thus, enmeshed in a transnational economic system not of their making, they were forced into work camps as laborers for the Russian fur trade.

Living conditions on the Pribilof Islands were understandably harsh. The changes in Aleut housing reflected the broader cultural transformations they experienced. Their earliest dwellings were usually fairly large, partly dug into the ground, and were either rounded rectangles or ovals in shape. Their residents would enter and leave through holes in the roofs, which were made of either sod, wood, or bone. After the arrival of the Russian fur traders, the houses of the Aleuts were no longer truly semi-subterranean, and they had interior walls made

Figure 5.11 Archaeological excavations revealed a large stone fire-place in the center of the floor of a sod-walled structure in the Pribilof Islands, Alaska. Russian and Aleut fur seal workers fueled their fires with seal blubber.
(Courtesy of Douglas W. Veltre.)

from blocks of sod (Figure 5.11). They also had doors and windows placed on the outside walls, and their roofs were made of dried grass held down against the wind with nets. These buildings were undoubtedly crowded, damp, and bleak.

The task of living in such conditions was challenging. Harvesting fur seals was exhausting work, because the Russians designed it to have an almost factory-like efficiency. Their government granted the Russian-American Company, formed in 1799, exclusive rights to all hunting activities in the region, and the entrepreneurial fur traders planned to make the most of the opportunity. Their goal was to obtain as many pelts as fast as possible, and get them to market while the prices were high. The chronic shortage of Russians willing to perform the work and live on the cold, tiny islands meant Aleuts would compose the labor force. Not only were they present in the region, they also knew how to survive in the harsh climate. More importantly, they knew how to catch the precious animals. They would thus perform the work of the company.

The Aleuts traditionally hunted marine mammals in a time-tested and ecologically sound way. Hunting individually or in a small group, they used their tracking skills, patience, and proficiency to bring down one or two animals. They used the pelts for clothing and other necessities, and consumed the meat. This time-honored practice dramatically changed with the development of economically based seal hunting. Under the direction of their Russian foremen, Aleut hunters were encouraged to conduct fur seal drives. Instead of killing individual animals on the spot, this new hunting method involved driving large numbers of seals overland to a specified killing ground. The killing ground was located close to the main settlement, so that the Aleuts would not have to haul the pelts far. This means of hunting was efficient but devastating to the ecosystem.

Source: Douglas W. Veltre and Allen P. McCartney. Russian Exploitation of Aleuts and Fur Seals: The Archaeology of Eighteenth- and Early Nineteenth-Century Settlements in the Pribilof Islands, Alaska. *Historical Archaeology* 36, 3 (2002):8–17.

Chapter 6

Pre-Excavation Fieldwork

Documents, Interviews, Buildings

Archaeology is a multidisciplinary enterprise. Whether studying the earliest humans in Africa or the Inka road systems high in the Andes, archaeologists of ancient history rely on artifacts, structural remains, food residues, and on information from many of the hard sciences. Archaeologists of ancient history often collaborate with biologists, climatologists, geologists, and chemists. Historical archaeologists also rely on the sciences, but their field is unique because of its strong reliance on sources of information not usually associated with excavation: historical documents, interviews with informants, and standing buildings. In this chapter, we explain how archaeologists use these so-called "nonarchaeological" sources in the study of the recent past.

Historical Fieldwork and Documents

Historians James Davidson and Mark Lytle note that writing history is a well-known, age-old way to organize knowledge, but if done badly can be easily dismissed. Misunderstandings about history often stem from the common assumption that "history" consists of a series of dry "facts." Many people believe the job of the historian is simply to discover the "facts"—like an archaeologist unearthing potsherds or a detective investigating a crime—and to compile them into a "history." To them, historians are like archaeologists. Instead of constructing history from sherds and soils, historians use scattered bits of information buried in documents and other textual materials. Sadly, many people first encounter history as a dull, seemingly relentless recitation of sterile dates and unrelated facts. Many people confess to dislike history simply because of the way it was originally presented to them. They have never been taught that history relates directly to our own times and, as such, that history is intimately important to each and every one of us.

Modern historians have striven to dispel the stereotype that history is dull and boring. In their fascinating book *After the Fact: The Art of Historical Detection*, Davidson and Lytle demonstrate how historians actually work. Rather than merely searching for new facts about old topics or simply rehashing a collection of old facts, historians engage in the serious evaluation and interpretation of their sources. Davidson and Lytle present several case studies ranging from colonial times to the Watergate break-in to show that "what happened in the past" is not necessarily the same as "history." In their essay on early photography, for instance, they show how photographers can shape impressions of past reality. The camera is often assumed to be an impartial observer, or what Davidson and Lytle call a "mirror with a memory." Photographers point it at something and the camera simply records the image on film. In actuality, though, the person behind the camera has the ability to insert his or her own biases into any picture. Images of lodgers in overcrowded late-nineteenth-century tenements or children playing in squalid alleyways may not truly represent "how things used to be." Some photographers may have staged their pictures or they may have removed important elements from the negative. Most people tend to accept old photographs as truthful, and so they become the visual memory of the past. But like any written account, they can be filled with biases.

The great French historian, Marc Bloch—a member of the French Resistance during World War II captured and executed by the Nazis on June 16, 1944, only ten days after D-Day—wrote that the "faculty of understanding the living is . . . the master quality of the historian." Writing history, technically termed "historiography," thus involves the interplay between the past (what actually happened) and the present (what the historian can document and is interested in studying). The past is not a huge file of dead facts, but a living body of knowledge from which people draw their interpretations using various perspectives and attitudes.

Nowhere does the interpretive task of the historian come across better than in T. H. Breen's study of East Hampton, a village located on the eastern end of Long Island, New York. Breen presents a history of this seventeenth-century town as an "interpretive journey." As he makes the journey, he holds firm to the idea "that people like ourselves have ultimately decided what will or will not be treated as a historical 'fact.'" Breen realizes that the existing histories of East Hampton are "products of an interpretive process that at the very best can generate only partial truths." When John Lyon Gardiner wrote the first history of the town in 1798, he portrayed East Hampton as a pastoral, idyllic place standing tall and proud for American Independence and staunch in its support of democracy. Gardiner believed the Native American Montauks were a blight on the town's history because he saw them as living in a degenerate condition. He regarded their extreme poverty as the result of their own "idle disposition and savage manners." For Gardner, East Hampton would have been a perfect place without them.

Today, Gardiner's eighteenth-century history seems ill informed at best and racist at worst. But he undoubtedly thought he was simply transcribing the town's historical "facts" for posterity. Other educated, literate members of his society (his audience) also probably assumed that the Montauks—and all other Native Americans for that matter—were degenerates with only themselves to blame for their debased condition. We know now that what Gardiner recounted were not the "facts," but only his interpretation of certain elements of the past. His perception was unfairly biased.

Historian Carl Becker told the assembled members of the prestigious American Historical Association in 1926 that "the simple historical fact turns out to be not a hard, cold something with clear outline, and measurable pressure, like a brick." He said historical facts have a much more nebulous character; they change and mutate with contemporary attitudes. A history written in 1926 would not be the same history written in 2016, even though both historians may cover the exact same period of history and use many of the same sources of information.

Breen understood this curious situation, and he became adept at writing several East Hampton histories at once. He saw the past from many different angles, traveling easily between the past and the present. He learned history is written by looking back at the past with different lenses. For example, he discovered a man named Samuel Mulford, East Hampton's most prominent citizen in the 1680s. Mulford owned a whaling company employing 24 men. He was also a Puritan and widely recognized for his dogmatic and rigid views on Calvinism. People who knew Mulford characterized him as "a long-winded, self-righteous bore." Using such comments, Breen develops an impression of Mulford's personality. As Breen observes, the written accounts make it possible to see Mulford as an ambitious man who could be obstinate and clever. Breen also discovers that Mulford had the curious nickname "Fishhook."

The story told in East Hampton is that early in the eighteenth century, Mulford traveled to London in the hope of obtaining a personal audience with the king. While waiting outside the palace, a clever pickpocket lifted most of Mulford's money. So distressed was the penny-wise Mulford that he promptly sewed a series of fishhooks inside his coat to secure his remaining cash. The storytellers say that all of London, and even the king himself, were impressed by Mulford's ingenuity.

Breen doubts the fishhook incident ever happened, and he proposes its truth is less important than the story itself. In fact, he believes that the story was really about the entire East Hampton community. A small town in the process of being overwhelmed by the world around it, East Hampton used ingenious methods—like Samuel Mulford's fishhooks—to protect and preserve itself. That the story uses Mulford as its focus merely shows how important he was (and still is) to the town's history.

Finding it difficult to shake the image of Samuel Mulford, Breen visited a direct descendant, the Presbyterian Reverend David Mulford, to learn more about the eighteenth-century eccentric. David Mulford lived in the house the Mulfords owned for more than three centuries. Breen hoped that Mulford, the family genealogist, could add to what he had discovered in the local archives. Breen also hoped that his visit might remind Mulford about letters or documents he had forgotten about but may have stored somewhere in his house. During their discussion, Breen tells Mulford what he knows of Samuel Mulford and the seventeenth century; Mulford in turn tells him about East Hampton's 300-year celebration in 1948, and of his father's "outspoken belief that the automobile had ruined the village." It was in these conversations that Breen traveled, sometimes unwittingly, between the past and the present. In the end, Breen had to admit that long after he had spoken with David Mulford, he continued to wonder whether he had used David to conjure up his image of Samuel. As Breen's experience demonstrates, writing history is not divorced from the perceptions and attitudes of the present.

The Historian's Craft

Breen's detailed, engaging account of how he unraveled the many histories of East Hampton, New York, illustrates that writing history—really the art of interpreting the past—is a field of expert research in its own right. Few archaeologists have extensive formal training in its intricacies or in the subtle nuances of historical research. Still, all historical archaeologists must understand the basics of historiography because at some point in their careers they will be called upon to conduct original archival research. Even if an archaeologist has the good fortune to collaborate closely with a professional historian, he or she must often read documents themselves. Having the eyes of an archaeologist, they may see something in a document that a historian, untuned to archaeological thinking, may have overlooked. In many respects, a historical archaeologist's abilities will show in the quality of his or her documentary research, for documents and artifacts are intimately linked in historical archaeology. (And documents, being produced by conscious human effort, are artifacts, too!) Breen's East Hampton study clearly illustrates the best historians are not necessarily detached scholars who know everything, but merely curious people who simply know where to find the pertinent information they seek. Their real skills as historians are revealed in their interpretations of what they find. Thus, being a historian is somewhat like being an archaeologist. Glass bottles and ceramic teacups and bowls—like legal papers, personal diaries, and correspondences—do not speak; they must be interpreted.

Historians study both primary and secondary sources. *Primary sources* are contemporary records, generally written by eyewitnesses or people who may have direct understanding or personal insight into the events or attitudes of the day. Breen used many primary documents in his East Hampton research. One of these sources is especially intriguing. In the late 1600s, the economy of East Hampton depended on whaling. Many of the town's most prominent citizens—Samuel Mulford included—were involved in the "whale design," the economy of whaling. The local residents knew that to hunt whales they would require the assistance of several common laborers. Most able-bodied workers in late-seventeenth-century New England were Native Americans. Needing laborers, the whalers of East Hampton entered into binding contracts with the Indians for the whaling season. But there were not always enough Native Americans to meet the demand, so the competition for their labor was fierce. In April, 1678, the Reverend Thomas James—an ambitious whaler—penned a document stating that he would offer "protest against any person or persons who have or shall contrary to all law of God or man, justice or equity, go about to violate or infringe" on his contracts with his native employees. This first-person document offers a clear picture of what Thomas James thought about people who would try to steal his Native American laborers away from him. He simply did not trust his parishioners.

Secondary sources are interpretations of primary sources, written after the events they describe. Breen's history is now a secondary source. Breen also read a number of other secondary sources to discover earlier interpretations of the town's history.

The historian's craft involves the practical element of knowing precisely where to look for primary sources, a task often requiring tact and ingenuity. Primary sources come from government archives, courthouse basements, dusty trunks found in attics, and even from auctions. The search for sources never ends, even after the historian has compiled hundreds of them. Even letters of Abraham Lincoln—one of the most well-researched figures in world history—occasionally turn up in unexpected places. In 1993, the Circuit Clerk of Tazewell County Courthouse in Pekin, Illinois, discovered 34 previously unknown Lincoln papers simply by pulling out a file marked "Re: Lincoln." These documents, written by Lincoln as a circuit-riding lawyer in central Illinois, include instructions to juries, bills of indictment, affidavits, and pleas. Lincoln rode a 15-county circuit twice a year and worked day and night when he visited local courthouses. William Beard, the assistant editor of the Lincoln Legal Papers project, described the documents as a "King Solomon's mine in Pekin." The discovery of these new papers, along with 75 others unexpectedly found at Illinois State University and at other Illinois courthouses, sparked excitement among Lincoln scholars around the world. Finding the Lincoln papers proves that documents from even the great figures of history, like important archaeological sites, still await discovery.

Primary source materials have major significance in historical archaeology, and some of the common places where they may be located are:

- Federal repositories (official, governmental correspondence; government maps and charts; photographic collections; statistical reports; acts and statutes; business charters; newspapers; military records; census rolls; immigration lists);
- State and provincial archives (official correspondence; local statutes; personal letters and diaries; militia records; photographic collections; newspapers);

- Private and university archives (special collections of correspondence and records of prominent individuals and important places; rare manuscripts and books; maps and charts);
- Local repositories (personal correspondence; land ownership records and plat maps; local tax rolls; birth and death records).

Most large archives and special collections facilities publish up-to-date catalogues of their holdings. Most of these facilities have websites and many have searchable databases. These computer-based sources are superb research tools because they allow historical archaeologists to perform some of their research right from their laboratories and offices.

A project at the Adobe Walls trading post site in the Texas panhandle demonstrates the value of primary sources in historical archaeology. This remote trading post came into being in 1874 when enterprising merchants followed the buffalo hunters onto the American Plains. The merchants only occupied their sod-and-picket post for six months, choosing to retreat to Kansas when local Native Americans began to harass them. When archaeologist Billy Harrison studied the post, he collaborated with historian T. Lindsay Baker. Baker sifted through nineteenth-century newspapers, including those with the romantic Western names of the *Dodge City Times* and *Leavenworth Times,* personal papers, letters, reports, and books and articles housed in no less than 55 separate repositories. These archives ranged from the National Archives in Washington, D.C., to a personal library in South Croydon, England. The historical documentation for this one small site, inhabited for only half a year, kept Baker busy for months as he located, read, evaluated, and interpreted the abundant material.

Harrison's excavations at Adobe Walls benefitted tremendously from Baker's historical research. While combing through the files of the National Archives in Washington, D.C., Baker discovered two sworn depositions relating to the trading post. In the first, made on October 11, 1892, Charles Rath, partner of the Rath and Company store, described his building at the post. As he remembered it, the store was built of sod, was 25 by 50 feet (7.6 by 15.3 m) in size, and had two "block houses" on opposite corners. He said these block houses measured 12 or 15 feet (3.7 or 4.6 m) square. The second deposition was made by Andrew Johnson, known as "Andy the Swede." In his statement, recorded the same day as Rath's, he recalled the Rath and Company store as being 24 or 25 feet (7.3 or 7.6 m) wide and about 50 or 60 feet (15.3 or 18.3 m) long. He said it was made of sod with a log roof. He also mentioned the two "block houses" as being about 12 by 12 feet (3.7 by 3.7 m) square. The presence of these eyewitness accounts meant that Harrison had some idea of what he would find when he began to excavate at the store site. He knew he was looking for a sod building that measured somewhere around 25 by 50 feet (7.6 by 15.3 m) in size. That the excavators found the actual building to measure 16.5 feet (5.0 m) by almost 53 feet (16.2 m) is not surprising (Figure 6.1). Some error in the informants' memories should be expected. After all, how many people actually know the measurements of the rooms in their house? Also, because the Adobe Walls trading post was occupied for such a short time, its residents cannot be expected to recall every minute detail about it. What is more surprising, however, is that Harrison found archaeological evidence for only one "block house," on the southeast corner. The building never had two blockhouses! The discrepancy between the residents' memories and the physical evidence cannot be explained. Perhaps another store built somewhere else had two blockhouses, and the men were simply confusing the two. The reason for the memory of two blockhouses is a mystery.

The Adobe Walls research highlights some of the difficulties inherent in using primary documents in archaeological research. The problems become even more acute when international relations or trade are involved. Such projects may require international travel and language

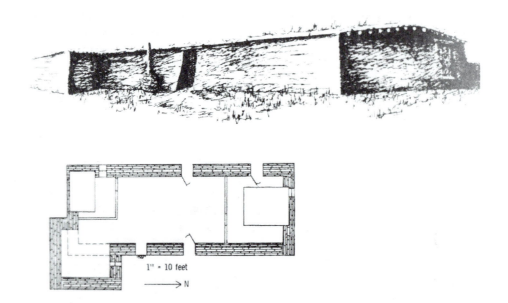

Figure 6.1 Excavated floor plan and artist's reconstruction of the Rath and Company Store, Adobe Walls trading post, Texas
(Courtesy of the Panhandle-Plains Historical Museum.)

skills. Quite apart from an expertise in sixteenth-century Spanish language usage and script, access to archives may be difficult to arrange, even with the cooperation of local scholars. The study of colonial sites in North America and elsewhere, for example, usually means acquiring a familiarity with the colonial archives of Spain, Portugal, Great Britain, France, the Netherlands, and other colonial nations. Such was the case when historical archaeologist Kathleen Deagan teamed up with historian Jane Landers in their study of Fort Mose, outside the historic city of St. Augustine, Florida. St. Augustine was the first permanent European city in the United States, and Fort Mose, more properly called "Gracia Real de Santa Teresa de Mose," was the creation of African American escapees from British plantations to the north (Figure 6.2). The Spanish welcomed these people fleeing from the Spanish Empire's longtime European enemy. The new arrivals founded Fort Mose in 1738, and it became the first legally approved free black community in what would become the United States. The residents of Fort Mose helped the Spanish defeat their former masters when the British attacked St. Augustine in the early 1740s. To learn something of the history of this important site, Deagan and Landers spent the first six months of their archaeological project becoming familiar with Spanish parish records held in Florida, and official governmental dispatches from Spanish archives. These Spanish records tell the "official" story of Fort Mose, or what the British derisively called simply a "Negroe Fort."

Deagan's archaeological research exposed some of the history of Fort Mose. The site of the fort was first identified by a crew working under the direction of Charles Fairbanks, a pioneer historical archaeologist from the University of Florida. Deagan was a student on this crew, and she returned to the site five years later as a professor to conduct a more detailed examination of the fort. She confirmed the fort's location, but for the next ten years was not able to obtain adequate funding for large-scale excavation.

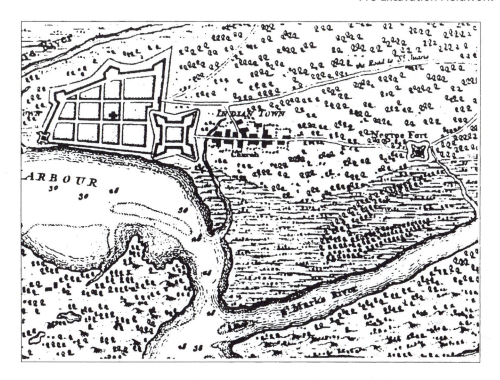

Figure 6.2 Detail of 1792 map of St. Augustine, Florida, showing "Negroe Fort"

(Map & Imagery Library, Special and Area Studies Collections, University of Florida, George A. Smathers Libraries)

When Deagan finally obtained the necessary funds, the archaeology at Fort Mose revealed several unique things about the fort, including details of its construction. The fort's walls were about 5 feet (1.5 m) tall, faced on the outside with marsh clay and planted along the top with prickly pear cactus. The fort's defensive moat was almost 7 feet (2 m) wide and about 2.5 feet (0.8 m) deep. It also had a watchtower or large building, and a smaller, circular wood and thatch building that may have been a dwelling. The artifacts from the site include lead shot, gunflints, white clay smoking pipes, brass buckles, bone buttons, and glass bottles. Native American pottery comprised a full 62 percent of the finds. Deagan identified these wares as coming from the local Timucuas. Most of the European ceramics in the collection are English rather than Spanish in origin. The English had begun to dominate the world ceramic market at this time, and smugglers were adept at bringing British goods into Spanish America. Deagan's archaeological program at Fort Mose, supported by Landers' extensive research in the relevant Spanish-language documents, provides exciting new information about early African American history.

Many historical archaeologists are using their insights, knowledge, and training to create "alternative histories." A society's most powerful and influential members have traditionally written official history or at the very least have had their positions made known. Individuals neither wealthy nor empowered may have had difficulty having their narratives committed to writing. Alternative histories seek to overturn this tradition by providing historical accounts of people who have been ignored or written about unfairly. Archaeologists are contributing important new pieces to the puzzle of the past, performing a task historical archaeologist Paul Shackel refers to as "reversing the narrative."

Jamie Brandon has provided an illustrative case study in his examination of a mill site in the Arkansas Ozarks. He begins with the present-day view of the "hillbilly," a person who is regarded as rural, anti-modern, socially backward, and white. This image of the hillbilly is part of the American, and undoubtedly also the world's, perception of how life in the Ozarks was (and is) lived. The problem with this image, however, is that it hides historical truth. As traditionally written, "hillbilly history" both creates a biased perception of daily life in general and specifically erases the African American contributions to the region. The false image allows biased history to continue being told.

Brandon's research at Van Winkle's Mill, built in 1850, revealed several important realities of the site's history. In the first place, Van Winkle owned 18 enslaved men and women. These individuals lived on the property and labored at the mill. The only known photograph of one of the African American mill workers shows him standing behind the large, extended Van Winkle family. Being in the background is a metaphor for the process of social marginalization. Census records make it abundantly clear that African Americans lived in the Ozarks both during and after enslavement. Their history constitutes an alternative history to the more widespread, unfair understanding of life in the Ozarks.

The alternative histories being constructed by Brandon and others are developed by understanding that many of the most well-known narratives of the past are biased and partial. One of the values of historical archaeology is the ability of its practitioners to write new chapters in local, regional, and global history, highlighting aspects of the past that have been ignored, marginalized, and forgotten about.

Oral Interviewing

Oral sources can be as valuable as written documentation. Anthropologists discovered early on that they would have to talk to people to learn about certain cultural practices. Anthropologists in the field ask numerous questions about a number of topics, including kinship terms, religious beliefs, attitudes about infanticide, and birth control methods. Anthropologists can directly observe practices and rituals, but beliefs and attitudes cannot be easily seen. People may seldom talk about them among strangers, and missionaries and early explorers may not have known about or even recorded such information. The only way to learn about oral cultures—those without writing—is to ask and to watch. Asking and watching is what anthropologists call "participant observation." It constitutes one of their fundamental research tools.

Polish-born Bronislaw Malinowski was one of the first professional anthropologists to spend a long period living among and studying people of another culture. His research among the Trobriand Islanders, near New Guinea, produced many important works that are now classics in the history of anthropology. His *The Sexual Life of Savages in North-Western Melanesia* created a public sensation when it appeared in 1929 because of its frank discussion of Trobriand sexuality. Malinowski is known among anthropologists for developing techniques of participant observation. His fieldwork involved extensive oral interviewing and face-to-face interaction. His diary entry for January 18, 1915, shows he was well aware of the difficulty of obtaining oral information: "Yesterday before noon, Pikana came. With great effort—for he was sleepy, kept yawning, and I had a headache and felt poorly—I wormed out of him material relating to kinship." The information "wormed" from Pikana with great difficulty forms the core of what many anthropology students learn about kinship today.

Historical archaeologists often sympathize with Malinowski. They search for what historian Carl Becker called the kind of history people "carry around in their heads." Everyone, no matter what his or her station in life knows some history that is unique and personal. The layout and use of the rooms in our house, when we graduated from high school, started college, and what our first job was like are all part of our "history." We remember what we thought about important national or international events, and how these things affected us and the people around us. These things we know; they are part of who we are.

Orally presented personal histories have been part of anthropological research for many years. Several committed anthropologists, like Frances Densmore, sought to save them from being lost forever (Figure 6.3). Collecting oral history is today a central task for many professional historians who use them to write about modern times. Oral anthologies have been compiled for events as distinctive as the Woodstock Festival and the attack on Pearl Harbor. Studs Terkel's bestselling *Hard Times: An Oral History of the Great Depression* is just one demonstration of how compelling oral histories can be. Even though Terkel modestly describes his book as "simply an attempt to get the story of the holocaust known as The

Figure 6.3 Anthropologist Frances Densmore getting an interpretation of a Blackfoot song
(MPI / Getty Images)

Great Depression from an improvised battalion of survivors," his informants tell stories with no equal. Before their collection, these deeply personal stories could not be culled from published articles, books, or newspapers. They existed only in people's memories. The oral historian, like the field anthropologist, commits these personal tales to the written page and gives them permanence.

Oral accounts are a nonrenewable resource. The people who remember Pearl Harbor, Woodstock, the Great Depression, or, for that matter the Boston Tea Party, have died, or will eventually die. The death of a generation is like burning an archive full of unique and non-retrievable information. In this sense, oral interviewing is similar to archaeology. The only difference is that an interviewer can learn about the past directly from people who lived it. They can ask questions, add unexpected information, and clarify obscurities or ambiguous statements.

The lines between oral history, anthropology, and historical research are often fuzzy. When Baker and Harrison studied Adobe Walls, they used interviews conducted with veterans of the post written down in the 1920s and 1930s. These transcripts were invaluable sources of personal information available from no one but a direct participant. Many of the informants—for example, J. Wright Mooar, a Chicago streetcar conductor turned professional buffalo hunter—remembered Adobe Walls and spoke about it in an insightful and personal way. "We had eleven outlaws hired," he recalled. "I remember some of them. They were good fellows. They stayed with us. We never had any preachers with us."

In 1922, during a visit to the old site, Andrew "Andy the Swede" Johnson and Orlando A. "Brick" Bond (Figure 6.4), two former residents of the post, drew a sketch map of the way they remembered the store. Billy Dixon was another man who remembered his experiences at Adobe Walls (Figure 6.5). Widely regarded as a hunter of rare ability, Dixon was awarded the Congressional Medal of Honor for his bravery at the Battle of Buffalo Wallow, a battle in

Figure 6.4 Orlando Bond and Andrew Johnson at the Adobe Walls Site in 1922

(Kansas State Historical Society)

Figure 6.5 Billy Dixon in 1876
(Kansas Collection, Kenneth Spencer Research Library, University of Kansas Libraries)

which six soldiers and scouts held off an overwhelming number of attacking Native Americans. He recalled the area of Adobe Walls as "a vast wilderness, inhabited by game—truly a hunter's paradise." Describing a fellow hunter, Dixon said that he was a man "who had lots of nerve and knew all the ins and outs of frontier life." These priceless accounts, seemingly from writers of Western fiction, are real.

We mentioned above how some eyewitnesses' comments about the construction of the Rath and Company store were confirmed by archaeological excavation. In many cases, the combination of oral information and archaeological findings serves to flesh out the small details of daily life. Many of Adobe Walls' men, interviewed in the 1920s, remembered the popularity of wild plums and coffee at the trading post. Accordingly, the archaeologists found 16 plum pits and 25 coffee beans from excavations in the area of the mess hall.

Oral remembrances can provide a range of information. Archaeologist Peter Schmidt used oral history in a somewhat broader way than the Abode Walls team when he investigated farming villages among the Buhaya living on the shores of Lake Victoria in Tanzania, East Africa (also see Chapter 1).

Relying on local informants, Schmidt learned a great deal about the political history of the Buhaya, their religious traditions, and their present-day land tenure system. He conducted two- to four-hour interviews in Swahili and then used what he learned to guide his excavations. Collecting such histories required persistence and patience. He had to visit some informants several times before he could make them comfortable enough to talk freely. Even then, most informants would agree to only one interview, thinking further discussion to be a waste of time.

Much of what Schmidt learned was not the kind of eyewitness information used by Baker and Harrison at Adobe Walls. Instead, his Buhaya informants spoke of the past by using mnemonic devices, mental images meant as memory aids. They used these mental tricks because they could not possibly have witnessed key events that unfolded centuries ago. They recited what they learned from their parents, and what their parents had learned from their parents, and so on, back several generations. After some experience with the informants and their way of thinking about the past, Schmidt came to understand how the people of this one part of Tanzania perceived their physical environment. He came to see the landscape as a complex mixture of folk belief, myth, and legend.

The significance of Schmidt's study to historical archaeology lies in his understanding that people have many different ways of remembering the past. Some are direct memories—resting on actual events seen and recalled or on reminiscences of respected individuals. At times the informants talked of events shrouded in folklore and tradition, accounts of a mythic, long-vanished past that were passed from father to son and mother to daughter over the generations. Schmidt's research in Tanzania proves that long-told stories can often be as useful as more recent information.

Oral information can sometimes contain a subtle mix of eyewitness account and oral tradition. Such is the case with Black Elk, holy man of the Oglala Sioux (Dakota), who at age 13 witnessed the Battle of the Little Bighorn. His autobiography stands today as one of the most beautifully told oral accounts in the world. In beginning his life story, Black Elk said that it was a tale "of us two-leggeds sharing in it with the four-leggeds and the wings of the air and all green things; for these are children of one mother and their father is one Spirit." Black Elk recounted the events of his life with a mixture of eyewitness detail and Oglala tradition. Speaking of the famous skirmish with Custer, he recalled that "it seemed that my people were all thunder-beings and that the soldiers would be rubbed out." His account is both spiritual and factual, personal and cultural at the same time.

In another study, Dana Ogo Shew and April Elizabeth Kamp-Whittaker used oral information linked to archaeological research to investigate daily life at the Granada Relocation Center in southeastern Colorado. The center, known more informally as Amache, was created in 1942 to house Japanese internees during World War II. It closed in October 1945, but at its height housed more than 7,000 people. During its three-year life, more than 10,000 uprooted Japanese men, women, and children lived at the center.

Living conditions at the center were uncomfortable and cramped. Regulations imposed by the War Relocation Authority were such that the daily lives the internees experienced before going to the center were completed disrupted. For one thing, being forced into communal living, they had to surrender their normal sense of privacy. Such private activities as bathing and dining became noisy group events rather than quiet family gatherings. Oral information, however, indicates that internees created family dining tables designed to maintain a sense of family cohesion. Traditional gender roles were transformed because men with strong ties to Japan had been arrested and held elsewhere. In addition, fathers, the traditional suppliers of food, were supplanted by the camp's administrators.

Even in the face of severe social disruptions, the oral information indicates that families were able to maintain a sense of togetherness and community. As one strategy, internees created clubs through which they could express themselves collectively. The Women's Federation, for instance, served as a conduit to the camp administration where internees could state their grievances and make demands. A series of religious and youth organizations crosscut other groups to create a web of interaction and association within the camp. Much of this information would have been lost without the oral information.

Oral accounts provide depth to the past. When used in conjunction with textual sources and archaeological data, they can be extremely powerful ways to interject a profoundly personal perspective on the past.

Beginning in the 1990s, a number of scholars became interested in the creation of memory. Researchers in many disciplines began intensive examinations of such topics as how memory is created, how social class influences memory, and how memory is linked to the building of monuments and other structures. A number of archaeologists were part of the movement to understand the role of memory in the construction of the past. The study of memory is particularly relevant to historical archaeology because many people from the recent past are still alive and can be interviewed. Several important studies of memory formation and maintenance have since been completed in historical archaeology.

In her study of the Hagg Cottages of Alderley Edge in Cheshire, England, Eleanor Conlin Casella employed oral histories to understand the creation of memory in the community. From the 1780s until the 1890s, the residents of Alderley Edge, located south of Manchester, were engaged in copper, lead, and cobalt mining. In addition to these working people, a few wealthy mill owners sought relief from the overcrowded, urban environment of Manchester and built elegant villas in the town. The specific area Casella researched was called "The Sandhills" because large amounts of acid-laced sand—a by-product of copper mining—had been dumped there.

Casella linked her archaeological excavations with oral interviewing to provide rare insights into the daily life of the working community. She was able to learn how the residents created a sense of community by maintaining fragile social bonds. The relations between individuals and social classes were complex and interwoven. When they interacted with the gentry, the residents of the Hagg Cottages participated in ties based on deference. Traditional paternalistic bonds ensured the landlord would care for the property in exchange for the tenants' annual rents. With their social equals, the residents found kinship through the practice of common labor. Connections formed from working together or even from having the same jobs. These bonds created lines of mutual assistance and a web of support within the community.

Most of the information Casella collected from the memories of former Cottages residents were available in no other sources. The knowledge held in the heads of people disappears when they pass away. Oral interviewing, while perhaps not immediately viewed as "archaeological," can be a key tool for historical archaeologists.

Architectural Fieldwork

Not all sites studied by historical archaeologists are empty fields or deserted city lots. The places often providing the most exciting information contain standing buildings, pieces of complex machinery, bridges, and abandoned mills. Historical archaeologists, though perhaps often viewed only as excavators, do not ignore these "large artifacts." In fact, historical archaeologists are frequently called upon to conduct surveys of standing buildings and other extant structures. Historical archaeologists are as interested in what rests above the ground as what lies beneath it.

Large-scale architectural surveys are often required when areas to be affected by wholesale land modification projects are to impact the landscape and everything on its surface, including existing buildings. Buildings, like oral interviews, represent a non-renewable resource. If preservation or moving structures are impossible, then archaeologists or architects may be called upon to document them before destruction. When the U.S. Army Corps of Engineers constructed a huge dam on the Savannah River, between Georgia and South Carolina, they created a gigantic artificial lake about 25 miles (40 km) long. The reservoir behind the dam rose about 60 feet (18.2 m) above the former riverbanks, and inundated a large number of archaeological sites.

The Corps of Engineers hired teams of archaeologists to excavate numerous sites of various ages within the dam area before the reservoir was flooded. They also hired a group of historical architects to document the standing buildings slated to be destroyed. The area to be flooded had once been home to enslaved and freed African Americans, to expansive plantations and small tenant farms, and diverse industrial complexes.

Structures are pieces of material culture, and they may reveal a great deal about past daily life. Some houses are examples of *vernacular architecture* or buildings constructed in agreement with cultural norms and without the aid of trained architects and builders. Others are examples of *formal architecture*. These are buildings designed by trained architects and built according to exacting plans.

Architect Linda Worthy, editor of the report detailing the buildings in the Savannah River area, stated that "The dwelling house is the most important component of the cultural landscape." Historical architects and folklorists have repeatedly shown that dwellings can be "read" like old books or abandoned landscapes to reveal histories that would otherwise remain silent. Only the language must be deciphered. Boarded-up windows, room additions, and altered rooflines all tell a story that can be interpreted once one knows how to read the evidence.

In compiling what they called the "more human history" of the Savannah River dam, architectural surveyors found and photographed 93 abandoned houses, including wood-framed farmhouses once inhabited by formerly enslaved tenant farmers, two-story plantation mansions of slave owners, and hewn-log cabins of the region's earliest European-American settlers (Figures 6.6, 6.7). Traveling an intertwined network of

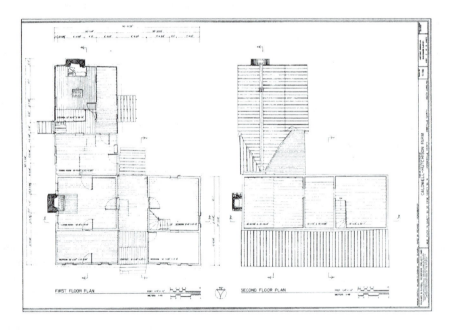

Figure 6.6 Floor plans of the late-eighteenth- to early nineteenth-century Caldwell-Hutchinson Farm, South Carolina

(NPS, Washington, DC)

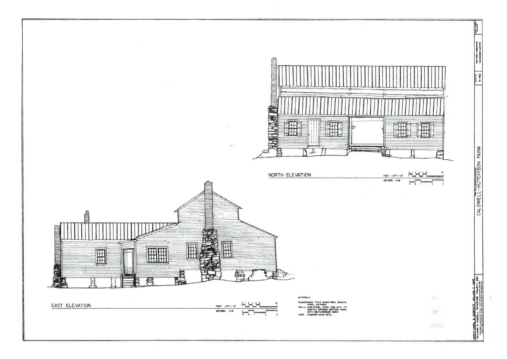

Figure 6.7 Elevation of the late-eighteenth- to early nineteenth-century Caldwell-Hutchinson Farm, South Carolina
(Courtesy of the Library of Congress.)

dusty backroads, they also discovered log barns and sheds, a blacksmith shop, and rusted iron bridges. These structures collectively tell a story covering the years from before 1860 to the mid-1950s, including the region's initial European American settlement, its creation as a rich plantation region based on the labor of enslaved African Americans, and its transition into a region of small tenant farmers clinging precariously to the near-exhausted red soil of the Upland South.

Detailed Architectural Surveys

The conduct of architectural surveys is highly specialized work. It requires careful mapping and precise interpretation of the buildings' physical characteristics. Many nations have established precise standards for architectural surveys. In the United States, the standards are set by the Historic American Buildings Survey (HABS), founded in 1933, and the Historic American Engineering Record (HAER), founded in 1969. Congress formally combined HABS and HAER in 1983 as HABS/HAER. The staff of HABS/HAER execute their measured drawings to precise specifications because these plans constitute a permanent, archival record of historically significant structures. Precise measured drawings have been completed for the Statue of Liberty in New York, for the original Smithsonian Institution building in Washington, D.C., the steam-powered hoist at the Quincy copper mine in northern Michigan, and many other important buildings, bridges, mechanical systems, historic ships, and landscapes.

HABS/HAER staff members were involved in documenting the architectural history of the White House in Washington, D.C. The removal of several layers of old paint from walls not exposed since 1798, revealed scorch marks from the British attempt to burn the mansion in 1814. With the paint removed, architects from HABS/HAER made exacting measured drawings of the windows, doors, and building facades. Their drawing of the main entrance reveals an ornate design of oak leaves and roses that harkens back to an age when formally trained architects ornamented their masterpieces with such ostentatious adornments.

HABS/HAER recorders also create a photographic record to amplify their drawings. Photographs are often preferred to measured drawings because they are quicker, easier, and less expensive to produce, particularly in digital format. These photographs are not simple snapshots, but highly professional images intended to convey a building's three-dimensional qualities, its spatial relationships with other buildings, its condition or state of preservation at the time of the photograph, and the texture of a building's many surfaces. Many of these photographs, artistic and beautiful in their own right, serve as the formal record of a building's design and construction.

In England, architectural surveying is handled by the staff of English Heritage's architectural investigators. These investigators have the goal of documenting the nation's incredible storehouse of historic buildings. They regularly collaborate with local bodies interested in historic preservation, and they make their materials available through the National Monuments Record. They also serve as consultants to bodies seeking advice on how best to protect significant examples of architecture.

An example of their work can be seen at Bletchley Park, the estate in Buckinghamshire where codebreakers toiled feverishly to break the German code during the Second World War. In 2003, a team of investigators began to study the standing structures at the estate dating from the time of the war (1939–1945). One of the team's interesting finds was that the authorities had constructed a series of wooden huts within which the codebreakers and their support staffs worked. Rather than being rigidly standardized as one might expect at a military base, the huts were placed in such a way that wartime departments needing to communicate with one another were located nearby to facilitate communication and collaboration.

Archaeologists can use computer software, such as CAD and animation programs, to document and even model standing pieces of architecture. Photogrammetry allows archaeologists to create files of 3D measurements from photographs. Using various programs, archaeologists can extrapolate how former buildings may have looked in the past, model locations of rooms, and assess how various rooms may have been used. 3D programs allow archaeologists to include shadows and changes in the lighting during the course of a day. Such visual recreations can be used in museum exhibits and other educational environments, as well as in serious research projects.

Archaeologists researching the Spanish colony of Floridablanca in Patagonia, southern Argentina, used architectural information to create a 3D image of settlers' houses. These houses were composed of nine terraced houses joined together and having a common tile roof (Figure 6.8). The creation of this image allows the archaeologists to obtain a thorough understanding of how the building fit into the landscape. It also breathes life into the archaeological site by making the history of the people's lives less abstract.

Figure 6.8 3D reconstruction of farmers' houses at Floridablanca, Patagonia, Argentina

(Buscaglia, Silvana, Maria Ximena Senatore, Eugenia Lascano, Victoria Bongiovanni, Matías de la Vega, and Ana Osella, To Protect an Order: Interdisciplinary Perspectives on Spatial Construction in the Spanish Colony of Floridablanca [Patagonia, Eighteenth Century], in *Historical Archaeology* 42, 4 [2008]:1–20.)

Other Architectural Research

Not many historical archaeologists can prepare measured drawings meeting the high standards of HABS/HAER or English Heritage's architectural investigators without considerable, specialized training. Nonetheless, historical archaeologists are often called upon to prepare measured drawings and take architectural photographs of standing structures. The level of detail will depend upon the amount of time available and the goals of the specific project. Some building surveys must be completed quickly. For others, the investigators may have the luxury of time and can provide thorough documentation of every aspect of a structure's architectural fabric.

In the 1980s, a new kind of historical archaeology, called buildings archaeology, began to emerge in Great Britain. Proponents of this non-excavation–based archaeology argued that archaeologists should be directly involved in the documentation, dating, and interpretation of the built environment. In *The Archaeology of Buildings*, Robert Morriss outlines the need for an archaeology of buildings and provides a useful guide for field archaeologists. Morriss explains how archaeologists should survey buildings, and he describes methods of archival research. He explains how archaeologists should evaluate the evidence provided by a building's walls, roof, flooring, and windows. The research, though focused on aboveground standing structures, is remarkably archaeological. Working much as field excavators, building investigators must learn to recognize significant features and to document the relationships of the features. They must also have considerable knowledge of the material culture used in buildings during various times in history, such as bricks, ceramic tiles, wood framing, stonework, and concrete).

Archaeologists from Southern Methodist University in Dallas, Texas, performed an architectural survey in north-central Texas as part of a larger study of the Richland/Chambers Reservoir project. Their work resulted in the documentation of 26 dwellings, four bridges, and 12 "special purpose structures"—storage sheds, various kinds of outbuildings, and even a store. Settlers in this part of Texas built these still-extant buildings between 1848 and 1945. The documentation provided by the survey team provided important information about the kinds of houses and other structures built in this region during an eventful 100-year period of history.

Building archaeologists can also document structures no longer existing. Morriss details research conducted at Caradoc Court, Herefordshire, England. The mansion, built in the 1600s as a timber-framed structure, was partially rebuilt in the 1860s. A devastating fire gutted the mansion before archaeologists could make an investigation of its history. Using an ingenious method of reconstruction, however, archaeologists salvaged what they could from the interior debris, and reconstructed the old house in the garden. They were able to move the various structural elements around in the garden to recreate much of the building's framing. They were aided by the unique character of hand-cut mortise and tenon joints. They were also able to document the remaining standing walls of the building once the debris was cleaned from the scorched interior. From all this evidence, the archaeologists learned that the builders had originally designed the mansion in a half-H plan, rather than the L-shaped plan as once assumed.

In some cases, archaeologists conduct architectural surveys of standing buildings to help them interpret what they have discovered through excavation. For instance, in his research in the Yucatán Peninsula in Mexico, Sam Sweitz examined standing houses in the region. These dwellings are constructed with rubble masonry walls around a series of wooden poles holding them up. The masonry walls are plastered with limestone mortar decorated in patterns made with broken pieces of limestone. The roofs are thatched. Sweitz found four variations on this vernacular building theme and used them to interpret Hacienda San Juan Bautista Tabi, a structure dating to the sixteenth century. His understanding of the site and the region would have been much less thorough without the architectural survey.

Historical archaeologists often must interpret the additions and modifications to standing structures just as they would soil strata discovered during excavation. Archaeologists know a building's history can be "read" like a landscape or archaeological deposit by careful study and analysis.

In 2004, Pamela Smith and Richard Smith were called upon to document the James Graham cottage near Adelaide, Australia, before it was demolished. To provide a full structural history of the building, they had to understand how it had been changed since first constructed. The cottage, built in 1849—only 13 years after the founding of the South Australia colony—had a complex history. Several renovations had occurred between 1850 and the mid-twentieth century. Modernization in the 1920s had effectively hidden the original cottage from view, making a study of the house's history difficult.

Faced with the problem of not being able to see the original structure, Smith and Smith devised a test they could use to identify the individual construction phases. The analysis is based on differences in the size and type of sand used in the mortar and the presence or absence of Portland cement, a product not available in the region until the 1880s. Having collected samples of mortar and render (painted stucco spread over brick faces as decoration) from inside and outside room walls, they submerged each one into 50 milliliters (0.10 pt.) of 10 percent (by mass) hydrochloric acid. They let the mixtures stand for 24 hours and then washed the granular matter left in each sample four times. Once thoroughly dried, they examined each sample under a microscope.

The analysis revealed six phases of construction at the cottage. The original, first phase was composed of a symmetrical four-room house with a slate roof and possibly a lean-to outside kitchen. Phase 2, probably dating 1860–1875, included the construction of two large rooms on the west side of the house. Phase 3, following closely after Phase 2, involved enlarging and enclosing the kitchen. The enclosure of the back veranda occurred in the fourth phase, probably between 1890 and 1900. The modernization in Phase 5 took place in the 1920s, and the final phase occurred in the 1980s when the local government renovated the house and converted it into a community center.

The research conducted by Smith and Smith at the Graham Cottage may not immediately seem like archaeology. After all, they conducted no excavations. All their research occurred above ground, as they essentially worked like architectural historians documenting the history of an old building. This research, however, highlights that twenty-first-century historical archaeology is a versatile discipline with links to many other disciplines. Historical archaeologists can use historical records, oral interviews, and architectural information to create powerful, rich pictures of the past. These images, constructed with materials gleaned from numerous so-called "nonarchaeological" sources, add a more human, personal touch to our current understanding of history. They help us appreciate the experience of living in the past. In the next chapter, we turn to the actual excavation of historic sites and the processing of the artifacts in the laboratory.

Site Visit: La Surveillante, Bantry Bay, Ireland, 1797

After a long and complex series of false starts, rumors, and international negotiations, the French military, under ultimate command of Napoleon Bonaparte, decided to assist the Irish in their quest for independence from Britain. Many radical Irish men and women had long wished to free themselves from their powerful neighbor to the east, and with the rise of the revolutionary United Irishmen in the 1790s, the dream seemed possible. The basic idea behind the plan, seen strictly from a military standpoint, was to have Irish citizens rise up against their English overlords and defeat them at home with the support of French allies. When the plan succeeded, the British island would precariously stand between two hostile powers: France to the east and the Hibernian-Franco alliance to the west. To bring the plan to fruition, the French planned to send a huge flotilla to rendezvous with the United Irishmen in Ireland.

The fleet left Brest under command of Vice-Admiral Morard de Galles in mid-December 1796. Their impressive armada was composed of 17 lines of battle ships, 13 frigates, six corvettes, and eight transports. One frigate specifically carried supplies of powder for the fleet. A force of 13,000 soldiers and cavalry were also on board under the command of General Lazare Hoche. They would comprise the landing party.

The passage to Ireland was doomed from the start. The formidable English Navy had blockaded Brest for months, and so running the blockage was no easy matter, especially at a time when ships' captains had to rely solely on the wind. Not knowing the precise location of the British vessels, and attempting to take advantage of favorable winds at night, the French armada was quickly thrown into confusion. One ship, armed with 74 cannons, was run aground, and more than 600 men were lost. The other ships became scattered in the dense fog, and the fleet became hopelessly separated. In the face of such chaos, the French captains agreed to meet off the coast of Mizen Head, on the extreme south-west corner of Ireland. They hoped to collect their accumulated strength and then continue with the planned invasion. The French sought to land at Bantry Bay, in the southwest, because of its ready access to the city of Cork. If they could control this important town, the British forces in the Province of Munster would be in serious trouble. The French would be able to open an undefended gateway for the importation of more troops. On December 21, the reduced fleet made for Bantry Bay, but overshot it because of poor visibility. On finally making the bay, the fleet was once again plagued by foul weather. Snowy gales blowing against the fleet threatened to spoil the invasion for good. At least two of the ships were blown 300 miles (483 km) off course into the Atlantic. Before long, British warships entering the bay added to the confusion of the French. *La Surveillante* was taking on water to such an extent that her crew decided to abandon and scuttle her. They did so on January 2, 1797, in 111 feet (34 m) of water. *La Surveillante* was a small frigate. Built in 1765, she measured about 143 feet (43.5 m) long. She was triple-masted and had two decks; the lower deck was the gun deck. *La Surveillante* was one of only 12 French ships to have her hull fitted with thin copper sheeting, installed to protect her from marine borers, barnacles, and other potentially damaging ocean-borne organisms. French naval engineers used bronze nails and bolts to fix the sheathing to the ship's wooden hull. They expected the protective cooper coating to last about five years. The French ranked their warships based on the number of cannon they carried. First-rate ships had 100 guns on three decks, and second-rate ships had 90 guns on three decks. Third-rate ships had 64 to 74 guns on two decks, and fourth-rate ships had 50 guns on two decks. Smaller frigates carried between 24 and 40 cannons, and so they were faster and lighter than the heavier, better-armed vessels. *La Surveillante* had 32 guns, 26 12-pounders and six 6-pounders. The crew may have scuttled the ship by raising the anchor up the main-mast and then letting it crash into the deck and hull. The ship's appearance on the ocean floor indicates that the crew did not attempt to remove her heavy cannons. They also did not remove many of their supplies of muskets or many of the other artifacts they carried onboard. The ship probably landed on her stern first and then listed slightly to starboard. With time, the wreck has worked its way into the seabed and now sits in Bantry Bay (Figure 6.9).

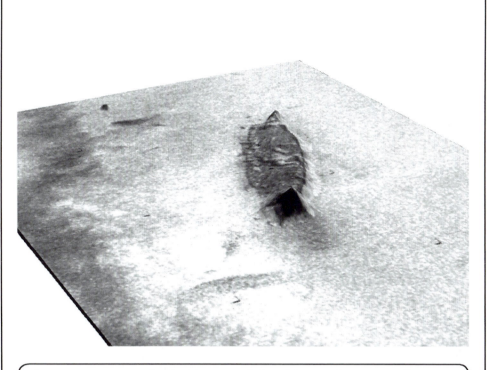

Figure 6.9 3D geophysical image of the shipwreck La Surveillante
on the floor of Bantry Bay, Ireland
(Courtesy of Colin Breen.)

Source: Colin Breen. *Integrated Marine Investigations on the Historic Shipwreck La Surveillante: A French Frigate Lost in Bantry Bay, Ireland, January, 1797.* (Coleraine: University of Ulster, 2001).

Chapter 7

Archaeological Fieldwork

Field and Laboratory

Archaeological research: The very words evoke images of heroes like Indiana Jones hacking their way through dense forests in search of stone pyramids, golden idols, and lost civilizations. Such stereotypes are today only the stuff of Hollywood fantasy; they reflect not what archaeologists really do, only what someone thinks they do. Magazines like *National Geographic,* along with well-produced television programs, paint a far more realistic portrait of archaeology today. Here, scientific excavation is the rule—instead of directing armies of workmen, archaeologists use toothbrushes, dental picks, and high-tech devices in pursuit of the past. The adventurer of yesterday is the time detective of today, logging as many hours in the laboratory as in the field, tracking down historical mysteries with all the scientific fervor of a latter-day Sherlock Holmes. Scientific excavations may appear less spectacular than the more well-funded, over-publicized treasure hunts of pseudo-archaeologists, but they are much more significant. Our fascination with them comes not from the discovery of buried gold, but from uncovering lost knowledge for future generations.

Archaeological stereotypes stress discovery and digging for the simple reason that exploration always engages the enthusiasm of a wide audience. However dazzling the finds, however significant the site, the archaeologist's most important and time-consuming task is not the actual excavation. Excavation, though infinitely exciting, is really a detailed record-keeping process. The notepad and the computer database are as symbolic of today's excavation as the spade and the trowel. This chapter presents some of the basic field and laboratory procedures used by historical archaeologists.

Archaeological Procedures

"All excavation is destruction." With these words, Sir Leonard Woolley, the British excavator of Ur—the great Sumerian city in today's Iraq—succinctly described archaeological excavation. Simply put, when archaeologists excavate a site, they destroy it. They generally destroy it carefully, taking it apart piece by piece, but nonetheless, they do demolish it. As archaeologist Kent Flannery once said, "Archaeology is the only branch of anthropology where we kill off our subjects!" In some ways, archaeological fieldwork is similar to a historian who burns all the documents he or she has read.

The conscious destruction caused by archaeological fieldwork may be difficult to imagine. We generally do not think of archaeologists as people who destroy the very thing they love. Instead, we often envision archaeologists standing boldly in the face of a raging bulldozer, willing to risk life and limb as the last line of defense against the wanton destruction of an important archaeological site. We see archaeologists as frontline warriors in the battle for historic preservation. But it is still true: Archaeologists, usually strong advocates of historic preservation, nonetheless destroy the archaeological sites they excavate. Archaeologists use subsurface surveying methods (see Chapter 5) to minimize the amount of a site's destruction, but site destruction is a sad but inescapable reality.

To understand archaeological excavation, imagine an old library card catalog file, the kind used before the introduction of today's familiar computerized databases. These files contained a single index card for each book in the library. On each card, the librarians had typed the name of the book, its author, the date of publication, the publisher, and its catalogue number (where you would find it in the library). Finding the location of a book on the shelf required thumbing through the files, searching alphabetically by the author's name, or by topic (such as "Amazon River, History of").

Suppose that the catalog has 40 drawers arranged in four rows and ten columns. Each row represents one layer of earth. Each card within the drawers represents one piece of archaeological information. This information can be an artifact, a posthole, a stone foundation wall, a trench, a soil color or texture, or any other element of the archaeological record. If the archaeologist has planned to obtain a 10 percent sample of the site, he or she will be able to look into only four drawers. The archaeologist will remove and keep the ones marked "artifact," but only record the information from the other cards before destroying them. He or she will only be able to write notes about the information contained on a card marked "soil color" and record the measurements written on a card marked "building foundation." Because all of the non-artifact cards must be destroyed (because they cannot be taken to the lab), future investigators will only have 36 drawers left to examine. They also will have the "artifact" cards and the notes the original archaeologist took from the other cards: soil colors, thicknesses of soil layers, width and height of stone walls, the distance between the building foundation and a fence line, and so forth. Once the study is finished, the destroyed cards will be lost forever. Only the written record of the destroyed cards will remain.

This example is fictional. Archaeological sites are not wooden file boxes filled with cards. Nonetheless, field archaeologists repeat much of the process just described. Some of the archaeological record vanishes forever (soil layers, delicate pit outlines), and some of it (artifacts, collected soil samples) ends up in a museum or university. Archaeologists destroy many archaeological features by the realities of excavation. When Kenneth Kidd excavated Sainte Marie I in 1941, the seventeenth-century Jesuit mission in Ontario mentioned in Chapter 2, he was only able to measure, record, and photograph the small postholes the mission's builders had placed beneath the still-visible wooden sill of the chapel's original wall. Kidd could not actually save the postholes themselves because they were simply dark stains in the soil. All anyone knows about these postholes today derives from Kidd's records and archaeological report; the holes themselves no longer exist. Kidd must be believed when stating that the posts had an average diameter of "4 inches" (10 cm) and an average depth of "about 20 inches" (51 cm). The postholes disappeared long ago.

Historical archaeologists generally follow the same excavation procedures as all other archaeologists. They excavate a colonial tavern in Cape Town, South Africa, with the same basic methods used to excavate an eleventh-century Anasazi pueblo in Arizona. Excavation is an unfolding process of carefully applied scientific procedures, techniques developed and refined by decades of archaeological research.

The Process of Archaeological Research

Excavation, like other research procedures, is slow and meticulous. Each excavation is unique in some ways, but six stages are common to all of them, extending from the earliest ideas about how to conduct the excavation to the final process of publication.

Research Design

All archaeological fieldwork begins with a carefully developed *research design*. A research design is an organized plan for carrying out the project. It includes explicit statements on how the archaeologist will attempt to answer the research questions posed before the excavation begins. The number of sites to be investigated, the size of the sample, and the kinds of specialists to be involved are all specified in the research design.

In an ideal world, an archaeologist would construct a research design based solely on the needs and requirements of the research. It would be comforting to think archaeologists can always conduct the research of interest to them in the best and most scientific ways. Much archaeology is conducted in this manner.

For example, when Prudence Rice was interested in learning about the development of the colonial wine industry in southern Peru, she created a research design involving surveys and the collection of data from an entire valley. History showed that the faraway Spanish mainland was incapable of supplying the region with wine for religious and secular purposes, so the colonists had to import and plant their own vines. The theoretical basis of Rice's research was rooted in world-systems theory, frontier theory, and various ideas about material and technological change. She located 130 different sites in the valley and conducted limited excavations at 28 of them. Her immediate research universe was one valley in southern Peru, but her analysis reached all the way to Spain itself. In this sense, her research design had few limits pressed upon it, except perhaps the normal ones accompanying any archaeological field project.

Most excavators find, however, that they must balance what they want to do with what they can realistically accomplish given constraints placed upon them. (And even Rice faced constraints.) Funding limitations, the availability of students and other field workers, the difficulty of obtaining permits and licenses, the presence of dangerous political situations, and environmental catastrophes can all affect archaeological research. Almost anything can happen to change the course of an archaeological field project. Even the most well-planned research design must be flexible enough to adapt to the changing conditions of fieldwork.

Archaeologists who work in the realm of cultural resource (or heritage) management are called upon every day to create research designs that are cost-effective and tightly scheduled (see Chapter 9). Cultural resource management (CRM) studies are completed to ensure that important archaeological sites and historical properties are not destroyed by construction projects before the sites can be adequately studied. Archaeologists in this environment regularly collaborate with private companies and governmental bodies, including those in charge of highways, municipalities, and environmental protection. CRM studies, being conducted for specific purposes, are usually restricted to a particular, well-defined place, such as the route of a new road.

For example, a team of archaeologists from Sonoma State University directed by Adrian and Mary Praetzellis, performed a study for the California Department of Transportation.

The goal of the highway department was to upgrade and widen the San Francisco Central Freeway in San Francisco. Federal law required the highway department to engage archaeologists. The archaeologists' mandate was to examine the construction area to ensure that no important sites would be destroyed before analysis. But, because the highway had a specific, predetermined route, the archaeologists were restricted to examining only those city blocks directly affected by it (Figure 7.1). They were able to excavate only within the designated

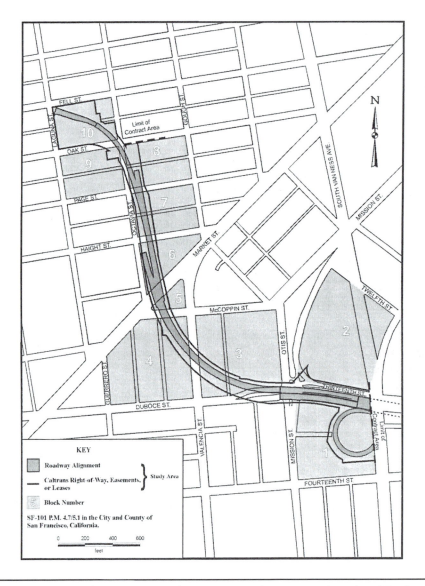

Figure 7.1 Central Freeway Replacement Project area, showing blocks included in research design

(From "The San Francisco Central Freeway Replacement project: Arch. Research Design and Treatment Plan" by Grace Ziesing, p. 04 © Anthropological Studies Center, Sonoma State University, 1998.)

city blocks. This restriction meant the archaeologists had to create a research design taking into account both the history of the city and the region, as well as more detailed information about the specific blocks that could be investigated. The archaeologists were able to overlay the route of the highway on historic maps of the city, and along with their archaeological findings, they were able to reconstruct the entire history of their project area.

The research design created by the archaeologists was successful because they planned it extremely well. They were able to use the limitations imposed upon them to present a thorough study of the area. The abundant information they provided did not lead to the reconstruction of the buildings or the creation of a permanent museum exhibit. The highway department's requirements made this impossible. But the research design enabled the archaeologists to document the settlement and growth of an important urban center. They also created an important artifact collection that archaeologists in other areas of the world can access for comparative purposes.

Implementation

Proposal and grant writing, fund raising, the hiring of a qualified crew, and the acquisition of all required permits—every archaeologist spends months on these mundane and sometimes frustrating tasks. But excavation cannot be done without them.

The process of implementation involves proposal writing and perhaps even the refinement of the research plan to accommodate the realities of time and funding. Construction, such as for the San Francisco highway project, is expensive, and construction engineers do not have the luxury of waiting while archaeologists delicately sift through the soil. Archaeologists thus often have a finite—and, in truth, usually far too short—time to complete their fieldwork. If an archaeologist knows only 52 weeks are available to complete an entire project, it does not make sense to plan 50 weeks of fieldwork and only two weeks for analysis and report writing. Archaeologists must be mindful of report deadlines because funding agencies expect to receive final reports within the time specified in the grant or contract.

The implementation phase should include weeks and months when the investigators complete their background research. This research includes a great deal of reading, both archaeological and archival. Oral interviewing and architectural analysis (see Chapter 6) may be required to have begun or even to be completed before the excavation starts.

Fieldwork

The time spent in the field varies infinitely with the research design and available time and funding (Figure 7.2). A complete excavation of a large colonial fortification might require a huge crew and months (and even years) of carefully uncovering foundation trenches, postholes, and building remains. Even more time is needed if the research plan calls for the excavation of villages placed outside the fort's walls.

Every excavation, however modest, requires keeping meticulous records, carefully handling all excavated material, and finding a place to store both. To create a place to compile notes and records, many fieldworkers construct on-site facilities, sometimes as simple as a tarpaulin strung between trees. Other excavators use rented on-site trailers or nearby houses. Archaeologists use these facilities to compile notes, create rough maps, wash and inventory artifact finds, and enter information into databases for future analysis. They may also use the temporary lab for emergency conservation work. In-field processing is preliminary to the permanent, more thorough laboratory analysis that follows any archaeological excavation. On-site processing has the advantage of allowing archaeologists to examine the objects as they are discovered, and enables them to adjust their research design while the excavation is still in progress.

Figure 7.2 Archaeology students excavate the floor areas of the inner and outer rooms of a two-room sod dwelling at the Zapadni site, St. Paul Island, Pribilof Islands, Alaska

(Courtesy of Douglas W. Veltre.)

Analysis

Most excavators think one month in the field requires at least three months in the laboratory. This estimate may be conservative because special circumstances may prolong the analysis for many months, and even years. This important time is when researchers process the information they have collected during fieldwork. This exacting research, so vital to good archaeological practice, is seldom understood by the public because it is not accomplished in the field, where people can watch archaeologists at work.

An archaeological lab usually has large, long tables for cleaning, marking, and analyzing artifacts. The laboratory workers have access to precise measuring tools (such as digital calipers), scales, and microscopes, while they enter information directly into computer databases. Some excavators use bar codes to mark bags of artifacts. Most field laboratories also have small libraries and artifact reference collections for comparison with excavated pieces. The field team must process and accession all the artifacts in a consistent format for future identification and for long-term storage. Most storage facilities now have curation standards to which field archaeologists must adhere if they wish to have their artifacts stored there. Archaeologists must obtain these standards (which probably vary from place to place) before they begin to catalog their specimens.

A flurry of activity begins once the materials are back at the home lab. Oral interviews must be transcribed from recording devices, architectural plans must be cleaned up and finalized (if they exist as part of the project), and all photos must be catalogued. The archaeologists must decide which photos, maps, and plans they wish to include in their reports and publications, and these must be finalized and readied.

When all the finds are properly accessioned, the research team examines each one, describes it, and prepares inventories and tables showing the kinds and quantities of artifacts they found at the site. In most cases, the analysis phase is when archaeologists may call on specialists to assist them. These individuals may be experts in radiometric dating (see Chapter 4), geology, or other sciences.

Laboratory-based research can be detailed and revealing. Analyses of animal bones (faunal material) and plant matter (floral material) are mainstays of laboratory research in archaeology in general and historical archaeology specifically. Research in these areas often proves invaluable for understanding the realities of past lived experience.

Plant and animal food remains require not only preliminary sorting on site, but careful analysis by specialists. Such finds are vitally important because they enable excavators to reconstruct the dietary habits of past households, neighborhoods, and communities.

Interpretation

Interpretation tests an archaeologist's skills, knowledge, creativity, and understanding. It is the process of making sense of all the accumulated data and of interpreting it in terms of theoretical perspectives. Historical archaeologists use a wide range of theories from anthropology and other fields—including history, sociology, geography, and political science—for this purpose (see Chapters 10, 11, and 12).

The interpretations historical archaeologists offer about the sites they study are varied and sometimes even controversial. No formula can be presented to show precisely how archaeologists frame their interpretations. Ideas about the past ultimately spring from an individual's attitudes, perceptions, interests, knowledge, creativity, and educational experiences. Interpretations also tend to be like fashion: They come into style, and after a while, they go out of vogue and are discarded.

Publication

No archaeological project is truly complete until the results are published. Without some dissemination of their findings and interpretations, the excavators have done nothing more than wrest artifacts from the ground. The act of recovery can be meaningful when a site is threatened with imminent destruction, but unless the results of an excavation are widely available, the archaeological information is effectively lost and the site is destroyed forever.

Specialist archaeological site reports are usually highly technical and are published in ways not readily accessible to nonarchaeologists. The report on the San Francisco freeway mentioned above, for example, was submitted to the California Department of Transportation. This report is a highly professional account of the research, with a great deal of important information, but nonarchaeologists are probably unaware this report even exists. Professional historical archaeologists know about it, but it is largely inaccessible to a wider audience.

To counteract the problem of making archaeological material available to a broad audience, some historical archaeologists write popular accounts of their research in addition to their highly technical site reports. Ivor Noël Hume is well known for his ability to make dense, complex archaeological information accessible to the public. His *Martin's Hundred: The Discovery of a Lost Colonial Virginia Settlement*, detailing the excavations at Wolstenholme Towne, Virginia, stands as one of the great popular accounts of historical archaeology. His book *If These Pots Could Talk: Collecting 2,000 Years of British Household Pottery* is a masterwork that recounts 40 years of knowledge about everyday British ceramics. Noël Hume wrote it for everyone interested in ceramics: collectors, archaeologists, amateur historians, and the general public.

Writing for the public is a major concern of all archaeologists, including historical archaeologists. Most archaeologists accept that their profession relies on the good graces of funding agencies and other bodies controlling financial resources or which have an interest in history and historical preservation. In his book *Writing About Archaeology*, Graham Connah asks "For who are we writing?" He observes that archaeologists have transformed what the world knows about the collective human past and acknowledges this has been a great gift to society. Too often, however, archaeologists tend to write only for other archaeologists, so much of what they produce is highly technical. Many archaeologists, however, think about their various audiences and write pamphlets, popular articles, and books for the general public, in addition to creating museum exhibits and other educational materials.

Excavation

The thrill of archaeological discovery is very real, but extreme caution is the watchword. British excavator Sir Mortimer Wheeler, one of the finest excavators in archaeological history, said that "It is essential to check any sort of excitement instantly, and to insist firmly on quiet routine." Professional archaeological excavation is as much science as a carefully controlled experiment in a chemistry lab, even though the conditions are usually far different. Field archaeologists must contend with the weather, tourists, insects, and maybe even local political situations, all of which may demand the archaeologists to think quickly and innovatively, but always with a concern for care. For example, when Noël Hume excavated at Martin's Hundred, his excavators found an early seventeenth-century close helmet, the first ever found in North America. A close helmet has a heavy visor that can be closed to cover and protect the entire head and face. The much-corroded find took many hours to remove in one piece from the ground, but the entire removal took place under controlled conditions. Everyone knew that undue haste could break the helmet into tiny pieces and it would be lost forever. Only complete patience and the utmost care could save the specimen.

The same may be said for every archaeological excavation conducted by professional archaeologists. Because excavation is a destructive process, archaeologists have an ethical responsibility to be careful and attentive. Edward Harris refers to this requirement as "the ethics of archaeological destruction of scientific evidence," and he is correct.

Mapping

People visiting an archaeological site for the first time may be surprised to find many excavators, perhaps even most of them, hunched over maps rather than actively digging in the ground. The public imagines archaeologists to be excavators first and foremost and they are not wrong. But archaeology without mapping would be a pointless scientific exercise, little better than looting. Maps—of the entire site, building foundations, the distribution of artifacts, and individual human-made postholes, pits, depressions, and other features—are every bit as important as the excavated artifacts. Archaeologists rely on their field maps to help them understand the site once they return to the lab and begin to analyze, interpret, and write.

One of the most important maps archaeologists make is the main site map. This is a plat showing the entire extent of the site, including the topography, the excavations, and everything else of note, such as the placement of standing structures, large trees, the limits of vegetation, and the location of nearby watercourses.

Archaeologists can make simple maps using nothing but a tape measure and a good compass. In most cases, however, archaeologists prefer more accuracy, and most have access to surveyor's tools useful for making accurate maps. A variety of tools exists, extending from simple surveyor's transits to sophisticated total stations and GPS devices.

Before the availability of total stations, archaeologists generally had to make do with second-hand surveyor's transits. These instruments, though easy to use, required the use of hand-held tape measures and the recording of all information by hand (Figure 7.3). Today, most archaeologists have access to total stations. A total station is a sophisticated surveying instrument able to record linear distances, elevations, and horizontal locations with a high level of accuracy. The total station shoots a laser or infrared beam to a prism located on a pole, the information bounces back, and is automatically recorded in a data logger located on one of the machine's tripod legs. The collected information can be downloaded from the data logger into a computer to generate maps and conduct analysis. Great accuracy is achieved because no need exists to stretch tape measures, which can droop or flutter in the wind, across the site.

Most field archaeologists also use a GPS (global positioning system) device to determine their precise location on the earth's surface. GPS receivers can be inexpensive hand-held models or expensive permanent stations. They work by linking to satellites orbiting the earth. Their accuracy varies with their quality, and for highly accurate surveys, many archaeologists use a DGPS (differential GPS). This system provides greater accuracy by calculating the difference between the estimated location and the actual location. In many cases, the use of a GPS receiver allows an archaeologist to tie his or her site's location directly to a national locational grid and to other georeferencing systems.

An increasing number of historical archaeologists are also using a high-tech mapping application called LiDAR, or Light Detection and Ranging. The system consists of an aircraft-mounted laser that can record thousands of elevation measurements per second with incredible accuracy (to about 15 cm or 6 in). They system's ability to record small changes in the earth's surface, added to its data being accessible for GIS analysis, makes LiDAR extremely valuable.

Archaeologists in Maryland used LiDAR to investigate two eighteenth-century plantations. The goals of the research were to study the garden landscapes in a more accurate way

175

Figure 7.3 Archaeology students survey the remains of Russian and Aleut sod houses at the Zapadni site, St. Paul Island, Pribilof Islands, Alaska

(Courtesy of Douglas W. Veltre.)

than is possible with existing two-dimensional maps and plans, and to evaluate the usefulness of LiDAR for such research. Once the data were retrieved, analyzed, and manipulated, the archaeologists were able to identify a number of features on the landscape, including even the location of past excavations and backdirt piles. The ability of LiDAR to show small changes in the topography of a landscape is a great asset to archaeological research because it means that areas of potential archaeological interest can be identified even if they are ephemeral or exhibit no surface expression. Such places may otherwise be easily overlooked.

Contexts of Space and Time

All excavation is based on the contexts of space and time (see Chapter 4). As a result, excavators must record data in two dimensions—horizontal and vertical. The horizontal dimension is maintained with the use of a site grid, a checkerboard of standard-sized squares placed across the entire site. There is nothing magical about the size of square chosen. Archaeologists decide in their research design which size will meet their needs for the particular site being excavated. Historical archaeologists sometimes disagree over the use of meters and centimeters or feet and inches, but regardless of the measurement scale used, each square in the grid receives a unique designation based on its distance from a datum point, or main point of reference, keyed into the site map. Field archaeologists can distinguish all the material from every excavation unit from all other finds, structures, and features by reference to the square's designation.

Archaeological grids work by reference to the main datum point. Upon approaching a site for the first time, an archaeologist planning fieldwork will establish a datum point, often referred to as the 0,0 (zero, zero) point. The excavators will record everything in reference to this point. It helps to imagine the entire site covered with an imaginary grid of regular sized squares. If a site has 1-meter-square grid placed over it, a spot located 10 meters due north of the 0,0 point will be designed 0E 10N and a point 10 meters due east will be 10E 0N. A point 5 meters east and 5 meters north would be 5E 5N. The corner of a brick fireplace might be located 25 meters east of 0,0 and 18 meters north, and designated as 25E 18N (Figure 7.4).

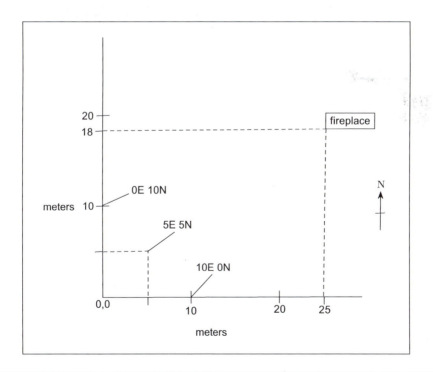

Figure 7.4 Simplified archaeological grid system
(Charles E. Orser, Jr.)

The strength of the grid system is that it can be expanded as necessary without changing any of the prior designations. In the example, the archaeologist could expand the grid to the south and west and not affect the grid structure.

This system may seem confusing at first, but it is essential to archaeological field research because this is how archaeologists know precisely where objects and human-made features are located in space. It does not matter what system an archaeologist adopts. Some archaeologists may write the north designation before the east, while others may use feet and inches rather than centimeters and meters. Other archaeologists may adopt a completely different system using numbers and letters for their grid identifiers. What matters is consistency. The excavation records will be a mess without the adoption of careful regularity. In the worst cases, the research may be useless.

The use of a reference point also allows archaeologists to keep accurate records on horizontal location year after year, and even permits someone else to excavate the same site and to use the identical grid years later. For example, when Samuel Smith, a historical archaeologist with the State of Tennessee's Division of Archaeology, excavated Fort Southwest Point, a late-eighteenth- and early nineteenth-century American military post in eastern Tennessee, he used a grid of 10-foot (3.1 m) squares (Figure 7.5). When he started, he thought the grid covered the entire site. But when he revisited the site two years later, he discovered he had to expand the grid to conduct further excavations on one end of the site. Because he used a uniform grid in the first place, he had no problem expanding it. Also, because the grid was regular, he was easily able to correlate the information from the new part of the site with the

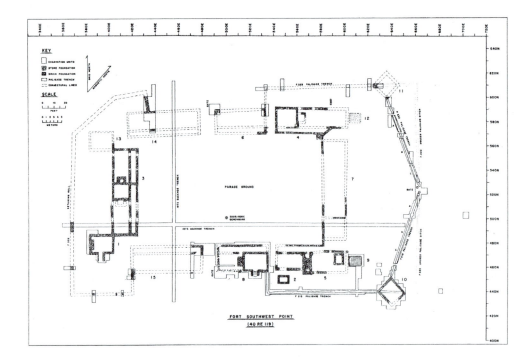

Figure 7.5 Excavations at Fort Southwest Point, Tennessee, 1973–1986, showing grid
(Tennessee Division of Archaeology)

material found earlier. The grid allowed Smith to keep track of the horizontal location of the 34,666 artifacts he found at the fort.

Space is horizontal; time is vertical. As we saw in Chapter 4, the context of time is based on the Law of Superposition, on stratified layers identified during excavation. At Fort Southwest Point, Smith divided the history of the post into five stages, based on historical documents: 1779–1796, 1797–1800, 1801–1807, 1808–1811, and 1812–present. He would have preferred to isolate each historical stage in distinct, easily distinguishable soil layers, but the correlation between the historical phases and the soil layers was not so clear. When he excavated a 40-foot (12.2 m) long trench through a depression in the soil, he discovered two parallel stone walls from a barracks building and no fewer than 11 separate soil layers.

Soil and artifacts are deposited in layers, so archaeologists like to excavate each layer separately. Historic sites can be particularly challenging in this regard, not only because they may have been occupied for only a few generations, or at most for a few centuries, but also because the occupation layers can be extremely thin (see Chapter 4). Consider a major city, like London or New York, where generation after generation has repeatedly rebuilt on the same spot. When contractors clear away the earlier buildings and their foundations, all that may be left for archaeologists are small lenses of soil and datable artifacts that can take months to analyze and interpret. Thin soils also appear at sites inhabited for brief periods.

As is true of the need of a horizontal grid over the site, archaeologists must also know where objects and features are located vertically. The Law of Superposition holds that objects, features, and soils found beneath others will be earlier in date if the landscape has not been disturbed. Thus, knowing where something was located vertically in terms of other things helps archaeologists interpret a site's history.

To keep records of vertical depth, archaeologists use a zero datum plane. This is an imaginary line, or plane, constructed over the grid. Archaeologists can establish this line with a surveying instrument, and given the hi-tech nature of today's machines, they can usually tie it directly to sea level if they wish. The use of this plane permits archaeologists to keep records on the depth of artifacts and features. Using a total station, they can even piece-plot every artifact they find in the ground. This means that they can obtain precise information about the horizontal and vertical position of every artifact and feature found during excavation. In many cases, archaeologists will measure objects in relation to the datum plane and in reference to depth under the surface. In any case, paying close attention to the vertical locations of things in the earth is a central aspect of archaeological field research. Failure to record such measurements is merely looting.

Methods

Like all archaeologists, historical archaeologists conduct both vertical and horizontal excavations, depending on their research design. *Vertical excavation* is used at small sites or in situations where the archaeological team has limited time and funds. This kind of investigation is intended to provide as much information as possible without excavating a large portion of a site. In vertical excavation, only small parts of a site are investigated with trenches and small excavations usually measuring less than 10 feet (3.1 m) square. Archaeologists refer to the smallest vertical excavations as "tests" or "test excavations."

One of the smallest testing methods is the "shovel test." Archaeologists use this method to determine the depth and horizontal extent of a site and to indicate the presence of artifacts and other features. Thus, shovel tests offer a quick way to assess the site's subsurface without major disturbance.

Shovel tests, holes about the size of a shovel, are manually dug into the ground. Archaeologists wishing to discover the horizontal extent of a site will often dig two perpendicular lines of shovel tests, one running due north–south and one running due east–west. This cross-shaped testing pattern will usually indicate the site's horizontal limits. When the artifacts no longer appear in the tests, chances are the boundaries of the site have been reached. In other cases, archaeologists will use clusters of shovel tests to identify activity areas.

The discovery of activity areas was the goal of the archaeologists planning to excavate at Sylvester Manor in Shelter Island, on the far eastern tip of Long Island, New York. The manor, established in 1652, was a source of provisions for sugar plantations in Barbados during colonial times. The estate originally encompassed all 8,000 acres (3,238 ha) of the island, but now includes only 250 acres (101 ha). In this large area is the still-standing dwelling house built around 1735. The long history of the manor—residents still occupied it when the archaeologists arrived in in the late 1990s—witnessed many activities and a diverse collection of residents and visitors, including Native Americans, enslaved Africans, and Europeans. Given the substantial history of the manor, coupled with the size of the estate, the archaeologists, under the direction of Stephen Mrozowski, dug a series of 50 by 50 cm (20 by 20 in) shovel tests in grids placed south, west, north, and east of the standing manor house (Figure 7.6). Concentrations of artifacts found within the shovel tests allowed the archaeologists to target specific locations for more intensive excavation. In an area termed the North Peninsula, for example, the shovel tests located a high concentration of seventeenth-century European ceramics and bricks. On the Southeast Lawn, the archaeologists excavated lines (or transects) of shovel tests placed every two and ten meters (seven and 33 ft). These tests revealed a large midden and an area of tightly packed cobblestones. The archaeologists focused much of their excavation on this part of the site.

Archaeologists at Fort Southwest Point, Tennessee, initially used vertical excavation as a quick and relatively easy way to locate building foundations. They used a mechanical backhoe to cut two long, perpendicular trenches through the center of the site (Figure 7.7). One trench, running southeast to northwest, was 185 feet (56.4 m) long; the other, running southwest to northeast, extended for 300 feet (91.5 m). The second trench crossed six different walls.

Archaeologists use mechanical equipment in rare cases or when time is extremely limited. The use of mechanical excavators speeds up the potential for discovery but increases the chance to damage or even destroy fragile archaeological features. As a result, archaeologists must consider the pros and cons of using machines and consider whether the benefits outweigh the possible harm to subsurface deposits.

In the second season of research at Fort Southwest Point, the crew excavated a number of 10-foot-squares (3.1 m). These excavations gave them more control than the mechanical excavation, but at the cost of much slower progress. The use of the smaller test excavations meant, however, that they could locate buried features more carefully. They could also simultaneously investigate several areas. They knew they could wait to conduct complete excavation of features until more funds became available.

Ten years passed before the State of Tennessee developed plans to reconstruct Fort Southwest Point. The archaeologists had to alter their research design from merely locating foundations and other features to large-scale archaeological investigation planned to provide information useful in the reconstruction. They continued to use limited vertical excavation to relocate the buried walls found earlier and to find still-undiscovered foundations. Their new research design, however, called for horizontal excavation.

Archaeologists use *horizontal excavation,* also called "area" or "block" excavation, to expose entire building foundations and large areas of sites. By exposing entire buildings,

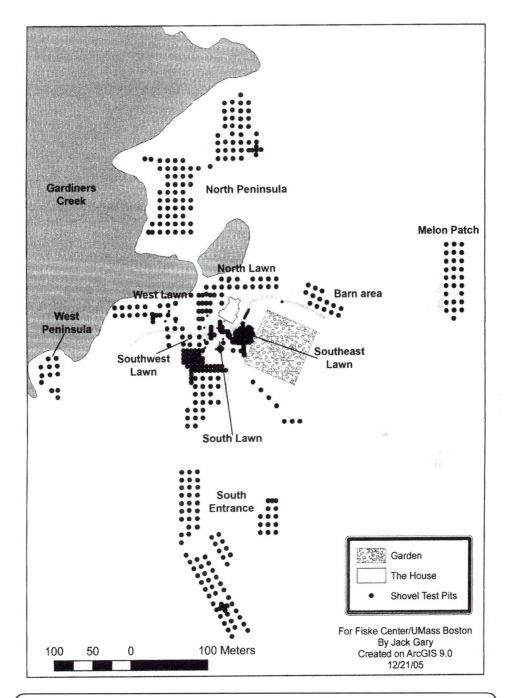

Figure 7.6 Sylvester Manor, Long Island, New York, site areas showing locations of shovel tests

(From Field Excavations at Sylvester Manor by Katherine Howlett Hayes in *Northeast Historical Archaeology* 36 [2007].)

Figure 7.7 Vertical trench excavation in the west wall of Southwest Point, Tennessee
(Tennessee Division of Archaeology)

excavators can study the architecture, as well as the spatial relationships between wells, out-buildings, houses, dumps, and other features, to say nothing of the internal alterations made to a building over long periods.

Horizontal excavation worked well at Fort Southwest Point because the archaeologists wanted to expose entire building foundations. Before horizontal excavation, a probable building called Structure 8 appeared merely as a large depression on the northeast side of the fort. Excavation over this depression measured roughly 30 by 46 feet (9.2 by 14.0 m) in size (Figure 7.8). The archaeologists perfectly planned their excavation strategy because the foundation of Structure 8 was only 22 feet wide and 43 feet long (6.7 by 13.1 m). The build-ers had positioned it directly in front of the fort's front wall so that anyone approaching the fort would have encountered it before the exterior wall itself (Figure 7.9). Careful excavation of Structure 8 allowed archaeologists to envision how it had been built. Constructed of logs, the building had two stories and a long porch on the front side. Inside were plank floors and a central chimney. It may have had windows, but only on the side facing the fort.

Archaeologists found three clay stairs leading down to the building's cellar. This find caused them to wonder whether the fort's residents had used this building for storing valuable goods when the fort served as the Cherokee Indian Agency in the early nineteenth century. Local Native Americans received ploughs, spinning wheels, and other "civilizing" items from the U.S. government at the fort during this period. The fort's designers may have constructed the steps into the cellar so that Native Americans could receive their objects without actually entering the fort itself (Figure 7.10).

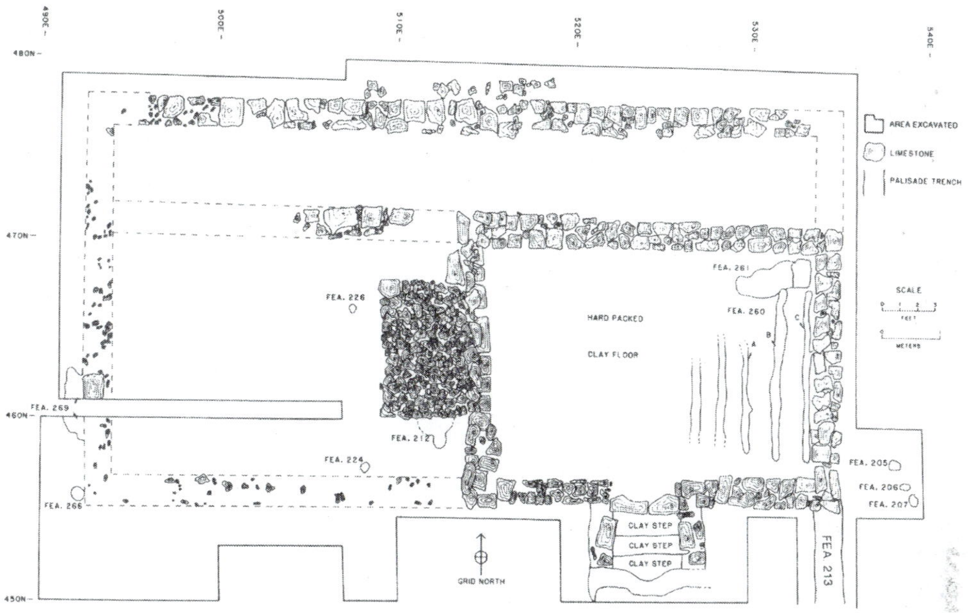

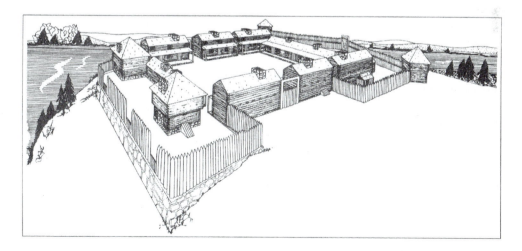

Figure 7.8 Map of horizontal excavation of Structure 8, Fort Southwest
Point, Tennessee

(Tennessee Division of Archaeology)

Figure 7.9 Artist's reconstruction of Fort Southwest Point, Tennessee,
based on archaeological findings. Structure 8 is to the right of
the main gate. The entrance to the cellar appears in front.

(Tennessee Division of Archaeology)

Figure 7.10 Structure 8, Fort Southwest Point, Tennessee, before and after horizontal excavation

(Tennessee Division of Archaeology)

Tools

Archaeological excavation is a deliberate, slow-moving process that requires infinite patience. Patience pays off, however, because, as excavations at Fort Southwest Point show, much can be revealed through painstaking excavation. The spade and the diamond-shaped mason's "pointing trowel" constitute the symbols of archaeological excavation. Today's archaeologists can use everything from backhoes to the smallest brushes and dental picks. Any digging tool, even a backhoe, can be useful in the hands of an expert. In most cases, archaeologists rely on trowels, shovels, and wheelbarrows to remove the earth from archaeological sites.

The archaeologist's trowel is a remarkable implement, used both for straightening the edges of excavations and smoothing stratigraphic profiles, and for exposing house foundations, hearths, and other features. It is most efficient when its long edges scrape delicately across damp soil, delineating the boundary between a dark, inconspicuous soil stain (like a posthole) and the surrounding lighter soil. No fieldworker ever walks without a trowel in hand, for it is the archaeologist's Swiss army knife.

Archaeologists sometimes discover, however, that a trowel is simply too coarse a tool for the job at hand. Cleaning delicate animal bones, exposing waterlogged plant remains, and removing soil from a decaying mud wall are all common archaeological tasks. The archaeologist hunched over an excavation carefully removing tiny grains of soil bears a striking similarity to a watchmaker bent over the tiniest screws, springs, and gears. Both jobs require patience and skill. Dustpans, whiskbrooms, paintbrushes, dental picks, and even sharpened pieces of bamboo come into play at critical moments. Dental picks are especially useful when cleaning bones because their many working edges allow archaeologists to scoop and scrape, lever, or dig tiny holes, just as your dentist does on your teeth. Many archaeologists make friends with their dentists just to acquire their worn-out tools!

Archaeologists regularly screen all, or in some cases a sizable portion of, the soil they excavate. This procedure is especially important in historical archaeology because screens catch the smallest artifacts—straight pins, glass beads, buttons—used in homes across the world in modern times. The size of the screen mesh varies with the problem at hand, but most historical archaeologists prefer quarter-inch (6.35 mm) or even 8-inch (5.08 mm) mesh to recover glass beads and other tiny objects. For example, the archaeologists at Sylvester Manor used both mesh sizes to ensure they would collect even the tiniest artifacts. Tiny artifacts, what James Deetz famously termed "small things forgotten," can offer important insights on the past. As such, historical archaeologists do everything in their power to collect them.

Field Recording

"Excavation, no matter how skillfully conducted, is sheer wasted effort unless the results are properly recorded." These words of Ivor Noël Hume, renowned excavator of Colonial Williamsburg, emphasize the need for careful record keeping in archaeological research. Without accurate records, even the best excavation is merely an exercise in destruction. In the final analysis, every archaeological excavation is only as good as the records that survive from it. Here are some of the day-to-day records kept on a well-organized excavation:

● *Field Notes.* Notes compiled during the progress of the fieldwork are the diary of the excavation. Their authors meticulously and thoroughly describe the daily activities on site. Field notes are the synthesis of the excavation and are the place where stratigraphy is initially analyzed and unfolding interpretations of the site are jotted down. They provide a record of the locations of structures and major finds. Field notes are compiled not only for the excavator's use but also as a permanent record for posterity. Visitors to archaeological sites are likely to see as many people writing in their field books as actually digging.

- Keepers of field notes should err on the side of over-coverage. Nothing is worse than inadequate notes omitting critical stratigraphic information or architectural data. The great Mesopotamian archaeologist Leonard Woolley used to inspect his assistants' field notes every evening. He was right, for these notes contain the only insights and observations of an excavation while it is occurring.
- Some archaeologists write their notes directly into their laptop computers or tablets while in the field. This practice is fine if at the end of the day they are able to create a backup copy. Too many things can go wrong, especially in often hot and dusty field conditions, to compile only a digital record of the excavation.

● *Site Maps and Plans.* This body of data from an excavation includes a detailed scale map of the entire site, drawings of each excavation unit with stratigraphic profiles, a complete stratigraphic sequence of the entire site, plans of all human-built features, and architectural drawings if appropriate. Being created in the field, they constitute a directly observed record of the archaeological contexts destroyed by excavation.

● *Artifact Inventory.* The inventory includes a complete list of all artifact finds. This list is most often stored on a computer, with specific find information entered into a database accessible using any number of search commands.

● *Photographic Record.* The photographic record accompanies the maps, plans, and field notes as primary documentation of the excavation. The photo record is today generally composed of digital images. These images depict the progress of the excavation from start to finish. Selected photos must appear in published reports, articles, and websites because they depict important finds and architectural elements as they appeared during excavation.

● *Administrative Records and Accounts.* These records contain the practical aspect of the archaeological fieldwork. They include information about the crew's labor: when each person worked and how many hours they spent in the field. They also include a running total of the project's expenses so that the chief archaeologist can keep track of the day-to-day costs of the excavation. These records collectively provide an irreplaceable archive of the project. Even after the archaeologists have published the final report of the excavation, the administrative records are a vital part of the archaeological record and should be preserved as archival records.

Conservation

The soil is often the archaeologist's worst enemy, for the chemicals within it and the conditions it endures can play havoc on the archaeological record. Miracles of survival sometimes come to light, like the early seventeenth-century silver teething stick found at Jamestown, Virginia. Most often, however, natural soil chemicals cause both perishable wood and other organic artifacts and food remains to deteriorate and often to disappear completely. When Kenneth Kidd discovered the postholes at the Sainte Marie I site, all that remained were dark stains in the soil where the posts had once stood. The earth's chemicals had caused the wood itself to rot away long ago.

Luckily, not all objects disappear completely, even in the harshest conditions. Ceramics, glass, and stone objects typically survive. Objects of iron, lead, pewter, copper, gold, and silver can endure with the proper soil and climatic conditions, but many will vanish in time. Leather, wood, and even paper sometimes remain over short periods or in waterlogged or very dry conditions. When excavating Fort Bowie, a nineteenth-century U.S.

Army post at Apache Pass, Arizona, for example, archaeologists found soda pop bottles with the remnants of labels still adhering to them. These bottles indicate the soldiers at the fort drank strawberry soda, sarsaparilla with iron, and orange cider. When archaeologists examined the remains of a Missouri River steamer named *Bertrand*—which hit a snag in the river and sank on April 1, 1865—they found several bottles and jars with their labels still intact. They also discovered numerous boxes stamped with the products' names, the wholesalers' names, their places of origin, and their final destinations in the American West.

Artifact conservation is a serious and difficult task, and conservator Per Guldbeck's description of the work as being similar to a surgeon saving someone's life after an accident is appropriate. Like surgeons, artifact conservators must be highly trained and have equal doses of common sense, knowledge of chemistry, and patience. Laboratory conservation is rarely dramatic. It is typically a slow process that involves weeks, even months, of delicate renovation, soaking organic materials in chemicals, and devising ingenious restoration techniques. The slow process of preserving wood from sunken ships can take years of preparation. The procedures, though often routine and well established, change as techniques become more sophisticated and as better products come on the market. The hardest part is often judging when the expense of permanent conservation is justified. Complete conservation is usually reserved only for special artifacts destined for museum display or for unusually important and unique finds.

Some of the most dramatic conservation efforts occur in the field, as archaeologists struggle to save a unique, delicate artifact from destruction. As mentioned above, Ivor Noël Hume's discovery of an early seventeenth-century close helmet at Wolstenholme Towne is a perfect example.

The excavators faced the challenging problem of how to remove the helmet so that conservators could stabilize it for study and museum display. When first discovered, the helmet was no longer actually iron; the soil had reduced it to a rusty ferrous shell encased in clay. Its discoverers would have utterly destroyed it if they had attempted to remove it like any other artifact. As a result, conservators devised a simple scheme to remove the helmet from the surrounding soil. They built a steel box frame around it then poured a silicone molding compound into the box. The 200-pound (91 kg) load was then winched out of the ground and taken to the laboratory for further conservation. The removal of the helmet from the field took two full days. By the time the excavators found a second helmet nearby, the conservators had devised a new system of recovery. They replaced the steel box and molding compound with strips of fiberglass screen softened with glue. They carefully placed these strips over the helmet's shell and applied wet paper and plaster of paris to the screen. The conservators used this method to remove the entire compound in an old tire. The second helmet was thus much lighter and easier to transport.

The second phase of the conservation process took place in the laboratory. Colonial Williamsburg conservator Gary McQuillen used small tools to remove the dirt from the inside of the helmet. He pried off the plaster and dissolved the screen and the glue. He used a tiny air-blasting gun to remove the surface of the rust, often leaving the helmet only a millimeter (0.04 in) thick in places. McQuillen's dedication and delicate work of conservation brought the helmet back to life, and it now serves as a triumphant centerpiece in the Winthrop Rockefeller Archaeology Museum at the Wolstenholme Towne site in Williamsburg.

Conservation can reveal information that may remain hidden on a poorly preserved artifact. A skilled conservator can reveal corroded design features, discover identifying maker's marks, and make otherwise deteriorated artifacts easier to identify and study.

Conservation has been highly successful at Fort Michilimackinac, an eighteenth-century French and British fortification in Michigan. Decades of excavation have yielded thousands of metal objects, including knives, forks, spoons, flintlock gun parts, and tools of all sorts. Most of these objects required conservation treatment before archaeologists could study them. Conserved military buttons have helped to identify individual regiments once serving at the fort. Records indicate the British Tenth Regiment served at Michilimackinac between 1772 and 1774. Many pewter buttons, emblazoned with a large "10," confirm the official documents. Other buttons, marked with a raised "RI 18," belonged to the British Eighteenth, or Royal Irish, Regiment. This unit is known to have served in the American Revolution in 1777, but records fail to show any of its members being garrisoned at Fort Michilimackinac. Only the buttons reveal this tiny piece of history.

Back to the Laboratory

For all the glamour of excavation, most research time is spent back in the laboratory, working on artifacts and other finds in far more detail than is possible in the field. It is here, in much greater comfort and with better facilities, that the long process of classifying artifacts unfolds.

Classifying and Grouping Historical Artifacts

Everyone arranges objects as part of day-to-day living. We classify eating utensils—knives, forks, and spoons—because each one looks unique and has a different function. Many of us even keep each kind of utensil in separate compartments in a special drawer. We classify roads according to their surface finishes and distinguish minivans from trucks. We group lifestyles, artifacts, even cultures, and make choices to discriminate between them. By the same token, archaeologists arrange artifacts, not in the same way we do in everyday life, but as a means of ordering their excavated data and facilitating analysis. Without some form of ordering system, a collection of artifacts may appear as a chaotic jumble of things that have no relation to one another.

Archaeological arrangements are artificial formulations based on criteria devised by archaeologists. Arrangement is a way of imparting meaning to artifacts. Archaeologists' classification systems do not necessarily coincide with those used by the people who made and used the original artifacts. Ordering creates units with meaning based on function (knives, forks, spoons), shape (round buttons, square buttons), style (red glass beads, blue glass beads, white glass beads with blue and red stripes), and material of manufacture (copper pots, brass pots, iron pots).

The arrangement of artifacts has four main objectives:

1. *To organize data into manageable units.* This means separating ceramic sherds from metal objects, bone tools from leather garments, and glass beads from glass container fragments. This work constitutes preliminary data processing.
2. *To describe units.* By identifying the individual characteristics (or attributes) of hundreds of artifacts, or clusters of artifacts, archaeologists can arrange them into relatively few units. Such units are economical ways of comparing large numbers of artifacts.
3. *To provide a hierarchy of units, which orders the relationships between them.* The units stem, in part, from the use of a variety of raw materials, manufacturing techniques, and functions.
4. *To study artifact variability.* Arrangement provides an easy way to compare different artifact assemblages, and to study the differences and similarities between them.

Archaeologists engage in two kinds of artifact arrangement: *classification and grouping*. In classification, the archaeologist uses units of arrangement that exist prior to excavation. Each category is mutually exclusive, so when archaeologists sort the excavated artifacts, they know immediately into which category a particular artifact belongs. Suppose a site dating 1750–1830 is excavated. Before beginning the excavation, the archaeologist may decide to sort the artifacts into six categories: ceramics, glass, iron, nonferrous metal, bone, and other materials (such as paper, coal, mortar). The central rule (the key attribute) in this classification scheme is "material of manufacture." The archaeologist could have chosen to sort the artifacts into only two classes (ceramics and non-ceramics), or three classes (glass, bone, and neither glass nor bone). None of them would be incorrect. The central point is that the units exist before the excavation, and after excavation the archaeologist must sort the recovered artifacts into the preexisting units.

No prearranged units exist in grouping. In this method of division, the archaeologist permits the artifacts to establish the units. A category called "iron" would not exist in a collection containing no iron objects. A collection with only ceramic and glass artifacts would have only two groups: ceramic and glass. Metal, iron, and other artifacts would not appear.

In their analysis of nineteenth- and twentieth-century Inuit sites on the coast of Labrador, Canada, for example, Melanie Cabak and Stephen Loring specifically examined a kind of European ceramic called "stamped earthenware." This term refers to an inexpensive white ceramic with a rapidly applied decorative technique. Potters would cut a design into a sponge and then dip the sponge into pigment. They would then press the sponge against the surface of an unglazed ceramic vessel, leaving the imprint of the design. They would perform this operation until they had pressed the desired pattern—usually geometric or floral—everywhere they wanted it on the vessel. Cabak and Loring examined a collection from a site called Nain that yielded 115 stamped sherds. They divided the types in the sample (the seven different motifs) into the five colors present: purple, green, blue, red/green, and polychrome (many colors). Archaeologists usually present this material in table form for the sake of convenience and ease in interpretation (Table 7.1).

Many archaeologists use complex computer algorithms to divide artifacts into discrete units. Historical archaeologists seldom use these approaches because written records can be useful guides to artifact nomenclatures used over the past 500 years. In cases where documents are not available, however, historical archaeologists must resort to more formal methods.

Table 7.1 Tabular presentation of stamped sherds from Nain Site, Labrador

Motif	Purple	Green	Blue	Red/Green	Polychrome	Total
fleur-de-lis	33	2	–	–	–	35
cross	2	–	–	–	1	3
leaf	–	–	3	–	4	7
floral	–	11	–	10	10	31
geometric	–	–	23	–	4	27
flag	–	–	–	2	–	2
unknown	3	2	–	3	2	10
Total	**38**	**15**	**26**	**15**	**21**	**115**

Historical archaeologists are often aided by *folk classification,* arrangements created by the people who made and used the excavated artifacts. These schemes can often be found in potters' records, corporate documents, newspaper ads, public notices, and other text-based sources. The original system employed by the artifact makers and users makes the task of ordering immeasurably more straightforward, because archaeologists' units may thus coincide with those actually used in the past.

Ceramics are perhaps the most common artifact type found by historical archaeologists. In this case archaeologists may benefit specifically from written evidence. For example, between 1640 and 1680, English artist Randle Holme decided to record and draw the objects, including ceramics, with which he was familiar. Holme was researching the symbols of English heraldry for a book. He discovered that descriptive terms for ceramics could be confusing. For instance, a "dish" could be described as a platter, dish, middling dish, broth dish, bason [basin], sallet dish, trencher plate or plate, and saucer. Later, the anonymous author of *The Complete Appraiser* (1770) was more precise than Holme. He used measurements to distinguish between the different kinds of ceramic vessels. He said "plates" were between 7.75 inches (19.7 cm) and 9.75 inches (24.8 cm) in diameter, whereas "dishes" ranged from 10.75 inches (27.3 cm) to 28 inches (71.1 cm) across.

The arrangements presented by Randle Holme and the author of *The Complete Appraiser* are folk classifications. Each sorted material culture—in this case, ceramic dishes—in a way that made sense to the people who used it. Folk ordering systems are important to historical archaeologists because they provide a foundation for understanding how people in the past used and thought about their material culture. As is true of all classifications, they exist independent of any excavated sample of artifacts.

In the early 1980s, five archaeologists collaborated to develop an ordering system for colonial ceramics from domestic sites in the Chesapeake region of Maryland and Virginia, based on folk classifications. Their Potomac Typological System, or POTS, was based on the work of Randle Holme, the author of *The Complete Appraiser,* and several probate inventories. They used probate lists to understand the range of vessels present in the colonial Chesapeake and to provide insights into the terms used to describe them. For example, the inventory of Francis Lewis, who died in 1677, lists "2 pewter dishes, 3 plates, 2 porringers"; the inventory of Robert Slye's slave quarters, for the year 1671, includes "1 iron bottle, 1 iron pot, 1 frying pan."

POTS is an elaborate, widely used system with a basis in solid historical fact. Twenty-eight separate types of ceramics used in the seventeenth century are identified (Figure 7.11). Their system includes vessel forms recognizable today: cups, saucers, jugs, and candlesticks. But many of the forms no longer used may seem curious. For instance, a "costrel" is a jug or bottle with two handles. Travelers and field laborers used these vessels as drink containers, much like canteens. A "sillabub pot" was a short, squat pot with two handles and a spout like a teakettle. It was used for serving sillabub (wine or liquor mixed with sweetened milk or cream), posset (hot, sweetened milk curdled with wine or ale), and wassail (ale or wine spiced with roasted apples and sugar).

Archaeologists who have investigated Dutch life, both in the New and the Old Worlds, have similarly used folk classification systems. Archaeologists excavating in places settled by colonial Dutch men and women, such as New York City when it was called New Amsterdam, have learned to identify the ceramic vessels they find by their historic Dutch names. For example, a *schotel* is a plate or dish, *melkteilen* are milk pans or bowls, and storage jars are a *voorraadpotten.* The same is true of archaeologists to have studied various African traditions. After excavating slave-made eighteenth- and nineteenth-century pottery in western Brazil, archaeologists Marcos de Souza and Luís Symanski realized they needed to look to

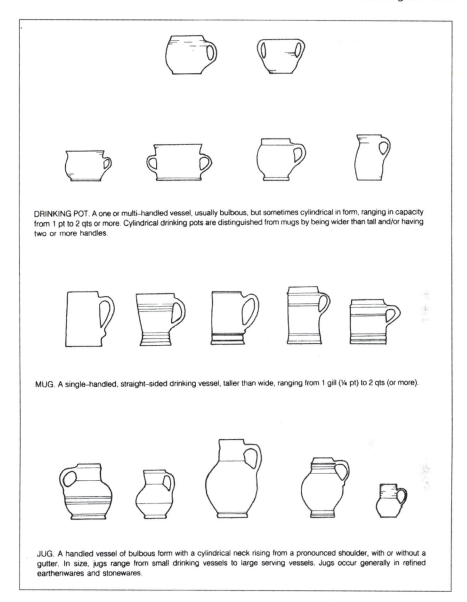

DRINKING POT. A one or multi-handled vessel, usually bulbous, but sometimes cylindrical in form, ranging in capacity from 1 pt to 2 qts or more. Cylindrical drinking pots are distinguished from mugs by being wider than tall and/or having two or more handles.

MUG. A single-handled, straight-sided drinking vessel, taller than wide, ranging from 1 gill (¼ pt) to 2 qts (or more).

JUG. A handled vessel of bulbous form with a cylindrical neck rising from a pronounced shoulder, with or without a gutter. In size, jugs range from small drinking vessels to large serving vessels. Jugs occur generally in refined earthenwares and stonewares.

Figure 7.11 Seventeenth-century ceramic vessel forms in the Chesapeake from POTS

(From A Vessel Typology for Early Chesapeake Ceramics: The Potomac Typological System, by Mary Beaudry, Janet Long, et al. in *Historical Archaeology* 17, 1 [1983].)

the pottery traditions of western and central Africa to obtain clues about the pottery's makers. Vessel forms such as cooking pots, domestic melting pots, and water jugs were common in both Brazil and Africa.

The ordering system POTS and other archaeological ordering schemes based on folk classifications are good examples of how historical archaeologists can use textual sources and archaeological finds to create useful analytical tools. Systems like POTS order the artifacts but retain the historical integrity of the folk classification.

Analysis

As the field of historical archaeology has grown and matured, its practitioners' analyses have gotten increasing sophisticated. Historical archaeologists today conduct a wide array of analyses on excavated materials, extending from animal bones to pieces of metal. Each analysis provides insights into the realities of past living experience that are unique and fascinating.

Zooarchaeologists specialize in the study of animal bones of all kinds. Most are trained in both archaeology and biology because their research goes far beyond the mere identification of animals once consumed for food. They separate domestic animals (e.g., cattle and sheep) from game (e.g., deer and rabbit). They calculate the minimum number of individuals in a collection as a way of establishing the amount of meat represented by the bones. They also look for revealing evidence of old butchering techniques, such as knife and saw cut marks. Cuts on bones provide information about how different ethnic groups and social classes used animals for food.

Zooarchaeologist Diana Crader studied the faunal remains excavated from one of the buildings inhabited by the enslaved at Jefferson's Monticello (Figure 7.12). She discovered the bones told a different story than the historical documents. Textual sources indicate that pork was a staple in the diet of the plantation's enslaved workers. Analysis revealed that while pig bones outnumber cow bones in the archaeological deposits, beef by weight was more important in the diet than pork. The bones found at one cabin indicate that Jefferson's enslaved ate both high-quality limbs and low-quality heads and feet. At another dwelling at Monticello,

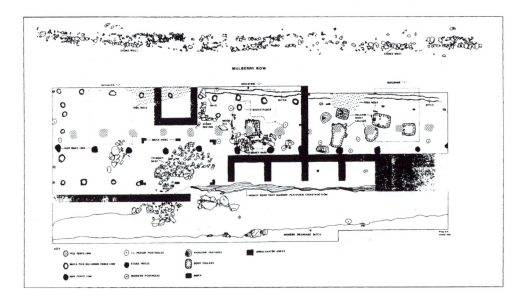

Figure 7.12 Mulberry Row slave quarters, Monticello, Virginia, as excavated in 1983–1984

(Reproduced by permission of the Society for American Archaeology from Slave Diet at Monticello, *American Antiquity* 55 [1990]:690–717.)

however, the bones told Crader that the enslaved did not eat high-quality meats. This evidence led her to conclude that Jefferson may have arranged his bonds men and women in a social hierarchy, in which some had a better diet than others. Proof of the social hierarchy among Monticello's enslaved community thus may be detected in archaeological deposits, but not in historical accounts.

Ethnobotanists, also called "archaeobotanists," are specialists in plant remains. These specialists have both archaeological and botanical training. They study both direct evidence for the human use of plants—seeds, nutshells, corncobs—and indirect evidence—leaves, bulbs, rinds, pollen. Like zooarchaeologists, their research goes far beyond the mere identification of domesticated and wild species.

In her research on the subsistence patterns of the colonial Spanish in Florida, Georgia, and South Carolina, ethnobotanist Margaret Scarry found evidence for a wide variety of plants at forts and town sites. These included Old World cultigens (watermelon, cantaloupe, peach, grape, olive), indigenous, New World species (squash/pumpkin, bean, maize), and exotic New World plants (lima bean, chili pepper). This evidence proves that Spanish settlers adopted a diverse strategy to ensure their survival. They introduced their own plants to the New World, they accepted many the Native Americans grew locally, and they imported still others from colonial outposts in the Caribbean, Mesoamerica, and South America. Spanish colonists adopted many plant foods from the local native peoples, but their food habits in general maintained many Spanish characteristics.

In collaboration with zooarchaeologist Elizabeth Reitz, Scarry was able to understand the natural world the Spanish encountered in what was for them a new world. Scarry and Reitz explored the Spanish response to their new environment in light of such anthropological issues as how the Spanish learned to live in the new environment, how the Spanish and the coastal Native Americans learned from one another, adopted elements of one another's culture and in the process created a hybrid, new culture. These important insights would be impossible without the evidence provided by historical archaeology.

In some cases, archaeologists may have unearthed something that requires radiography (X-ray) to be interpreted. The need for radiography is fairly common in underwater archaeology. Objects resting on the seabed for hundreds of years may be completely covered with accretions. Radiography allows archeologists to see through the accretion mass. It can be used with ceramics, metals, paper, and human remains as well.

Radiography was central, for example, in solving the riddle of the date of small metal statues of St. Peter found in Austria. Statuettes of saints are known to have been made throughout medieval times but no written documentation has been found to indicate such figurines were made in the nineteenth century. Thus, when a metal St. Peter statuette was discovered at a site near Innsbruck, the question of its date was foremost in importance. Radiography—in addition to highly scientific metallurgical analysis—provided clues that the statue had been made in the late nineteenth century. Plastic statuettes are sold today in Rome, but surprisingly little knowledge remains about objects produced as recently as the nineteenth century. Radiography provided information on how the statues were made, using technologies perfectly consistent with nineteenth-century methods.

In another study, archaeologists used an analytical tool called total reflection X-ray fluorescence (TXRF). In 1997, a team of archaeologists from the Argentinean National Institute of Anthropology began excavating the wreck of the British warship H.M.S. *Swift* sunk off the coast of Patagonia in 1770. By 2006, they had excavated a large portion of the officers' quarters, where they discovered a small cylindrical glass bottle with its cork intact and liquid still inside. The placement of the bottle suggested it belonged to one of the ship's officers. Seeking to learn the contents of the bottle, they used TXRF to determine the chemical composition of the liquid. The analysis revealed the presence of a compound called mercurous chloride (Hg_2Cl_2). Physicians had prescribed mercury compounds for centuries to cure several ailments, the most notable being syphilis. It also had uses as an antiseptic even though its side effects included tooth loss; ulcerations of the mouth, throat, and skin; brain damage; and even death. Mercury was only replaced by penicillin in the twentieth century. Archaeologists rarely discover whole glass bottles with liquids still inside. When they do, however, TXRF analysis is a valuable tool.

In another study, archeologists also called upon metallurgical specialists. This project was geared toward understanding the production of metal at a Spanish colony in today's New Mexico, dating 1540–1680 C.E. Because mining was an important historical industry in this part of the Spanish Empire, the archaeologists used the multidisciplinary approach common to all historical archaeology. However, since the project specifically concerned metal production, collaboration with specialists was required. In this case, scanning electron microscopy equipped with high-tech imaging detectors was used to identify the metals present in slag and other samples taken from the site. The results did not confirm the presence of gold or silver in the samples even though these were the metals most often sought by Spanish colonists. Instead, the samples contained lead and copper. The archaeologists' conclusion is that the colonists may have tested the local ores for copper, lead, and perhaps even silver. Though the results are not as straightforward as might be wished, the laboratory analysis was extremely important because it provided concrete evidence for past activities at the site. It also offered additional research questions for future investigation.

Archaeologists have also used metallurgical analysis to compare artillery shells fired during the American Civil War. They compared samples from the Confederate and Federal armies fired during the battles of Pea Ridge, Arkansas (August 1861), and Wilson's Creek, Missouri (February 1862). Finite element analysis, optical and scanning electron microscopy, chemical profiling, and hardness testing produced two significant findings for future consideration. First, differences in the amount of carbon present in the ordnance of the two armies could be used for the spatial analysis of shell location on the battlefields. As was true at the site of the Battle of the Little Bighorn (see Chapter 3), mapping the artillery shells could provide information about the course of the battles and the location of batteries. Second, the shells of the Federal Army were found to be more uniform than those of the Confederates. Further research may show that the Federal Army, with considerable industrial resources behind it, may have obtained their ordnance from fewer sources than the Confederates, whose economy was largely based on agriculture. This sort of research offers unlimited potential to furthering the goals of conflict archaeology (see Chapter 3).

A number of historical archaeologists have also followed the lead of their colleagues investigating ancient history by attempting to identify the sources of various artifacts. Artifact sourcing typically involves the geochemical analysis of an artifact's physical properties and comparison with natural rocks and other materials from the earth.

An analysis of eighteenth-century ceramics discovered in the San Francisco Bay area of California was designed to determine whether excavated wares had been locally made or imported. The production of ceramics was not an indigenous industry. Native Americans made low-fired, coarse pottery; they did not make high-fired coarse or glazed wares before contact with Europeans. As a result, the ceramics at the archaeological sites are associated with the colonial Spanish. To unravel the mystery of the ceramics' origin, an archaeological team led by Russell Skowronek used neutron activation analysis to identify the chemicals in six assemblages of ceramics excavated from colonial Spanish sites. The ceramics were architectural (bricks and tiles), plain earthenware, lead-glazed earthenware, and majolica (a tin-glazed earthenware). The analysis revealed that the architectural ceramics, the plain earthenware, and the lead-glazed earthenware were produced somewhere in the region at newly built kiln sites. The majolica, however, had come from outside California, probably from potteries in Mexico. At least half of the majolica had probably been produced by one specific, albeit unidentified, ceramic house.

In another study, Alan Vince and Allan Peacey conducted a geochemical analysis of English clay smoking pipes. Tobacco smoking was introduced into the British Isles in the late sixteenth century and the manufacture of pipes quickly became a London-based monopoly. In less than 100 years, however, small shops across the countryside had begun producing clay pipes of their own. An understanding of the network of shops making smoking pipes shows how the industry spread and provides a model for understanding how industries and their artifacts diffuse through a landscape. Given the complexity of the analysis, and the potentially broad distribution of pipes and clays, Vince and Peacey focused on one region having eight pipe production sites dating roughly 1620–1740.

Pipeclay (also called "ball clay"), the material from which white clay pipes are made, is composed mostly of silica, kaolinite, and muscovite. The clays appear naturally in various places throughout England. Source identification rests upon matching the chemical composition of pipeclay deposits with excavated clay pipes. In this analysis, Vince and Peacey used Inductively Coupled Plasma Mass Spectroscopy, a test measuring the major elements present in small samples. The analysis, though tentative, found differences in the composition of the clay in the pipes. It also revealed that the region's pipemakers used clays originating about 28 miles (45 km) from their shops rather than clays located only seven miles (11 km) away. The exact reason of the selection of clays is unclear, but the test results provide new avenues of research.

Gunflints, studied by historical archaeologists since the 1960s, are common artifacts on colonial-era sites associated with Europeans and with native peoples in contact with Europeans. The gunflint, now largely a forgotten technology, was an important piece of equipment during the days of the flintlock musket. The flint, which is a small piece of chipped chert, fit into the gun's lock. Flintknappers produced two kinds of flints. A spall type with a rounded heel, and a blade type with a squarish heel. To shoot a flintlock, the shooter pulled back the lock and when the trigger was squeezed, the lock with the flint in its jaws moved forward and struck the pan. This action caused a spark to ignite the gunpowder, thus propelling the lead musket ball from the gun's barrel. The expression that someone or something is a "flash in the pan" comes from the days of the flintlock musket. It means the person or thing is a momentary sensation, destined not to last long, like a flash in the gun's pan that fails to ignite the gunpowder.

In the 1990s, archaeologists from the Texas Historical Commission (THC) began to excavate a shipwreck in Matagorda Bay called *La Belle*. This ship, belonging to the French explorer La Salle, was lost during a storm in 1686. Included in the wreckage were 316 unused gunflints. Shortly after beginning the shipwreck study, the THC started to excavate a related terrestrial site called Fort St. Louis. This was the fort La Salle planned to use as his base of operation until he could locate the mouth of the Mississippi River.

Gunflints were originally a European product made from chert containing over 97 percent silica. Gunflint sourcing is difficult because the chert occurring in western Europe and England is relatively uniform in composition. Advances in Inductively Coupled Plasma Mass Spectrometry makes it possible to identify the subtle variations in the chemical compositions of cherts used for gunflints.

The analysis of the Texas gunflints began by collecting chert samples from known gunflint producing areas in France and England. Both countries supplied most of the gunflints to North America during the time of La Salle's expedition. The analysis identified three distinct sets of gunflints. One group consisted of Fort St. Louis gunflints probably made locally by Spanish or indigenous individuals associated with them. A second group, from both the fort and the shipwreck, derived from British chert, and the third group, also from both sites, originated in France. The source of some flints could not be identified. This finding is important for many reasons, but one interesting element is its demonstration of the increasingly multicultural nature of artifacts after about 1492.

In addition to the high-tech tests that can be called upon, historical archaeologists have also devised their own analytical tools. Though much less sophisticated than geochemical and other scientific procedures, they nonetheless are extremely important to the discipline. They constitute important laboratory activities.

One of the most important analytical methods used in historical archaeology involves ceramics. In Chapter 4, we explained a dating technique called mean ceramic dating. This dating technique, devised by a historical archaeologist, is conducted using sherd counts, or the number of ceramic fragments present in a sample. Though important, the number of sherds has little correlation to the number of actual vessels once present at an archaeological site. As Barbara Voss has stated, "People don't use sherds, they use vessels." People use plates, cups, saucers, bowl, and many other vessels for certain tasks. Thus, to conduct a study of social past life using ceramics as a variable—instead of using them merely for dating—archaeologists must also know the number of vessels present. The reason is clear. Suppose a household member drops two plates. One breaks into four pieces, while the other shatters into 30 pieces. The archaeological sample is composed of 34 sherds but only two plates were present.

The number of vessels may reflect a host of social elements, including personal preference, cost per vessel, availability in the market, and traditional values of the household. Historical archaeologists are interested in each of these social variables. The number of sherds in an assemblage, however, is not a social variable. Rather, it refers to a number of physical and environmental factors, including the chemical composition of the ceramics, the floor material upon which the plates were dropped, the condition of each plate before being dropped, and the natural forces acting upon the plates once they were deposited in the soil.

To identify the number of vessels present rather than just the number of sherds, historical archaeologists use a method called the minimum number of vessels (MNV). Archaeologists calculate the MNV by examining the number of rim and base sherds present, in addition to other attributes such as material of manufacture (fine earthenware, coarse earthenware, stoneware, and porcelain), decoration style and color, and body type (bowl, plate, cup).

A hypothetical example in Table 7.2 demonstrates how to make the calculation. In this example are 100 sherds that have been divided into piles of fine earthenware, coarse earthenware, stoneware, and porcelain. In this example, the sherds have been grouped by simple form: rim, base, or body sherd. Looking at the sample, we immediately know between four and 100 possible vessels are present. Why? Each ware type is represented, so we know at least one vessel each of fine earthenware, coarse earthenware, stoneware, and porcelain is present. And, because the sample has 100 sherds, we know this must be the maximum number of possible vessels, provided each sherd represents one vessel.

Though not impossible, this scenario is extremely unlikely given the way ceramics break. The maximum number of vessels is unimportant because it overestimates the number of vessels present. This conclusion completely overlooks the fact that some of the sherds will probably crossmend (fit together). If two rim sherds fit together, they represent one vessel, not two.

Table 7.2 Hypothetical example of MNV calculation by sherd form

Ware Type	Rim	Base	Body	Total	MNV
Fine earthenware	5	2	10	17	2
Coarse earthenware	15	5	20	40	5
Stoneware	5	2	10	17	3
Porcelain	5	6	15	26	10
Total	30	15	55	100	20

Total number of sherds = 100

The next step in the process is to examine each sherd in comparison with every other sherd, to arrive at the MNV. This analysis consists of determining the similarities among the individual sherds. If two rims are present but one has a diameter of 2 inches (5 cm) and one 3 inches (8 cm), two vessels are present. If both of the rims measure 2 inches in diameter, then the minimum number is one, because we cannot know whether they are from the same vessel. If one of them has a red decoration and one a blue decoration, however, then two vessels are present. Body sherds are generally not useful for MNV calculation unless they contain distinguishing decorations or identifiable structural features (handles, spouts, obvious curvature that may indicate vessel shape). The successful calculation of MNV usually develops over time, as an archaeologist learns the different kinds of ceramics present at various times in history. In the example, the minimum number is arbitrarily set at 20 vessels: two fine earthenware, five coarse earthenware, three stoneware, and ten porcelain.

Once the number of vessels is calculated, the archaeologist can begin to ask socially and culturally significant questions. For example, if porcelain was the most expensive of the four ware types, why does it appear in such a high percentage? Does the greater number of coarse earthenware vessels mean the residents of the site were engaged in storage activities rather than dining? If so, why are only three stoneware vessels present? Was the excavation strategy correct for the site? Should more excavation have occurred?

The analyses historical archaeologists perform will continue to develop as new technologies are invented and as innovative methods are devised. Each new technique will help archaeologists develop better interpretations of daily life during the past 500 years. The use of high-tech testing makes historical archaeology more exciting than ever.

Site Visit: Fresh Water Pond, New York City, 1810–1834

In its earliest years, the City of New York was restricted to the tiny southern tip of Manhattan. As the area's population grew, the city expanded northward into a region of pastures and simple roadways. A major geographic feature of this area was a large, circular body of water known as the "Collect Pond" or the "Fresh

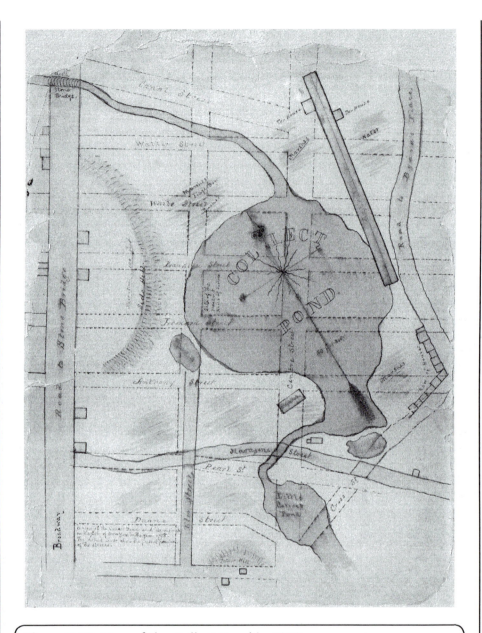

Figure 7.13 Map of the Collect Pond in 1840
(CPC Collection / Alamy)

Water Pond" (Figure 7.13). The availability of useful water had encouraged several industries, including tanneries, to locate near the pond. From this rural location they could make their products unhindered, and then transport them for
sale to the city at relatively little expense. Late-eighteenth-century tanneries,

however, were not environmentally friendly, and they quickly polluted the pond. With urban expansion, city leaders realized the industries occupied increasingly valuable land. Thus, seeking to integrate this area into the fabric of the city, they order the pond filled and a new street, Anthony Street, to be constructed across its southwestern edge. By 1814, the Fresh Water Pond had completely disappeared. Some of the industrialists sued the city for forcing them to uproot their businesses, but other owners saw a bright future in renting space to newly arrived households and shopkeepers. The area just south of the Fresh Water Pond came to be called the Five Points, because of the five corners created by the intersection of Anthony, Cross, and Orange streets.

Many of the men and women who moved into the working-class neighborhood near the old Collect Pond were free African Americans. They came as a result of emancipation, and many of them followed the earlier migration of other African American families. They also believed they could live in the burgeoning city relatively anonymously and find work with little problem. Early nineteenth-century census records reveal this area had the highest percentage of free black households in lower Manhattan. The heads of these households were artisans—shoemakers, carpenters, and laborers—or seamstresses and domestics.

Between 1810 and 1820, many free blacks in the city lived with white families. New York state law decreed that all children born into slavery after July 4, 1799, were legally free. Even so, the law also said that females were required to be "in service" until age 25, males until 28. The "in service" requirement effectively meant that many legally free men and women were essentially enslaved within white households. Some individuals were able to negotiate the terms of their indenture and to make cash payments to ensure their freedom. When freed of their indenture commitments, many African Americans chose to move to the Five Points area. Some support groups, such as the African Mutual Relief Society, offered assistance and aid to in-migrating African Americans.

New York's African American community also established numerous cultural institutions in the area, including several churches of different denominations and schools. These centers had many functions, including providing the community's civic leadership and offering the nucleus for political activities. The community also started a newspaper called *Freedom's Journal* that argued against slavery, oppressive anti-black legislation, and colonization.

The African American community was understandably opposed to the continuation of enslavement, and they staged anti-slavery protests in 1810, 1819, 1826, and 1832. Human bondage was *the* controversial issue of the nineteenth century, and debate over it threatened to destroy the United States. Many European immigrants who settled in New York in the early decades of the nineteenth century did not necessarily share the African American community's views on slavery, and conflicts erupted as both views were given voice.

Working-class people from both the African American and the European immigrant communities also tended to view each other as possible competitors for jobs. Many Europeans had moved into the cheap accommodations of the Five Points area, and the proximity of individuals with widely differing viewpoints fostered conflict and disagreement. Public meetings were organized to promote both abolition and anti-abolition perspectives, and violent mobs often surged through the city's streets. Conflict culminated with five nights' of violence during the summer of 1834, with pro-slavery supporters attacking the homes of prominent non–African American merchants and ministers who argued for abolition. Vandalism soon spread beyond their homes and even the African Mutual Relief Society was attacked. Windows were smashed, and several residences and businesses were burned to the ground. Such racism and hostility, coupled with rising rents and competition over jobs convinced many of the neighborhood's African Americans to seek employment and residence elsewhere.

Source: Claudia Milne. On the Grounds of the Fresh Water Pond: The Free-Black Community at Five Points, 1810–1834. *International Journal of Historical Archaeology* 6 (2002):127–142.

Chapter 8

Artifacts in Historical Archaeology

In the "Adventure of the Blue Carbuncle," Dr. Watson arrives at 221B Baker Street, London, to find Sherlock Holmes contemplating "a very seedy and disreputable hard-felt hat, much worse for wear, and cracked in several places." From this hat, judged by Watson to be rather ordinary, Holmes brilliantly deduces a wealth of information, as only he can do. The great detective concludes the owner of the hat was an intellectual man, he was once prosperous, he is middle-aged, and he recently has had his hair cut. Holmes also figures the owner's wife has ceased to love him and the man has no gaslight in his house.

Almost everyone in the Western world is familiar with the exploits of the illustrious, though fictional, Sherlock Holmes. His deductive methods will live forever. Some readers may be surprised to find his name in a book about historical archaeology, but though Holmes was only the literary creation of a British physician, the insightful sleuth has much in common with modern archaeologists. When Holmes says in "The Boscombe Valley Mystery" that his method is "founded upon the observation of trifles," he could have been speaking as an archaeologist. Historical archaeologists, no matter what historical era they study, focus on portable artifacts. These often-fragmentary things are the many mundane objects ordinary people used in their daily lives, things sometimes so trivial their users may never have consciously thought about them. They may simply have taken the objects for granted, much as we do with many of the things around us. For historical archaeologists, the trifles bear a striking resemblance to things used around the world every day today: glass bottles, ceramic dishes, mirrors, buttons, thimbles, and hundreds of other things. Similarities between things today and those of the recent past are part of what makes historical archaeology a unique and fascinating field of study.

Artifacts and Material Culture

Archaeologists are known for using the terms artifact and material culture and they often use them interchangeably. They write about the "material culture" of a particular site when referring to collections of artifacts, and sometimes they write "artifact" when meaning "material culture."

In its simplest sense, an *artifact* is anything made or modified by conscious human action. A stone arrow point, a soft drink bottle, a carved wooden mask, and a table are all artifacts. Humans are constantly surrounded by artifacts: we cook with them, eat from them, drive in them, sleep on them, and get buried in them. The artifacts we use help to define who we are. The term material culture includes artifacts, but is generally conceived of more broadly. Material culture includes all elements of consciously created human expression, including landscapes, words, a marching band's design on an athletic field, the distance we stand from someone when speaking to them, and so forth.

The stone circle known as the Big Horn Medicine Wheel lies in the mountains of northern Wyoming. Most Americans know of the Big Horn Mountains through their association with "Custer's Last Stand" (see Chapter 3), but they were more importantly home to Native Americans for thousands of years before Custer was born. Native Americans built the Big Horn Medicine Wheel sometime in the ancient past. The wheel looks like a stone wagon wheel with a central "hub" out of which radiates a series of "spokes." A stone "rim" connects the ends of the spokes. Archaeologists have hotly debated the meaning of the wheel, and they have put forward a number of interpretations. Ancient Native Americans may have used the wheel as an observatory or a monument to deceased, revered leaders. It may have been the focal point for the vision quests of adolescents who fasted and prayed in the hope the Great Spirit would lead them to adulthood, or it may have been a symbolic representation of the universe. Many Crow people on the northern Plains today regard the wheel as a sacred site, and argue that no one needs to explain it to them; they know its meaning the way any believer understands what is sacred within their belief system.

The Big Horn Medicine Wheel is a fascinating object, but is it an artifact? The stones of the wheel cannot be considered artifacts in the strictest sense of the term because they were not actually modified by human action. Only their place on the earth's surface was changed. The only difference between the stones of the wheel and others nearby is that the former are arranged in such a way as to resemble a wheel. If any one of the stones were found somewhere else, an archaeologist would not consider it an artifact. Arranged as a medicine wheel, though, the stones are collectively an example of Native American material culture. The medicine wheel makes a cultural statement about past ideas even though archaeologists do not agree on its precise meaning. Material culture thus includes objects that may have been shaped by humanity but not necessarily physically altered. A gravel road is an example of material culture, but the thousands of tiny pebbles in the road are not artifacts by themselves.

A house presents more of a challenge for a historical archaeologist to classify as artifact or material culture. A house is clearly something made by conscious human activity, but is it an artifact? Houses are composed of hundreds of things that clearly *are* artifacts: nails, roofing tiles, floor boards, and plaster walls—but is a house an artifact in the same way a bottle is?

In the final analysis, the difference between an artifact and material culture is perhaps not significant. To simplify matters, we consider an artifact to be any readily *portable* object, and material culture to be all the physical expressions created by human action, such as landscapes and clusters of industrial buildings.

What is important about artifacts and material culture is that both require interpretation. Artifacts require interpretation because they are not passive creations. People do not simply make tools, use them, and then forget about them. Artifacts impose structure on people's lives in the same way people impose structure on an artifact in the process of fashioning it. The relationship between humans and things may best be considered by thinking about a small farmhouse.

Farmhouses, like all buildings, are built in ways that make cultural sense to their builders. When War of 1812 veteran Charles Ames moved from New England to Indiana in the early nineteenth century, he built a house true to his memories of New England. Let us suppose

Ames was used to looking at his fields out of his back door in New England, but in Indiana the topography made it impossible for him to see his pastures from home. The house in Indiana thus has structured Ames's life. He could adopt a number of strategies to survey his fields in the manner in which he was accustomed. He could design his house differently, he could alter the landscape, or he could change the way he checked his fields. Regardless of his decision, Ames's material culture—his new house in Indiana—has affected his behavior.

Material culture can structure human actions in powerful ways. In one study, archaeologist Gregory Monks argues that the architecture used by the Hudson's Bay Company at Upper Fort Garry in today's Manitoba, Canada, served as a form of nonverbal communication. The mighty Hudson's Bay Company built the fur trading and commercial post in 1836 and used it as an administrative center for their activities in the Red River/Assiniboine River region. Monks does not accept the conventional idea that the fort was built simply as a backdrop to be used by traders and governmental officials in the course of their daily affairs. In other words, he refuses to interpret the structure as merely functional. He proposes instead that Upper Fort Garry was an active participant in promoting the quasi-military and economic goals of the Hudson's Bay Company. The placement of the flagpole—with its British Red ensign proudly emblazoned with "HBC"—standing directly opposite the entrance, the construction of an interior wall to separate living quarters from storehouses, and the expansion of economic areas at the expense of living and administrative zones were not simply done for convenience. Monks believes these changes were meant to symbolize something much more profound: that the Hudson's Bay Company gave its economic motives greatest importance. The movement of the outer wall to make the once-interior sales area accessible from outside the fort was perhaps the clearest nonverbal message the company could send. They were saying they wanted local trade, but only on their terms. The quality of material culture to embody several meanings, such as at Upper Fort Garry, makes it a centrally important, though often frustratingly complex subject for historical archaeologists.

Interpreting Artifacts

In *Reading Matter: Multidisciplinary Perspectives on Material Culture,* Arthur Asa Berger presents a hypothetical situation in which the offices of six scholars look down upon and surround a small courtyard. On a picnic table in the center of the courtyard, the scholars can see a McDonald's hamburger, some French fries, and a milkshake. The scholars are a semiotician (someone who studies signs or symbols), a psychoanalytic psychologist, an anthropologist, a historian, a sociologist, and a Marxist political scientist. On looking at the objects, each scholar perceives something different. The semiotician views McDonald's as a symbol of America, its standardization and its efficiency, and the psychologist sees the success of McDonald's as an example of the need for individual gratification but also an indication of creeping depersonalization. The anthropologist perceives the hamburger and fries ritualistically and contemplates how the McDonald's experience has entered American folklore. The historian considers the food an example of the history of a successful corporation and a visible reminder of the growing importance of corporations in American history. The sociologist sees in the same meal a representation of youth culture and the way in which immigrants work their way into the American social order through low-paying jobs. Finally, the Marxist political scientist sees the objects as examples of how different socioeconomic classes of people are exploited by multinational corporations and how McDonald's hides the class differences inherent in capitalism by providing practically identical, inexpensive products to all members of society.

Berger's hypothetical situation vividly shows how scholars from diverse disciplinary backgrounds and with disparate perspectives can interpret the same objects differently. The intricate process of interpretation can be made even more complex by adding, for example, more anthropologists and historians, each of whom have slightly different perspectives on culture and history. No matter how many scholars are added, what is missing from Berger's mix is a historical archaeologist. How would a historical archaeologist see Berger's fast-food meal?

The easy answer is that individual historical archaeologists may perceive the objects in each of the ways outlined by Berger. Because historical archaeology is a field reaching across disciplines (see Chapter 1), its practitioners are perfectly free to borrow ideas from numerous perspectives. American studies scholar Thomas Schlereth has outlined nine diverse perspectives he terms "conceptual positions" that students of material culture can adopt: art historic, symbolist, cultural historic, environmentalist, functionalist, structuralist, behavioralist, nationalist, and social historic. He places historical archaeology in the cultural historic category, but it is obvious today that the field has much more to offer than simple historical reconstruction. In fact, historical archaeologists have conducted research in all of Schlereth's categories, as well as others.

For the sake of brevity, we present the interpretation of artifacts from just three broad perspectives: as historical documents (Schlereth's art historic, cultural historic, nationalist, and social historic), as commodities (Schlereth's functionalist and behavioralist), and as ideas (Schlereth's symbolist and structuralist). These three categories of interpretation are not mutually exclusive; each builds upon the other, starting with the use of physical things as historical documents.

Artifacts as Historical Documents

All archaeology is based on the fundamental assumption that artifacts provide information about the past. For more than a century, most archaeologists have considered artifacts as the equivalent of historical documents. John L. Stephens, the nineteenth-century American explorer of Copán, the majestic city of the Maya, understood this usage. On beholding a finely carved stela, or upright stone slab, Stephens remarked that it proved "as a newly discovered historical text might have done, that the peoples who once occupied the American continent were no savages." He likened the stelae of the Maya to historical documents because they provided information about life in ancient Mexico. Historical archaeologist Ivor Noël Hume once gave Stephens's comment a more modern twist by proclaiming artifacts to be the "signposts of the past."

The idea that artifacts can be read as historical texts has much to do with the technology of artifact production. People who made artifacts in long distant eras probably relied almost exclusively on cultural conventions when it came to design. They developed the technology, the decorations, and the styles of their objects over many years. Archaeologists of antiquity can chart changes in artifact design or decoration but often only broadly. For instance, when Donald Lehmer compiled the cultural chronology of a region in the United States that archaeologists call the "Middle Missouri"—the Missouri River valley in North and South Dakota— he knew that pottery with surfaces roughened with cord-wrapped sticks characterized what archaeologists have dubbed the Initial Coalescent Variant of the Central Plains Tradition. He also knew that the people who lived during the more recent Extended Coalescent Variant did not cord-roughen their pottery. Archaeologists of the American Plains generally agree the Initial Coalescent Variant dates to about 1400–1550 C.E. and the Extended Coalescent Variant dates to about 1550–1675 C.E. In South Dakota, therefore, an archaeologist could date a cord-roughened sherd found along the Missouri River to sometime within a 150-year period. The precise placement of this sherd within this time span, however, may remain a mystery.

Historical archaeologists often have a distinct advantage over their colleagues who investigate deep antiquity when it comes to using artifacts as historical documents. Historical archaeologists can often recognize changes in artifacts in terms of years or sometimes even days rather than in generations or centuries. The fine-grained understanding of artifacts as historical documents often exists, particularly in the most recent years, because most historical artifacts were manufactured by factories or corporations. These corporations, because they were economic concerns, often kept careful, detailed records as part of their responsibilities to their shareholders. Corporate archives can thus provide abundant information about the changes in design, style, and decoration of specific artifacts. The fine-grained analysis of some artifacts in historical archaeology mirrors the microstratigraphy historical archaeologists often encounter in the field (see Chapter 4).

A famous designer of eighteenth-century ceramic artifacts was Josiah Wedgwood, a man widely celebrated both for his beautifully crafted wares and for his business acumen. Wedgwood, who justifiably viewed his ceramic paste formulas and his decorative innovations as trade secrets, is known to have kept detailed records of his patterns, shapes, and decorations. His decorative designs on plates, called "Old Feather Edge," "New Feather Edge," "Queen Pattern," and "Royal Pattern," are well known today because of his factory records (Figure 8.1). Archaeologists conducting excavations throughout the British colonial world have repeatedly found ceramic sherds in these patterns.

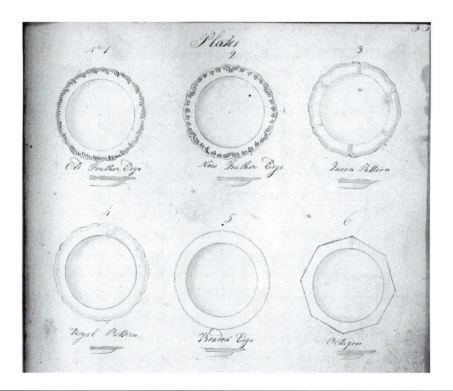

Figure 8.1 Plate drawings from Wedgwood's 1802 drawing book
(Wedgwood Museum / WWRD)

Historical archaeologists use artifacts as historical documents in many ways. They most frequently use them to date specific occupation layers in the soil. The common Coca-Cola bottle provides an excellent case in point.

The Coca-Cola Bottle

Coca-Cola was invented in Atlanta, Georgia, by pharmacist John S. Pemberton in 1886. Pemberton's creation became such a popular beverage that in 1892 he called his business "The Coca-Cola Company." With the prospect of Coca-Cola becoming a major sensation, the company registered the now classic "Coca-Cola" logo with the United States Patent Office in 1893. In the earliest years of production and distribution, bottlers paid little attention to the packaging in which Coca-Cola was sold, and they indiscriminately used straight-sided bottles of whatever color they could get. In 1916, however, the company decided to adopt a standardized, patented bottle design to protect its popular product from the countless imitators who sought to cash in on Pemberton's soft drink gold mine.

Many early twentieth-century manufacturers of liquid foodstuffs chose to patent their bottle designs rather than the bottle's actual contents. To patent a bottle's contents required announcing the product's formula, something few manufacturers of highly sought-after products wished to do. All Coca-Cola sold between 1916 and 1923 thus came in bottles reading "Bottle Pat'd Nov. 1915" on the base. This bottle had the classic shape now associated with the drink. The company patented a new design on Christmas Day, 1923, so all Coca-Cola sold between 1924 and 1937 came in bottles reading "Bottle Pat'd Dec. 25, 1923." Other design innovations followed in 1937, so that all Coke bottles sold between 1937 and 1951 read "Bottle Pat. D-105529." The company first used the word "Coke" on their bottles in 1941, and between 1963 and 1965 they also included "6½ oz." on one side panel.

The changes in the common Coca-Cola bottle form the official patent history of one of the world's most widely known products. With their relatively tight dates, Coca-Cola bottles found at archaeological sites can function as documents in a way not often duplicated by artifacts not produced in factory or corporate settings. When David Gradwohl and Nancy Osborn found a bottle with the easily identifiable "Coca-Cola" script painted on it at Buxton, Iowa—a coal mining town with a large African American population—they immediately knew the bottle dated after 1893.

In addition to telltale designs and identifiable product names, many mass-produced objects contain manufacturers' marks that can serve as valuable chronological markers. The manufacturers' symbols were company icons and identifiers, but archaeologists can use them as time markers. Ceramics and glass bottles are two noteworthy examples.

Ceramic Maker's Marks

The practice of placing maker's marks on the bottom of ceramic vessels goes back centuries. A Roman potter named M. Perennius lived sometime between 100 B.C.E. and 100 C.E. Renowned for his skill at copying Greek designs, he was widely considered a ceramic genius. He stamped his pottery "M. PERINNI," "M. PEREN," or "M. PERE." Archaeologists excavating in Rome, northern France, and Spain have found his marks to be a wonderful time marker. Perennius is said to have employed 17 slaves in his pottery works, the most famous being a man named Tigranes, who was so proud of his work that he stamped it "TIGRAN," "TIGRA," or just plain "TIGR." Following a tradition thus dating from classical times, potters have etched their wares with a variety of initials, shapes, and symbols that forever serve as their personal, unique marks. Archaeologists also call maker's marks *bottom marks* because potters usually placed them on the underside of their vessels.

Large pottery houses in operation during the Industrial Revolution of the late eighteenth century adopted the same procedure to mark their products. The most well-developed set of maker's marks appear on post–Industrial Revolution British ceramics, but American potters quickly followed suit by marking their wares as well. Potters on both sides of the Atlantic compiled a massive array of unique and distinguishing marks. As may be expected, the number of symbols expanded with the rapid growth of the ceramics industry and the increase in competition between potteries. Before 1770, English potters seldom marked their wares but after this date, they almost always did. Ceramic scholars have spent years compiling reference works of ceramic marks, and many published catalogues are available for use by historical archaeologists.

Historical archaeologists use these catalogues to identify and date the marked ceramics sherds they find. For example, a sherd marked with a globe having the word *MINTON* written across it is a product of the Minton pottery of Staffordshire, England. Established in 1793, the Minton pottery used the globe from about 1863 to 1872. In 1873, the Mintons added a crown to the top of the globe and an *S* to the word *MINTON* (Figure 8.2). In addition to such individualized marks, many English potters incorporated the British Royal Arms into their marks. These logos are characterized by a lion (on the left) and a unicorn (on the right) flanking an oblong shield with a crown on top of it. The marks included a quartered shield with a smaller shield in the middle before 1837, but the small shield was removed after this date.

Ceramics from Victorian England, made from 1842 to 1883, carry one of the most diagnostic bottom marks a historical archaeologist can find. This mark appears as a diamond having a small circle on top, with numbers and letters on the inside corners of the diamond. These distinctive marks indicate the factory had registered the design or shape of the vessel with the British Patent Office. Because the purpose of the symbol was to protect the pottery from piracy for at least three years, the bottom mark contains an exact date of registry. The

Figure 8.2 Marks from the bottom of Minton ceramics. Without crown: about 1863–1872, with crown: about 1873. The word *England* was added below the crown in 1891. The symbol on the right was used from about 1912–1950.

(From *Encyclopedia of British Pottery and Porcelain Marks* by Geoffrey Godden. New York: Bonanza, 1964.)

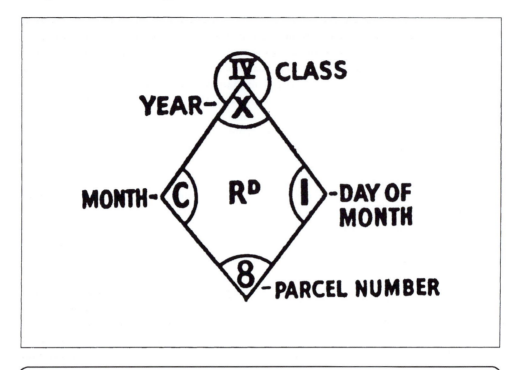

Figure 8.3 British registry mark, used from 1842–1867

(From *Encyclopedia of British Pottery and Porcelain Marks* by Geoffrey Godden. New York: Bonanza, 1964.)

Patent Office assigned codes to ceramic manufacturers and required them to place them in the corners of the diamond. An archaeologist can identify an English ceramic made during the 1842–1867 period by the "C" in the left corner of the diamond, an "I" in the right corner, and an "X" in the top corner as having been registered at the British Patent Office on January (C), 1 (I), 1842 (X) (Figure 8.3). This date has little to do with when the ceramic vessel may have been used. It serves, however, as a *terminus post quem*, or "date after which" it was made. The 1842 date on the vessel itself indicates this piece could not have been used *before* 1842. Only more detailed knowledge of the site itself will provide a *terminus ante quem*, or "date before which." If other sources confirmed the site was completely abandoned in 1862, the ceramic sherd with the diamond-shaped mark can be dated 1842–1862.

A recognizable portion of the mark must remain visible on the sherd to be useful for archaeological dating. Archaeologists are often frustrated by only finding a tiny, unidentifiable fragment of a mark.

Bottle Maker's Marks

Glass bottles can also carry maker's marks. The first known marked glass reads in Greek "Ennion made it." Happily for historical archaeologists, most glass manufacturers have followed Ennion's lead. To identify maker's marks on glass, historical archaeologists can use catalogues of marks complied by glass specialists in the same way they employ books of ceramic marks.

Glass manufacturers, like potters, often used distinctive marks to identify their wares. For example, a "C" with a square around it on the bottom of a bottle indicates the Crystal Glass Company of Los Angeles, California, made the bottle between 1921 and 1928. The words *KEARNS & CO.* identify a bottle made by the Kearns, Gorsuch Bottle Company of Zanesville, Ohio, between 1864 and 1876, and the letters *ABGM Co.* indicate a bottle was manufactured by the Adolphus Busch Glass Manufacturing Company of Belleville, Illinois, sometime between 1886 and 1928.

As is the case with marked ceramics, archaeologists can use glass marks to identify the object's producer and the date ranges of its manufacture. Historical archaeologists can also use the marks in conjunction with ceramic marks to narrow down the site's dates and to understand the distance artifacts had to travel to reach the archaeological site. This information sheds important light on marketing and artifact distribution, information perhaps existing in no other source.

Archaeologists excavating early twentieth-century sites along the Pacific coast noticed embossed numbers on the rims of common milk bottles. Rather than being placed on the bottom, these marks were at the top. Being unable to find any information about these numbers in the archeological literature, the researchers read contemporary industry materials. In sources such as *Pacific Bottler*, *Milk Dealer*, and *Glass Container*, they discovered that the numbers were actually codes for the dates of manufacture. Between 1917 and 1938, at least five companies located in California (Sacramento, Los Angeles, and San Francisco) used these codes. They indicate the month and year of manufacture, and were used by manufacturers to keep track of the bottles. At the time, glass milk bottles were usually returned and reused. This research shows that historical archaeologists, by continuing their research into maker's marks, can always discover something new, even in the least likely places.

Technological Attributes

The prevalence of artifacts like glass bottles and ceramic plates with clearly identifiable marks increases with time, so late-nineteenth- and early twentieth-century sites are more likely to contain marked and readily datable objects. As a result, historical archaeologists who study sites dating before the late nineteenth century often do not have the advantage of discovering easily identifiable, marked ceramics and glass. With the lack of supporting documentation, historical archaeologists have had to learn to date artifacts by their *attributes*, or physical characteristics.

The physical attributes found in objects made by non-industrialized peoples are largely the result of culturally recognized and understood conventions. For example, beautifully decorated Mimbres black-on-white pottery from southwestern New Mexico (1000–1130 C.E.) is emblazoned with bold geometric designs and delicately drawn animal figures that would be immediately recognized by every member of that culture. The physical attributes of these ceremonial bowls are culturally expressive; they depict legends of creation and other aspects of Mimbres belief.

In contrast, the physical attributes of objects made by industrialized societies often relate more to a manufacturer's efforts to produce objects consumers find appealing or that simplify the manufacturing process. As a result, the physical attributes of many objects discovered by historical archaeologists have much to do with technological change and innovation.

Glass bottles provide an excellent example of how technological change can be documented through time using artifacts. Since antiquity, glassmakers have produced bottles using their own air. Glassblowers, after placing a ball of molten glass on the end of a hollow rod, use forced air from their lungs to shape a vessel. They "free-blow" bottles and other vessels using only their skill and experience. The process leaves visible stretched air bubbles in the body of the glass. Also visible is the distinctive rough mark on the bottle's base, called the *pontil scar*, where the glassblower broke the glass rod free from the bottle. Glassblowing was a slow and laborious process, and the uniformity of the individual bottles rested with the skill of the glassblower.

As producers of recognizable liquid foodstuffs began to link their products with their containers, like Coca-Cola, they began to require standardized bottles. To meet this demand, glass producers began to produce bottles in molds. Around 1750, glassblowers started to blow bottles into hinged, two-piece molds. The protrusions on the bottle mouths (called the "finish") were made by hand using a shaping tool run around the outside of the top of the bottle before it cooled. When the bottle had sufficiently cooled and hardened, the glassmaker removed it from the mold. Molded bottles exhibit a seam line running from near the top to bottom of the bottle, and diagonally across the base. The seam does not appear where the bottle maker ran the shaping tool around the bottle mouth because the action of the tool erased it.

Glass factories used the two-piece mold until about 1880. English bottle-maker Henry Ricketts patented a three-piece (or "Ricketts mold") in 1821. Manufacturers used this mold, characterized by a seam running around the bottle's shoulder, until about the 1920s. Michael Owens, general manager of the Toledo Glass Company, invented the first fully automatic bottle-making machine in 1903, and today, after a series of improvements, the modern bottle was produced. Today's bottles show evidence of their manufacturing technique by the presence of a seam extending from the tip of the mouth to the base. Even the finish is machine-made. Given the bottle's technological history, their visible attributes—seam lines, pontil marks, and bubbles—all serve as valuable chronological indicators.

Other attributes, such as the type of closure, are also chronologically significant. Bottle makers used threads on bottle necks only after about the mid-1850s. Before then, they capped their bottles with wax, corks, or some other clever method designed to keep the liquid inside. The greatest innovation in bottle closure came in 1892 when William Painter patented the "crown cap," readily recognized today as the familiar bottle cap. Painter called his invention the "crown cork" because it "gives a crowning and beautiful effect to the bottle." Painter's official patent for his "Bottle-Sealing Device" gave a less poetic description of his achievement, calling it "a metallic flanged sealing-cap adapted to receive the head of a bottle and containing a concavo-convex sealing disk" (Figure 8.4).

Even the common, everyday nail has a well-documented manufacturing history. Today's round-headed, fully machine-made wire nail only dates to the 1850s. Before then, nail producers used a variety of other methods to make their products. Completely handmade nails can be recognized by their hammered heads, flattened points (when viewed from one side), and irregular shapes. Blacksmiths who made nails completely by hand found it a tiresome and monotonous process. With the rise of greater industrialization, nail manufacturers, like their glass- and ceramic-making colleagues, sought more efficient and quicker ways to produce huge quantities of uniform nails. Nails made between the 1790s and the 1820s were thus cut with a die from a flat, solid sheet of "nail plate." These nails are recognizable by their rectangular, rather than round, cross sections and by their hand-hammered heads. By the 1880s, the modern wire nail (with round heads and shanks) were much less expensive to manufacture than their machine-cut cousins, and so they were cheaper to purchase. Most builders shifted to using the less expensive round nails at about that time. Historical archaeologists must be careful when attempting to use nails for dating purposes because some building restorationists still prefer to use old nail styles for the sake of authenticity. Also, many builders may have

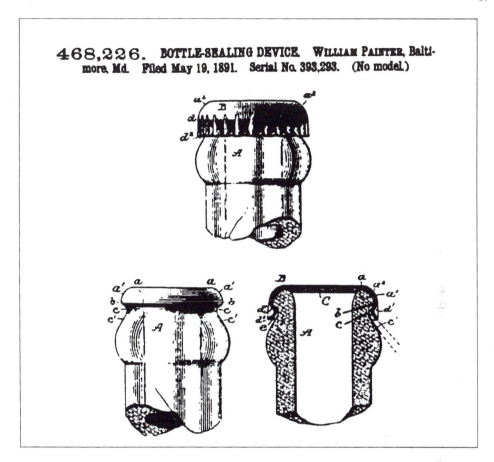

Figure 8.4 Patent information for common bottle cap, 1891
(U.S. Patent Office)

salvaged nails from old buildings and reused them in new constructions. The presence of old nails in a new building can make accurate dating difficult.

The list of potentially datable artifacts is enormous. Lighting devices, locks, horseshoes, smoking pipes, glass beads, dolls, tin cans, hair combs, and many other objects were all produced with different technologies through time. Historical archaeologists can use these artifacts to help date soil layers, wells, privies, trenches, and even entire sites. Even the most prosaic artifacts can become important historical documents.

As historical archaeology has matured as a discipline and as the number of excavated sites has grown accordingly, a number of innovative excavators have developed searchable, online databases of artifacts. One of the most well-used resources is the Digital Archaeological Archives of Comparative Slavery, or DAACS. This database was developed in 2000 using a grant from the Andrew W. Mellow Foundation. Housed in the Department of Archaeology at Monticello, Virginia (Thomas Jefferson's home), the project is directed by Fraser Neiman, its creator, and Jillian Galle, its first manager. The goal of DAACS is to catalogue and make available artifacts discovered at archaeological sites inhabited or associated with the African American enslaved. The database includes artifact information from a number of sites throughout the Chesapeake, South Carolina, Tennessee, and the Caribbean islands of Jamaica, Nevis, and St. Kitts. Archaeologists studying New World African slavery make frequent use of this important database, and its contents and prominence will surely grow as more sites are added to it.

Other organizations have developed similar searchable databases. Historical archaeologists find these to be incredible resources because they can quickly check comparative sources without having to travel far and wide to museums and universities. Today, for example, a historical archaeologist conducting research into the colonial Dutch settlement of lower Manhattan can rummage through the collections of repositories in the Netherlands and never leave home.

Artifacts as Commodities

Artifacts produced during the most recent decades were mass produced and were intended for sale on a large scale. Most historical artifacts were thus *commodities,* objects created specifically for exchange.

The manufacture and sale of commodities extends back thousands of years. Renowned British-trained Australian archaeologist V. Gordon Childe remarked how the presence of cylinder seals throughout ancient Mesopotamia and the Indus Valley provided the "earliest recorded instance" of the transportation of artifacts over vast distances. Many archaeologists think the Kulli merchants, early traveling salesmen of the third millennium, connected the Mesopotamian world with the Harappans in the Indus Valley. The Kulli lived in Baluchistan, a region straddling western Pakistan and southeastern Iran.

Most communities, no matter how small and self-sufficient, generally maintained a series of connections with the outside world. These linkages might include connections with nearby neighbors, with communities across a region, and with a world market. They might entail the trade of both necessities and luxuries. Archaeologists are interested in studying short- and long-distance connections because of their commercial, political, and social significance. Sites inhabited during the past 500 years offer rich potential for such research.

Using Historical Records in Commodity Research

Historical records from certain periods can provide abundant information about the kinds of commodities available and the criteria people used to select them. Probate records, store advertisements, business catalogues, and even storekeepers' inventory books can be mines of information about consumer preferences, market availability, and price.

Historical archaeologists have found probate records to be an important source of information. Shortly after a person's death, assessors walked through the deceased's home and recorded the objects they saw. The compiled inventory was a list of objects that could be assessed for taxes, valued for inheritance purposes, or evaluated in preparation of an estate sale. Probate inventories can be extremely informative for archaeologists for three reasons: They can help identify objects found in archaeological deposits, they can describe perishable household effects (such as books) that leave no durable archaeological evidence, and they can provide information about objects that were never actually at the site, like cattle herds, farm implements, and carriages. Probate inventories reveal what objects surrounded a person immediately before his or her death. The probate list of James Edward Calhoun, of rural Abbeville County, South Carolina, makes the point.

James Edward Calhoun was the cousin of John C. Calhoun, ardent defender of the American South's slaveocracy. James Edward—world traveler, speaker of 17 languages, and scholar—served as the astronomer with the Stephen A. Long expedition of 1823 as it traveled along the old fur trading routes of the Upper Midwest. Settling down on two cotton plantations in northwestern South Carolina—named Midway and Millwood—Calhoun promised to become a full-fledged member of the South's antebellum slave-owning elite. When his young wife died in 1844 during a horrific epidemic, Calhoun gave up the life of the highborn southern gentleman and soon became known as the "Hermit of Millwood." Upon his death in 1889, assessors carefully inventoried Calhoun's personal property.

Millwood Plantation was located in South Carolina's backwoods, but Calhoun's probate list includes numerous objects that belie his seclusion: a pair of dueling pistols, three gold watches, a telescope, two surveying compasses, a Chinese clothes basket, a silver dog whistle, a silver tea service, $100 worth of Confederate war bonds, and the usual assortment of buttons, dishes, tools, rifles, and agricultural implements one might expect to find in a southern planter's home.

As an added bonus for historical archaeologists, auctioneers held an estate sale after the inventory, and this additional list can be used to assess the relative value of the items Calhoun owned. The Chinese clothes basket sold for $1.55, the dog whistle for $5.00, and the gold watches for $22, $40, and $41. All told, Calhoun's estate sold for $1,644.27, not a paltry sum in rural South Carolina in 1889.

Calhoun obviously cared for the valuable items he owned, otherwise they could not have been available for sale after his death. Archaeologists who excavated his homesite found little of extraordinary value there. The archaeology did tell them, however, that he ate from dishes decorated with a blue pattern called "Italian Flower Garden," that he used a variety of patent medicines, and that he smoked a small pipe that had a face etched into it. These less-valuable objects did not appear in the probate inventory because Calhoun had discarded them. The archaeology, in conjunction with the probate inventory, however, provides the full range of objects Calhoun owned and used during his lifetime.

Our fast-paced, rapidly changing modern world seems to operate because of advertising and aggressive marketing. Inventive merchants devised the methods of modern advertising in the late nineteenth century. A classic example is the Sears Roebuck Catalogue. Back in the 1890s, Sears executives reasoned that if most American consumers could not visit their store in Chicago, they would take their store to their customers "through the agency of Uncle Sam's Mail." Their method was the now-ubiquitous mail-order catalogue. Sears used more than 700 tightly packed pages to list everything from underwear to cast iron pots, from shovels to French bust developers. Calling themselves the "Cheapest Supply House," the Sears executives bragged that "Nearly all our customers send cash in full. It's the best way. If you send too much money we will always refund the balance with the bill." And so they did, ushering in a revolution in retailing.

Archaeologists use contemporary advertisements, such as those in the Sears catalogue, to develop ideas about what goods were available in different regions at various times. These sources also provide interesting information about consumer attitudes because marketers wished to capitalize on the public's widely held perceptions. The selling of St. Jakob's Oel, a popular late-nineteenth-century patent medicine, provides an excellent example of nineteenth-century advertising techniques (Figure 8.5).

Charles A. Voegeler of Baltimore, Maryland, first marketed St. Jakob's Oel in the 1880s under the name of "Keller's Roman Liniment." Voegeler put a picture of Caesar on the label to imply that his product came originally from the ancient Romans. He rested his hope

Figure 8.5 Late-nineteenth-century advertisement for St. Jacobs Oil
(Transcendental Graphics / Getty Images)

on the idea that people would assume what was good for the world-conquering Romans would be good for them as well. But when the Roman motif did not sell as well as Voegeler had hoped, he changed the name of the product first to "St. Jacob's Oil" and then to "St. Jakob's Oel." The spelling change allowed him to market the oil as if it were made by German monks living in the fabled Black Forest. The connection with the ancient Romans was severed.

Advertisements in the *Chicago Tribune* show the way in which Voegeler adjusted his claims for the sake of sales. An advertisement dated January 1, 1880, stated that St. Jakob's Oel cured "rheumatism, neuralgia, pains, soreness, stiffness, cuts, [and] sores." Three days later, advertisements claimed the medicine cured "backache, toothache, headache, swellings, sprains, bruises, burns, [and] scalds." Two days later, Voegeler added "chilblains [the inflammation of the hands and feet because of exposure to the cold], wounds, [and] corns." Did the readers of these ads realize that St. Jakob's Oel was getting better day by day? In any case, Voegeler was definitely not shy about promoting his product. On one of his promotional cards he depicted a red-robed, hooded, white-bearded monk standing in New York Harbor in place of the Statue of Liberty. Instead of a torch, the monk holds up a shining bottle of St. Jacob's Oel!

Historical archaeology shows that Voegeler's cure-all sold well. Excavations at the Drake farmstead in northern Illinois (inhabited from 1838 to 1896) proved that the Drake family bought at least 51 bottles of this "German" remedy in the decade it was available. At the documented price of 50 cents a bottle, the Drake family spent over $25 on this one patent medicine, a not inconsiderable sum at the time.

Using Artifacts in Commodity Research

Apart from historical records, the artifacts themselves tell archaeologists much about their roles as commodities, not only from their labels or attributes, but also from their distribution within sites and across entire regions. Historical archaeologists often have a unique opportunity to obtain a good understanding of the kinds of material objects consumers purchased over wide areas. Perhaps even more revealing, they can often discover things intended to be hidden from public view. For example, while excavating at colonial Jamestown, Virginia, John Cotter was surprised to find the left half of a male pelvis and the bones of the left leg and foot in a seventeenth-century well. Are the bones evidence of an unsolved or perhaps even undetected murder of a person dismembered after death? Cotter was at a loss to explain why part of a human body lay in the well, for there were no obvious signs of violence. These bones cannot be considered commodities, but they demonstrate how wells and other archaeological features can be used to hide elements of daily life, and how they can provide archaeologists with important, often unique, information.

It may be possible to hide some things from your neighbors, but the prying eyes of the archaeologist can see into every corner of a site. When David Hurst Thomas excavated Spanish colonial and Native American sites on St. Catherine's Island, on the Georgia coast, he discovered the Franciscan missionaries there required their Indian charges to accept all the outward trappings of devout Christianity. The archaeology proves the priests encouraged the Native Americans to adopt the Christian manner of burial: unmarked graves beneath the church floor and hands crossed over the chest with feet pointed toward the altar. But the priests also compromised because they allowed the Native Americans to deposit objects in the graves. Placing artifacts with the dead was a common custom among many Native American cultures. Many of the artifacts excavated on St. Catherine's Island were clearly aboriginal in nature—a shell gorget, several

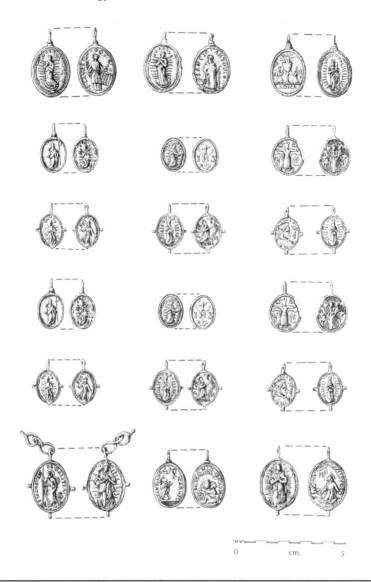

Figure 8.6 Religious medallions from St. Catherine's Island

(From "Saints and Soldiers at Santa Catalina: Hispanic Designs for Colonial America" by David Hurst Thomas in *The Recovery of Meaning: Historical Archaeology in the Eastern United States*, edited by M.P. Leone and P.B. Potter, Jr., Washington, D.C., Small Institution Press © Eliot Werner Publications.)

stone projectile points, and a "chunky" stone, possibly used in a game. Other grave objects were European commodities—whole ceramic vessels, mirrors, and bronze religious medallions (Figure 8.6).

Church leaders frowned on the deposition of objects with the dead, but the missionaries at St. Catherine's Island apparently decided to overlook this traditional practice in their effort to convert the natives to Christianity. Not every colonial Spanish site, however, indicates a willingness to accede to native practice. Graves found at mission sites in Florida are often devoid of artifacts. The precise reason for this difference remains a mystery, but it does illustrate an important reality of Spanish colonialism—that the missionaries' approach to conversion was flexible. Local priests apparently had some latitude when enforcing Church regulations, or else they simply turned a blind eye to some traditional, Native American practices.

Archaeologists have studied the flow of commodities through large trade networks by calculating the distance artifacts had to be transported to reach the site of their use and final deposition. Historical archaeologists, by using company records, patent information, and other sources of information—in addition to direct information from artifacts themselves (see Chapter 7)—are often able to establish exact manufacturing locales of artifacts found at archaeological sites. The amassed information can reveal clues about the long-distance connections past peoples maintained.

Excavating at the Moser farm in extreme northwestern Arkansas, occupied from about 1875 to 1919, archaeologist Leslie Stewart-Abernathy discovered that people in the remote Ozark Mountains maintained diverse connections with the outside world. The site itself was rather small, but the cultural boundaries of this homestead extended far beyond the farm's fences. In fact, the Moser site yielded artifacts from all over the world. The farmers who once lived there ate from dishes made in Ohio and England, administered to their ailments with "Dr. King's New Discovery for Consumption" from Chicago and "Dr. Jayne's Expectorant" from Philadelphia, and canned the vegetables from their gardens in fruit jars with zinc lids and white glass lid liners made in West Virginia and New York. Stewart-Abernathy's excavations show that the inhabitants of the Ozarks, a region often assumed to be well out of the commercial mainstream, participated in the world's marketplace as much as families located along major trading routes.

The presence of exotic commodities at archaeological sites of recent date is easy to understand because the roots of our own economic lives were forged during the fifteenth and sixteenth centuries. In her long-term study of historic St. Augustine, Florida, for example, Kathleen Deagan has documented the wide range of goods available to colonial settlers. Spanish settlers founded St. Augustine in 1565, and the town served as the headquarters for Spain's economic, military, and religious activities in eastern North America, called "La Florida," until 1821. The main cultural ties of the citizens of St. Augustine were with Spain itself, but Deagan's excavations proved the residents also received goods from many other places. She found several kinds of Native American pottery from throughout Florida, red-painted wares from Mexico, coarse ceramics from Italy, and porcelain from Asia. Such research demonstrates that the residents of even remote colonial settlements on the fringes of huge empires could use artifacts imported from far afield.

A residence excavated in Plymouth, England (called the Kitto Institute site) demonstrates that the distribution of commodities was widespread. An examination of the 201 ceramic vessels found at the site, which dates to the 1625–1630 period, indicates the residents used commodities from all over Europe. Included in the collection are six blue and white porcelain vessels from China, vessels of five different decorative types from Spain and Portugal, and eight different types from France. Also included are ceramics made in Germany, the Netherlands, and throughout England.

The numbers and kinds of commodities used at specific sites, like the Kitto Institute site and St. Augustine, allow archaeologists to investigate lines of inquiry that may never have occurred to them without understanding the important role of commodities in the modern world. But even commodities were never simply economic objects, meant only to be purchased, used, and then discarded. Throughout the time of their use, all objects—including commodities—were imbued by their owners with various meanings. The search to discover these meanings is one of the most challenging and yet exciting elements of today's historical archaeology.

Artifacts as Ideas

One of the most interesting, yet difficult, aspects of understanding artifacts of any date is to determine what they actually meant to the people who used them. It may be relatively easy today to envision how artifacts serve as historical documents (objects that relate information about the past) or as commodities (things bought and sold in past marketplaces). But it may be more difficult to understand that the past meanings of artifacts may not be so obvious or straightforward. Many archaeologists now think of artifacts as "signs." A sign, as defined by the Italian semiotician Umberto Eco, is anything that "can be taken as significantly substituting for something else." Eco has become famous outside the narrow field of semiotics for his novels, especially *The Name of the Rose* and *Foucault's Pendulum*. Although Eco's books can be read simply as good stories, semioticians have pored over them in search of much deeper meanings.

Signs are strongly associated with physical things, especially when artifacts are defined as communicative objects—bits of information intended to invoke an image. The Coca-Cola Company's famous red and white sign is an excellent example. On one level it simply advertises the soft drink product, but on another level it has become synonymous with the United States and globalization. When Americans see this symbol in distant lands, they may be reminded of home; when non-Americans see the red and white logo, they may think of the creeping presence of American consumerism. In both cases, the Coca-Cola logo—and indeed all corporate logos—stand for something not embodied by the product itself.

Ideas underlie all physical things and give them meaning. Even our early human ancestors living at Olduvai Gorge, East Africa, put ideas into their simple stone choppers. They made such artifacts to be multipurpose tools, designed to accomplish tasks related to survival, such as breaking bones during food preparation. Archaeologists can understand the functional value of such artifacts through experiments. They can replicate the tools with authentic methods of flintknapping, and they can use the tools to smash bones and scrape meat from them. These experimental archaeologists can examine their tools through microscopes, looking for the telltale signs of edge wear also observable on ancient stone tools. If the edge wear patterns match, the chance is good that both tools were used in the same manner.

But what about other, apparently non-functional attributes of artifacts, elements like decorations on pottery that have no obvious connection with physical survival? What do these things mean? Without supporting documentation, archaeologists are on their own when it comes to providing interpretations. In these cases, they may decide to use an ethnographic analogy (see Chapter 3), but in other cases they may be completely mystified. The first farmers along the Danube River in ancient Europe etched spirals and meandering designs into their pottery, and today no one knows precisely what these designs were meant to represent. Were they simply decorative or did they identify clan membership or some other social variable?

The meaning of artifacts from the more recent past may be easier to interpret because of their role as commodities. Artifact designers of the past 500 years produced artifacts in the hope they would become "objects of desire," things people wanted but did not always actually need. The question archaeologists, as well as modern advertisers and product manufacturers ask is: What makes an artifact desirable? Does an object's appearance alone, often meant to represent something else, make people willing to pay for it? Do ideas existing behind artifacts allow them to become expressions of something else?

Different Interpretations of the Ideas behind Artifacts

Many archaeologists who study artifacts as ideas have used a theory called "structuralism." Structuralism is a complex and hotly debated theory that has as one of its main goals the understanding of the basic, universal patterns that structure human ideas and thereby actions. The most fundamental universal pattern is binary opposition, an idea structuralists propose as basic to the production of meaning. Some of the opposites that material culture specialists have used in studying objects are: bright/dull, light/dark, modern/classic, expensive/cheap, handcrafted/mass-produced, and luxury/everyday. When exploring the role of binary opposites in structuring Anglo-American material culture during the colonial period, James Deetz used the categories private/public, artificial/natural, and complex/simple (see Chapter 10). Deetz proposed that the distinction between individual and shared table settings represented the private/public dyad; the difference between blue and white ceramics and brown, green, and yellow ceramics represented the artificial/natural opposite, and multicolored versus blue and white dishes represented the complex/simple binary opposite.

Deetz used these binary opposites to illustrate the "oppositional structures" underpinning the colonial Anglo-American worldview. Deetz's plan was not to perceive artifacts as historical documents—objects merely found in the ground instead of in an archive—or as commodities, but rather as an avenue for understanding the mentality of colonial English men and women. His foundation for such an approach stemmed from his belief that material culture is more democratic than documents, meaning that people may select objects based on unconscious principles and desires unexpressed in writing, or perhaps even realized at the time. In addition, people in the past did not create deposits of artifacts with the same intentions they had when they wrote documents. In fact, they could never have imagined that anyone would care about their discarded trash! They undoubtedly could imagine, however, that they were leaving written documents for posterity (see Chapter 3).

Ann Smart Martin, a material culture specialist who has used archaeological materials in her research, has adopted a different way of exploring artifacts as ideas. Like Deetz, Martin investigated eighteenth-century sites in the eastern United States, but her focus was on objects made of pewter rather than ceramic. Pewter, an alloy made with a combination of lead and tin, was a common material for the manufacture of drinking and eating utensils during colonial times (Figure 8.7). When thinking about pewter and its widespread use in the past, Martin was struck by the archaeological collections she studied: While they were typically rich in ceramic sherds, they were usually devoid of pewter objects. Colonial chroniclers, on the other hand, often mentioned artifacts made of pewter in probate inventories and other writings. So why do historical archaeologists find so few pewter objects in their excavations?

The scarcity of pewter in relation to ceramics may relate to simple physics: Ceramics break and are discarded, pewter dents but does not break. A person can drink from a dented pewter mug, but he or she cannot eat from half a ceramic plate (at least not very easily). This simple reality is no doubt true, but Martin also sought a deeper meaning for the relationship between pewter and ceramics. Her research convinced her that the meaning of the different proportions of ceramics and pewter may relate to simple consumer preference for ceramics over pewter, or else to a deeper meaning in which pewter represented "conservative stability and wealth" in a rapidly changing society. Martin concluded that the difference between the presence of pewter (as traditional objects) and ceramics (as modern objects) was not based on

Figure 8.7 Pewter objects made in colonial America
(Courtesy of the Winterthur Museum.)

physical differences alone but on a subtle idea of social standing. Pewter and ceramics were chosen by people because of the ideas behind each.

In another study, archaeologist Paul Shackel described how many of the mundane objects of daily life can provide unique insights about artifact meaning and reveal how artifacts present and encapsulate ideas. Shackel used a combination of historical and archaeological sources to show how one object, the common toothbrush, can be immensely important in helping archaeologists to understand past ideas.

Archaeologists have traditionally given toothbrushes little thought. When they found them during excavation they often gave them a functional meaning: People used toothbrushes for dental hygiene. But by using historical records, Shackel was able to show a deeper importance

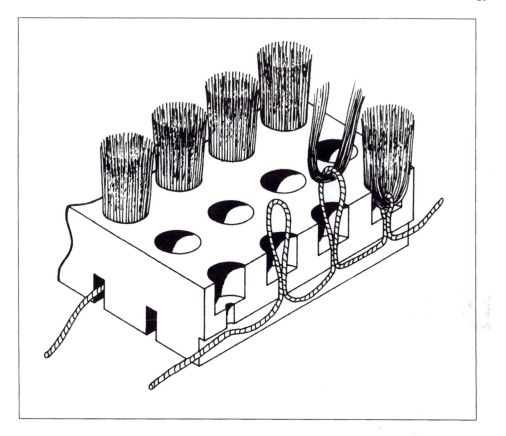

Figure 8.8 Putting the bristles in a toothbrush

(From *Personal Discipline and Material Culture: An Archaeology of Annapolis, Maryland, 1695–1870* by Paul A. Schackel © 1993 by the University of Tennessee Press. Reprinted by permission.)

for how toothbrush manufacturers made their products. He specifically investigated the placement of the bristles into the head of the toothbrush and its relation to the larger concerns of social order and discipline (Figure 8.8). Most people may find such a topic to be unworthy of intensive study, but this was precisely Shackel's point: meaning resides within all artifacts, even the most commonplace among them.

Chinese inventors created the toothbrush, but Western travelers did not bring them home until 1498. Today we use synthetic-fiber bristles, but European toothbrush makers in the past used stiff hairs from Polish, Russian, Chinese, Japanese, and Tibetan boars. Rather than simply viewing the change from hog bristles to nylon as technological alone, Shackel proposed that the change in bristle placement on the toothbrush—from widely haphazard to neat rows—reflects a deeper understanding of social and workplace order. He believed an *idea* of orderliness began to permeate society to such an extent people *expected* orderliness in all elements of society, including in their toothbrushes. Shackel envisioned the neat rows of bristle holes in the common toothbrush as a sign of the increased importance of personal discipline in Western society. The toothbrush thus symbolizes discipline and order. Its neat rows of bristles were not meaningless. Rather, they reflect a wider principle of Western society: Order is better than chaos.

Not all archaeologists agree that accurate meanings of past ideas can be discerned from artifacts. One school of thought holds that all perceptions and perspectives about the past are filtered through our own life experiences and education. They argue that because no one can ever really "know" the past, most of what we say about it actually derives from our own times. In other words, we construct a past that has meaning to us.

Archaeologists of this school argue that no matter how much we may wish to understand the past, we can never truly know it. This point was made as long ago as 1926 by historian Carl Becker, who said that "the historical fact is in someone's mind or it is nowhere." Some archaeologists have used this idea to give meaning to artifacts from ancient times. How can anyone alive today really know the ideas of a potter who lived along the banks of the Danube River and put designs on her pots a thousand years ago? Interpretations of meaning come from somewhere and for many archaeologists the only place can possibly be the "here and now."

In contrast, historical archaeologists can rely on numerous pieces of well-documented information to study the meanings of artifacts in the past. Contemporary writings do much to help them "get inside people's heads" and to see something of the world as the writers saw it during their time. The presence of documents, however, does not mean the search for meaning in past artifacts is either straightforward or readily agreed upon. On the contrary, this kind of research will always provide controversial interpretations. But rather than being put off by the points of contention, historical archaeologists embrace them because they provide intriguing insights into past life. The study of meaning—from the lowly toothbrush to the grand formal garden—will continue to attract the historical archaeologist's attention for many years.

Site Visit: Mobile, Alabama, 1702–1711

The French, not to be outdone by the other European superpowers who were harvesting the riches of the New World, strove to establish their own empire in North America. In addition to their successful efforts in Canada, they also cast their eyes on the Gulf of Mexico, and settled in a region that would come to be called French colonial Louisiana. The French sought to establish themselves between the Spanish at La Florida (to the east) and Nueva España (Mexico) to the west. So, in 1702 Pierre Le Moyne d'Iberville began a settlement that was designed as the military, economic, and political linchpin of the French empire in Louisiana. This settlement is known today as Old Mobile. This French center lasted only nine years, when the decision was made to move the town to the location of today's Mobile, on the mouth of Mobile Bay.

As was true of all colonial adventures, the new settlers had to decide how they would interact with the native peoples who had lived in the region for generations. The French at Mobile encountered several cultures, including the Mobiles, Tomés, Creeks, Choctaws, and Chickasaws. These longtime occupants of the region had developed histories interwoven with intermittent trade contacts and warfare.

In one of those strange twists of historical fate, the French and the Spanish (whose nearest settlement was the presidio at Pensacola, just west of Mobile) were uneasy allies throughout the life of Old Mobile. Their connection was uniquely European, because they were drawn together by the War of Spanish Succession (1701–1713). Their uncertain relations along the Gulf Coast in far-away North America derived from two circumstances: They were both seeking to control land in North America (often the same land), and they had different ideas about how to interact with the local Native Americans. But even so, the French at Mobile and the Spanish at Pensacola learned that they had to depend upon one another because of the chronic shortage of supplies caused by the unreliability of ships coming from Europe. They undoubtedly also shared some sense of being culturally European and religiously Roman Catholic in an environment in which they were surrounded by indigenous peoples who were certainly not European or Christian in behavior or tradition.

French Mobile was in many ways a typical European colonial town. The colonists designed a settlement that made cultural sense to them. They built more than 100 houses on a regular grid of streets, using names that would have been at home in Paris. They constructed their houses using a method called *poteaux sur sole* (post-on-sill). In this kind of construction, a wooden sill was laid on the ground and hewn wooden posts (like today's wall studs) were set on top of them. They filled the interstices with a mixture of clay and other materials to provide both strength and insulation. The houses also had several rooms and fireplaces. Smaller houses, possibly used for soldiers, had only one room and were made with the less-substantial *pieux en terre* method, in which upright posts were set into narrow trenches (Figure 8.9). These buildings were less substantial and more temporary than the residential dwellings. At one edge of town, the colonists constructed Fort Louis, a simple wooden stockade overlooking the river.

The residents of Old Mobile were mostly men, but with time the colony's promoters were able to convince a few French women to emigrate to the settlement. The residents also purchased Native American women and children to serve as domestic servants. Enslaved Indians comprised perhaps as much as a quarter of the population. Priests in the colony disapproved of the cohabitation of French settlers and Native American women, and so they promoted the emigration of more French women and even the introduction of enslaved Africans.

The high percentage of native peoples at Old Mobile meant the objects used every day reflected a combination of Native American and French forms of manufacture and design. In addition, the town's connection with La Florida meant that much of the material culture was Spanish. The members of a household at Old Mobile may have used an equal amount of French tin-glazed faience, Spanish tin-glazed majolica, and unglazed pottery made by the Apalachees in Florida. The residents also used a substantial amount of fine Chinese porcelain,

Figure 8.9 Barracks to garrison French troops at Old Mobile, 1702–1711

(Courtesy of Gregory Waselkov.)

the quality and styles of which were comparable to examples found throughout Europe.

The food consumed by the residents of Old Mobile was also a cultural blend of New and Old World species. They ate native maize and European fava beans, and they learned to harvest the wild foods around them. They ate white-tailed deer, as well as muskrat, beaver, opossum, squirrel, and fish.

Source: Gregory A. Waselkov, ed. French Colonial Archaeology at Old Mobile: Selected Studies. *Historical Archaeology* 36, 1 (2002):1–148.

Chapter 9

Historical Archaeology and Cultural Resource Management

Students of historical archaeology will encounter cultural resource management (CRM) at some point during their careers. In fact, most archaeologists practicing today work in the CRM environment. This is true throughout the world, wherever governments are concerned about preserving and protecting their historic properties. The growth in CRM research has been partly responsible for the increased worldwide interest in historical archaeology. CRM research has also done much to promote archaeology to the public. In this chapter we present some basic information about cultural resource management to explain the nature and importance of this activity to historical archaeology.

The Changing Face of Historical Archaeology

Historical archaeology as practiced at the beginning of the twenty-first century is different from much of the historical archaeology that was practiced before the mid-1970s. Not only have theoretical and methodological emphases changed over time, but the very nature of the workforce has also undergone transformation. Only a few years ago, the vast majority of professional archaeologists taught in academic departments or built educational exhibits for museums. Archaeologists were largely engaged in pure research, activities specifically designed to produce knowledge about the past. The central idea was that scholarly books and museum exhibits would serve the public good by providing information about the latest advances in knowledge about human history and culture. The situation is vastly different today, as archaeologists have found a diversity of homes. CRM historical archaeologists may be employed by governmental agencies (municipal, state, federal) responsible for protecting cultural heritage, by for-profit engineering companies engaged in large construction projects, by privately owned firms dedicated solely to archaeological consulting, or by indigenous tribes seeking to control, preserve, and protect their cultural heritages. A few universities maintain CRM research units within departments of anthropology or as separate entities.

Given the significance of CRM, it became clear by the early 1990s that the profession of archaeology had changed. To understand the magnitude of the change from pure academic to sponsored research, the Society for Historical Archaeology conducted a survey of its members in the late 1990s. The survey showed that most practicing historical archaeologists were engaged in CRM research in some fashion. Fully 71 percent of the survey respondents reported they had completed a cultural resource management study during the 1993–1998 period. Only 29 percent of the responding members said they had engaged in any teaching during the same period. These employment figures represent a major shift in the practice of historical archaeology (and archaeology in general). By the year 2000, many more individuals were employed in historical archaeology than ever before, but their main activities occurred within cultural resource management rather than in universities or museums (Figure 9.1). What has brought about the shift from educational instruction to sponsored research conducted under contract?

Perhaps ironically, part of what caused the expanded employment opportunities for historical archaeologists was the economic expansion that occurred throughout the world after the World War II. The expansion of cities, the construction of strip malls in once-empty fields, and the unrelenting use of agricultural land for new homes, small businesses, and industries destroyed archaeological sites at an ever-increasing rate. As the dual process of construction of the new/destruction of the old was advertised and explained to growing numbers of concerned citizens, individuals committed to saving the past began to stress the need for increased preservation and protection.

Figure 9.1 Double fireplace foundation discovered at Ashland-Belle Helene Plantation, Louisiana, as part of a project conducted for the Shell Chemical Company by archaeologists from Earth Search Inc.

(Jill-Karen Yakubik and Rosalinda Méndez, *Beyond the Great House: Archaeology at Ashland-Belle Helene Plantation*, Baton Rouge: Louisiana Division of Archaeology, 1995, p. 20.)

Some concerned individuals developed organizations dedicated to preservation and protection, but these groups were usually concerned only with the homes of prominent members of history or with fairly small geographical areas. For example, the Society for the Preservation of Old Dwellings, now called the Preservation Society of Charleston, South Carolina, was originally created in 1920 specifically to save the Joseph Manigault House, built around 1802. In the late 1940s, a group of concerned citizens united to create the National Trust for Historic Preservation. Their goal was to acquire and maintain historic American houses, and their first property was Woodlawn Plantation in Virginia, a mansion built in 1805 and given by George Washington to his nephew. Organizations such as these were instrumental in saving and restoring historic properties, but their mandate was usually limited and their vision was usually toward saving properties and houses associated with America's famous early citizens. What was needed was governmentally imposed regulations that would set limits on the destruction of important archaeological sites and historic properties. Only through such legislation could historic preservation spread throughout the United States and include within its purview sites associated with people not included among society's elites.

A Short Overview of CRM Legislation in the United States

Many countries have enacted laws to protect their antiquities. In the United States, Congress passed the first act of this kind in 1906. Titled "An Act for the Preservation of American Antiquities," it called for the protection of "historic landmarks, historic and prehistoric structures, and other objects of historic or scientific interest" located on land owned or controlled by the federal government. In 1935, Congress enacted another law, "An Act to Provide for the Preservation of Historic American Sites, Buildings, Objects, and Antiquities of National Significance." This act significantly broadened the reach of the earlier law by stating that the preservation of "historic sites, buildings and objects of national significance" was national policy. The framers of the act noted that places deemed important should be maintained for the "inspiration and benefit of the people of the United States." One of the main features of this act was to mandate control of the effort to the Department of the Interior through the National Park Service (which had been created ten years after the passage of the 1906 act). The identification of the National Park Service was important because the prior act had left implementation variously in the hands of the departments of war, agriculture, and interior, depending upon the location of the sites or properties.

The next step in the federal archaeological protection process occurred in 1966 when Congress passed "An Act to Establish a Program for the Preservation of Additional Historic Properties Throughout the Nation." This act stated "the spirit and direction of the Nation are founded upon and reflected in its historic heritage," and recognized "ever-increasing extensions of urban centers, highways, and residential, commercial, and industrial developments." An important feature of this legislation is that it created the National Register of Historic Places, the list of National Historic Landmarks, and the State Historic Preservation Offices (SHPO). What would be most significant for archaeologists—and what would cause the numbers of CRM archaeologists to rise—was the part of the Act designated Section 106.

Section 106 mandates the whenever federal funds are being used in the United States to build a road, realign a bridge, construct a new courthouse, or for any other land modifying purpose, archaeologists (and historians, historical architects, and other scholars required for the project at hand) must be enlisted to ensure the construction does not have an adverse effect on "any district, site, building, structure, or object that is included in or eligible for inclusion in the National Register." The importance of Section 106 has meant that archaeologists and cultural resource managers often refer to the required archaeological research as fulfilling the Section 106 process.

For archaeology, one of the key elements of the 1966 bill was the establishment of the National Register of Historic Places. The National Register is an official list kept by the Department of the Interior of sites, properties, and districts deemed important enough to be preserved. One of its most important features, as it pertains specifically to historical archaeology, is the official decision that sites, properties, and districts more than 50 years old fall within its purview. This requirement meant that in the year 2000, sites dating before 1950 could be listed on the National Register. In 2010, the date of inclusion was 1960, and so forth.

The 50-year sliding scale for potential eligibility meant that archaeologists interested in pre-European periods of American history could no longer ignore modern-era sites when they conducted CRM field research. The addition of the 50-year cut-off date was a tremendous boon to historical archaeology because all organizations doing CRM research required individuals with knowledge of and training in the archaeology and history of the past 500 years. With the legislation in place, CRM field archaeologists were required to examine modern-period sites provided they were at leas 50 years old. When they walked down the right-of-way of a future highway searching for evidence of archaeological sites, they knew that modern-period sites were included in their mandate. Ignoring historical archaeology might mean violating the cultural resource protection law.

As important as the 1966 legislation was to mandating the significance of history, heritage, and archaeology as national policy, no archaeologists were involved in formulating it. In 1968, two well-respected archaeologists, Carl Chapman and Charles R. McGimsey III, traveled to Washington, D.C., to alert Congress that more needed to be accomplished to protect the archaeological sites of the United States. With time, they and others wrote a draft of new legislation and convinced one Senator (Frank Moss of Idaho) and one Representative (Charles Bennett of Florida) to present the bill to each legislative house. This law, the "Archeological and Historic Preservation Act"—but widely known as the "Moss-Bennett Bill"—was approved in 1974. This act was designed to amend the "Reservoir Salvage Act of 1960," a law providing archaeological research in areas slated to be flooded by the building of dams and the subsequent creation of large reservoirs. The legislation mandated that all governmental agencies must be aware of the archaeological and historical sites and properties in the projects they conducted, monitored, or assisted. One implication of the law was that funding for archaeological research dramatically increased after 1975.

These laws and other legislation helped create CRM archaeology in the United States. As Charles R. McGimsey III has explained, the path to obtaining the legislation was never easy, and the laws were never perfect. Every advance seemed to be accompanied with a setback. The laws in the United States are still not without flaw. The most serious deficiency is that private property is not included in any legislation. One of the major complaints of American archaeologists is that landowners are free to modify their land as they see fit regardless of the presence of important archaeological and historical properties.

Readers in other countries can compare and contrast the development of CRM law in the United States with what has occurred in their nations. Some places have stronger laws than the United States, and some have weaker laws. The destruction of archaeological sites is a worldwide problem (see Chapter 13), and archaeologists are constantly striving to find ways to save them. The loss of modern-era sites is as serious as the destruction of ancient sites. In fact, the problem may often be more immediate for historical archaeology because many people fail to appreciate the value of excavating archaeological sites already known in "history." This book shows the fallacy of such thinking, but it continues to exist nonetheless.

CRM Research

CRM archaeology is designed differently from the pure research efforts of academic archaeologists. Archaeologists whose main responsibilities rest with providing instruction in colleges and universities can spend years or even decades carefully studying one topic before they feel fully qualified to write about it in full. The past, like today, was complicated, and archaeologists' efforts to comprehend it may require considerable time and attention. CRM archaeologists are under much tighter constraints than academic archaeologists because they seldom have the luxury of spending years unraveling the nuances of a site's history.

Unlike purely academic archaeologists, CRM archaeologists conduct research for a specific sponsor who requires clearance for a construction project or other landscape-modifying endeavor. Cultural resource archaeologists are sometimes referred to as "contract," "commercial," or "consulting" archaeologists to indicate they work under the terms of legal contacts specifying the precise work they will perform for their client, who pays the bill. For example, archaeologists working in CRM may be under contract to survey the right-of-way for a new highway or they may conduct limited excavations at a town lot slated for the location of new federal housing projects. They may also perform extensive excavations at sites deemed especially significant within an area to be disturbed by large-scale construction (Figure 9.2). Archaeologists' clients can range from small, local water districts to huge federal

Figure 9.2 Excavation of the Paddy's Alley site in north Boston, Massachusetts, found as part of the massive Central Artery Project

(From *Highway to the Past: The Archaeology of Boston's Big Dig* edited by Ann-Eliza H. Lewis. Boston: Massachusetts Historical Commission, 2001, page 43. Courtesy of the Massachusetts Historical Commission, Office of the Secretary of the Commonwealth.)

agencies, with their fees reflecting the amount and level of research to be performed. Obviously, long-term, research-intensive projects in a densely settled urban center will cost more than a one-day survey of a cell tower pad.

How do CRM archaeologists acquire the information that allows them to make informed recommendations about important sites and properties? They use the same methods used by all archaeologists. They conduct background research by reading the reports of other archaeologists, and they perform field surveys and excavations (Figure 9.3). Historical

Figure 9.3 The floor of a Chinese business in Sacramento, California, excavated by historical archaeologists from Sonoma State University under contract with the U.S. General Services Administration

(From *Historical Archaeology of an Overseas Chinese Community in Sacramento, California, Volume 1: Archaeological Excavations* by Mary and Adrian Praetzellis, p. 143. © Anthropological Studies Center, Sonoma State University, 1997.)

archaeologists conducting CRM research also rely on documentary and often oral evidence to support their recommendations. Only by conducting thorough research can they make a strong case for preservation and protection.

As part of their contracts, CRM archaeologists are required to complete and submit detailed, fully professional reports of their investigations. These reports typically contain a complete history of the region under study, a statement about past archaeological research at the site or in the immediate area, a detailed explanation of the methods they used to examine the area to be modified, a thorough statement of their findings, qualitative and quantitative descriptions of the artifacts found, and their recommendations about each individual site they discovered or examined. Some of the questions they will address are: Did they find anything during their field survey? If so, what? Did they discover anything that could be deemed "significant" enough for listing on the National Register of Historic Places? Is anything important enough to demand further study? Should the construction project proceed without further archaeological study?

The largest reports of investigations can fill hundreds of pages and include everything from a full history of the site and region to a detailed study of excavated plant seeds. For example, the report on the excavation of one city block in lower Manhattan, in the historic Five Points neighborhood, contains seven volumes and thousands of pages. The report detailing the excavation of the materials from 290 Broadway, also in lower Manhattan, includes four large volumes.

In addition to the client, governmental archaeologists—most directly on the state level—constitute the primary audience for CRM reports of investigations. These men and women are trained archaeologists who are charged by their governments or agencies to ensure that all archaeological and historical contract work has been done professionally and thoroughly. They are the individuals who are ultimately responsible for ensuring the protection of sites within their jurisdictions, and they make the final decisions about which sites to protect based on the CRM archaeologists' findings and recommendations.

The reports of CRM archaeologists are invaluable sources of information about the archaeological history of an area. The archival and field research they conduct under the terms of their contracts make them experts on the places they have studied. One frequently cited problem with these reports, however, is that they are seldom widely distributed. Part of the restriction on distribution is purely practical because CRM reports contain the precise locations of archaeological sites. Information about site locations must be kept from looters who would thoughtlessly destroy precious archaeological sites if they knew where to find them. The sensitive nature of the information contained in most contract reports is the reason governmental agencies are their primary repositories. In other cases, the information in a report may be so politically sensitive the sponsoring body may not want it released to the public. The proprietary rights of the sponsors who originally paid for the research may be at issue, and the increasing level of security around the world may also inhibit access to some archaeological material. For example, archaeological surveys conducted for federal agencies on the grounds of nuclear power plants may be much more difficult to obtain in the future because of governmental concerns about terrorism.

The governmental archaeologist's office is usually the first stop when CRM archaeologists are contracted to survey a particular area. In the United States this is usually the State Archaeologist's Office or the State Historic Preservation Office (which are often the same place). Archaeologists in other countries will check with the nation's assigned cultural authorities. In the Republic of Ireland, for example, the authority rests with the National Museum of Ireland. In any case, archaeologists planning to conduct a CRM study must check site databases and examine all previous reports completed for the area to be investigated. The often-limited distribution of CRM reports has led many archaeologists to refer to them as a "gray literature": They exist, but in a shadowy and often inaccessible way.

To address the problem with "gray literature," a non-profit organization called Digital Antiquity has created tDAR, the Digital Archaeological Record. The organization's goal is to make obscure information more available to professional archaeologists. Housed at Arizona State University, tDAR database allows archaeologists to search for reports that may be extremely difficult to obtain in hard copy. The creation of digital archaeological archives is a huge benefit to all archaeologists, not just those involved with CRM projects.

Cultural resource professionals must concern themselves first and foremost with the concept of "significance." This idea, though easy to understand in principle, is not as straightforward as one may think. The legislation in the United States requires the investigators to deem a site or property significant before placing it on the National Register of Historic Places. CRM archaeologists spend a good deal of time thinking about significance because it forms the cornerstone of the preservation legislation.

The idea behind significance is largely practical. Faced with expanding economic growth (what developers tend to call "progress"), even the most die-hard preservationists admit that some archaeological and historical sites will be destroyed by new construction. The destruction of old buildings and archaeological sites has occurred in one form or another for centuries, and archaeologists accept this reality. Not everything can be saved. As a result, preservationists realized long ago they had to devise measures permitting someone to decide which sites and properties are especially important and must be saved if at all possible. This plan of action was reasonable, but how could anyone decide what sites from the past are important enough to preserve? Someone interested in the ancient Maya may not attach much importance to a nineteenth-century shipwreck off the coast of Italy. A maritime archaeologist, however, may view the Italian wreck site as tremendously significant. At the same time, ideas about what should be saved can change over time. The once-prevalent idea that the houses of the wealthy and powerful should be saved before the houses of non-elites is no longer mainstream.

As may be expected, different nations may have dissimilar ideas about what is significant. In the United States, the issue of significance was written into the legislation. According to the 1966 act, a site is deemed significant if it is eligible to be listed in the National Register of Historic Places. To be registered, an archaeological site or historic property must be deemed significant in at least one of the following areas:

1. integrity;
2. importance at the local, state, or national level;
3. appropriate age (over 50 years); and
4. exhibit exceptional value if not meeting any of the other requirements.

Integrity is the central feature for deciding whether a site or property is eligible for the National Register. To have integrity a site must be able to convey its significance. This usually means a site cannot be damaged to such a degree that it no longer can provide useful evidence. A small eighteenth-century fortification so looted by relic hunters that it can no longer yield useful archaeological information is a prime example.

Once a site has been judged to have integrity, the law provides four criteria to determine significance. A site or property must:

A. be associated with events that have made a significant contribution to the broad patterns of American history; or
B. be associated with the lives of significant persons in the past; or

C. embody the distinctive characteristics of a type, period, or method of construction, or represent the work of a master, or possess high artistic values, or represent a significant and distinguishable entity whose components may lack individual distinction; or

D. have yielded or may be likely to yield, information important in history or prehistory.

When assessing a site's suitability, archaeologists thus must consider the site's association with important events and people, its architecture, and the cultural and historical information the site has the potential to contribute to the general storehouse of knowledge. CRM archaeologists must fully understand these criteria to enable them to make informed recommendations about the significance of specific sites. Since 1966, more than 76,000 sites and properties have been listed on the National Register, and the governmental database has information on more than one million individual properties.

In their important guide to archaeological significance, historical archaeologists Donald Hardesty and Barbara Little present a case study of the iron and steel resources of Pennsylvania for the years 1716–1945. The archaeological examination of their last two periods, covering the years 1867–1901 and 1902–1945, would have been largely impossible within a CRM environment without the 50-year requirement of the legislation. Without this mandate, archaeologists may not have been interested in early to mid-twentieth-century sites. They may have written them off as "too modern," something still occurring in many countries without a recent cut-off date.

Many countries still wrestle with the idea of preserving and protecting modern-period sites. This debate rages everywhere, including in countries with extremely long histories. In the Republic of Ireland, for instance, the National Monuments Act, first passed in 1930 and amended in 1954 and 1987, states that a site must predate 1700 C.E. to be protected. Documented Irish history began several centuries earlier, so the period of literate history covered by the act is actually quite long. The wording of the legislation means, however, that a site dating after 1700 is not automatically covered by the legislation. This restriction thus ignores many sites with major importance to Irish history. Several sites historical archaeologists would consider important have possibly been ignored by Ireland's contract archaeologists. They may not even consider post-1700 era sites to be archaeological. The omission of post-1700 sites constitutes a significant problem in Irish preservation law. In all fairness, the federal archaeologists who work for the National Museum of Ireland and for the Office of Public Works Heritage Service understand the limitations of the legislation. Their efforts are extremely positive because some day people may look back and wonder why no one protected the eighteenth- and nineteenth-century sites once dotting the Irish countryside. Nations across the globe are deciding with increasing frequency that modern-period sites are a legitimate focus for archaeological research. These decisions, when positive, help to advance the cause of historical archaeology.

In their essay "Cultural Resource Management and the Business of Archaeology," archaeologists Christopher Bergman and John Doershuk state that the CRM professional must have knowledge about a diverse number of things, including:

- all regulations concerning CRM legislation;
- all permit requirements of the agencies involved in the contract;
- the specifics of the client's industry, financing, and construction schedule;
- the project's guidelines;
- the limits of their professional capabilities to meet the terms of the contract;
- ways to adapt their archaeological methods to the needs of the client;
- how to identify and document all possible archaeological and historic sites that may be found in the area specified by the contract; and
- how to negotiate the various differences of opinion that may arise.

This list aptly demonstrates the difficulty of conducting good CRM archaeology. Public relations skills exist outside the demands of the archaeology itself. Cultural resource specialists must be good field archaeologists, expert researchers, good writers, and be skilled at personal relations.

A Few Pros and Cons of CRM Archaeology

Cultural resource management, like any profession, has pros and cons. Not everyone agrees about these because individuals have different views, attitudes, and experiences. Every individual must decide whether a career in CRM archaeology is right for them. Many highly talented, creative archaeologists have worked in CRM for years, and have provided major advances to knowledge about human history. Some of the largest, most successful projects in the United States have been completed within a CRM environment. For other individuals, CRM archaeology is not a good fit, and so they are better suited to teaching archaeology in a college or university, or creating exhibits and other educational materials in a museum setting.

The Pros

Without question, students of archaeology will benefit from gaining experience in CRM archaeology. The CRM environment is usually fast-paced and rapidly changing. In CRM, an archaeologist will conduct primary research on a huge number of vastly different archaeological sites and historic properties, and they will gain abundant personal experience in diverse areas. In the course of a single day, a CRM archaeologist conducting a survey in the western United States may examine an ancient Native American encampment, an early twentieth-century mining settlement, and a nineteenth-century battlefield. Commercial archaeologists in Europe may be called upon to investigate an ancient megalithic monument, a fourteenth-century castle, and an early nineteenth-century miner's cabin all in the same field trip. Contract archaeologists acquire an immense amount of knowledge about every investigated site: its history, cultural importance, current condition, and ultimate significance. They will draw maps of the sites and collect artifacts they see lying on the surface. They will be required to recognize artifacts from many different periods of history, extending from flint scrapers to machine-cut nails. They will be the first person to handle artifacts that may have lain in the earth for hundreds or even thousands of years, and they may have access to sites tourists can only see from behind a fence. Students of archaeology can quickly gain vast experience in cultural resource management, and much of what they do can be exciting and profoundly interesting.

Travel is another element of CRM archaeology. Archaeologists under contract are often required to travel great distances and to stay in numerous locations for long periods of time. Archaeological travel is a wonderful learning experience, both in terms of the historical and cultural knowledge that can be gained and the personal growth that accompanies it. Broad experience helps individuals become better citizens of the world. CRM archaeology provides an excellent way for archaeologists to immerse themselves in the life of a place they may never have visited otherwise. And, because they may stay in one location for several weeks, they can make new friends and learn unfamiliar cultural and regional traditions.

Archaeologists working in CRM environments also have the opportunity to sharpen their research, writing, and critical thinking skills. Cultural resource archaeologists must write fully competitive, professional proposals that outline their qualifications and provide their exact plans for meeting the terms specified in the request for proposals. Because they work in the business world, they know that other archaeologists will be bidding on the same contract. As a result, they must make their proposals as sharp and as detailed as possible. They must demonstrate their knowledge of archaeological methods and express their familiarity with the region in question. They must show they are qualified and eager to do the research. They must also submit a detailed budget, along with a time schedule to prove they can complete the research on time and under budget. Contract archaeologists are seldom able to petition for an extension of time or for more funding because their research is conducted to satisfy the schedules of their sponsors. In most cases, CRM archaeologists are constrained by the terms outlined in their proposals. For this reason, they must fully understand the abilities of their staffs. Any overages are likely to come directly from their bottom line. This can be a significant problem because most CRM firms are for-profit concerns. In the CRM environment, a firm that overestimates the abilities of its staff or underestimates the costs needed to meet the requirements of the contract will probably not be in business for long.

Writing proposals forces archaeologists to organize their thoughts and sharpen their abilities to work within a specified time frame. These are skills all archaeologists should acquire regardless of their work environment, and experience in cultural resource management provides these skills in abundance. CRM archaeologists, because they often write proposals for nonarchaeologists, must learn to use clear language devoid of archaeological jargon. Learning to write clearly and efficiently is a skill students can use in whatever profession they eventually choose.

For projects specifically involving historical archaeology, contract archaeologists must know where to find the most appropriate archival repositories. They will have to conduct their background historical research in the most efficient way possible. They must learn how to extract the most pertinent information from the most important sources and not allow themselves to be sidetracked. Old newspapers can be tremendous sources of information about modern-period archaeological sites and the people who once lived in them. Most nineteenth-century newspapers, however, include large sections of product ads, many of which were printed on the front page. These old ads are often fascinating, and readers may easily become enthralled by their wild claims and unique ways of promoting their products. But unless a CRM archaeologist has a specific, contract-related reason for studying these ads, the time spent reading them may be difficult to justify to his or her sponsor. That is not to suggest the reader will not have acquired a great deal of interesting and potentially important information. It may be difficult to make a highway engineer understand, however, why the report is late because the archaeologist became immersed in ads for nineteenth-century patent medicines! In any case, knowledge of how to locate, use, and read archival materials is a positive element of CRM archaeology that serves the needs of historical archaeology extremely well.

Experience in CRM archaeology has many benefits, both for the profession of historical archaeology and for individuals engaged in it. It provides a wonderful way to contribute to the creation of archaeological knowledge, to become acquainted with artifacts from many periods of history, and to visit numerous interesting places. But as is true of any pursuit, CRM archaeology has a negative side, too.

The Cons

Consulting archaeologists must travel. While this may be interesting and exciting at the beginning, some people find the constant need to be on the road tiresome. CRM archaeology can require a great deal of relocating because archaeologists must go the projects' locations. They cannot conduct field surveys from the library or laboratory. Much of the traveling is seasonal and hectic. Fieldwork is not possible in environments with cold winters and deep snowfalls, so most CRM archaeologists use the time to write final reports, prepare proposals for new projects, and plan for work already obtained. One problem with seasonality is that some

CRM firms must reduce their staffs during non-fieldwork periods. Excavation may require a large crew, and when the fieldwork is finished, not everyone is needed to prepare the final report. As a result, employment in CRM research can be seasonal and short-term, unless an individual has worked his or her way into the administrative level. Many CRM firms will hire field workers only for specific projects and then be forced to let them go when the project is completed. Long-term employment may be difficult to obtain with the smallest CRM companies. Managers of such firms may be required to scramble to maintain their payrolls during slack periods. Most managers strive to keep a core of highly qualified staff members, but in the worst economic times, even this may not be possible. The largest firms can often employ field workers as lab technicians when the weather precludes fieldwork.

An article about the realities of archaeological fieldwork in Great Britain in the 1960s is revealing. This research occurred before the development of CRM archaeology, but the conditions discussed mirror the general situation still prevalent in much contract archaeology. In their account, Anwen Cooper and Thomas Yarrow note that most of the important archaeological field research conducted in Britain in the 1960s was undertaken by a "notoriously diverse team" comprised of professionals, archaeology students, and a class of people they describe as "artisans, draft dodgers, DJs, and day-release prisoners." Cooper and Yarrow stress two elements of this last group: they are seldom if ever mentioned in the archaeological literature, and they lived by traveling around Britain's "digging circuit." One participant in the circuit specifically mentioned the constant movement required of the job. The need to go from place to place following the archaeology is also a significant element of CRM archaeology. Britain's itinerant archaeologists effectively formed a sub-culture. Many of them were highly skilled excavators with extensive knowledge of archaeological history, but none of them were professional archaeologists even though their contributions to the archaeological profession were immense.

Another problem with cultural resource management can involve the workload itself. Contract archaeologists obtain a great deal of extremely valuable experience, but often because they must work on several projects at once. The time limits placed on the completion of a project—imposed by the funding organization—sometimes means the research may be hurried to meet the deadline. Deadlines are established as part of the original contract. These dates can seldom be renegotiated to any significant extent. Construction engineers and real estate developers expect to receive clearance for their projects on time so they can begin construction. CRM projects thus run for a set period of time and no more. A project effectively disappears when the deadline comes and the final report is submitted. Once this happens, another project must begin immediately. The reality of CRM archaeology is that the members of a firm must be working on proposals for new projects while they are completing the research and report preparation for their current projects. The managers of cultural resource firms must worry about cash flow just like any other businessperson. They cannot afford to overextend themselves with too many employees, and they cannot afford to miss deadlines.

CRM archaeologists do not have the ability to control the extent of their research, and they cannot always focus on specific research topics that interest them, unless they do so on their own time. What is eligible for study by a cultural resource management team is specified in the contract, and archaeologists who go beyond these specifications are liable to find themselves outside the scope of the contract.

In Chapter 7, we mentioned research conducted under the direction of Adrian and Mary Praetzellis in San Francisco, California. They performed this CRM research project in the route of the San Francisco Central Freeway under contract with the City and County of San Francisco. The Praetzellises and their team of archaeologists at Sonoma State University are some of the most qualified CRM historical archaeologists in the world, and their work stands as models for those wishing to learn the proper way to approach contract archaeology. Their summary for the San Francisco Central Freeway project provides an excellent overview of the restrictions CRM archaeologists can face in their research:

> The Central Freeway Replacement Project will involve the retrofitting and widening of the existing elevated structure between South Van Ness Avenue and Fell Street. Ten city blocks will be affected by the Central Freeway Replacement Project. Subsurface impacts associated with the retrofit phase are currently anticipated on only four of the project blocks, but project plans for the widening of the freeway have not yet been finalized, so the entire right-of-way requires careful study for archaeological potential.

What this means is that the archaeological research team was restricted to the ten blocks that would be affected by the highway work and no more. They would be outside the limits of the contract if they chose to conduct field research on properties and sites outside the right-of-way. Their map of the project area shows that Block 3 is bounded by Otis Street on the east, Duboce Street on the south, Valencia Street on the west, and McCoppin Street on the north. The projected path of the freeway cuts through the southern part of the block and swings up through its western half (Figure 9.4). Archaeological and historical sites in

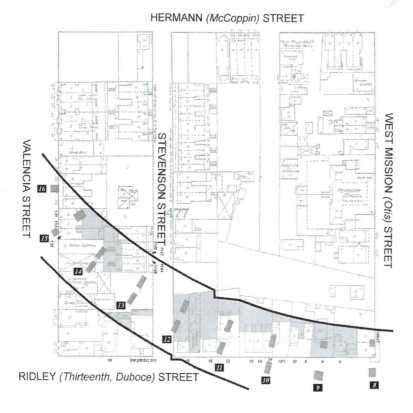

Figure 9.4 Highway right-of-way for the San Francisco Central Freeway Project

(Anthropological Studies Center, Sonoma State University)

237

the path of the freeway in Block 3 are eligible for study under the terms of the contract, but any sites south of Duboce Street are not eligible (at least under the terms of the contract). Such limitations are common in CRM research, and contract archaeologists have learned to live with them.

Some Ethical Issues in CRM Archaeology

Archaeologists often confront ethical challenges. These challenges involve how they should interact with indigenous peoples and descendant communities, whether they should conduct research on artifact collections they know to have been looted, and how to conduct research at sites some people judge to be sacred. One of the hallmarks of archaeological research is that archaeologists are always confronting new ethical challenges. CRM archaeology is often in the forefront of many difficult issues because of the sheer amount of research being conducted around the world.

Some of the ethical issues faced by CRM archaeologists are unique to their environment. Because they operate within the competitive business world, CRM archaeologists are often engaged in a delicate balancing act between their desire to perform good archaeology and the practical requirement to maintain the financial viability of their consulting companies. Contract archaeologists cannot simply choose what to study and ignore the rest. They are required by law to meet their obligations once they have a contract in hand. Any contract archaeologist who decided that he or she would only take contracts restricted to a narrow research topic would not be in business for long. As a result, CRM archaeologists with a specialty in historical archaeology must also be knowledgeable about the artifacts and settlements of earlier eras. In the largest firms, CRM archaeologists may be able to specialize in historical archaeology, but even in this case, they cannot concentrate only on one period of history. A historical archaeologist interested in colonial America must also know about late-nineteenth-century industrialism and many other topics as well.

Cultural resource professionals are often called upon to make choices that defy easy resolution. They must often make decisions within a rapidly changing environment and collaborate with a constantly changing set of clients' representatives. Some of the clients and their agents may be hostile to archaeology, believing it to be an unnecessary burden, something designed only to waste their time and consume their financial resources. They may even believe the CRM archaeologists have a vested interest in prolonging the work to maintain their employment. Some people are simply opposed to archaeology because they mistakenly believe it to be "anti-progress." Many developers perceive the saving of old buildings and buried archaeological sites as slowing or even stopping the progress they view as required of a capitalist economy. Without constant expansion, they say the economy will collapse or stagnate. Archaeology provides an easy and visible target for individuals who fail to realize that a respect for the past constitutes part of a healthy society. Some of the problem rests with the archaeology profession's general lack of successful public education, a trend that archaeologists are always striving to correct (see Chapter 13).

In the worst possible situations, cultural resource archaeologists may find themselves in conflict with their sponsor. Unscrupulous real estate developers may ask the archaeologists they have hired to "forget" they saw an archaeological site or to make recommendations that serve the sponsor's needs but will forever damage the integrity of an archaeological site. This situation represents a major ethical dilemma. On the one hand, the archaeologist is working on behalf of the sponsor, but on the other, the sponsor is asking the archaeologist to violate standard professional ethics.

CRM archaeology in the United States is usually defined by three "phases." Phase I generally refers to a pedestrian, or walkover, survey, where the archaeologists simply conduct a visual inspection for artifacts and other cultural materials. It may also include shovel testing. Phase II usually means limited excavation used to judge the subsurface integrity of a site. The excavations may be 1 by 1 meter (3.3 x 3.3 ft) excavation units placed at locations indicated by the Phase I findings. Phase III refers to more intensive excavation. Thomas King, longtime expert on American CRM archaeology, refers to this three-phase system as "find it/assess it/dig it up (Phase I-II-III)."

Suppose archaeologists are under contract to conduct a Phase I survey of a piece of ground located near a white sandy beach slated to become the site of a luxury apartment complex. In the course of the survey, the archaeologists discover what might have been the encampment of individuals engaged in an eighteenth-century anti-tax revolt. A single document found in the local archives mentions a site in the vicinity but does not provide a precise location. The field archaeologists cannot determine whether the identified spot is the historic site from the surface features and artifacts alone. They also cannot access the extent of the site or even learn whether the soil conditions have preserved anything without further exploration at the Phase II or possibly even Phase III level. The problem, however, is that the developer is eager to get his buildings up before the summer so that he can start renting the apartments to work-weary vacationers. He does not want to pay for further archaeological research, and he wonders why "his" archaeologists are doing this to "him." He asks them to forget about the site, and if they cannot do that, perhaps they can downplay its importance in their report. What do the archaeologists do? Do they report the developer to the authorities and possibly lose future contracts in the area? Do they agree to the developer's demands and ignore their professional ethics?

Fortunately, CRM archaeologists seldom encounter such crass behavior during the course of their work. Most developers understand the need to preserve and protect a nation's heritage, if sometimes only reluctantly. But CRM archaeologists must be aware that such encounters do occur, and they must consider how they will respond to such challenges.

Another ethical issue of CRM archaeology concerns the treatment of field crews. Hired field workers are often termed "archaeological technicians" in contracts. As noted above, Cooper and Yarrow commented on how the labor of field archaeologists is usually overlooked by professional archaeologists who need workers to complete their research and CRM projects. In *Archaeology as Political Action*, Randall McGuire writes about the class structure of CRM archaeology. He notes how CRM field crews work in often-harsh conditions, for short periods with little long-term job security, and for relatively low pay given the skills needed to do good archaeology. The wage structure of CRM firms is unequal, in the sense that management receives much higher pay than field workers do. This practice conforms to the typical business model of any for-profit company. He also observes something well known in professional archaeology: that field workers are widely known as "shovel bums," a term remarkably consistent with the view in 1960s England that field crews formed a unique subculture, something like a professional underclass. (In fact, archaeologists looking for work can access a website called Shovel Bums.)

In the 1990s, a group of fieldworkers attempted to create a labor union called United Archaeological Field Technicians. This group sought to bring together field technicians into a collective bargaining unit. The effort ultimately failed even though it had an affiliation with the AFL-CIO. The union disappeared without having much impact. The reasons for failure are undoubtedly complex, but two factors may help explain the union's demise. First, it is possible that fieldworkers serious about a career in archaeology believed they would eventually climb of ranks in CRM and become managers themselves. As such, they may have been unwilling to be seen in the role of questioning the basic labor structure of CRM archaeology. Second, it could be possible, since archaeology is essentially an upper-middle-class pursuit, that many people drawn to the profession may have little prior experience with trade unions and so misunderstand or are wary of them.

In March 1995, owners of a few archaeological CRM firms came together and founded the American Cultural Resources Association. The ACRA is a trade association composed of professional consulting firms. One goal is to monitor cultural resource activities in the United States and to be advocates for commercial archaeology on state and federal levels. Another goal is to develop universal standards for field technician pay rates and to make their code of ethics the standard in the profession. However, since about 1,300 CRM firms exist in the United States as of early 2014, whether this can be accomplished is unclear. The disparity of size (with a handful of large companies dominating) and the simple need for firms to compete against one another may make the task impossibly complex.

To summarize, CRM archaeology constitutes a significant element of today's historical archaeology. Like anything else, it has good and bad points. Generally, however, students of historical archaeology will benefit from some exposure to the world of contract archaeology because of the range of experiences offered. Even so, aspiring archaeologists should be aware of the downsides, too.

Site Visit: Hacienda Tabi, Yucatan, Mexico, 1876–1911

With the independence of Mexico from Spain, a small class of landowners, mostly of European descent, exerted their authority within the emerging socio-political system. Mexico was once the jewel in Spain's colonial crown because of its incredible riches in gold and silver. With independence, wealthy landowners decided to gain control economically. With the cessation of colonial control from Iberia, several members of the European elite increased the size of their landholdings. Needing laborers to work their fields to produce an income from their vast estates, these landowners established ways to dominate the indigenous Mayas. One place that experienced the changes wrought in the late nineteenth century was Hacienda San Juan Bautista Tabi, a prominent sugar estate in the Yucatan peninsula (Figure 9.5).

Haciendas were large estates worked by indigenous villagers. Like the classic New World slave plantation, hacienda workers were kept in a kind of legal bondage. The estate owners did not actually own their bodies as in slavery, but as workers, they were hopelessly in debt to them. Workers in debt were legally bound to their estates until they could repay what they owed. Debts were amassed through a series of well-crafted schemes, including allowing workers to purchase on credit vastly overpriced commodities at the hacienda store. Because workers seldom made enough money to pay off their debts, they were required to continue to live (and to work) on the estate to which they owed money. Such practices perpetuated the presence of poverty-stricken workers on estates year after year.

Figure 9.5 Hacienda Tabi, Yucatan, Mexico
(© Michael Calderwood.)

The practice of debt peonage in Mexico was always oppressive, but it became even more so during the rule of President Porfirio Diaz (1876–1911). During this period, many haciendas, including Hacienda Tabi, established categories of debt, setting the amount of work for individual peons. Individuals with fewer than 100 pesos of debt, "temporary workers," usually only had to work during harvest. People with more than 200 pesos of debt had to work every day except Sunday. They also could not leave the estate without their supervisor's consent.

Given the nature of hacienda labor, it was inevitable that conflicts would arise between owners and workers. Part of the ongoing struggle was reflected in the physical construction of the haciendas themselves. The physical layout of Hacienda Tabi had two main elements: a large, open "great yard" around which were situated the owner's estate house, surrounded by the church, sugar mill, and stables. The second structural element was the workers' village. It was designed on a grid of 14 square-to-rectangular residential blocks arranged around two sides of the owner's complex. Two open plazas were included within the village grid, and four streets ran out of the settlement in the cardinal directions.

The first hacienda zone, with the estate's principal buildings, was intended to express the power and dominance of the hacienda owner. His house was a long, spacious, two-story building, with elaborate staircases, numerous decorative arches, and massive windows. Its two floors contained about 27,770 square feet (2,580 sq m) of floor area. The proximity of the house to the stables and the sugar mill was designed to indicate the owner's control over these economic realms. The nearness of the church reinforced the idea that the economic and political orders were upheld by the religious order. People from the village wishing to enter the church first had to walk into the "great yard" in front of the owner's elaborate house. This path reminded them of the power the owner's family (and his entire class) held over people like them. But the effect of viewing the huge landowner's house was more than merely symbolic. The estate's workers also realized it housed two tiny confinement cells on the west end of its lower floor. These cells measured only 8 feet (2.5 m) square. Hacienda workers could be confined at any time in these cells for disobeying the rules or for exhibiting behavior forbidden by the estate owner. Workers could also be whipped as part of their punishment.

The houses of the hacienda workers were rectangular in design with rounded corners. They had only about 344 square feet (32 sq m) of floor space. They were built either of perishable materials or more durable stone blocks. The quality and size of the houses varied with their occupants' jobs. Salaried workers on fixed wages had higher prestige than workers paid only by the amount of work they performed. Salaried workers thus lived in more substantial and slightly larger houses than task laborers. Four qualities of workers' houses at the hacienda tended to reflect the estate's hierarchy of work.

Source: Allan D. Meyers and David L. Carlson. Peonage, Power Relations, and the Built Environment at Hacienda Tabi, Yucatan, Mexico. *International Journal of Historical Archaeology* 6 (2002):225–252.

Interpretation in Historical Archaeology

Chapter 10

Theory in Historical Archaeology

Of all the subfields of archaeology, none is more multidisciplinary in its perspective than historical archaeology. Historical archaeologists draw on ideas and concepts from many disciplines, including anthropology, history, geography, sociology, political science, and landscape architecture among others. In this chapter, we discuss some of the theoretical approaches that form the basis for interpreting archaeological materials found at modern-period sites. Given the range of ideas in historical archaeology and the profession's recent and continuing growth, the comments here cannot be exhaustive. Rather, our goal is to provide an overview of interpretive perspectives rather than a how-to primer on "the best way" to interpret the past 500 years of human history. Archaeologists today acknowledge that many perspectives exist about the past and accept that no one interpretation may capture the full complexity of any past sociocultural situation.

Many students may shy away from the theoretical aspects of archaeology. This is unfortunate because theory forms the discipline's core. No one should be afraid of theory; it simply constitutes the ways in which various archaeologists have thought about the past. Each archaeologist brings to the field his or her own preconceptions, outlooks, and experience, and as archaeologists struggle to make sense of the past, they tend to present it in different ways. Each archaeologist emphasizes certain elements of the past and downplays others based on what they believe to have been most important. Some archaeologists concentrate on settlement patterns while others focus on patterns of subsistence. Variation in approach is normal because the subject matter is vast. Human history represents a complex and interconnected web of personal interactions, motivations, and actions, and deciphering them with archaeological information is difficult. Given the complicated nature of human existence, one reasonable place to begin is with one's understanding of "how the world works": what is important to emphasize and what we can afford to ignore.

Archaeologists can disagree about one another's interpretations, and sometimes these arguments can be heated. Individual archaeologists, as scholars believing in their interpretations, tend to stand by them until overwhelming counter evidence causes them to change their minds. This is how science and knowledge advances. Disagreements over theory are honest differences of opinion. Rather than viewing them as setbacks, controversies usually result in advancing knowledge. Theory presents a rich area of study for all archaeologists, including those examining modern history.

In this textbook, we can only present three broad theoretical approaches in historical archaeology: humanistic, scientific, and humanistic science. These are not the only approaches possible, nor are they mutually exclusive. Considered together, they illuminate the universe of interpretations possible in the field. Those presented here have been created, in general, with knowledge and acknowledgment of the others. Our perspective is that humanistic scientific archaeology is prevalent in the twenty-first century because historical archaeologists trained as anthropologists seek to do good science (by excavating their sites systematically and analyzing their finds carefully) while also attempting to provide concrete information about how men and women lived in the past. At the same time, however, not all historical archaeologists are trained as anthropologists. Historical archaeologists educated in a traditional European manner, for example, may have little or no anthropological training. This does not mean, of course, that their research suffers. Rather, their general historical focus provides yet another way to interpret the past.

Individual archaeologists are constantly striving to develop new theoretical approaches to understand history. The three interpretative strands presented here are somewhat chronological in the sense that humanistic interpretations tended to come first and humanistic science later on. Even so, any individual archaeologist is free to choose among them at any time in their career or to create an entirely new approach.

Humanistic Historical Archaeology

Humanism is a philosophy focusing on the inherent dignity of humanity, on the potentials, sensibilities, and actions of real men and women. The humanistic approach in archaeology is expressed by historical reconstructions attempting to put today's visitors in touch with their historical counterparts by showing how people in the past lived. Historical reconstructions at "living museums" seeking to place modern visitors "inside" the past are humanistic in their basic framework. As we have seen at Colonial Williamsburg, Virginia, and Greenfield Village, Michigan (Chapter 3), the act of taking visitors back in time usually involves not only documents, but also artifacts and buildings. The material remains of the past—chairs, glass tumblers, knives and forks—can create powerful impressions in the minds of onlookers. Museum reconstructions are vivid ways to bring the past alive using both commonplace and exotic artifacts to recreate the human dimension of a once-bustling building or community.

Humanistic historical archaeology is often associated with the physical reconstruction of buildings, but not invariably. In a classic study of the late 1960s, Robert Ascher and Charles Fairbanks provided a compelling picture of the experience of the enslaved by adopting a humanistic approach. They excavated the ruins of a cabin on Rayfield Plantation on Cumberland Island, off the coast of Georgia. Some of the largest and richest estates in the hemisphere were located in this region. Ascher and Fairbanks estimated that enslaved men and women had lived in the cabin from about 1834, when Robert Stafford bought Rayfield, until the end of the American Civil War in 1865. A brick chimney was all that stood a century later. Ascher and Fairbanks's goal in excavating the cabin was "to discover and convey a sense of daily life as it might have been experienced by the people who lived in the cabin." They adopted a unique approach to help bring enslavement to life. They interspersed their archaeological report—the stratigraphic drawings and excavation photographs—with a literary "soundtrack" taken from primary documentary sources.

They quoted the great African American orator Frederick Douglass speaking about what it was like to be considered property: "I had now a new conception of my degraded condition. Prior to this, I had become, if not insensible to my lot, at least partly so." Ascher and Fairbanks also found a list of the enslaved in an archive, men and women who had been sold to Stafford as part of the plantation in April 1834. This simple list, when united with the physical remains of the cabin, offered a profoundly human portrait of lives lived in bondage. Such a picture adds depth to the archaeological finding that "Life inside the cabin produced an ash layer that eventually spilled out of the fireplace and onto the floor where the sand turned a darker color through time and use." Through their masterful combination of historical and archaeological source materials, Ascher and Fairbanks linked the differences they observed in the soil layers at the cabin site with the lives of once-living men and women. They created a human picture of enslavement and placed readers in the cabin without actually building a physical replica. Their illustration of a tiny, blue-glass bead found inside the cabin makes readers wonder about the person who had worn this bead. What had his or her life really been like? Human enslavement was not an abstraction to Ascher and Fairbanks; it was the deeply personal, lived experiences of real men and women in the past.

The roots of humanism in historical archaeology extend to the field's earliest days, to a time when historical archaeology was associated almost totally with the discipline of history. When John Cotter excavated Jamestown, Virginia, in the 1950s, one of his primary goals was to summarize the archaeological findings "so as to indicate the way of life" developing in seventeenth-century Virginia. When Kenneth Kidd studied the mission of Sainte Marie I in Ontario, Canada, in the 1940s, he wanted to provide information about "the activities of the Jesuit Fathers in the decade of their residence among the Huron Indians." Cotter and Kidd each viewed his research as the study of history in a humanistic way. In 1964, Ivor Noël Hume famously described the fledgling field of historical archaeology as the "handmaiden to history." He meant this memorable phase to suggest that historical archaeologists complement the humanistic side of historical study. In this view, historical archaeologists find their greatest contribution to knowledge in the realm of humanistic interpretation.

The humanistic approach remains a pervasive and fruitful thread through historical archaeology to this day, even though many archaeologists have adopted a more overtly scientific approach. The scientific approaches, however, do not diminish the importance of the humanistic approach, and both exist in today's historical archaeology.

Humanistic Archaeology at Kingsmill

A model example of humanistic historical archaeology is William Kelso's 1984 study of seven plantations at Kingsmill, near Williamsburg, Virginia. Kelso, director of archaeology for the Association for the Preservation of Virginia Antiquities, is a social historian who has considerable experience and expertise using historical archaeology as a tool for understanding colonial Virginia. He is most recognized today as the excavator of the first settlement at Jamestown, Virginia.

The subtitle of his book *Kingsmill Plantations, 1619–1800: Archaeology of Country Life in Colonial Virginia* aptly summarizes Kelso's perspective, for he was interested in presenting an image of past life in Virginia during the seventeenth and eighteenth centuries. Accordingly, he concentrated on three elements of the past: historical narrative, artifacts, and people. He reconstructed the historical context of colonial Virginia from primary documents, and recounted the rise of the tobacco economy, the events of Bacon's Rebellion in

1676, and the steady advance of the Virginian frontier as it moved inland from the coast. Kelso realized that historical events are situated in physical spaces composed of things: "colonial Virginians surrounded themselves with an evolving material culture" that written records alone cannot fully document. In other words, interpreting the historical setting in full requires the combination of textual and archaeological sources, a central feature of historical archaeology.

Housing represents an important example of material culture, and one of Kelso's goals was to explain the changes in housing styles in colonial Virginia. History shows that many English men and women in colonial Virginia ceased living in small "earthfast" homes—structures having dirt floors and upright support posts buried in the ground—and began to build brick homes. The growth of the plantation economy made the transition possible, but estate records indicate people furnished their homes with such a wide variety of goods that generalization is extremely difficult. An individual family's dishes, their wine bottles, and their personal ornaments thus can only be understood from direct archaeological fieldwork at their specific homesite. In other words, *as individual humans* their experiences in the world can only be fully grasped by the examination of their house.

The concept of human uniqueness is a characteristic of the humanistic approach. In general, humanistic archaeologists tend to shy away from overarching concepts and generalizations, seeking instead to concentrate on the lives of individual lived experience.

Without people, none of the historical events of the Kingsmill area (recounted in historical records) and not one material object (illuminated from the archaeological research) could exist. To help bring the historical actors into focus, Kelso concentrated on the area's elites because they were people who wrote about themselves and who in turn were written about by others. Enslaved men and women were seldom written about in any great detail, and they rarely had the opportunity to write about themselves.

Kelso introduced individuals such as Humphrey Higginson, who arrived in Virginia in 1635 and married into the huge estate. Shortly afterward he added another large tract to his "growing Kingsmill estate." George Percy, Jamestown's lieutenant governor, also appears. He described the Kingsmill area in 1607 as a bountiful paradise: "The soil was good and fruitful, with excellent good timber. There are also great stores of vines in bigness of a man's thigh, running up to the tops of trees in great abundance." He also saw many squirrels, rabbits, and birds.

Kelso's archaeological research at the seven Kingsmill sites encompassed the full range of colonial society, including the excavation of planter's mansions and slave quarters. Using horizontal excavation, he was able to provide maximum information about housing conditions and site layout (Figure 10.1). The social distinctions between owners and enslaved men and women are overtly expressed in housing. Large-scale eighteenth-century planters chose prominent locations for their mansions and built impressive, formal gardens. Enslaved men and women dug root cellars under their homes, possibly without their masters' knowledge, and made do as well as possible given the circumstances (Figure 10.2).

Images of past life at Kingsmill Plantation emerge through Kelso's humanistic perspective. His stated goal was to "reconstruct the setting within which landlords and laborers went about their lives within Virginia's tobacco empire." The richness of the archaeological findings coupled with a detailed textual record of daily life in this historically significant part of the United States makes for an interpretation rooted in the image of real people in the past actively going about their daily activities. The people are not abstractions, but individuals just like us in ways that are universal to the human experience.

Figure 10.1 Horizontal excavation of Burwell mansion and kitchen, Kingsmill, Virginia, 1975

(Virginia Department of Historic Resources)

Figure 10.2 Excavated root cellar of a slave cabin, Kingsmill, Virginia

(Virginia Department of Historic Resources)

Scientific Historical Archaeology

When American archaeologists fully "discovered" anthropology in the 1960s (Chapter 2), they also embraced the scientific method. In their attempts to make anthropological archaeology more rigorous, a number of excavators urged their colleagues to conduct research having explicit scientific goals. They argued that archaeologists should be able to meet the highest scientific standards in their research and be able to devise intricate models of past societies testable with carefully designed hypotheses. Archaeologists should strive, they said, to contribute to knowledge of human life by discovering general laws of behavior. In their view, the final goal for scientific archaeologists should be to explain the complex cultural processes that govern human life throughout history, including the past 500 years.

Interest in scientific archaeology exploded in the late 1960s and 1970s. The leading proponent of an explicitly scientific perspective in historical archaeology was Stanley South. His *Method and Theory in Historical Archaeology*, first published in 1977, was a clarion call for historical archaeologists to be overtly scientific in their research.

South believed that the route toward a scientific historical archaeology must start with archaeologists being able to recognize patterns among the artifacts they excavate. He posited that men and women who lived within the same cultural tradition should have left the same kinds of artifacts, in roughly similar percentages, in the soils of their past residences regardless of their individuality. Patterns recognizable in the artifacts should reflect the cultural patterns of the people under study. Sites inhabited by peoples from different cultural traditions should exhibit distinct artifact patterns when compared. How can archaeologists discover the patterns? According to South, the answer rested in quantifying the artifacts into discrete categories. The categories he devised were: kitchen, bone, architectural, furniture, arms, clothing, personal, tobacco pipe, and activities. South employed these general classes of artifacts during his study of a number of British colonial sites—from dwellings to forts—in the Carolinas.

To discern the pattern represented in any artifact collection, an archaeologist must compute the percentage of each class. Some sites are characterized by large numbers of architectural artifacts (like nails) but have almost no tobacco pipes, whereas others have high percentages of kitchen (dishes and bottles) and architectural artifacts but very few furniture objects. For South, these patterns are highly significant because they directly reflect the residents' cultural pattern. As they are deep-seated cultural patterns, archaeologists should be able to identify them at other sites, too.

Archaeologists can use the patterns to construct broad theories of behavior. When an archaeologist discovers a new pattern among the artifacts at another site, the conclusion must be that whomever lived at that site had a different culture than the people who created the already-identified patterns found elsewhere. South believed that the continuing process of site excavation, pattern recognition, and site testing would lead to a truly scientific archaeology that could be as rigorous as chemistry or physics (Figure 10.3). His methodology, he believed, would give historical archaeology the attention and respect it deserved.

Many archaeologists immediately found South's approach appealing. It presented a straightforward way to analyze the mass of archaeological finds from the smallest to the largest site. Proper artifact identification and careful comparison was all that was required to determine whether a newly excavated site's artifact pattern conformed to any of the existing patterns.

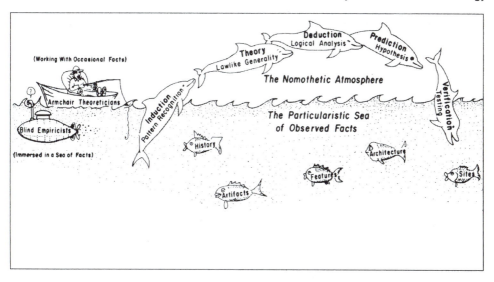

Figure 10.3 South's flowchart showing the scientific method. The archaeologist should follow the path of the dolphin.

(From Stanley South, *Method and Theory in Historical Archaeology*, New York: Academic Press, 1977.)

Scientific Historical Archaeology at Camden

Archaeologist Kenneth Lewis conducted a study explicitly following the scientific methodology outlined by South. Lewis focused on a town called Camden in north-central South Carolina, the same region in which South invented the pattern concept.

During the height of the American Revolution in 1780, British soldiers built Camden in the Carolina backcountry. They intended it as one of a chain of posts across the state needed to secure the region for the British Empire. The town's geographical position made it a perfect communication hub for the frontier, and the British soon used it as a central redistribution point for war munitions coming inland from Charleston. They fortified the town (Figure 10.4), and fought two battles nearby. Camden continued to function as a frontier center after the war, and rapidly grew in regional importance. As the town prospered, new residents moved to the north side, and by 1812 they had abandoned much of the old town.

In the mid-1970s, Lewis was given the opportunity to excavate part of the old town. The Camden Historical Commission wished to develop the site, and they needed specific architectural information only archaeology could supply. To provide the information, Lewis excavated along the southwest palisade and on a small part of the town's interior. Rather than present a humanistic portrait of daily life in Camden, Lewis chose an overtly scientific research plan focusing on the town's place in the South Carolina frontier.

He began by constructing a frontier model emphasizing cultural changes as people learned to adapt to a frontier environment. The creation of models testable with archaeological data is a hallmark of scientific archaeology. Lewis constructed his model using a number of generalizations drawn from anthropological and historical literature. His first generalization is that organized societies will react or adapt to a frontier in a patterned (or non-random) way. This

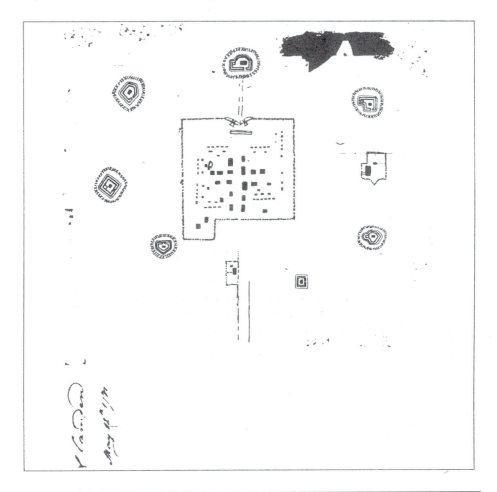

Figure 10.4 1781 map of Camden, South Carolina
(Courtesy of the South Carolina Institute of Archaeology and Anthropology, University of South Carolina, Columbia.)

patterned reaction, being cultural, will be based on the people's traditional concepts of how to live. Another generalization is that frontier colonies expand in size as new people move in.

Lewis devised hypotheses from the generalizations and tested them with archaeological and historical information. One hypothesis was that "the colonial settlement tended to lie adjacent to the significant routes of transportation and communication connecting Camden with the outside world." Another is that the nature of the settlement as a frontier town should mean that most of its buildings were associated with the transfer and storage of commodities and with the periodic gathering of people for special events, such as markets and trials. The implication is that most of the structures in the settlement should have been special-use buildings rather than dwellings.

One of the hallmarks of scientific archaeology is that the hypotheses and their outcomes must be explicitly expressed so that other archaeologists can investigate them if they wish. In this way, scientific archaeology overtly maintains its connection to the scientific method.

Figure 10.5 Row of bricks in excavation unit at Camden, South Carolina, 1975

(Courtesy of the South Carolina Institute of Archaeology and Anthropology, University of South Carolina, Columbia.)

Lewis used vertical excavations—small trenches and test units—to evaluate his 11 hypotheses (Figure 10.5). For example, the spatial distribution of architectural artifacts—nails and bricks—convinced him that 17 buildings had indeed been built next to the roads running through old Camden. This finding led him to conclude that the hypothesis about the settlement pattern tended to be confirmed: "The general form of the colonial occupation at Camden is basically that of an English two-row settlement, with a single main street and 2 cross-streets."

Lewis's study of Camden is scientific in tone and scope. He included no artifact photographs or drawings, and he did not focus on important individuals or interpret how significant historical events affected the townspeople. His focus was on the process of frontier settlement, as he sought to explain how the settlement pattern of the town changed over time, how Camden found a place in the frontier economy as a communication center, and how Native American villages were not a barrier to the expansion of the frontier. He provided a picture of how Camden, as a frontier town, was part of a larger process of European settlement and life in the New World, but he did not dwell on how individuals lived on a daily basis. His study of Camden helped bring science to historical archaeology by emphasizing scientific precision, modeling, and theory building as a way to examine changes in a historic community over time.

Humanistic Science in Historical Archaeology

Interest in scientific historical archaeology peaked in the early 1980s, and since then, most historical archaeologists have pursued a perspective not easily characterized simply as either humanistic or scientific. Perhaps the best term for this varied perspective is "humanistic science," because most practitioners have adopted something from both humanism and science. Most historical archaeologists seek to contribute to knowledge about past daily life, as would a humanist, but as archaeologists, most would also not wish to leave social science behind. By its very nature, archaeology requires scientific thinking and precision, and archaeologists will never abandon methods of measurement and analysis extending back to the Enlightenment. At the same time, however, archaeologists have overwhelmingly abandoned the idea that cultural life can be reduced to a few artifact patterns and that hypothesis testing always represents the best approach.

As a result, most historical archaeologists adopt a middle course and blend the humanistic tradition with scientific perspectives. Historical archaeology provides new information by blending anthropological archaeology (a social science) with history (a humanity).

The union of science and humanism has bred many innovative perspectives and has fostered dynamic excitement in the field. Historical archaeologists are today actively pushing the boundaries of knowledge by presenting and exploring new approaches and interpretations. Here we focus only on two major theorists, James Deetz and Mark Leone, both of whom have a considerable following in historical archaeology. While other archaeologists have modified and refined their approaches, an understanding of their perspectives is useful for comprehending the theoretical direction of much contemporary historical archaeology.

Historical Structuralism

The approach used by James Deetz may best be described as *historical structuralism*. Deetz began by studying the Arikaras, the village-dwelling, horticultural Native Americans who lived along the Missouri River in today's South Dakota. His doctoral dissertation, published in 1965, was part of the movement to test the waters of process-oriented, scientific archaeology. Using archaeological information collected from Arikara sites, Deetz sought to determine whether he could observe a correlation between the pottery they made and the dramatic social transformations they experienced after contact with European explorers and fur traders. The number of Arikaras dropped precipitously as they suffered from newly introduced diseases. Having experienced extreme depopulation, they steadily moved their villages north further and further up the Missouri River, and combined reduced villages into new, larger villages. They also changed their ideas about where newly married couples should live. The Arikaras traditionally had a post-marriage residence rule stating that newly married couples should live in the villages of the bride's family. As they moved their villages north, they abandoned the custom of matrilocality for a more liberal view that was not so strict about post-marriage residence. After depopulation, the Arikara relaxed their residence rules. Deetz wondered whether depopulation, village agglomeration, and flexible post-marriage residence behavior—significant cultural transformations when combined—could be observed in their pottery. Why pottery? Because women made the Arikaras' pots, and girls learned the craft of pottery manufacture from their mothers and grandmothers. Deetz wanted to know whether the movement of girls away from their maternal kin had any effect on the way they made their pots.

When Deetz studied the pottery excavated from a number of village sites along the Missouri River, he saw that over time the pottery did indeed show an increased irregularity in design. He expected that with the decline of matrilocality, female potters moved away from the villages of their birth and their maternal kin. In the new arrangement, any village could contain female potters originally from several earlier villages. The mixing of women from different maternal lineages meant that several styles of pottery could appear within the same village, as women continued to make pottery familiar to them. Deetz's research suggested the maximum stress among the Arikaras occurred between 1720 and 1750, the time of greatest variability in their pottery.

Deetz's study quickly became a classic because his method was scientific and his perspective was anthropological. Over the next several years, however, Deetz turned away from the study of contact-period Native Americans to investigate America's earliest English settlers. He developed his structuralist approach as part of this effort.

Structuralism is a perspective that aims to discover a culture's hidden themes and relations. As a major theoretical approach in anthropology, it began with the work of a number of French scholars, most notably sociologist Emile Durkheim and cultural anthropologist Claude Levi-Strauss. They and their followers developed structuralism partly in reaction to functionalism, another influential theoretical perspective.

Functionalists are generally interested in learning how institutions work together and perpetuate culture. Proponents of functionalism tend to see culture as composed of several individual institutions that, like the pieces of a jigsaw puzzle, can be assembled and understood in their totality. The job of the functionalist anthropologist is to study cultural institutions—marriage, kinship, cosmology—and to determine how they fit together.

Structuralists found the functional view inadequate because it never explained a culture's deeper structures. For example, what are the underlying ideas actually making social institutions work? Instead of being interested in the pieces of the puzzle—as functionalists—structuralists are interested in the driveshaft that causes the machine to cut the pieces into their individual shapes. Their interest lies in the deep structures of culture, including practices its members may undertake, perhaps even unconsciously.

Deetz was drawn to structuralism, but only when combined with a significant degree of historical analysis. He drew much of his intellectual inspiration from the research of folklorist Henry Glassie. In his widely read *Folk Housing in Middle Virginia*, published in 1975, Glassie presented a structuralist interpretation of the vernacular architecture in two Virginia counties. His goal was to write a "grammar" showing the choices individual builders had available to them when they built a new house. For example, when deciding on the location of house's features—fireplaces, stairways, halls, porches—builders faced almost countless options. They could place a stairway in a public or a private space, enclose a porch to make another room, or cluster outbuildings in one spot or scatter them across the backyard. That vernacular builders consistently chose certain options meant they all followed some deep structure, some patterned cultural logic. Structuralists tend to believe this logic is similar to the grammar of a language.

Glassie focused specifically on standing buildings, but Deetz chose several kinds of material culture to study the deep structure of the colonial mind. Arguing that material culture is "the track of our collective existence," Deetz examined tombstones, house designs, ceramic colors, customs of eating, and music, and he discerned significant changes in each over time. For example, eighteenth-century tombstones exhibit a dramatic change. In the early years of the century, craftsmen put images of skulls on gravestones, but in the later years they carved angelic cherubs on them (Figure 10.6). During the same period, butchers ceased hacking cuts of meat from carcasses using chopping tools and began to remove them carefully with saws. Deetz also noticed that ceramics also underwent a transformation. By the late eighteenth century, bone white dishes had replaced the once-fashionable brown, green, and yellow dishes.

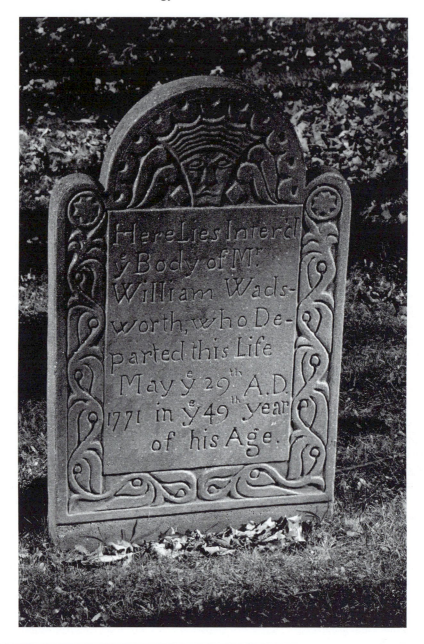

Figure 10.6 Colonial tombstone of William Wadsworth
(Lee Snider / Photo Images / Corbis)

Deetz perceived these dramatic changes in material culture as purposeful and inter-connected. Tombstone carvers simply did not grow tired of the death-head patterns, just as ceramic makers did not stop making earth-tone vessels on a whim. Deetz argued instead that all of the changes he observed in material culture—from houses to cuts of meat—represented what he called the "Georgian mind set." This term refers to the way English men and women saw the world during the reigns of the English King George—I, II, and III (from 1714 to 1820). A series of structural rules—a grammar—operated behind this mind set to arrange culture, to order things in a certain way. Deetz believed every culture has these rules and that archaeologists can observe them in material culture even though the culture's members themselves may not have been aware of them. The death's head on a tombstone is a powerful emotional device connoting Puritan orthodoxy, whereas the angel suggests a liberalization of Puritanism and the rise of a different belief system. The use of a saw to remove meat from a carcass denotes the rise of individualism through the use of "portion control." Hacked cuts were imprecise and impersonal; sawn portions were neat and individualized. The popularity of white dishes symbolized a movement away from nature and toward artificiality. The change in dish color was not merely a technological innovation; it hid a deeper meaning, a structure that the entirety of a culture's material objects represents in various ways.

Many of Deetz's colleagues and students followed his theoretical lead. These archaeologists have for the most part sought to use his ideas and general approach as a starting point for their own research. One such archaeologist is Martin Hall. He built on Deetz's historical structuralism by adding the idea of "discourse." A "discourse" is created by the interaction, the "conversation," among material objects, written texts, and spoken words. The conversation takes place within a specific historical context. No formal laws of the human mind exist in such settings because discourses make their own rules as they develop. The rules make sense within the cultural tradition, and much of the discourse is symbolic.

Hall used Westover Plantation, the colonial estate owned by the powerful Byrds of Virginia, to illustrate his point. A purely structural analysis of the plantation would tend to push the Byrds, as historical actors, into the background. The way they built their mansion, the position of their slave quarters, and the very dishes from which they ate would all be structured by the Enlightenment mind, a frame of thought including "the Georgian mansions of England, Mozart's music, Jane Austen's novels, and formal gardens." In Hall's discursive analysis, the Byrds moved to center stage as members of the ruling elite. He believed their architecture and displays of public wealth were really symbolic reminders of their supreme social power. When considered in its totality, "the material world of Westover and the actions of patriarch, family, and slave would be statements in a discourse."

Hall perceived the world of artifacts as a uniquely powerful realm where individual men and women used material things to resist the influence of domination and to redefine themselves within the changing social order. Moving to South Africa (Figure 10.7), Hall demonstrated how Europeans at the Cape of Good Hope used colonial ceramics in this manner. The Dutch East India Company adopted a three-tiered hierarchy of ceramics. They put common, cheaply made red-bodied wares decorated with bright green and yellow glazes on the lowest level. Above them they placed coarse porcelains imported to the Cape from Indonesia. They regarded the rare, fine porcelains from the royal kilns of China as the finest ceramics. But Chinese porcelain vessels were far more than merely elegant, domestic wares. They were also important in an elaborate ceremony of display that included drinking tea and holding formal dinner parties. Elite families proudly displayed their fine porcelains as symbolic reminders of their social power and importance. Not surprisingly, sherds of such delicate wares occur frequently in the archaeological sites once inhabited by members of the Dutch colonial elite. But Hall also found fragments of fine porcelains in the homes of the enslaved, together with the coarse red-bodied wares common among the lower levels of society. Coarse porcelains, the domestic wares most common in the deposits left by Dutch soldiers, were absent from the houses of enslaved Africans.

257

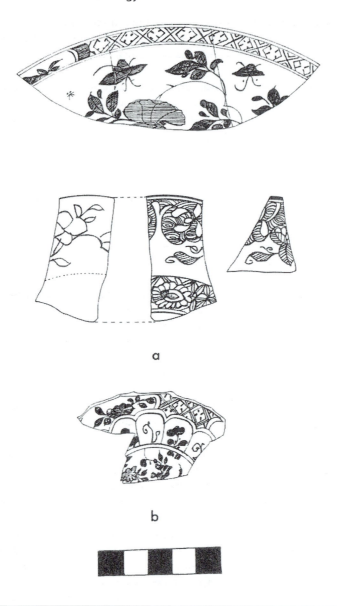

a

b

Figure 10.7 Pieces of early eighteenth-century fine Chinese porcelain dinner plates from Cape Town, South Africa

(The South African Archaeological Society, Goodwin Series: *Historical Archaeology in the Western Cape*, vol. 7 by Martin Hall et al. June, 1993, p. 49, fig. 16.)

Enslaved men and women conceivably could have been issued ceramics different from those commonly used by Dutch soldiers. But how can the fine porcelains present in the slave quarters be explained? Hall believed that enslaved individuals stole fine dishes as a gesture of defiance. On a deeper level, though, these same porcelains symbolically "turned the world

upside down, allowing the repressed victims of a patriarchal world to reconstitute daily a 'space' for themselves." Fine porcelains had a meaning for the enslaved that was distinct from that of their Dutch masters. They were symbolic markers to be sure, but markers with far different meanings.

Hall expanded the boundaries of historical structuralism, and his approach is innovative and interesting. He and Deetz, however, are not the only historical archaeologists who have combined science and humanism in an effort to understand the historical past. Another approach espouses what may be called "critical materialism."

Critical Materialism

Critical materialism is our term for an approach combining "critical theory" with "materialism." Materialism is an ancient perspective maintaining that the reality of physical matter takes precedence over ideas and thought processes. Critical theory, a twentieth-century refinement of the nineteenth-century ideas of Karl Marx, was proposed by scholars of the Frankfurt School of sociology in the 1920s, among them Theodor Adorno, Max Horkheimer, and Herbert Marcuse. These scholars argued that knowledge is never truly neutral because it is affected by the investigator's class interests. In other words, individual researchers, no matter how conscientious and careful they may be, cannot escape their class backgrounds. Rather than pretend that research is unbiased and free of judgment, critical theorists argue that analysts should recognize the hidden prejudices inherent in their research. They should understand that research is "reflexive"; it reflects back on itself. With this perspective in mind, critical theorists argue that research is never passionless and atheoretical. This is especially true in historical studies because of the significant degree of interpretation required.

Historical archaeologist Mark Leone developed an approach linking materialism and critical theory. He concentrates on the close relationship between a society's class structure and its technology.

Leone began his career like Deetz in processual archaeology. In a study of Mormon fences, Leone emphasized a perspective in which archaeology is a science of technology. Leone as anthropologist was interested in how technology affects culture and how cultures manipulate technology. As a historical archaeologist, he was equally intrigued with technology's historical aspects.

Nineteenth-century Mormons built fences and walls, and they continue to build them today. A traditional historical explanation for the Mormon use of fences held that the use of this technology was merely a throwback to their days in New England. When the Mormons traveled west through Illinois and the Great Plains, finally settling in Utah, they took the idea of fences with them. Fences thus represented something the Mormons knew from the past. Leone, however, was dissatisfied with this simplistic explanation and asked a perceptive question: Why did the same settlers not bring other elements of New England material culture with them? Why just fences, and why do Mormon farmers continue to build similar fences today? Leone believed that Mormons used fences to divide their space in ways making sense within the context of their religious beliefs. Technology, as represented by fences, was embedded in Mormon life at every level. The use of space, their subsistence strategies, and their ways of interacting socially were all tied to technology in some way. Leone proposed that Mormonism could not exist without their way of dividing up space. In their world, technology and space were employed in tandem to make life work. Fences and religion reinforced one another.

A strong thread of mental process ran through Leone's Mormon study, in that a relationship was seen to exist between fence technology and the ideas that caused Mormons to build them. Significantly, Leone also argued that archaeology, though seemingly only about the past, is conducted in the present. Archaeological research is a product of the present. This understanding became a standard precept of late-twentieth-century archaeology and is a widely held view today.

His examination of Mormon culture soon led Leone to consider critical theory as a framework to understand the relationships between class position, ideological belief, and the modern uses of archaeology. Critical theory has a wide following outside archaeology, in legal scholarship, history, geography, and several other disciplines. Archaeologists espousing this approach argue that the scientific objectivity sought by processual archaeologists like Stanley South is not really possible. Artifacts do not "speak" for themselves; archaeologists are not simply translators. Artifacts are not value-free even when they are quantified and expressed as frequencies and percentages. Archaeologists create artificial categories when sorting artifacts, and the very act of creating these categories is a biased process. Why, for example, did South have a separate category for "smoking pipes" rather than just including them under "activities"? Why was "kitchen" a category instead of "food preparation"?

Critical theorists believe that archaeologists give artifacts meaning; they are interpreters rather than translators. That these meanings sometimes may have importance outside archaeology should be celebrated as a way for archaeology to develop a greater sense of relevance within modern society. For Leone, archaeology has political and social functions allowing it to address questions with contemporary social relevance. (This again has become standard thinking in twenty-first-century archaeology; see Chapter 13.)

The complex relationship between politics and archaeology has surfaced in the many controversies over the excavation and reburial of Native American skeletal remains and grave goods. Archaeologists may perceive the excavation of Native American graves as constituting an important avenue for learning about the health, diet, and physical condition of past populations, but many Native Americans view burial excavation as desecration. Excavation, though clearly "about" the past, takes place in the present and affects living people. The graves, though ancient, are not just "of the past"; they belong in the present just as much as in the past.

Leone has focused much of his attention on a major historical phenomenon of the modern era—the growth of capitalism—as it was expressed in Annapolis, Maryland. He views capitalism as a way of organizing life, as a way of setting up social categories. For him, capitalism is not merely an economic system, something removed from social analysis. Capitalism is part and parcel of each and every segment of life, a culture in and of itself. All activity in Annapolis, both past and present, had/has an umbrella of capitalism spread over it. But making this claim is not enough because an important issue for Leone is how to address capitalism's operation "on the ground," or in other words, in people's daily lives. Another way to state this is: How can historical archaeologists study capitalism?

Annapolis has a rich historical tradition, and Leone was able to begin his study with probate inventories. From these lists of personal property, he constructed four wealth-holding groups for the years 1690–1775. Though probate records were seldom kept for enslaved and free African Americans, poor whites, and most women, they nonetheless include a large segment of the historical population. Historians have shown that capitalism had an increasing influence on life in Annapolis throughout the eighteenth century. When they compared the early years of the century with later decades, they discovered that with time more people worked for wages, merchants made more money, and more consumer goods entered the city. Leone took these facts as a starting point and combined them with his ideas about the importance of class.

Working closely with colleagues Parker Potter and Paul Shackel, Leone showed how people's lives became more standardized over time and how there existed an "increasing interchangeability of things, acts, and persons." In the early seventeenth century, men and women often acted communally. They slept in the same rooms, they ate their meals from one or two bowls, and they did not use personalized silverware. With the rising influence of capitalism, however, people's lives became more regulated and consequently more interchangeable with everyone else's. Men and women now paid attention to clocks, they had a certain time for lunch, and they each had their own dishes and forks for dining. This was when potters developed the various kinds of ceramic vessels mentioned in the POTS program (see Chapter 7).

Leone and his colleagues excavated three domestic household sites in Annapolis to study the social changes occurring between the late seventeenth and the mid-eighteenth centuries. One site each represented the upper-wealth group, the middle-wealth group, and a household whose members had climbed from the lowest wealth group in the 1740s to the highest group over the next several years. To measure social change using glazed ceramics, Leone, Potter, and Shackel devised a clever formula. Their idea was that an increase in ceramic variation would signal the increasing impact of capitalism on the daily lives of ordinary men and women. Greater ceramic variability meant greater and more diverse purchasing from an ever-increasing stock of potential objects. Leone and his colleagues took the number of types of ceramics in a sample, combined it with the number of plate sizes—which they termed "type-sizes"—and divided it by the number of types present. They then multiplied the quotient by the number of plate sizes to produce an index number. The index number of a soil layer containing five type-sizes, three different ceramic types (porcelain, pearlware, whiteware), and four different sizes of plates, would be calculated as: $(5/3)(4) = 6.67$ (Table 10.1). The higher the value, the greater the variation.

When they computed the index value for the three sites at Annapolis, the values indeed increased over time. For example, at the Hammond-Harwood House, belonging to the upper-wealth household, the value increased from 2.0 in the mid- to late eighteenth century to 27.0 in the late eighteenth to early nineteenth century. At the Thomas Hyde House site—where the household moved from the lowest wealth group to the highest—the index values started at 1.0 in the early eighteenth century. By the mid- to late eighteenth century the index value was 2.0, and by the late eighteenth to early nineteenth century it was 24.5. The value was 73.1 for the mid-nineteenth century. The message from these values was inescapable, and Leone and his associates concluded the variation in dish sizes and ware types reflected a new etiquette based on increasing individuality.

Leone and his colleagues' research indicates that changes in material culture between the seventeenth and the nineteenth centuries do not simply reflect transformations of some deep

Table 10.1 Ceramic index for Annapolis, Maryland

Plate Diameter (Inches)						
Ceramic Type	4	5	6	7	8	9
Porcelain	—	—	—	—	×	—
Pearlware	—	—	—	×	—	×
Whiteware	×	—	—	—	—	×

Source: Mark P. Leone, Parker B. Potter, Jr., and Paul A. Shackel. Toward a Critical Archaeology. *Current Anthropology* 28 (1987):288.

mental construct. They represent wholesale social changes brought about because of and through human experiences within the historical process of capitalism.

Interpretive Historical Archaeology

Interpretive archaeology, a complex approach to archaeological interpretation, is one part of a broader theoretical development termed "postprocessual archaeology." Rather than constituting a unified perspective similar to the scientific processual archaeology of the 1960s, the term "postprocessual archaeology" is meant to indicate archaeological concepts created after (actually "post") processual archaeology. Postprocessual archaeology thus includes many perspectives, with interpretive archaeology being just one of them.

Interpretive archaeology was originally proposed by Ian Hodder, who also coined the term "postprocessual archaeology." As outlined by him, interpretative archaeology contains three essential elements. First is that archaeologists should adopt a "guarded objectivity" in their research into the past. This means archaeologists must acknowledge that the knowledge they produce is created dialectically as a product of both past and present. Archaeological information does not exist in the past alone; it is a product of today as much as of the past. As a result, when an archaeologist excavates an arrowhead made of chipped French bottle glass, he or she must understand that the resultant interpretation comes both from the present (the archaeologist's mind) and from the past (the maker's mind). One implication of this idea is that subordinate groups, such as ethnic minorities, should be able to use archaeological knowledge for present purposes. In other words, archaeological "data" is not intended to sit quietly on the library's shelves unused and ignored by people alive today. Archaeological images of the past—as interpretations of eras long over—should have meaning today. Secondly, Hodder postulates that archaeologists must move themselves away from such a strong reliance on theory and seek to tell relevant human stories. Rather than presenting archaeological findings as cold, dry hypotheses, intricate statistical tests, and complex theoretical arguments, archaeologists should present images of the past that exhibit a sensitivity and general understanding of the human condition that unites all people. Archaeology that is intensely scientific robs the past of its essential human character. It reduces past men and women—like us in so many ways—to lifeless automatons. In this sense, interpretive archaeology shares the perspective of humanistic historical archaeology. Third, archaeologists writing history should treat their work reflexively, critically engaging with other interpretations as they form their views about the past. This means interpretive archaeologists should acknowledge that their interpretation is one of many that may be proposed. No interpretation of human culture and society should be expected to represent the ultimate "truth." History is a complicated mix of individuals, events, and accidents that can never be known with certainty. Some speculation may be required to make sense of the past.

Interpretative archaeology is thus an outgrowth of many intellectual traditions and theoretical strands. It draws upon diverse traditions including feminism, structuralism, Marxism, and many others. As a result, it can be difficult to characterize as a unified way of thinking about history.

The key to interpretive archaeology is the word "interpretive." The goal of the interpretive archaeologist is to write narratives that ultimately make a human connection between the past and the present. Interpretive archaeology is meant to be expressive and emotive.

In her explanation of interpretive historical archaeology, Laurie Wilkie employs the example of a tiny porcelain soap dish she discovered at a plantation site in Louisiana. She uses this seemingly insignificant object to evoke a sense of human commonality between people seeing

the object today and its past owners and users. The plantation, built in the late eighteenth century and inhabited until the 1950s, was home to many African American families as well as the estate owner's family. In her study of the plantation as an archaeological site, Wilkie did what historical archaeologists do: she studied census records, interviewed local people, and excavated the remains of a house that had been reduced to a pile of bricks and refuse. Her analysis of the information she amassed led her to conclude the home was once inhabited by an African American woman named Silvia Freeman. A widow, Freeman lived in the house with her five children while she was employed as the planter family's cook. Research indicated that because Freeman was paid only about $4 a month, she was frequently forced to borrow against her future paychecks. The low rate of pay—and the subsequent need to spend wisely—suggests the toy soap dish was probably a treasured object purchased for a child. The child must have eventually lost it while playing outside the house, and someone must have unknowingly swept it up with other trash. Wilkie found it under what would have been the house when still standing on brick piers.

The idea in interpretive archaeology is that anyone with children hearing the tale of the toy soap dish should be able to make an immediate connection with the Freeman family. They would understand the parental desire to provide playthings for their children even in cases of severe economic stress. The common human understanding evoked by the family's story when coupled with the soap dish should transcend differences in racial assignment, ethnic heritage, class standing, gender, and all other dimensions of social difference. In short, the goal of the interpretive archaeologist is to transcend the disconnections that may occur through the distance between past and present. When the connection is correctly made, everyone should be able to empathize with the Freemans on a basic human level.

In her study of Sylvestor Manor, on the eastern shore of New York's Long Island (also see Chapter 7), Katherine Howlett Hayes adopts the interpretive approach. Because the manor has been occupied since the mid-seventeenth century, many human connections may potentially be made.

One of Hayes's specific interests is attempting to understand how mundane artifacts either worked to bring people together or keep them apart. This line of research is pertinent because Europeans, Native Americans, and African Americans all interacted at the estate at one time or another.

Hayes believes that one class of artifact found during excavation, personal objects, perhaps more than any other, "help us to envision the historical actors." These artifacts—personal adornments and objects used in leisure and amusement—though perhaps foreign to the present are nonetheless common enough to allow us to establish a human connection between today's society and the manor's past residents. Some artifacts may even have had "boundary crossing" characteristics in the past, meaning they may have brought past people together by providing shared meanings. One example found at the estate is a silver coin with an X scratched on one side and an X in a triangle on the other. These markings are reminiscent of divine symbols used by local Native Americans. At the same time, however, archaeologists who have excavated sites associated with enslaved Africans have discovered artifacts with similar X scratches. Thus, if the X marks were intentionally made—and they certainly seem to have been—then they crossed the boundary between two diverse belief systems, one African, the other Native American.

In interpretive archaeology, crossover artifacts may evoke the sense that different human cultures may not be so different after all. Artifacts shown to have defied the boundaries of time and heritage may be the most evocative of all.

* * *

To summarize, historical archaeologists, like all archaeologists, use theoretical ideas to help them devise meaning from the past. Archaeologists want to know what things—artifacts, landscapes, buildings—"mean" and how people have used and interacted with these created things. Meaning, of course, is a difficult subject, and archaeologists have developed different ways to understand it. Past archaeologists may have thought that a particular object or landscape had a single, correct meaning, but today's archaeologists are more willing to admit the possibility of many meanings. Important variables contributing to the different meanings may relate to conditions in the past, whereas others may reflect the archaeological interpreter's experiences, education, and interests.

A good analogy for thinking about theory in historical archaeology is to envision a website where music can be purchased and downloaded. Rather than list the styles of music randomly, the webmaster has arranged them in categories accessed through different links. People searching for jazz will click the jazz link, but others will choose the blues link. Others will go directly to the classical part of the site. Many people will make their way through several categories, finding something they like about each one of them. Archaeological theories come and go like trends in music. The music store of 1980 did not look like the virtual music store of 2010, and the internet store of 2011 was not an exact duplicate of the store in 2012. Scholars pick and choose theories, though the process is more complicated than simply looking for music. Some archaeologists are drawn to class analysis, and others to the mental constructs underlying the creation of bottles, dishes, and houses. Still others find value in the scientific perspectives developed in the 1960s.

Individual archaeologists, perhaps like musical purists, tend to defend their own way of looking at the past because they honestly believe their perspective provides the greatest insight into historical reality. In the final analysis, most experts are willing to accept that several equally valid perspectives may be used to interpret the past. They may believe their way is best, but most are open-minded enough to accept that other ideas may also have merit.

Whatever their theoretical perspective, archaeologists are engaged in the analysis of daily life extending from the individual scale to that of the entire globe. The availability of historical records, memories, and other "nonarchaeological" sources of information gives historical archaeology vitality and makes its research exciting. In the next two chapters, we present some ways historical archaeologists have investigated various scales of life in the past 500 years. As was true in this chapter, our goal is not to be exhaustive, for this is impossible, but to touch upon a few trends.

Site Visit: Ross Female Factory, Tasmania, 1848–1855

Van Diemen's Land (or Tasmania, as it was renamed in 1855) is an island off the southeastern tip of Australia. Between 1803 and 1854, the British government shipped 74,000 convicted felons to the penal colony on Van Diemen's Land. Roughly 12,000 of these prisoners (about 16 percent) were women.

The British built a network of female prisons on Van Diemen's Land. They named one of them the Ross Female Factory. "Factory" was short for "manufactory" because the theory behind such institutions was that imprisoned women would learn to better themselves through productive labor. Most prisoners were assigned to work for non-convict settlers, for local merchants, or on public works projects.

The Ross Female Factory began as a male-only institution, but in 1847 a plan was formulated to convert the prison into a facility that could house women and their children. As a male prison, the Ross institution was initially (in 1833) composed of four brick huts with thatched roofs. In 1834, the prison authorities decided to modify the living arrangements and built a long brick building with a thatched roof. They also added a mess room, a cookhouse, houses for an overseer and a constable, two sheds, and a muster yard. The structures were arranged in a neat square with the muster yard in the center. The prison underwent significant physical alteration after the women arrived. New fences were built, and stone floors were replaced with wooden floors. Six solitary confinement cells were constructed, and a bake house was among the new facilities. Windowpanes were installed, and all wards received a coat of whitewash. The women usually slept in hammocks, but 30 iron bedsteads were ordered for the hospital. A boundary fence was built to prevent convicts from engaging in unauthorized communication with the outside world.

The women prisoners at the Ross Female Factory were usually sent there as a secondary measure. Most had originally been transported to Van Diemen's Land from Britain because they had been convicted of petty theft or of a crime against property. They could also be sent there for illegitimate pregnancy, public drunkenness, or homosexuality.

Once at the institution, the superintendent divided the women into three groups. All were assigned to the "crime class" upon arrival. This designation meant they had to work in the prison laundry or perform sewing under contract for local settlers. After a period of good behavior, a woman could be assigned to the "hiring class." Members of this group were assigned domestic duties on nearby farms, or else they worked in the hospital, nursery, or held semi-supervisory roles. The third division, the "punishment class," was composed of women who flaunted the rules, disobeyed the jailers, or were caught in possession of forbidden objects. These women were confined to solitary cells, usually with decreased food rations. They could also have their heads shaved and be made to wear iron collars as further signs of humiliation. The solitary cells were separated from the main prison compound by 9-foot (2.7-m) high wooden fences.

The women's solitary cells measured only about 4 by 6 feet (1.2 by 1.8 m), making them smaller than the men's cells (Figure 10.8). Their walls were made of rough-cut sandstone rubble, and were about 20 inches (50 cm) thick. They had earthen floors situated below the level of their doors, giving the cells a dark, dungeon-like quality.

The solitary conditions faced by the women from the "punishment class" were harsh and brutal, but this does not mean the women were completely broken. It is likely that while in solitary confinement, they participated in an

Figure 10.8 Solitary Cells, Ross Factory Archaeology Project 1997
(Courtesy of Eleanor Casella.)

underground trade network using buttons or the occasional coin as monetary tokens. They probably used this currency to obtain objects not allowed in solitary, like tobacco and alcohol. Once they had gotten such items, they hid them under the cells' earthen floors. They also dug pits into the floors to store bottles, foodstuffs, white clay tobacco pipes, and other banned objects.

Prison authorities must have discovered both the secret exchange network and the women's method of hiding contraband because they had new floors of hard clayey silt laid down in the cells. The clay surfaces were both easier to inspect and considerably more difficult to excavate surreptitiously. The clay floors had a detrimental impact on the secret trade, but it did not end it.

Sources: Eleanor Conlin Casella. To Watch or Restrain: Female Convict Prisons in 19th-Century Tasmania. *International Journal of Historical Archaeology* 5 (2001):45–72; Eleanor Conlin Casella, *Archaeology of the Ross Female Factory: Female Incarceration in Van Diemen's Land, Australia.* (Launceston: Queen Victoria Museum and Art Gallery, 2002).

Chapter 11

The Historical Archaeology of Individuals and Social Groups

Historical Archaeology and Matters of Scale

Historical archaeologists have always thought about analytical scale. The nature of the field gives its practitioners the ability to investigate sites that are small and "local," situations and processes that are "global," and connections between the local and the global. Given this variability, one question archaeologists of the past 500 years have asked themselves is: how is it possible to be interested in the globalized world and yet excavate individual sites?

Many of the most common artifacts discovered in historical archaeology have traveled great distances to reach their final resting places in the soil. To illustrate the point, Martin Hall and Stephen Silliman use the example of the common white clay smoking pipe. They observe that even though these ubiquitous archaeological finds may have been manufactured in the Netherlands in the seventeenth century, archaeologists discover them throughout the world wherever the Dutch lived in colonial days: New York, Brazil, South Africa, the Caribbean, and Southeast Asia. Historical archaeologists find the widespread presence of such finds—across widely diverse environments—difficult to ignore, and so a major task facing historical archaeology today is finding ways to study the small and unique while also thinking about the large and commonplace. Elsewhere, we explain the historical archaeologist's need to "dig local, think global." Historical archaeologists have a special ability and responsibility, given their broad and diverse sources of information—extending from interviewing informants to examining seeds—to find linkages between the local and the global. Only through this effort will they be able to offer knowledge about the contemporary world using the lenses of the past.

One way to envision the problems historical archaeologists face when thinking about local-global connections is to envision the scale of archaeological research as a continuum extending from the level of the individual to the various interlinked, intra- and transcontinental networks of interaction.

In a famous example, French historian Fernand Braudel proposed that the past can be viewed as consisting of three scales: individual time, social time, and geographical time, or long-term history. Individual time is the history of people "in reference to the environment within which they are encompassed." Social time is the history of "groups and groupings," and long-term history is "traditional history," the history of "oscillations" and trends. In archaeology, the individual scale consists of studies of artifact styles and particular sites. These are elements of the past that are influenced by specific events and by the actions of individuals. The social scale involves the study of social groups and the larger circumstances that affect families, kin networks, economic classes, and other groupings of people. In modern history, this scale is likely to involve the large trends that extend across national and even international boundaries. Long-term history concerns the unfolding of history over several generations.

Historical archaeologist Paul Shackel used Braudel's framework in his study of the development of personal discipline in Annapolis, Maryland, between the years 1695 and 1870. For him, individual time could be observed in the archaeology conducted at individual house lots, with the primary data being the artifacts collected from each site. He specifically noticed how ceramics and toothbrushes (both of which he found during excavation) were used to create a sense of individuality in the home. In interpreting Braudel's middle scale of history, social time, Shackel concentrated on what occurred in Annapolis from the late seventeenth to the late nineteenth centuries. His sources for this analysis were contemporary newspapers, personal letters, travelers' guides, and probate lists. To examine long-term history and its relation both to the individual house lots and the city as a whole, Shackel drew back even further and examined the history and social impacts of etiquette. His goal at this scale was to understand why the residents of Annapolis cared about whether they used the "proper" kind of plate or whether they "appropriately" managed their time. Shackel's use of Braudel's three scales allowed him to offer many insights he may otherwise have overlooked had he concentrated only on individual house lots.

The archaeological focus on individuals and their households as the smallest analytical units has appeared desirable because much research in historical archaeology is conducted at a discrete place typically defined as a household. Even scholars who have adopted a global viewpoint, such as world-systems theorists, acknowledge the household as a primary unit of analysis.

The focus on households in archaeological research, besides having a practical element, has important connections to anthropology and history. These links demonstrate the inherent multidisciplinary nature of historical archaeology and stress the importance of small units of analysis. Households constitute a basic unit of daily life because they provide an environment encompassing just about every feature of the socialization process. As noted below, however, the household as the central unit of analysis is not universal in historical archaeology because it cannot address situations where entire communities were the unit of residence, such as the closely knit residences in Chinatowns.

Much of the rationale for the analysis of small units derives most recently from the similarities between archaeology and microhistory (see Chapter 3). Both household archaeologists and microhistorians study small social groups (and sometimes individuals), investigate little spaces and short periods of time, use sources that may be extremely narrow in scope, and defy the artificial boundaries established by separate academic disciplines.

Historical archaeologists throughout the world are investigating individual domestic house sites. At the same time, some archaeologists are examining the sub-household level, taking microhistory at its smallest unit of analysis, the individual.

The idea behind of the local level of analysis derives from the concept that even the small and seemingly insignificant things help humans to manipulate, define, and signal their social roles and identities. This scale of research is inherently interesting because it can provide in-depth insights into the ways social groups use material culture.

The household constitutes a small and reasonable scale of archaeological research, but considerably more difficulty is introduced when archaeologists attempt to broaden the scale to include several households. Community studies also have a long tradition in historical archaeology, with much of the research being conducted in urban neighborhoods. Equally significant are neighborhood-type studies being conducted in seemingly non-neighborhood groups of households like work camps and state-run institutions, like prisons and almshouses. A main feature of these studies rests on the idea that the people in the neighborhood or community interacted on a daily basis and that the networks of relations they created—material, economic, religious, and otherwise—formed the various social units in operation. Much of the theoretical foundation of such research is rooted in the archaeology of social inequality.

Community studies are relatively easy to conceptualize, particularly when the archaeological focus is the urban neighborhood. Individuals in the various households can be expected to have interacted in regular ways with their neighbors. This idea allows powerful insights into past daily life, particularly in situations where the community was a tightly knit social unit.

Historical Archaeology and Individuals

Much of the archaeology practiced over the past decades has investigated the lives of people who are mostly anonymous. Ancient Bronze Age Britons, Near Eastern farmers, and all those individuals who struggled to build the Great Pyramid at Geza are unknown by name. From the ancient world, archaeologists only tend to know the names of the powerful, such as King Tutankhamun, Cleopatra, and Alexander the Great. The same has been true of much historical archaeology, as much early research focused on the wealthy and powerful (see Chapter 1).

In the beginning, restorationists and pioneer historical archaeologists were drawn to famous places like Jamestown, Colonial Williamsburg, and Monticello. And, in locales with historically known individuals, historical archaeologists have had success directly relating artifacts to identifiable men and women. For example, while excavating the overseer's cabin at Cannon's Point Plantation in Georgia, archaeologist John Otto found a glass disk engraved "Hugh F. Grant" and "1829." This disk, possibly a lens of some sort, was undoubtedly owned by Hugh Fraser Grant, the son of a wealthy planter who lived in the area. Records show that Grant was 18 years old in 1829. Wealthy planters' sons often worked as overseers so that they might learn the business of running a large plantation before they acquired their own estate. Thus, Grant may have served as the Cannon's Point overseer before his marriage in 1831. In any case, the etched inscription makes it abundantly clear he once owned the lens.

Another example comes from the site of Ferryland, Newfoundland, Canada. Sir George Calvert, the First Lord Baltimore founded this settlement in 1621, and in 1638 Sir David and Lady Sara Kirke arrived to take up residence there. The year before, Charles I had granted Kirke a monopoly on trade to the island and the right to levy taxes on all visiting non-English ships. Sir David was eventually recalled to court, where charges had been filed against him. In 1654 he died in a London prison. Lady Sara, however, remained in Newfoundland throughout.

Archaeologists excavating at Ferryland have found thousands of fragments of tin-glazed Portuguese earthenware called faience. Seventeenth-century faience is a thick-bodied ware with a buff-colored paste and a glaze having a bluish-white tint. Some of the fragments in the collection are marked "SK" at locations easily linked to the Kirkes' time on the island (Figure 11.1). Working with comparative samples from the era, as well as historical records, Barry Gaulton and Tânia Casimiro were able to associate the marked ceramics with Sara Kirke.

Figure 11.1 SK faience from Ferryland, Newfoundland, Canada
(Courtesy of Barry Goulton.)

For those who could afford them, personalized earthenware was a popular consumer item in seventeenth-century England and Portugal. Many vessels were marked both with the maker's and the recipient's initials. As a result, a reasonable conclusion is that the wares found at Ferryland were once in the possession of Lady Sara Kirke, a wealthy member of the community. Such finds are rare, but archaeologists do find them from time to time.

One thing making historical archaeology somewhat unique within archaeology is that given the range of research materials available, its practitioners can often associate artifacts and buildings with men and women who were not prominent in society. The presence of census records, land deeds, maps, diaries, and other unique textual source make it possible to associate some artifacts with obscure individuals from the past. For example, Lucy Foster (see Chapter 2) and Sylvia Freeman (see Chapter 10) were both hard-working African Americans who were neither famous nor wealthy. In fact, just the opposite was true. And, if it were not for the archaeological research occurring at the women's homes, few living individuals would have ever known about them.

In many cases, however, historical archaeologists cannot associate specific artifacts with specific people even if the names of the people are known. The names of family members living in a New York City tenement might be listed in official census rolls. These lists may reveal the size of the individual families, their relationships, occupations, and ages, but it will be impossible, except in rare cases, to associate individual artifacts excavated from the back yard privy with any specific tenement resident. The most an archaeologist will be able to conclude is that someone from the building deposited the objects.

Archaeologists studying the nineteenth-century Boott Cotton Mills in Lowell, Massachusetts, faced this problem. The historical documents told them many things about the place:

that wealthy entrepreneurs from Boston incorporated the mill on March 22, 1835; that they named it after Kirk Boott, their agent; and that two other agents were named Benjamin French and Linus Child. The documents reveal much about the prominent men of Boott Mills, but it says little about all the others who worked there. What about them?

More than 1,000 laborers—950 women and 120 men—produced about nine million yards of cloth annually in the mill. These now largely forgotten men and women made it possible for the well-documented Boston entrepreneurs to grow wealthy. Mill workers and other industrial workers usually constitute an anonymous labor force, individuals mentioned only rarely in factory records. Some of the Boott Mills workers' names are known. In 1860, 32-year-old James Stoddard was a mill hand; 34-year-old Mary Hanscom was a seamstress, and 24-year-old Charles E. Dodge was a belt maker. The mill records reveal little else about them. Only archaeological excavation has the potential to give voice to these now-silenced men and women. Diet is one avenue of research because historical archaeologists frequently excavate quantities of animal bones (see Chapter 7). Analysis of these bones, when used in conjunction with textual information, can provide significant information about the health of past social groups, such as the Boott Mills employees.

Account books compiled by mill officials provide the formal version of the mill hands' diet. A report published in 1886 listed the food provided for 66 men and 11 women for one month (Figure 11.2). It included 400 pounds (149.2 kg) of roast beef, 272 pounds (101.5 kg) of beefsteak, 160 pounds (59.7 kg) of ham, and 70 pounds (26.1 kg) of salt pork. The workers also consumed mackerel, cod, and other fish, as well as an assortment of beans, rice, squash, and cheese.

The account books initially appear to present a thorough and complete understanding of the mill hands' diet, but archaeological research provides a richer view. Animal bones and plant remains excavated from the boarding house site offered fresh insights. The published lists provided for "the demands for nutrients to 75 laboring men at moderate work for 30 days, or 1 man for 2,250 days." The faunal remains suggested, however, that the people in the mill found it desirable, and perhaps even necessary, to supplement their diet with other foodstuffs. Zooarchaeologist David Landon's analysis reveals families at Boott Mills also ate turkey, chicken, and mutton—foods not mentioned in the records. Sheep bones in the archaeological collection proved the workers ate inexpensive shank cuts and forequarters. The absence of these foods in the historical sources may suggest workers purchased these foods on their own. Ethnobotanist Gerald Kelso discovered that in addition to undocumented cuts of meat, the mill hands also ate grains, grapes, and blackberries or raspberries. The archaeological remains cannot indicate which employees ate what, but the presence of the undocumented foodstuffs at the boarding house provides a collective picture of the workers' diet. On an individual basis, some people may not have liked grapes and mutton and so did not consume them. Archaeologists must generalize—on the group level—because such personal preference can never be known.

One strength of historical archaeology is that it can sometimes flesh out the more commonplace details of the lives of society's anonymous working people—men and women like Stoddard, Hanscom, Dodge—and the hundreds of others who toiled alongside them every day at the Boott Mills. More often, however, individuals are blurred in the archaeological record with other individuals. Their names are lost to history, and so they come down to us through their artifacts and food remains, as members of once well-defined social and economic classes, as males and females, as ethnic groups. How do archaeologists study such complicated groups?

As may be supposed from the previous chapter, no one answer is possible. Different archaeologists approach the study of social groups in different ways using diverse ideas and

DIETARY NUMBER, A 1.

Description : Boarding-house in Lowell, Mass., of 77 persons, 66 males and 11 females Boarders, mill operatives. Time, one month. Estimated as equivalent in demands for nutrients to 75 laboring men at moderate work for 30 days, or 1 man for 2,250 days.

ANALYSIS.

Kinds.	FOOD-MATERIALS.			NUTRIENTS.		
	Prices per lb.	Quantities.	Costs.	Protein.	Fats.	Carbohydrates.
	cents.	lbs.		lbs.	lbs.	lbs.
Beef, roast,	10	400	$40 00	60.4	79.9	–
Beef steak,	14	272	38 08	39.4	42.4	–
Beef, corned,	7	350	24 50	40.3	99.8	–
Beef tongue,	10	62	6 20	9.2	9.5	–
Beef stew,	5	167	8 35	23.4	52.3	–
Beef, tripe,	6	20	1 20	4.2	0.2	–
Pork, roast,	10	150	15 00	17.1	54.3	–
Ham,	11	160	17 60	23.4	54.9	–
Salt pork,	10	70	7 00	2.0	53.6	–
Lard,	8	260	20 80	–	257.4	–
Haddock,	7	168	11 76	13.9	0.2	–
Halibut,	12	50	6 00	7 6	2.1	–
Mackerel,	3	40	1 20	4.0	1.6	–
Salt fish (cod),	4½	50	2 25	8.0	0.2	–
Total meats, fish, etc.,	. .	2,219	$199 94	252.9	708.4	–
Milk,	2	3,024	$60 48	102.8	111.9	145.2
Cheese,	11	63.5	6 98	17.2	22.5	1.5
Butter,	22 and 10	291	54 54	2.9	254.6	1.5
Eggs,	14	107	14 82	12.4	10.9	0.6
Total dairy products and eggs,	. .	3,485.5	$136 82	135.3	399.9	148.8
Flour,	3	1,568	$47 04	174.0	17.2	1,182.3
Sugar,	7½	600	45 00	–	–	580.2
Molasses,	4½	99	4 50	–	–	70.3
Beans,	3	124	3 74	28.8	2 6	66.6
Rice,	8	25	2 00	1.9	0.1	19.9
Oatmeal,	4	25	1 00	3.8	1.8	16.8
Potatoes,	1	2,520	25 20	47.9	5.0	463.7
Squash,	1½	250	3 75	1.3	0.3	13.3
Onions,	2	26	50	0.3	–	2.0
Beets,	5-9	90	50	1.6	0.1	9.0
Turnips,	5-6	120	1 00	1.1	0.2	6.1
Tomatoes,	5-6	120	1 00	1.6	0.4	5.4
Apples,	1⅔	300	5 00	0.9	–	32.7
Raisins,	12½	24	3 00	0.6	0.1	15.1
Currants,	10	15	1 50	0.3	–	9.5
Corn starch,	9	12	1 08	–	–	11.0
Crackers,	5	48	2 40	5.1	4.8	34.0
Total vegetable food,	. .	5,966	$148 21	269.2	32.6	2,537.9
Total animal food,	. .	5,704.5	336 76	388.2	1,108.3	148.8
Total food,	. .	11,670.5	$484 97	657.4	1,140.9	2,686.7
Meats, fish, etc., per man per day,	. .	.99	$0 09	.11	.31	–
Dairy products and eggs, per man per day,	. .	1.55	06	.06	.18	.07
Animal food, per man per day,	. .	2.54	$0 15	.17	.49	.07
Vegetable food, " "	. .	2.65	07	.12	.01	1.13
Total food, " "	. .	5.19	$0 22	.29	.50	1.20

Figure 11.2 Account book of food for millworkers, Lowell, Massachusetts, published in 1886

(From *Food Consumption: Qualities, Costs, and Nutrients of Food Materials* by W. O. Atwater. Massachusetts Bureau of Statistics of Labor 17: 270, 1886.)

concepts. This chapter presents only a few examples. Once again, the material presented here is not exhaustive. Our goal is to provide insight into some of the ways historical archaeology can illuminate the living conditions encountered by past social groups.

Cultural Complexity and Social Stratification

Historical archaeologists investigate complex, socially stratified societies, including literate, pre-industrial, and industrial civilizations. *Social stratification* means that a society is divided into two or more groups ranked relative to one another according to some measure.

Many years ago, anthropologist Elman Service divided human societies into pre-state and state-organized societies. Pre-state societies consisted of hunting bands and simple horticultural societies. These social organizations were either egalitarian in organization, or incorporated minor social differences based on sex, lineage, or some other factor. State-organized societies—Sumerians, ancient Egyptians, Aztecs—were marked by a highly stratified social organization headed by a small class of (often heredity-based) rulers and nobles. Aztec society, for example, was composed of nobles, commoners, and slaves, but within these broad social groupings were numerous economic classes, such as merchants, priests, and warriors. Early pre-industrial civilizations depended on simple technologies and the manual labor of hundreds and perhaps even thousands of individuals. They usually had highly centralized governments, and many of their institutions persisted for long periods. Each of these societies included numerous, often competing social groups. But, even though stratified, they did not have a capitalistic—or profit-centered—economy designed to be global. The worldwide search for wealth characterizing capitalism was one prominent feature of the so-called Age of European Exploration. Since 1492, human societies have been composed of monarchs, captains, generals, priests, merchants, and humble folk.

Given the historical variation, and the range of systems of social stratification theoretically possible, how do archaeologists identify distinct social groups in archaeological deposits? How do artifacts, food remains, structures, burials, and other pieces of evidence help archaeologists untangle the social complexities of the past 500 years?

Historical records may indicate that certain groups of people—enslaved Africans, Native American women, European immigrant laborers—once lived at a particular site. The archaeological problem in such cases is not simply to identify these groups from the remains they left behind, but to try to understand how each group used its material culture to indicate and symbolize their collective identity.

Social identity is a difficult subject because it can change over time and with the situation. But the study of social identity and its material associations is what makes historical archaeology an important social science. Before historical archaeologists can perform the more difficult work of relating artifacts, buildings, and landscapes with certain past social identities, they must first be certain they can actually identify the past groups in the archaeological remains. Given the fluid nature of social identity, archaeologists typically think in terms of the totality of a person's social standing as their identity.

Cemeteries, although controversial to excavate, often provide important clues about social stratification. Archaeologists generally assume that in death, men and women tend to reflect the social standing they held in life. They consider clothing, ornaments, and grave objects to represent the totality of a deceased person's social position at the time of death. One reason archaeologists associate grave appearance with past social standing stems from the difference among burials in the same cemetery.

In her examination of a seventeenth-century cemetery used by the Narragansetts in Rhode Island, archaeologist Patricia Rubertone investigated 56 burials. Included in the sample were 15 males, 28 females, and 13 unknown individuals. As a group, the burials contained a wide variety of European materials—glass wine bottles, brass kettles, lead shot, buttons—and Native American objects—pottery vessels, textiles, shell beads. But the distribution of objects in the graves was not consistent. A burial of a three-year-old contained a bracelet made of glass and brass, a glass medicine bottle, an iron hoe, and a metal spoon, while the burial of a 15-year-old female contained only a single shell. Some burials had finger rings, others had none. Three adult women's burials contained hoes, whereas only one adult male had one.

Archaeologists assume that differences in artifact association must mean something. But what? How do archaeologists unravel the meaning of such obvious differences? One way to discover something about social stratification in the complex societies studied by historical archaeologists is with a focus on social class.

Social Class

"Class" is a difficult concept, and social scientists disagree about its precise definition. Some say a person's social class membership has to do with his or her "life's chances," the opportunity to acquire property, education, and material things. Others contend that class membership, and even life chances for that matter, relate more to a person's relationship to production. The mark of difference is that some people own factories and agricultural land whereas others work in the factories and on the land. In this formulation, individuals are either owners (haves) or workers (have-nots). Other people equate class strictly with income. The more money a person has, the higher their social position in society. In one well-known definition, anthropologist Marvin Harris defined a class as a group of people who have a similar relationship to the structure of social control in a society and who possess similar amounts of power over the allocation of wealth, privilege, resources, and technology. In short, definitions of class abound.

An important point about classes is that an individual's membership in a particular class can change as that person acquires (or loses) something of value to the society, such as wealth, power, position, or education. Furthermore, men and women in a class system only know their position in a relative way. For example, everyone may have some idea whether they belong to the upper, middle, or lower class, but not necessarily to what part of the class. Are they upper middle class or the lower upper class? Making this decision requires a firm under-standing of what constitutes the difference. For archaeologists, material culture constitutes a key variable. The difficulty of reaching an agreement about the true nature of class makes it difficult for historical archaeologists to understand past class-based social systems.

Historical archaeologist Steven Shephard studied the relationship between material cul-ture and class membership in Alexandria, Virginia. Alexandria began as a small trading post primarily for tobacco in the early 1730s, but soon grew into a major mercantile center. At its height, the city boasted a population stratified into classes extending from enslaved African Americans at the bottom to wealthy planters and merchants at the top. Shephard examined three early nineteenth-century sites in the city in the hope of isolating material evidence of class membership. City records indicated the residents of two sites could be classified as hav-ing been within the middle class (based on income and occupation). The inhabitants of the third site were in the much poorer lower class. From the thousands of artifacts excavated by the city's archaeological staff, Shephard decided to focus on glazed ceramics because these objects can be studied in terms of quantity, quality, and variety. Alexandrian families usually purchased large quantities of ceramics during the course of their lives. Their vessels could be of vastly different qualities, from fine imported wares to everyday kitchen pieces. Shephard, examining a sample composed of around 1,300 bowls, cups, saucers, and plates from different neighborhoods, noticed that the middle-class households had a greater quantity and variety of dishes than did the lower-class household. Middle-class families also had more matching pieces and of greater variety than the poorer household.

Shephard's findings may appear somewhat obvious. Given today's class differences, we can easily imagine men and women in higher social positions having a greater variety of dishes than someone lower down the social ladder. Shephard's conclusion, however, that "the quantity and quality variables are the strongest correlates of class membership," provides an avenue of inquiry others can follow.

One obvious factor influencing the ability of class members to acquire certain dishes (or anything else for that matter), hinges on whether they can be obtained. No one can buy what is not available. The upper class may be expected to have had a greater ability to obtain the goods they want, but only if available. If upper-class families wished to live off the beaten path far from highways or railroads, would they have had difficulty obtaining some artifacts?

Sherene Baugher and Robert Venables decided to test this idea by examining ceramic artifacts excavated at seven eighteenth-century sites in New York State. They chose two sites in the country, and five sites in New York City—two on Staten Island, three on Manhattan. They used historical records to establish that each site was inhabited by upper- or middle-class households. One site was inhabited by Sir William Johnson, the famous Englishman who was the liaison between the British government and the powerful Iroquois. Less well-known people, but no less wealthy, lived at the other sites. Having used documents to establish the class affiliation of the sites' residents, Baugher and Venables compared the artifacts from each location. They focused on ceramics but found few differences between the collections. Each site contained the expensive, imported porcelains and finely made white tableware archaeologists usually associate with eighteenth-century wealth. Baugher and Venables did observe a difference in inexpensive tableware: kitchen pieces made locally and directly purchased from their producers. This finding suggests that the household members probably saw no reason to spend money importing mixing bowls, churns, and jars when they were easily available locally for less cost. And in any case, these pieces were for kitchen use only, out of the public eye. It seems, therefore, that a household's location played some role in artifact acquisition. Even elites in the backwoods could buy the things they wanted, but they also made conscious decisions about their purchases, sometimes buying objects made locally. Then as now, class helps shape what individuals can acquire. Upper-crust, colonial New Yorkers, regardless of address, could easily mimic the fashions of London and other European capitals, at least in public.

In another essay entitled "Steps to an Archaeology of Capitalism," Robert Paynter stated that historical archaeologists can do much more than simply identify the presence of classes at past archaeological sites. He proposed that historical archaeologists can make significant contributions to the theory of class. The potential to make this contribution exists because material culture plays such a large role in many class theories.

In discussing glass bottles—objects frequently found by historical archaeologists—Paynter stated that the transition from mouth blowing to machine manufacture was more than simply a technological innovation (see Chapter 8). Much of it was associated with the relations between glassblowers and factory owners. The impetus for the development of bottle-making machines occurred because labor strikes and work stoppages by glassblowers made the industry a risky proposition for factory owners. In response to the risk, bottle manufacturers sought to circumvent work-stopping labor problems by decreasing the number of "troublesome" employees. An automatic bottle maker was one obvious way to do this. When put in this light, the bottle fragments found by historical archaeologists during excavation represent much more than a mere technological improvement; they symbolize the way one class—glass-factory owners—reacted to the protests of another class—glassblowers.

A new generation of historical archaeologists are investigating class with great vigor. Much more remains to be done on the subject of class identification and meaning, but current research points in new and interesting directions. Today's historical archaeologists are busy examining how social classes were created and maintained, how class members used material objects to identify themselves, and how various social classes struggled for control, power, and dignity.

Gender

Men and women constitute the two most basic groups in the vast panorama of human history. Archaeologists for years found it easy to speak of these two groups in simplistic terms. Ancient men hunted, so all stone arrowheads and spear points were "male" objects; women cooked, so all potsherds were "female" objects. Scholars usually assumed that a society's "movers and shakers" were men; they were responsible for cultural change and technological advancement. Women stood behind the scenes: homemaking, weaving, and cooking.

Western convention recognizes only two sexes. We imagine sex to be based on physiology rather than behavior. Not every culture, however, makes this assumption. The eighteenth-century Tahitians of the south Pacific recognized three sexes: male, female, and mahu. The mahu were permanent transvestites who were not regarded as oddities. Neither were they considered to be male or female. Visiting Europeans were horrified by the mahu. John Turnbull described them in 1813 as "a set of men . . . whose open profession is of such abomination that the laudable delicacy of our language will not admit it to be mentioned." The famed William Bligh, captain of H.M.S. *Bounty,* later set adrift by his mutinous crew in 1788, said of one particular mahu, "The Women treat him as one of their Sex, and he observes every restriction that they do, and is equally respected and esteemed." Many Native American societies also recognized three sexes. Among the Crows of Montana, for instance, the berdache—identified as individuals who have "two spirits"—was the equivalent of the Tahitian mahu. Finds-Them-and-Kills-Them, a Crow berdache, dressed like a woman and performed the domestic chores of a woman. Other Crows saw him not as a deviant male, but as a member of a third sex.

Westerners also tend to equate sex with gender. But gender refers to culturally prescribed behavior. Among the Tahitians and the Crows, Westerners would see two sexes and two gender roles: male and female. The mahu and berdache would constitute deviant males. The Tahitians and the Crows, however, would perceive two sexes and three gender roles: male and female; and male, female, and transvestite behavior.

Numerous archaeologists, some working in collaboration with ethnographers, have dispelled the Western perception of equating gender with sex. Archaeologists have learned to evaluate the many roles, systems, and ideologies involving gender. As historical archaeologist Donna Seifert has observed, "women are not defective men; pregnancy, childbearing, and nursing are not necessarily disabilities; women's behavior, experience, and history is not deviant behavior because it is not the same as men's." The study of gender is not just about women; it is about women and men interacting to create and maintain society. When archaeologists learn about women's roles in the past, they are simultaneously enlightened about men's roles. Giving women a voice in the past provides a deep, realistic understanding of history and culture.

Donna Seifert investigated "Hooker's Division," a nineteenth-century red light section of Washington, D.C., Hooker's Division was named for Major General Joseph Hooker, who in 1863 as commander of the Army of the Potomac, ordered the city's prostitutes to concentrate in one part of town. The city council forced Hooker to take this drastic step because they were growing increasingly concerned about the burgeoning number of off-duty soldiers flooding the nation's capital. Soldiers fresh from battle, bored, and perhaps away from home for the first time, went looking for fully stocked saloons and bordellos. They found both in Hooker's Division.

Remarkably, even though prostitution is considered "the world's oldest profession," archaeologists before Seifert had not studied it in great detail. Rather than seeking to examine Hooker's Division as a way to learn about one particular group of women, Seifert chose to envision prostitution as a kind of gender relationship. Serving as a sexual partner in this situation represented a necessary job rather than an expectation of marriage. Gender relationships and expectations within society permit prostitution to flourish.

Examining the materials excavated from Hooker's Division, Seifert found clothing artifacts—such as buttons—present in much greater quantity than at other, more purely residential parts of the city. Buttons from Hooker's Division came from a variety of garments, ranging from fancy ladies' robes to everyday men's and women's shirts and coats. Excavation revealed several men's trouser buttons, perhaps lost by the brothel porters, or by the young men who ventured into the neighborhood.

Seifert also discovered that objects of personal hygiene and adornment (mirrors, combs, and jewelry) occurred more often in the red light district than at other, nearby residences. A jar of "Valentine's Meat Juice," for the cure of "social diseases," reveals information about the health concerns of the ladies in Hooker's Division and the realities of their occupation.

Seifert's findings are important because they provide a voice for women too long absent in archaeological accounts. Several archaeologists have since followed her lead in studying the realities of prostitution, including seeing the situation as representing a gender relationship. Prostitutes worked to support themselves and their families as part of this relationship. Prostitution is not simply an aberrant whim that "just happens" to some women; it has economic and social roots relating to and reflecting gender roles in society.

In some cases, simply the act of demonstrating the presence of women at a site is enough to shake forever the foundations of once-cherished androcentric, or male-focused, interpretations. Archaeologists have done a superb job of placing women at sites where they have long been invisible. Logging camps, like military forts, are usually perceived as bastions of manhood. A common image presents manly lumberjacks tramping into virgin forests ready to do battle with nature. They turn trees into usable lumber using only brute strength and willpower. Women, when mentioned in the historical records of the lumber industry, usually live "in town." Traditional histories thus tend to project only one image of logging: that it was a male-only activity.

The reality of logging was far different from the image. Archaeologist Janet Brashler concretely proved that women were involved in logging. Examining historic photographs and reading numerous historical reports, she learned that women lived in most logging camps. Rather than being a rarity, women were an integral part of the timber industry. Brashler rooted her research in the idea that gender is an organizing principle of group relations. This perspective allowed her to look beyond the image of the all-male shantytown. She discovered that many logging camps were inhabited by families. Dogway, West Virginia, for example, was a temporary logging town established by the Cherry River Boom and Lumber Company. Residents lived there from about 1910–1915 to 1927. Brashler made numerous surface finds at this abandoned town, including intricately decorated dishes, cast iron stove parts, rusted barrel hoops and springs, and different colored glass fragments. She also saw crumbled brick chimneys, caved-in root cellars, old railway grades, and 60 old railroad cars that had been converted into housing.

Brashler gave women a voice within the sphere of the Cherry River Boom and Lumber Company. Archaeologists interested in the gender relations of the logging industry face a challenge as they attempt, in Brashler's words, "to define more clearly the artifact assemblages found in family camps, single-gender camps, family shanty camps, camps with red-light districts, and camps where one or two women might have been present as the wives of the foreman or cook." How can the artifacts unearthed from logging sites be used to give voice to the women of the logging industry? How do the rusty tin cans, bent metal plates and cups, broken glass bottles, and iron pot fragments represent logging-oriented gender roles?

Circumstances prevented Brashler from excavating any of the logging camps she found during her surveys, so she was forced to work entirely with materials collected from the surface. Her research nonetheless challenged archaeologists to look for women where their preconceived notions suggested they were absent.

Many people often assume the earliest European colonists and explorers were men. After all, no women accompanied Columbus on his first or second voyages to the New World. But several archaeologists are rapidly changing this male-only view of colonialism. History records that Spanish women engaged in numerous trades, from folk medicine to textile production, even though they were generally expected to be homemakers. In the sixteenth and seventeenth centuries, Spanish women generally went to the New World as the wives of wealthy aristocrats. The main responsibility of these women was to maintain the Spanish colonial household.

Authors of colonial Spanish documents usually ignored the typical Spanish wife. Luckily, however, archaeologists can unearth evidence of their presence. At Puerto Real, Haiti, Charles Ewen found material evidence for the presence of women in the deposits of the sixteenth-century Spanish town site. At one high-status residence, he found a lace bobbin made of bone, a number of glass beads, a ring fashioned from jet (a dense, black coal), and a pendant in the shape of a unicorn. Nothing else is known of the woman, or women, who used the bobbin or wore the ring, pendant, and beads, but now with their presence acknowledged, archaeologists can continue to search for them. At a seventeenth-century Spanish mission site in Tallahassee, Florida, Bonnie McEwan has excavated objects similar to those found in Haiti: jet rings, metal sequins or beads, small brass rings, and a quartz pendant in the shape of a teardrop.

McEwan's and Ewen's research demonstrates that women lived in colonial Spanish communities and that Spanish wives had a dramatic role in shaping colonial society. Colonial Spanish wives made their impact felt by interacting with the female Native American and African American domestics who worked alongside them in their homes. Spanish women were important transferrers of culture through instruction in language, religion, and other aspects of European tradition. The continuity with Spain women sought in their colonial homes was impressed upon domestic servants because Spanish wives were ultimately responsible for ensuring the home conformed to the Spanish ideal. Spanish women were thus on the front line of cultural change, bringing Spanish culture to non-Spaniards and deciding which elements of non-Spanish culture to adopt in their homes. Spanish women thus played an important role in bringing Spanish culture to the continent their nation had only just discovered.

A number of historical archaeologists have begun to look closer at gender relations in colonial situations. For example, in her study of colonial San Francisco, one of the social variables Barbara Voss examines is sexuality and gender relations. She begins by noting that archaeologists have for too long theorized identity as static. Because her interest is ultimately in studying ethnogenesis—or the birth of new cultural identities—she perceives social identity as fluid. Identity, being a process rather than a state of being, is free to change over time. She also notes that identity is "overdetermined." This means that identity is so complex that analysts cannot expect to disentangle one dimension of social variability from another. Many historical archaeologists now hold this view. Voss argues that sexuality is closely related to gender, and that sexuality is as important to identity as ethnicity.

Voss's goal is to understand the ethnogenesis of Californio identity during the years 1776–1821. Californio is a self-identification that emphasizes Spanish heritage even though most of the settlers in the region around San Francisco were of mixed Mexican, Indian, African, and European ancestry. The sense of Iberian identity, and the strong role of the Catholic Church in the Spanish New World, meant that sacred precepts often dictated how identities would be formed. The social positions of men and women were defined according to Biblical tradition. Women were subordinate to men because Eve had been created from Adam's rib and placed on the earth to serve him. The Church also took the word "position" literally. The sexual position they mandated was the "missionary position." Any other position was deemed a perversion because it would metaphorically suggest that women were superior—literally "over"—men. The Church also held authority over baptism and marriage, rituals that helped to determine identities of gender and sexuality.

The religious mores advanced by the Catholic Church had implications for material culture. Clothing was one arena where social differences were determined by law and conservative conventions. People of African heritage, for example, were forbidden by law to wear silk, lace, precious stones, pearls, and anything made of gold or silver. Only elite Spanish women were permitted to wear embroidered headscarves. First violations would be punished by confiscation, but thereafter by whippings.

Voss discovered, using the combination of historical analysis and archaeological excavation commonplace to historical archaeology, that people were able to negotiate their identities with their dress (Figure 11.3). The women, for example, fastened their garments with cloth belts and ties rather than with the more Spanish buttons and buckles. Others in the community were doing similar things, leading Voss to conclude that over time the residents of colonial San Francisco were transforming themselves. They were undergoing ethnogenesis, with a significant element of the transformation involving sexual identity.

Figure 11.3 Copper-alloy uniform buttons and glass beads from midden deposits at the Presidio of San Francisco
(Courtesy of Barbara Voss.)

In another study, Diana DiPaolo Loren writes about how Natchez woman, living along the Lower Mississippi River, changed their patterns of dress after coming into contact with French traders. She notes how glass beads, though small in size, had a tremendous impact on Natchez concepts. They are tangible manifestations of cultural change. Many Native American cultures, perhaps including the Natchez, perceived beads as helping to protect the spirit in the afterlife. Hence, mourners often placed trade beads in graves along with their deceased kin. The large number of trade beads found at archaeological sites outside burial contexts, however, implies that Natchez individuals began to use them as adornments over time. The increased wearing of beads suggests the creation of a new concept of self, another transformation of identity.

Historical archaeologists investigating gender roles and, indeed, other social elements of daily life, have tended to envision the household as a unified body composed of individuals who work together toward the common good of the group. Conflicts, though we may imagine them to have occurred, are largely left unnoticed in the background. Archaeologist Hadley Kruczek-Aaron, however, has challenged this perspective and in the process has provided a sophisticated view of gender roles.

Kruczek-Aaron focused on the estate of Gerrit Smith (1797–1874), a famous politician and reformer who lived in New York State. Historical records report that the Smith household was the scene of two interpersonal struggles: one between the household's women and their working-class, female housekeeper and nanny, and the other between Gerrit Smith and his wife Ann and daughter Elizabeth. One of the conflicts existing between Smith and his daughter Elizabeth concerned the latter's interest in fashionable things. Smith's personal philosophy was founded on simple living, whereas Elizabeth wanted to live surrounded by the most recent amenities available. Documentary sources indicate that Smith won many of the contests over fashion. Their home was described as decorated in a minimalist fashion, with simple furnishings and no mirrors, expensive carpets, or heavy drapery. Excavations revealed, however, that Smith did not win every battle. The discovery of intricately decorated, transfer-printed dishes proves that the Smith women asserted control over at least one domain of material culture—their dinner wares. The women could use these decorative pieces as display items within their otherwise simple surroundings to impress their friends and visitors. The romantic patterns on the dishes led Kruczek-Aaron to conclude that the designs challenged the "thoroughly Spartan existence" the Smiths were supposed to have lived. The importance of Kruczek-Aaron's research stems from her interest in depicting gender roles as negotiable social factors. Her perspective is insightful because she understands that gender roles change through time. The study of gender and gender roles continues to offer promise to historical archaeology by helping to overturn long-held stereotypes about men and women, while at the same time demonstrating the interpretive potential of historical archaeology.

Archaeologists have also studied gender using African American graves. In their research, Kristin Wilson and Melanie Cabak used information associated with 336 individuals from six cemeteries in the American South dating to the late nineteenth and early twentieth centuries. Their goal was to discover whether differences in gender could be discerned from the material culture found within the graves. Research of this kind concentrates on gender as a condition fixed in death (and commemorated in graves) rather than gender as a fluid process.

Wilson and Cabak's analysis revealed differences between African American male and female graves. One of their surprising discoveries is that the graves showed little continuity between the belief systems of West Africa and the southern United States. Women's identities tended to reflect their roles as caregivers for children and other women. Pierced coins—associated with providing protection from sickness and evil—occurred only in graves of women and children. Women had more personal adornments than men, but the graves of younger women contained more jewelry than the graves of elderly women.

Ethnicity

Historical archaeologists investigated ethnicity before they began to study class membership or gender relations. In fact, ethnicity was historical archaeology's first foray into historical sociology.

Experts disagree on a precise definition of ethnicity, but in general they consider an ethnic group to be an assemblage of people who share enough physical and cultural characteristics to define themselves as "us" and to define everyone else as "them." Ethnicity refers to the characteristics a group accepts as pertinent to them. Ethnic groups can be "nationalities," such as the Croats and Serbs in Bosnia-Hercegovina, or "people," such as the Romani (Gypsies) or Irish Travelers of Europe. Historical archaeologists in the United States have focused most of their attention on African, Hispanic, and Asian ethnic groups, although they have also examined several European groups as well.

For all its study by historical archaeologists, the correlation between ethnicity and material culture remains poorly understood. Sherene Baugher and Robert Venables had explicit historical information concerning the ethnicity of the people who lived at four of the seven sites they studied in New York State. Sir William Johnson, who lived on the Mohawk River, was Irish; Robert Livingston, who lived on the Hudson River between Albany and New York City, was of Scottish and Dutch ancestry; Jacob Rezeau, who lived in the center of Staten Island, was French; and Christopher Billopp, who lived on the southern tip of Staten Island, was English. Even with this knowledge, Baugher and Venables were unable to observe any clear evidence of ethnic difference among the archaeological remains at the sites.

Lu Ann De Cunzo drew the same conclusion in her study of Paterson, New Jersey. She examined the artifacts from six nineteenth-century privies. Paterson was founded in 1791 by the Society for the Establishment of Useful Manufacture. The town was the first planned manufacturing community in America, and even though the town was not a great success at first, it soon became the destination of several immigrant groups, including people from Great Britain and Ireland.

The six privies De Cunzo studied were associated with Irish and English settlers. She scrutinized the artifact collections from each privy, but found no clear evidence of Irish or English identity. She found no clay pipes with Irish slogans imprinted on them, no insignia related to Irish independence, nothing symbolizing pride in the British Empire. She could not discern any difference in the quantity and diversity of ceramic and glass objects in the privies. The medicine bottles, ceramic plates and cups, and liquor bottles indicated nothing particularly suggestive of ethnicity. In short, De Cunzo was unable to distinguish any material differences between historically documented Irish and English households. Most likely, then, people of English and Irish heritage probably expressed their ethnicity through their secular and religious associations rather than in their material possessions. Both Irish and English immigrants strove to be "American" at the expense of any clear material expression of their individual ethnic identities. In other words, they engaged in consumption like all the ethnic groups who lived around and among them.

The New York and New Jersey examples show just how difficult it is to distinguish ethnic groups from household artifacts alone. For this reason, many archaeologists originally turned to the identification of "ethnic markers." Ethnic markers are individual artifacts or groups of artifacts that undeniably indicate the presence of certain ethnic groups at archaeological sites. The opium smoking-pipe brought to the United States by nineteenth-century Chinese immigrants is a classic example of a supposed ethnic marker. Opium pipe bowls have a distinctive appearance, and historical archaeologists can easily identify them once they know their characteristics. Made of either pottery or stone (such as jade), the bowls resemble fancy doorknobs that have a hole, the "smoking hole," running downward through their center. This bowl was attached to a long pipestem and completed the opium pipe, or "pistol" (Figure 11.4).

When Roberta Greenwood conducted research on Main Street in Ventura, California, she used opium pipes as ethnic markers. She found small glass medicinal vials and opium pipe bowls in a mix of nineteenth-century artifacts. These objects immediately signaled the presence of Chinese residents in the area. Greenwood's general expectation was that in a community containing men and women of both Chinese and non-Chinese heritage, some artifacts could be singled out to represent each group. Her reasoning made sense because archaeologists at the time did not know much about the material expressions of ethnic group affiliation. Well over half the artifacts she found in her excavations were of Chinese origin, including rice bowls, tea cups, ginger jars, and soy bottles. She identified other ceramic cups, plates, bowls, and chamber pots as non-Chinese artifacts.

Greenwood then proposed that several kinds of artifacts, in addition to opium pipes, could be viewed as ethnic markers. Her pioneering research followed conventional wisdom at the time, and her assumptions are difficult to criticize. She was following a new line of research, and she had little comparative information to consult. Greenwood no longer holds the views she published in the 1970s, and she, like all historical archaeologists, now acknowledges that easy interpretations rest too strongly on ethnic stereotypes. How can we ever assume a porcelain tea cup or a soy bottle was used only by Chinese men and women, especially in cases where the deposits are ethnically mixed?

The problem of association is perhaps best expressed by the opium pipe bowl. Many people associate opium smoking with Chinese immigrants to North America, and pictures of Chinese men smoking opium are legion. But was opium smoking strictly a Chinese habit?

Ruth Ann Sando and David Felton studied the store records of the Kwong Tai Wo Company for the years 1871–1883. The store was located in northern California, but its precise location is unknown. The purpose of their analysis was to provide archaeologists with a more comprehensive view of the kinds of material objects Chinese residents had available to them. For instance, the Kwong Tai Wo records offer information about the kinds of ceramic tableware Chinese people bought and used, and they present a rare commentary on where the main profits of the business lay. For the 12 years covered by the account books, the total value of the ceramics mentioned is only $266.80. For the ten years from 1873 to 1883, the total value of the opium sold exceeded $2,850.

The Kwong Tai Wo store sold at least ten different kinds of opium, some with exotic names meaning "Abundant Luck," "Abundant Memory," and "Everlasting Peace." Archaeologists throughout the American West have found can lids bearing the names of these varieties. One thing Sando and Felton learned in their research was that opium use was a widespread feature of nineteenth-century American life for both Chinese and non-Chinese individuals. Although Chinese people generally took their opium by smoking and non-Chinese in medicines, many non-Chinese also smoked it. This evidence shows that associating opium pipes found at archaeological sites with Chinese inhabitants is far too simplistic a conclusion. As historical archaeology became more sophisticated in the 1990s, historical archaeologists began to place far greater emphasis on context when attempting to associate specific artifacts with past ethnic groups.

Some ethnic markers do appear in the archaeological record. Mark Leone and his colleagues excavating in Annapolis, Maryland, unearthed a steel comb at an apartment house site called Gott's Court. Gott's Court was home to about 25 African American households

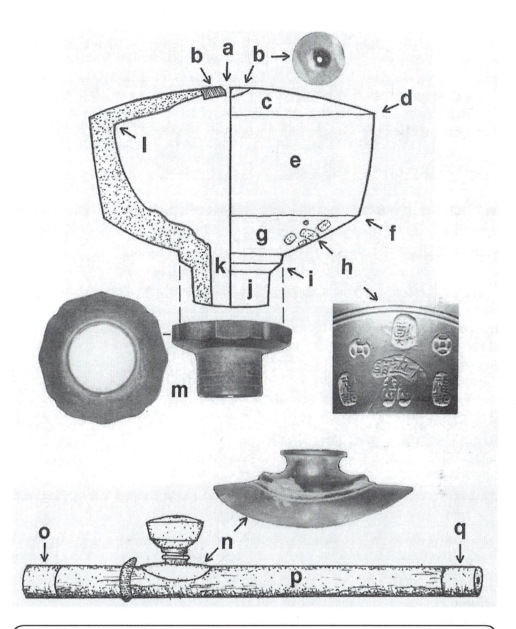

Figure 11.4 Parts of an opium pipe: a. smoking hole, b. insert, c. smoking surface, d. rim, e. side, f. shoulder, g. base, h. stamps, i. flange, j. stem, k. basal hole, l. rim joint, m. metal connector, n. saddle, o. end piece, p. pipe stem, q. mouthpiece

from 1906 until the mid-1930s. Leone and his team excavated the site as part of their project to understand and interpret the history and culture of historic Annapolis. The enigmatic comb was one of the most intriguing finds they made at the site. Not knowing the past function of the comb, they began their inquiry by searching old catalogs and scouring archaeological site reports. Their hope was that someone else had found a similar comb and knew its function, but they had no success. No other archaeological specimens were known to exist. When a photograph of the comb appeared in the *Washington Post,* an African American housekeeper visited the archaeological lab and told the archaeologists that their mystery object was a hot comb used by African Americans to straighten their hair. The archaeologists were excited that their mystery artifact had been identified, but they still had much to learn about its past function. They initially interpreted the comb as a way African Americans could strive to integrate themselves into the job market. Straighter hair might be a feature that potential non-African American employers would view as a positive sign of personal attitude. African Americans with whom the research team spoke, however, said this was not the case. They said the hot comb was used, not as a tool of assimilation into white society, but as a way to ensure cultural survival. African Americans could use the comb to make it appear they had been assimilated, when in fact this was not true. The use of the comb was simply a prudent way to negotiate the rules of white society. The hot comb is clearly an ethnic marker, but one having a profound symbolic meaning.

Do white clay smoking pipes proclaiming "Erin Go Bragh" (Ireland For Ever) symbolize Irish ethnicity? Does a blue bead found in the remains of a plantation cabin mean it was worn by an enslaved African American? Do the brightly colored yellow and red majolica ceramics from the Iberian Peninsula always signal the presence of Spanish or Portuguese colonialists? Historical reality is much more complicated than any stereotype would admit. As Lu Ann De Cunzo's research in New Jersey demonstrated so well, ethnicity can be extremely difficult to discover at archaeological sites. Even when census rolls, personal letters, and land deeds allow historical archaeologists to determine the ethnicity of the people who once lived at a property, the artifacts are rarely equally forthcoming about their past owners' ethnicities. Ethnicity remains a difficult topic of great interest to many historical archaeologists.

Race

Ethnicity and race are closely intertwined, and both present formidable challenges for historical archaeologists. Both social dimensions are difficult, and sometimes well-nigh impossible, to identify in archaeological deposits.

Most people tend to confuse race and ethnicity, so much so that the two have become practically synonymous in everyday speech. Even experts can sometimes make the mistake of confusing the two concepts. V. Gordon Childe, one of history's greatest archaeological thinkers, said in 1926 that "The correlation of cultural with racial groups is generally hazardous and speculative." Childe actually meant "ethnic" groups, and his wording was unfortunate because he made this statement in his widely read *The Aryans: A Study of Indo-European Origins.* The book was so well known that even Nazis read it because they generally approved of the way Childe depicted the Aryans. Childe, a lifelong socialist, was never able to forget (or forgive) how the Nazis had misused his serious work of archaeological interpretation to justify their own pernicious deeds.

As a scholarly matter, race and ethnicity are easy to separate. Race is usually used by one group to designate people in another group. The racial designation is generally intended for people of a lower social standing than the people identifying the "races." Thus, race is a term imposed from outside a group, and people who have been lumped together as a "race" are said to be "racialized." The process of assigning and identifying "races" is called racialization. Race is usually narrowly defined on the basis of an outward characteristic, most notably physical appearance. Anthropologists today completely reject the term "race" as a valid human category, understanding that only one race exists—the human race. They see human physical diversity simply as variety. In 1945 British anthropologist M. F. Ashley Montagu referred to race as humanity's "most dangerous myth." Conversely, ethnicity is designated from the inside. People use ethnic terms to identify themselves because of some shared or perceived identity. Ethnicity is not derogatory because it is a self-identification.

Showing the fallacy of racial categories does not necessarily mean that historical archaeologists can afford to ignore race, or that the impact of racial identification is negligible on living men, women, and children, past and present. Some people in the past did use racial categories to designate certain human groups, and their social behavior was affected by their usage. Ideas of racial inequality have been common throughout world history (and still are), but can they be identifiable in archaeological deposits?

A number of historical archaeologists are diligently working to unravel the archaeological mysteries of race. Paul Mullins, a leading figure in this effort, proposed that African Americans, as part of the wider American consumer society, faced special challenges because of racism. As a result, they invented ways to use mass-produced objects in unique ways. He said that racism forced African Americans to create special ways to represent and hide their cultural integrity as a means of survival in a harsh, apartheid society. The purchase and use of material things by men and women of African descent was thus always constrained by discrimination, law, economics, and social barriers.

To support his idea, Mullins excavated at the Maynard-Burgess House in Annapolis. Two African American families, first the Maynards and then the Burgesses, occupied the property from 1847 to 1980. One of Mullins' findings was that the families used fish and other seafoods as an important way to circumvent the normal economic system. These were foods they could acquire themselves without having to visit the market. Excavated faunal remains show that by the late nineteenth century, however, the Maynards began to rely on store-bought foods. By the beginning of the twentieth century, the household relied almost exclusively on professionally butchered meats. Bottles excavated from the house also show that by 1890, the Maynards purchased brand-name foods and canned very little of their own food. Hundreds of fragments of tin cans and a large collection of bottles from professionally packaged foods—coupled with only two canning jars and one ceramic crock—combine to show the Maynards had fully bought into the American national market. Like most urban dwellers, they no longer preserved their own foods. They preferred instead to visit stores and buy them. Bottles from 26 nationally advertised brands of medicinal products—like mineral water and Bromo Seltzer—show the Maynards relied on over-the-counter products rather than on home remedies.

In addition to glass bottles, butchered animal bones, and medicine bottles, Mullins discovered several sherds of ceramic tableware. These dishes resembled those excavated at Gott's Court, mentioned above, in that they were mismatched. Mullins believed the African Americans in Annapolis used a specific strategy to obtain their ceramics. They may have purchased a few new vessels, but they probably obtained much of their tableware through barter and informal exchange. As one woman told the research team: "I don't remember us having any good china sets, you know. . . . I think a lot of stuff was passed down from grandparents to parents." Mullins believed the mix of ceramics found in the excavations at the Maynard-Burgess House demonstrated that the Maynard family felt little need to present "the appearance of assimilation" to the outside world. African Americans did not feel the need to appear to be part of white society when they were at home and out of the public eye. Mullins believed his research showed that African Americans bought into the American consumer society along with everyone else, but they were more likely to hide their affluence because of racist attitudes in society. As a result, the consumerism of African Americans was tactical; it was designed to negotiate the tricky social terrain defined by racism and marginalization.

Mullins's study of the Maynard-Burgess House demonstrates the difficulty inherent in the archaeological study of racism. Straightforward interpretations are impossible because racial designation seldom exists by itself. It is usually coupled with socioeconomics or some other measure of social inequality. The Maynards, like the men and women at Gott's Court, negotiated with white society in subtle ways that did not compromise their integrity. Hardly surprising, their methods of negotiation are difficult to identify today, for they were both complex and clandestine. They can only be identified from the dispassionate evidence of distinctive artifacts, which the negotiators bought, used, and threw away.

In another study of race, from Virginia and Jamaica, Ywone Edwards-Ingram demonstrated the often-subtle character of racial negotiation. She examined the role medicine could play in the social relations created between enslaved African Americans and their Anglo-American masters. Her specific interest was in the use of plants for medicinal purposes. She discovered that enslaved men and women were often able—sometimes on the sly, sometimes openly—to visit their own doctors and healers, men and women who, like them, were held in lifelong bondage on the same plantation. Enslaved Africans may have felt a sense of personal power when visiting these traditional healers. They also may have appreciated the cultural aspect of using African doctors, because in doing so, they were preserving something of their traditional way of life.

Most people today may not think of medicine as cultural, but Edward-Ingram's study clearly illustrates the importance of context. African Americans relied on cures with African connections. They employed charms, specific colors, certain materials, and ritual behaviors rooted in Africa. Enslaved African Americans could use plants for food, but they could also use them for curing in situations where their owner purposefully withheld medical care. African American women could also use plants to induce abortion. The use of plants to end pregnancy was an act of personal power because the enslaved could consciously choose not to increase the slave owner's supply of human chattel. By ending a pregnancy, they saved another life from enslavement.

White slave owners attempted to use their conceptions of race to instill a sense of inferiority on enslaved men and women. Slave owners could force their power and authority over their workforce by withholding food and other supplies, including medicine. Gathering plants, for various purposes, was one way enslaved individuals could negotiate the racial hierarchy in which they found themselves. They could use their cultural knowledge of plants as a form of social power. This knowledge indicates the complex nature of racial negotiation, as African Americans confronted racism on a daily basis.

Age

Archaeologists, including historical archaeologists, ignored the serious study of children for many years. In most cases, when archaeologists discovered porcelain tea cups and doll parts, metal soldiers and tiny cannons, and clay and glass marbles, they just assumed children were present in the past and left it at that. In some ways, the identification of children through toys was similar to the identification of ethnic groups through opium pipes and shamrock-decorated smoking pipes. The correlation was not exact because ethnicity is a self-defined identity and childhood is a biological fact. Childhood may be biological, but different cultures perceive it in vastly different ways. For example, the Maasai of Kenya and Tanzania expect their five- and six-year-old children to perform useful tasks for the community. Boys as young as four may care for young animals and may be expected to recognize their family's cows. Young girls in the society form into social groups with their own rules, independent of the adults. In nineteenth-century Ireland, a man was considered a boy regardless of biological age until he was married. In the United States, children under the age of 16 were considered eligible for heavy labor in mills and factories until the practice of hiring them was outlawed by the Fair Labor Standards Act passed in 1938.

The presence of toys may in fact indicate the presence of children at a site. For example, when archaeologists excavating the 1913–1914 campsite of the massacred strikers at Ludlow, Colorado, found a children's tea set in the rubble, it confirmed the historical accounts of families among the strikers. Similarly, the discovery of porcelain doll heads, legs, and arms at San Pedro Sirís, an autonomous Maya village in Belize occupied from the late nineteenth to the early twentieth century, substantiates the children's use of European toys.

Research identifying children at past settlements and villages is important, but the archaeology of children also has a more profound significance. Jane Baxter, a leader in the field, outlines several reasons why the archaeology of children is necessary. For one thing, it reflects the broader trends in archaeological scholarship. The archaeological "discovery" of children is akin to the greater emphasis archaeologists have placed on identity and gender since the 1970s. The acknowledgment of children represents the maturity of archaeology as a way of investigating all past social life, even that of its smallest members. The goal of finally making children visible is simply good archaeology. Emphasis on the lived experience of children also means archaeologists must rethink some of their long-held assumptions. Rather than simply representing a temporary state of being, childhood encapsulates the period of enculturation. Children learn their culture's mores, social roles, expectations, and limitations. When viewed from this perspective, the archaeology of childhood has important anthropological implications. Without acknowledging the central place of learning in preparation for adulthood, archaeologists must envision their archaeological subjects as adults who sprang fully formed from nowhere. In other words, it makes sense to incorporate children's' lives into the human story; without them the story is incomplete. At the same time, an interest in the lives of children allows archaeologists to broaden their range of collaboration with other scholars. Child development experts can assist archaeologists as they strive to interpret the intricacies of childhood in the past. Archaeologists of ancient North Americans, for instance, have used psychological studies by child development scholars to investigate the cognitive skills required to make and decorate pottery. In Europe's post-industrialized world, many children were forced into mines and factories to become contributors to the household economy of lower-class families. Thus, many children were producers of crafts and commodities alongside adults.

Jonathan Prangnell and Kate Quirk investigated the social roles of children in a mining community called Paradise in Queensland, Australia. Paradise was established in the late 1880s in response to the discovery of gold-bearing reefs. The community was the very definition of a boomtown. In 1890, it had 40 residents, but by the following year, the population had exploded to 600. The popular conception is that mining camps were masculine, rough places. Historical archaeologists have done much to dispel this inaccurate perception. For most of its existence, women and children composed most of the inhabitants of Paradise. Historical records indicate that many of the miners had large families and, preferring not to abandon them for the mines, they brought their wives and children with them. Documents also reveal that children in Paradise often forged social bonds between families, with some children being named for members of other families. Children in the community thus were important members of social networks.

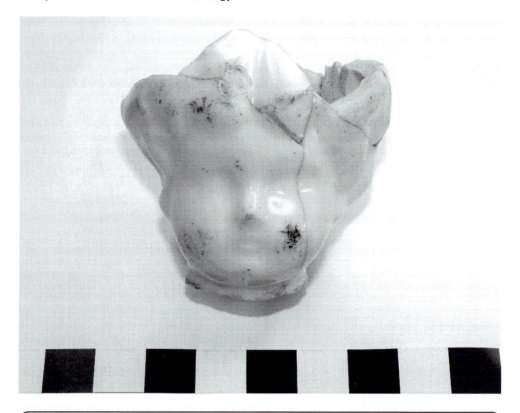

Figure 11.5 Ceramic doll's head from Paradise, Queensland, Australia
(Courtesy of Jonathan Prangnell.)

Excavation revealed pieces of inexpensive ceramic dolls (Figure 11.5) and tea sets, probably from Germany, and ceramic marble stoppers from Codd's water bottles. These were bottles, patented in 1870, containing a marble in the neck. The carbonation in the liquid would kept the marble against the stopper. The method was effective as a bottle closure, but children often broke the bottles to obtain the marble. Archaeologists also found pieces of slates with perfectly spaced, scored straight lines, indicating that children in the community had been learning to write.

The research also revealed that a number of the children in the town were employed. Some worked for family businesses, performed household chores, and tended gardens. Others—boys and girls—were employed as servants, in the mines, or in support services for the mines, such as hauling.

In short, the archaeological research at Paradise demonstrates that children played substantial and important roles in the community. Rather than being "seen and not heard," as might have been true of many upper-class Victorian homes, the impoverished children of the Australian goldfields were expected to contribute to the economic health of the family.

In another study of children, this one in nineteenth-century Rio de Janeiro, Brazil, archaeologist Tania Lima investigated the role of toys and games in transmitting the moral values of European Brazilian society. As in most cases, excavation revealed doll parts and dishes specially made for children. She observes that many of the toys found reinforced gender roles through their material of manufacture. Whereas marbles generally used by boys were hard and durable, the porcelain doll parts used principally by girls were fragile and delicate. From today's perspective we might argue that the relationships between toys and gender roles are more fluid, but such was not the case in nineteenth-century Brazil (or in the United States for that matter). In Brazil, the roles of boys and girls were prescribed and reinforced by what Lima terms "indoctrination." Girls were socialized by their mothers with tea sets, and boys were given whips so they could learn at an early age their place as punishers in a society based on human bondage.

The study of children is a growing realm of study in historical archaeology. Much will be learned as research expands throughout the world and as increasing numbers of archaeologists take up the challenge of interpreting childhood in many different ways and in diverse social and historical contexts.

Social Class, Gender, Ethnicity, Race, and Age

We have explored social class, gender, ethnicity, race, and age as if they are separate domains of social life. In doing this, we may have implied that archaeologists can deftly extract these complex subjects from a past society and individually put them under a microscope of interpretation. But the separation of class, ethnicity, gender, race, and age is only an analytic convenience. The separation has no reality in any human society. Social scientists (including archaeologists) considering such complex social variables must guard against "essentialism," the idea that some categories are inherently correct and exist in all times and places. All notions of social class, ethnicity, gender, race, and age exist within particular social settings and they have meaning only within those contexts. Ideas about each are free to vary with time and place, and meaning in one culture would not necessarily have meaning in another.

No single individual is just an African American, just a member of the middle class, or just a woman. A person can be an African American woman who belongs to the middle class, but she cannot occupy only one category. Why? Because in complex, highly stratified social organizations, any single individual is simultaneously a member of many groups. Because historical archaeologists know this, they are constantly trying to decide how best to study the social complexities of past societies. In Steven Shephard's study of classes in Alexandria, Virginia, mentioned above, middle-class households were headed by men who were of European-American descent. They were often owners of a small number of enslaved men and women of African heritage. The nearby lower-class neighborhood was inhabited by free African American unskilled laborers. The prostitutes in Hooker's Division researched by Donna Seifert were working-class women who were trying to feed their families; they were not simply women who had gone astray. The women living in the Gerrit Smith house were not just women; they were women of European descent and members of both the elite and the working classes.

Class membership, gender role, ethnic affiliation, and racial assignment are like the strings of a net; they are interconnected and inseparable. The groups we have illustrated provide historical archaeologists with a means of organizing their analyses and framing their interpretations. But as the analyses and perspectives of historical archaeology have grown more sophisticated, a number of archaeologists have consciously sought to study social groups as intertwined, complex networks of social actors. One of the first studies of this sort, even though it is far from perfect, concentrated on a slave plantation in the American South.

John Otto, who excavated at Cannon's Point Plantation in Georgia, was one of the first historical archaeologists attempting to study an antebellum slave plantation as if it were composed of men and women who were not just slaves or slave owners, but who were members of several social groups at the same time.

Otto used his knowledge of history, historical sociology, and cultural anthropology to construct a model of plantation society in the antebellum South. Social groups formed a central feature of his model. He proposed that the plantation's inhabitants were simultaneously members of at least three social groups, which he termed "statuses." A "racial/legal status" created two groups of people: free (white planters and overseers) and unfree (black slaves). Three groups existed as a "social status": managers (planters), supervisors (overseers), and the enslaved (workers). An "elite/subordinate status" created two more groups: elites (planters) and subordinates (overseers and the enslaved). The groups existed side by side, and each individual on the plantation belonged to all three of them. An African American field hand would belong to the unfree racial/legal group, the worker group, and the subordinate group, all at once. A German overseer would share the "free" group with the planter family but also the "subordinate" group with the enslaved men and women.

The spatial arrangement of Cannon's Point Plantation meant it was an easy matter to link distinct sites with planters, slaves, and overseers. The planter's house was located on the extreme northern end of the island, overlooking the salt marsh. As was typical of the slave-owning South, the planter's part of the site contained several buildings: his house, a detached kitchen, a few small sheds and outbuildings, and some small cabins, reserved for the enslaved men, women, and children who labored inside the master's house. The cabins of the field hands were located farther away and close to the agricultural fields. The overseer's cabin was situated between the homes of the field hands and those of the house servants, probably to increase surveillance over the enslaved work force (Figure 11.6).

Having associated specific sites with slaves, overseers, and planters, Otto believed it would be possible to examine the artifacts unearthed from each site to learn how they reflected the three different "statuses" existing within his model of plantation society. To learn the differences between his "racial/legal status" groups, he grouped together the artifacts found at the planter site and at the overseer site (because both were free whites). He then compared them with those unearthed at the site associated with the enslaved (because they were unfree blacks). To study the "social status" groups, he compared the three sites individually, and to investigate the "elite/subordinate status," he grouped the artifacts from the sites associated with the overseer and the enslaved (the subordinates) and compared them with those from the planter site (the elites).

Otto's comparisons showed differences. Liquor bottles from the three sites represented the racial/legal status. The planter and the overseer sites contained more gin bottles than the homes of the enslaved, but the latter contained more ale, port, and wine bottles. Food remains reflected both the racial/legal status and the elite/subordinate status. The animal bones proved that the enslaved were more dependent on wild animals than either the white planter or the overseer households. Wild species such as deer composed a full 45 percent of the meat diet of the enslaved. The planter family ate fewer wild animals, but the number of species in the faunal sample from their house site was larger than that from either the overseer or the enslaved sites. Ceramic vessel forms reflected social status because each plantation group used different forms. In the planter deposits, flatwares—plates, deep soup plates, and platters—constituted more than 80 percent of the ceramic collection. Excavations in the overseer's site yielded only 28 percent flat vessels, and in the enslaved area only 19 percent of the excavated ceramic vessels were flat forms. But over 40 percent of the vessels in the cabins of the enslaved were bowls; in the overseer deposits, 25 percent of the ceramics were bowls. Ceramic decoration seemed to reflect the elite/subordinate status because the planter site had many more transfer-printed vessels than either the overseer or the slave sites. Otto

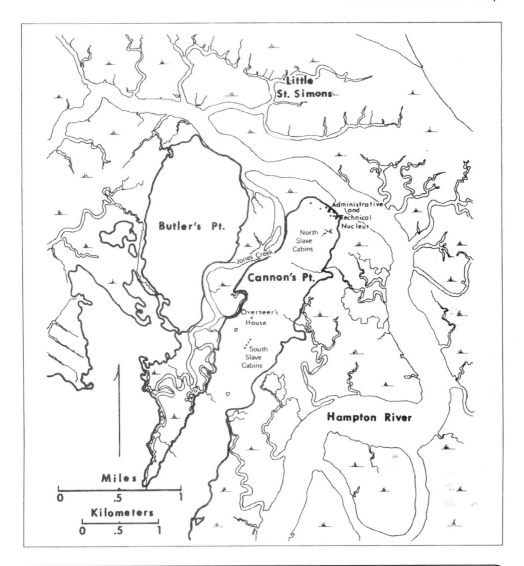

Figure 11.6 Location of planter, overseer, and slave sites at Cannon's Point Plantation, St. Simons Island, Georgia, 1794–1860

(From J.S. Otton, *Cannon's Point Plantation 1794–1860: Living Conditions and Status Patterns in the Old South* © 1984 Elsevier.)

used these complex artifact comparisons to conclude that the three statues can be identified in the archaeological deposits at Cannon's Point Plantation. He cautioned, though, that some artifacts may signal different things and that diversity may exist because plantation society was complex. Regional and local traditions, and even personal decisions, could affect the structure and design of any particular plantation.

Archaeologist Lynn Clark provided another study that demonstrated the interconnections between various social groups. Clark was also interested in how archaeologists can discern interactions between ethnicity and class. Rather than excavate, as Otto had done, she chose to study gravestones, a common piece of material culture readily available above ground. Interested in learning whether ethnic symbols on tombstones could be associated with lower-class standing, she selected a sample of more than 1,000 gravestones in Broome County, New York. The ethnic groups who lived in the county were German-Jewish, Italian, Irish, and Slovak immigrants. Her reasoning was that as immigrant men and women climbed the social ladder in late-nineteenth- and early twentieth-century America, they had to appear to surrender their ethnicity. They had to assimilate into mainstream American society and downplay their distinct European heritages. She thought people in the lower class would have been less likely to have given up their ethnic symbols because they would not be trying to assimilate. They could continue to use gravestone symbols to stress their ethnic uniqueness. She also thought that gravestones should become more alike in the middle class because such people would have been more likely to have left their ethnic symbols behind as they were Americanized.

Clark's gravestone survey indicated that ethnic groups and social classes had a wide variety of available options. Upper-class white-collar workers traditionally established their place in the social order by demonstrating their wealth and power. The greatest display of wealth in any cemetery is a mausoleum, and before 1940, all mausoleums in the cemeteries Clark studied were built by upper-class professionals or administrators. These people were either assimilated Americans or Irish in heritage. After the 1920s, however, upper-class Americans, Irish, and German Jews displayed their wealth less frequently on their gravestones. After about 1940, though, blue-collar Italians began to build mausoleums. By the 1950s and 1960s, Italians often built large mausoleums, whereas the upper class had stopped doing so. Jewish graves were distinguished by their widespread use of epitaphs, but particularly so after the 1930s.

Clark's work in "above-ground archaeology" shows how ethnicity and class are intertwined into a complex bundle that archaeologists can unravel only with the greatest difficulty. Today's archaeologists often find it impossible to decide whether a people's actions were guided by their class position, ethnic affiliation, or some complex combination of both. Archaeological solutions to the puzzles of past society become even more elusive when gender and concepts of race are thrown into the mix. The creative research projects mentioned throughout this chapter—and a growing number of archaeologists are conducting these important studies in many places around the world—show how difficult it is for archaeologists to attempt social analyses. Even historical archaeologists, scholars who often have the benefit of highly useful texts, cannot assume to make easy social interpretations. Archaeologists who try to assign people from the past to groups are sure to encounter pitfalls. Class, gender, ethnicity, race, and age are important issues that will challenge historical archaeologists for many years to come. They represent cutting-edge sociological issues in the field for the foreseeable future.

Site Visit: Nain, Labrador, 1820–1880

The Inuit of Labrador had encountered European visitors for at least 250 years before the Moravians established a mission there in the mid-eighteenth century. First the Vikings had come, and then European fishermen had realized in the sixteenth century that the bountiful waters of the north Atlantic were a rich source of cod and other northern fish species. Before long, vessels manned by French, Basque, and Portuguese crews plied the coasts of Inuit territory. The Inuit were not always pleased to find European foreigners in their territory, and they often staged raids against them. British entrepreneurs quickly understood these raids were bad for business, and their government urged the Moravian Brethren—organized in 1457 in what is today the Czech Republic—to establish a Christianizing mission among the Inuit.

The Moravians accepted the challenge, believing they could serve several important functions. They could bring Christianity to the Inuit, act as a buffer between them and the incoming Europeans, and keep the Inuit away from the vices of the European sailors. Their first mission, in 1752, ended quickly, however, when the Inuit murdered five of its members. Undaunted, they tried again in 1771 and established a mission settlement at Nain. They followed this success with two other missions, one north of Nain in 1776 and one south in 1782.

Missions have obvious religious goals, and the Moravians made it clear they wanted to convert the Inuit. But the impact of missions is never only religious, because missionaries also impart their views on morality, law, and economics to their native audiences. Natives who frequently visit or live around missions may slowly acquire the foreigners' attitudes as well as their religious beliefs. One implication of missionary work, particularly in the eighteenth and nineteenth centuries, was that part of the Christianizing process involved accepting foreign material culture. As the Inuit on the coast of Labrador learned about Christianity and the European way of doing things, they also developed an interest in possessing products manufactured in Europe. The desired objects were initially related to survival, with steel fishhooks and hunting gear being much sought after. But by the mid-nineteenth century, the Inuit had become dependent on European foods, and regularly consumed biscuits, dried peas, bread, and tea. In the mission's early years, the Inuit bartered their sealskins, caribou hides, and fish for the desired European goods, but over time, they began to work for the missionaries for wages, which they used to purchase items from the mission store.

The Labrador Inuit, like many native peoples around the world, were drawn to European glazed ceramics. A particular kind of ware traded to the Inuit, and readily accepted by them, is called "stamped earthenware." Ceramists also refer to it as "sponge-decorated" or "cut sponge-decorated," because the decoration is put onto the white-bodied vessel using the root of a sponge into which a design has been cut (Figure 11.7). The sponge is dipped in pigment and pressed onto the vessel. A light glaze and firing fixes the image to the vessel. The stamped decorations could be either monochrome or polychrome, but the pigments used were typically vibrant blues, pinks, greens, browns, reds, purples, and yellows. The designs could take many forms with floral and geometric motifs being especially common.

Cut sponge-decorated wares were generally inexpensive to purchase, and so they were often used by people on the lower end of the socioeconomic spectrum.

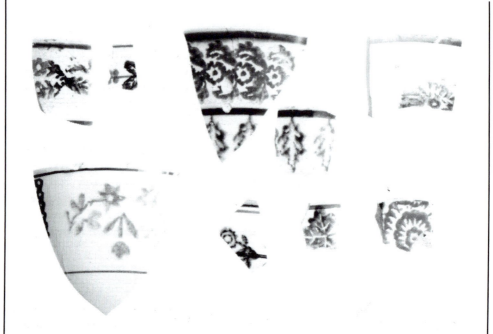

Figure 11.7 Cut-sponge decorated whiteware from Nain, Labrador
(Photo by Stephen Long.)

They became popular in the 1840s and were made until the 1930s, with their peak of popularity being the 1880–1910 period.

The Inuit at Nain had at least 37 different stamped vessels. Most were small hollow vessels (saucers, cups, and mugs), followed closely by bowls. The vessels had monochrome decorations in purple, green, or blue, in six decorative motifs: fleur-de-lis, stylized cross, leaf, floral, geometric, and flag.

The presence of stamped earthenware ceramics at the Nain mission indicates the Inuit in the settlement experienced a significant shift in their dietary habits during the nineteenth century. Before the missionaries had arrived, their food consisted of whale, seal, walrus, and polar bear, supplemented with wild berries, shellfish, and waterfowl. The presence of the missionaries altered their traditional pattern to be sure, but the Inuit were not totally changed. For example, they tended to use small- to medium-sized bowls rather than plates. In addition to using the bowls to serve and eat their traditional stews, they also filled them with oil for dipping their meat. The also used bowls as blubber lamps, and they regularly used teacups for many different sorts of beverages including tea.

Source: Melanie Cabak and Stephen Loring. A Set of Very Fair Cups and Saucers:
Stamped Ceramics as an Example of Inuit Incorporation. *International Journal
of Historical Archaeology* 4 (2000):1–34.

Chapter 12

Global Historical Archaeology and Modern-World Archaeology

In the previous chapter we explored some ways historical archaeologists have investigated individuals and groups using a combination of excavation and historical research. Investigations of this nature constitute the smallest scale of archaeological analysis because they concentrate on small places and individual people. This research, though concentrated on the small, is nonetheless extremely complicated and multifaceted. But it represents only two scales of analysis possible in historical archaeology. A growing number of historical archaeologists are interested in finding ways to connect the small and the site-specific to the wider worlds in which past people lived.

Historical archaeologists face serious conceptual and practical issues when attempting to move beyond the community and the city and into the wider world. Archaeological analysis is extremely well suited to small-scale study and tightly focused interpretations of individuals, artifacts, and discrete places. Much cultural and historical knowledge has been created through such studies. Without question, however, the development of global studies is extremely important to furthering historical archaeology's sophistication in the twenty-first century.

In this chapter we explore two larger scales of analysis in historical archaeology. The first, global historical archaeology, involves the spread of historical archaeology throughout the world. It demonstrates the important contribution the field can make to post-1500 sites and peoples wherever they were located. One of the goals of global historical archaeology is to transform the discipline into a truly worldwide practice. The second kind of expanded-scale historical archaeology is modern-world archaeology. This approach seeks to understand how the world we live in today came to be. The central foci of analysis are four prominent elements of post-1500 life: colonialism, Eurocentrism, racialization, and capitalism. A central question is whether archaeologists can invent ways to conceptualize extra-site interactions and connections in innovative ways that move beyond simply noting that similar artifacts occur in diverse places in the world.

Global Historical Archaeology

Historical archaeology is today being practiced in every corner of the globe, from Argentina to Alaska, India to Russia, Portugal to Indonesia. The range and diversity of research being undertaken makes a summary difficult. Thus, in this part of the chapter, we present overviews illustrating some of the research being performed, with the understanding that this information is necessarily incomplete. We focus here on the culture contacts that occurred after 1492, concentrating on the Dutch Empire. The Dutch Empire provides a good example because their agents traveled the globe and made contact with diverse non-European cultures.

Culture Contacts

Peoples from different cultures have been in contact for thousands of years, and archaeologists have examined these situations in every part of the world. Ideas about contact as an anthropological topic have changed over time, and archaeologists have steadily developed increasingly sophisticated ways to interpret it. In historical archaeology, the term "culture contact" typically refers to the meeting of indigenous peoples and incoming Europeans, but historical archaeologists can also investigate contact situations not involving Europeans. The key characteristic is the meeting of two cultures with diverse origins, traditions, and customs in the post-1500 era.

What is often called the European Age of Discovery had a profound and often catastrophic impact on indigenous peoples around the world. Cultural anthropologists, archaeologists, and historians have long been intrigued by the post-Columbian "clash of cultures," and their research has proven that the interactions were never one-sided. Rather, cultures in contact learn from one another. Indigenous peoples across the globe were impressed by the durability of the Europeans' iron axes, the power of their firearms, and the way their brass kettles could withstand intense heat without cracking. Many indigenous peoples thus rapidly incorporated foreign objects into their daily lives. Several cultures living in Mesoamerica adopted Old World cereal crops, cattle, goats, and sheep without hesitation because they understood their advantages for survival. The same societies, however, did not merely adapt foreign objects; they also donated to the Europeans. Sixteenth- and seventeenth-century Native American farmers were expert agriculturalists, and Europeans soon carried amaranth, potatoes, tomatoes, and tobacco back to the Old World. These crops had major impacts on European life. For example, the South American potato rapidly became a staple of the Irish diet, so much so that when the crop was struck by a devastating fungus in 1845, people referred to the starvation that followed as "The Great Irish Potato Famine." New World tobacco, which created the same cultural impact, also caused an entirely new artifact to be invented and used throughout the world—the white clay smoking pipe.

The process of cultural and social interaction was extremely complex and often quite subtle. The history of the process varied with location. Multicultural contacts of all sorts created what anthropologist Nicholas Thomas has termed "mutual entanglements." When viewed through time, these entanglements appear as shared histories.

Many cultural changes resulting from decisions made in good faith by one generation could have dramatic and dangerous effects on their descendants. The Khoikhoi herders of the Cape of Good Hope at the southern tip of Africa were under such pressure to trade their cattle to beef-hungry Dutch visitors that they bartered away both their surplus bulls and their cows. Many Khoikhoi, because they had no breeding stock, were without cattle a generation later.

Cultures in contact tend to view one another through well-defined cultural lenses. People with no prior knowledge of a foreign culture usually find culturally reasonable ways to understand people who are different. For example, upon first contact, some Maori of New Zealand considered Captain Cook and his men gods who had come from across the horizon. For their part, Cook and his crew were horrified to find freshly butchered human bones in abandoned Maori camps. Europeans for generations considered the Maori fierce cannibals, to the point that passing ships hesitated to land among them.

French historian Fernand Braudel wrote that indigenous peoples around the world were affected by "the mighty shadow cast" over them by western Europe. But they were not necessarily destroyed by this shadow. What many Europeans took to be submission and acquiescence were in fact complex strategies for survival. Many Aztec communities in Mexico sought to minimize their contacts with their new colonial Spanish masters. The Aztecs' conversion to Catholicism was actually a careful blending of cultural elements. They adapted their traditional religious beliefs and social ties to the realities of the new society, one wherein they were economically marginal and on the bottom of the social ladder.

Blendings of European and indigenous cultures—often referred to as creole or hybrid societies—are reflected not only in surviving native belief systems and oral traditions, but also in subtle changes in artifacts of every kind. Historical archaeology has a major role to play in untangling culture contact situations because judicious excavation often reveals fascinating, heretofore unknown information. Historical archaeologists in the twenty-first century understand that indigenous peoples were far more empowered than archaeologists once thought.

The following examples provide instances in which global historical archaeology has cast significant new light on complex cultural interactions occurring during in the past 500 years. We use the Dutch world empire as a focal point only for convenience to illustrate the kinds of research projects archaeologists have conducted and to suggest areas for future research.

The Dutch Empire

In July 1581, the northern provinces of what is today the Netherlands declared their independence from Spain. About 75 years earlier, the Netherlands, then called the "Low Countries," came under Spanish rule when Charles V inherited it from the dukes of Burgundy. The Dutch fought for their freedom until 1648, when the King of Spain finally agreed to recognize their independence.

The Dutch became major players in world history during the seventeenth century. This so-called "Golden Age" saw Dutch sailors establish a maritime empire that at its height accounted for half of the world's shipping. Amsterdam grew to become the world's most active commercial city, and the Dutch enjoyed the highest standard of living in Europe.

Europeans became increasingly convinced, during the fifteenth century, that great wealth could be made outside their continent. The brutal conquests of the Spanish in Mexico had brought vast amounts of gold back to Madrid and helped them create an impressive empire. Other Europeans desperately wanted their share of these riches, and so each nation-state devised its own strategy for moving into the burgeoning global market.

Seeking to create their niche, Dutch entrepreneurs in 1602 combined to form the Dutch East India Company, known as VOC (Verenigde Oostindische Compagnie). The agents of this company created a vast trading network lasting until 1795. They drove English and Portuguese merchant ships from Indonesia, which they named the "Netherlands Indies." They built a capitol in the region and named it Batavia (today's Jakarta).

The success of the Dutch East India Company encouraged other entrepreneurs to develop the Dutch West India Company. The focus of this enterprise rested on the riches of the New World and Africa. In today's United States, the Dutch built a city called New Amsterdam (now New York) in 1624. They colonized much of the area around the city, and also captured islands in the Caribbean from the Spanish.

The vast Dutch Empire went into steady decline beginning in the 1670s. France and England, both searching for greater control of the world's wealth, formed a secret alliance against the Netherlands and attacked it in 1672. The Dutch survived this assault and, after a period of peace, the English once again declared war on the Netherlands in 1780. The Dutch had supported the Americans' War of Independence. The English defeated the Dutch in 1784, and only 11 years later, the French occupied the country and renamed it the Batavian Republic. The occupation spelled the end of the once-powerful Dutch Empire.

The story of the Dutch Empire has been repeated by other nations who have sought to control the world's economy. During its heyday, the Dutch built settlements across the globe. Historical archaeologists have investigated several of these colonial outposts in Africa, North America, the Caribbean and South America, and Asia. Their studies show the extent of global historical archaeology and indicate the future promise of continued research.

Dutch explorers, traders, and colonists built an extensive network of villages, forts, and cities around the world. In this chapter, we visit a few of their settlements to illustrate the richness of research in historical archaeology. We focus on sites revealing information about contacts between Europeans and non-Europeans. Of all the historical processes occurring since about 1415, none have been more dramatic and significant than the multicultural contacts developing as a result of Western exploration and colonization.

Africa

European contacts with African cultures were as complex as similar contacts throughout the world. The Portuguese were attracted to the African coasts by gold and slaves. These trading ventures were so profitable the Portuguese sought to control access to the interior by fortifying strategic locations. In 1482, a full decade before Columbus set foot in the Americas, the Portuguese Crown authorized building an imposing fort on the coast of modern Ghana in West Africa. This fort, named the Castle São Jorge da Mina and lying on a rocky headland, was designed to protect what the Portuguese hoped would be a lucrative gold trade with the interior (Figure 12.1). A small African community called Elmina soon developed under the castle walls because Africans, not Europeans, controlled the trade with the gold-mining peoples far inland. The Portuguese held the castle for 155 years and maintained a precarious control over the "gold coast" as the Dutch rose to power. In 1637, the Dutch succeeded in capturing the castle. It proved a profitable investment for them for over two centuries, until the Gold Coast was ceded to the British in 1872.

Fante people inhabited the area around Elmina before the Portuguese arrived, but other indigenous groups soon moved in, realizing the material advantage of living near an important European trading post. The size of the African community quickly swelled. By 1700, as many as 15,000 inhabitants lived in more than 1,000 stone houses. The townspeople, although culturally Fante, regarded themselves as a politically and even culturally distinct people. After a series of conflicts, the British bombarded Elmina both from land and sea, destroying it on June 13, 1873. They leveled the town's ruins and used the site for a parade ground.

Happily for archaeologists, the site remained undeveloped. Elmina offers a unique opportunity to examine how some Africans learned from and taught the Europeans who lived alongside them. Archaeologist Christopher DeCorse has probed the settlement for several

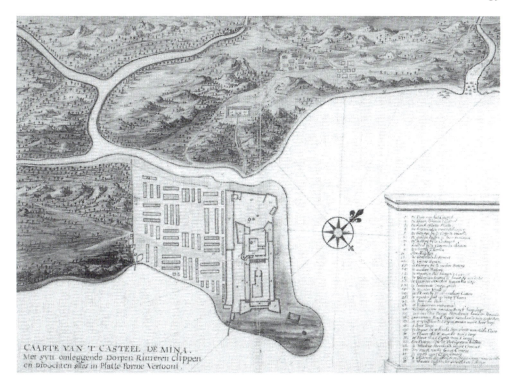

Figure 12.1 Elmina Castle, ca. 1637

(Nationaal Archief, Den Haag, Verzameling Binnenlandse Kaarten Hingman: Eerste en Tweede Supplement, nummer toegang 4.VTHR, inventarisnummer 619.77.)

years. He excavated 3,011 square feet (271 sq. m) and exposed another 600 square feet (54 sq. m). These excavations yielded more than 100,000 artifacts. His research has permitted an intimate look into African–European interaction along the Gold Coast.

Most of the artifacts DeCorse excavated date to the eighteenth and nineteenth centuries. Many document the connections between Elmina and the rest of the world. White clay tobacco pipes came from England and the Netherlands, porcelain was made in Chinese factories, and glass bottles once held American patent medicines. An almost whole, gray stoneware jug from Germany was brilliantly decorated with blue rosettes and ribbons. In its center the letters "A R," refer to Queen Anne ("Anne Regina"), the English monarch from 1702 to 1714.

DeCorse's research also documents cultural change in the cosmopolitan community beneath Elmina's walls. Many Africans and Europeans visited the fort, not only from overseas but also from far in the interior. During some periods of the fort's history, Mande traders and Asante people from the interior were active participants in the town's daily life. At other times, European slavers brought Africans from deep inland both to labor locally and for export to Brazil and other parts of the New World. The Dutch were also active slave traders during their time at Elmina, transporting thousands of captive Africans to their plantations in the Netherlands Antilles.

Archaeology indicates the people of Elmina were selective in the cultural changes they were willing to accept. For example, the presence of buttons and buckles within the artifact collection attests to changes in dress. Slate pencils and writing slates show that at least some of the townspeople were literate. In contrast, European burial customs and cemeteries—including one reserved for the Dutch—did not come into general use before 1873. DeCorse found burials beneath all the house floors he excavated, even those having less than 12 inches (30 cm) of soil above bedrock.

DeCorse's excavations provide a unique picture of cultural continuity within an environment of continual economic and political change. Many Africans were changed by regular contact with Europeans, but many were not. In addition, those who accepted changes were not overwhelmed by European ways. They simply adapted to new circumstances in a purposeful way, adopting new artifacts and customs when it was to their advantage to do so.

Stating that the twenty-first century is forged from deep historical roots is a truism. Nowhere is this sentiment truer than in South Africa, where the complex politics of today result from centuries of interaction and misunderstanding between indigenous African peoples and foreign Europeans, including the Dutch. Historical documents and oral traditions reveal much about the interactions between these different peoples, but historical archaeology is rapidly filling in many gaps in the story and providing fresh insights.

When Portuguese captain Bartolemeu Diaz anchored in Mossel Bay, east of the Cape of Good Hope in 1488, he found himself in a peaceful and beautiful bay surrounded by green hills. Skin-clad herdsmen grazing large cattle on the lush grass soon fled at the sight of Diaz's ships. These people were Khoikhoi, nomadic cattle herders and foragers, people with simple possessions, but a highly sophisticated adaptation to the unpredictable semitropical environment of the Cape. The Portuguese, and the Dutch who followed them, considered the Khoikhoi little more than animals, people without an intelligible language or any recognizable religion. Sailors, recounting that the Khoikhoi smeared themselves with rancid butter, mentioned that they could be smelled from thirty paces. The Europeans called them by the derogatory name "Hottentots."

The Khoikhoi, however, were vital to the passing ships of Europe because they supplied fresh meat to crews wrestling with scurvy. These visitors generally left the Khoikhoi alone. With no reports of gold being found in their territory, the Europeans had no interest in their land. The policy of non-involvement changed in 1652, when the Dutch East India Company built a small fort at the Cape. The dynamics of cultural interaction were transformed at once because the European newcomers were colonists, farmers in search of land and grass for grazing. Seeking pastureland rather than gold, they soon encroached on the territory of the Khoikhoi and restricted their movements. The Dutch also forced them to trade their cattle, even their much-needed breeding stock. VOC agents told the colonists to "tolerate, negotiate, manipulate" the local people. Most followed this advice to such a devastating degree that the traditional culture of the Cape Khoikhoi vanished within a century. The survivors eked out a living as ranch hands or domestic servants; others moved far inland to escape the Dutch.

The outlines of this story are well known, but many details remain a mystery. To uncover more details about Khoikhoi/Dutch cultural interaction, Carmel Schrire embarked on a study of Oudepost I, "Old Post." The Dutch constructed this small, stone fort in 1669 to show the increasingly aggressive French that they "owned" the Cape. The French soon lost interest in the area, so the four to ten Dutchmen who lived at the post until 1732 spent their days trading with the neighboring Khoikhoi. Schrire's work included a major excavation of buildings associated with Oudepost. The area around the post had not seen much settlement after 1732, so the sites were largely undisturbed by subsequent residents and clandestine looters.

Historical records mention the construction of the VOC outpost, but only archaeological research could provide precise details. No map or plan of the remote post is known to

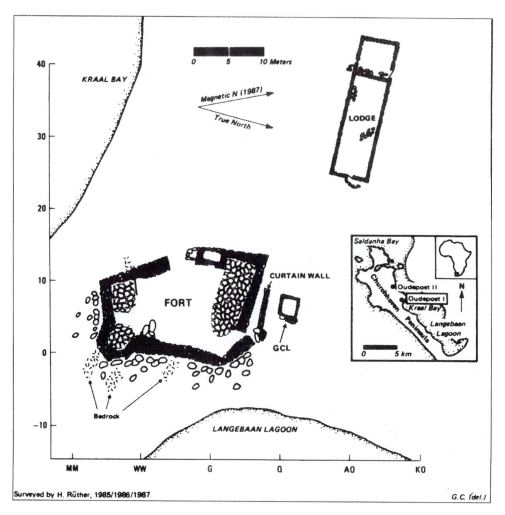

Figure 12.2 Building foundations at Oudepost I, South Africa in 1987
(Courtesy of Carmel Schrire.)

exist. Schrire's excavations revealed that the Dutch built three small buildings on the beach at Oudepost I (Figure 12.2). One was an irregularly shaped fort encompassing more than 4,400 square feet (400 sq. m). The second building, placed to the northwest, was a long, rectangular structure measuring 18.5 by 65.1 feet (5.6 by 19.8 m). This building may have served as the garrison's barracks, because Schrire found domestic artifacts and food remains associated with it. The third structure, whose function is unknown, was located directly north of the fort and measured only 9.3 by 10.6 feet (2.8 by 3.2 m).

Excavation revealed that Dutch settlers constructed the buildings with rocks collected from the shore. Schrire learned that the garrison did not deposit their refuse in one particular dump but tossed it everywhere, leaving a broad layer of seventeenth-century glass, ceramics, gunflints, and metal across the site. The presence of Khoikhoi pottery, stone tools, and bone spear points in the midden attests to their connection with the outpost.

Historical accounts provide abundant evidence for interaction between Khoikhoi inhabitants and Dutch settlers. For example, in 1670 the fort's commandant reported that a small band of Khoikhoi had arrived to offer their services in fighting the French. In 1726 another post commandant wrote that he had hired a Khoikhoi man, whom he referred to as a "Hottentot," to tend the post's sheep in return for being "properly supplied with liquor and tobacco." The important issue interesting Schrire was thus not *whether* the Khoikhoi and the Dutch interacted at Oudepost, but rather *how* they interacted.

The faunal remains tell part of the story. The authors of historical texts dwell on the importance the Dutch placed on the cattle trade. Their relentless demand for meat, gained either by trade or theft, is thought to have put tremendous pressure on local Khoikhoi groups. Cattle bones are indeed commonplace in the archaeological deposits at Oudepost I, but the archaeological remains also provide a much more complete picture of Dutch subsistence. Instead of relying completely on sheep and cattle, the Europeans also adopted elements of the Khoikhoi's traditional subsistence strategy. The Dutch settlers partly followed the hunter-gatherer lifestyle the Khoikhoi had practiced for generations. Schrire's findings provided irrefutable proof of this Dutch strategy, as large numbers of fish, mammal, and bird bones were excavated from the fort's middens. Domesticated species accounted for only about 28 percent of the animal bones found at the site.

Oudepost I offers insights into Dutch/Khoikhoi interaction, and also a brief, albeit telling, glimpse into the thoughts of at least one Dutch member of the garrison. An unknown soldier has left a tantalizing clue of his service at the post by etching a simple palm tree onto an ostrich egg shell (Figure 12.3). Palms did not grow at the Cape then, so Schrire imagined

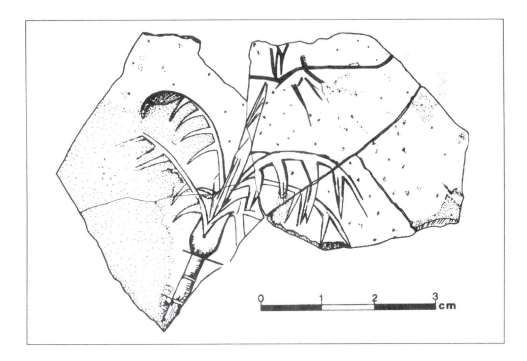

Figure 12.3 Etched ostrich shell found at Oudepost I, South Africa
(Courtesy of Carmel Schrire.)

a lonely soldier creating the image while pining for his days in the warmer, more hospitable Southeast Asia.

The Cape Khoikhoi did not survive permanent European settlement in their homeland. Oudepost I flourished at a time when Dutch farmers were staking out ranches deep inside Khoikhoi territory, disrupting centuries-old seasonal movements that prevented the herders from overgrazing their large territories in the interior. By the late eighteenth century, the numbers of the Cape Khoikhoi had dropped dramatically. Early European records chronicle their fate, leaving historical archaeologists to fill in the details of their day-to-day existence through the most mundane artifacts never appearing in written documents.

Research by Stacey Jordan, a student of Schrire's, has provided an excellent view of how Dutch settlers at the Cape sought to create a way of life similar to what they had known at home. When Dutch settlers first went to the Cape, they took with them pewter plates and cups and wooden vessels. These were the containers used on Dutch ships at the time. After 1666, they increasingly used Asian porcelains, but they did not have access to their traditional coarse red earthenware. Dutch potters had made coarse earthenware vessels since the fourteenth century.

Coarse earthenware was a common kind of ceramic produced in Europe during the Middle Ages, and it is still made today. Coarse earthenware is low-fired and often glazed—on the interior, exterior, or both sides—in earth-tone colors. Today's terra cotta flowerpots are red coarse earthenware, but usually made with finer pastes than many older vessels (Figure 12.4).

In the absence of their familiar dishes, Dutch settlers at the Cape were forced to eat with their hands out of large pots. Some of the men even used shells as spoons, in a method that would have appeared barbaric to many people still living in the Netherlands. In 1663 the commander at the Cape sought to change this behavior by asking the VOC to send potters from home. They approved the request, and the first coarse earthenware pottery was established at the Cape two years later. The commander was so happy he wrote in his diary, "This morning, for the first time, diverse kinds of baked and glazed earthenware were taken from the oven in the new pottery and found to be very good." Some were even sold in the public market, undoubtedly to the joy of other Dutch colonists.

Jordan's analysis of the coarse earthenware excavated from the Cape shows that Dutch potters made vessels for different purposes. They made storage pots of various sizes, and pots, pans, skillets, pot lids, and drainers for food preparation. They also made saucers, plates, bowls, and pitchers for serving food, and special vessels for heating and lighting their homes. Jordan believed these European-style ceramic vessels were more than simply functional. In addition to having specific uses, she thought the ceramics were also an attempt by the Dutch East India Company to maintain a sense of Dutch identity. The Company's representatives in the Cape—the elite officers and administrators—may have sought to use Dutch ceramics as a way to maintain the class structure of the Netherlands. Settlers who used familiar ceramics, even though made in Africa, reinforced the idea that they were neither the wealthy entrepreneurs who ran the VOC nor indigenous Khoikhoi. They were simply working people of Dutch heritage living far away from home.

Traveling to the Cape of Good Hope was not without risk, and the Dutch East India Company lost many ships to storms, reefs, and bad judgment. One such ship, the *Oosterland,* was found by sport divers off the Cape in 1988 and investigated by archaeologists in the early 1990s. Dutch shipwrights built the ship in the Netherlands in 1684, and it became an important part of the Company's trading fleet, making three successful voyages to Asia. But it also had a checkered history. Its sailors had to turn back on her maiden voyage after only two weeks because of bad weather, and in 1697, 11 people on board died from the drinking water and at least 35 others were made seriously ill. While waiting in 1697 at the Cape to

Figure 12.4 Unglazed coarse earthenware sherds
(Courtesy of Barbara Voss.)

rendezvous with other ships for the long journey home, a northwesterly gale caused another ship to crash into the *Oosterland*. The wind shifted the following day, forcing the ship adrift. When it hit the seabed, the ship's mast splintered and the hull broke apart. Only two people survived out of the 300 on board.

The wreck lay only about 918 feet (280 m) offshore, under only about 20 feet (6 m) of water. The archaeologists used sonar (Chapter 5) to chart the wreck's precise location on the sea floor. Their excavations—the first systematic maritime field school in South Africa's

history—revealed the kinds of objects the ships of the VOC transported: stoneware jugs of German manufacture; clay pipes from the Netherlands; porcelain vessels made in China; spices; porcelain statuettes in the shape of ducks, eagles, and Buddhist lions; and wicker baskets containing blue dye.

North America

Giovanni da Verazzano is the first recorded European to visit the area that would later become New Amsterdam and then New York. Sailing along the coast in 1524, Verazzano encountered native people dressed in multicolored birds' feathers who greeted the ship with great joy. Verazzano sailed under the French flag, and it was not long before Portuguese and Spanish cartographers were showing the location on their maps and charts.

The expansion of the Dutch Empire meant they would be looking for places around the world to settle, and the region observed by Verazzano appeared to offer a fertile opportunity. In 1609, Henry Hudson set sail from the Netherlands to explore the region, arriving in September. Hudson and his crew discovered that while some Native Americans were happy to see them, others were not so impressed, and one attack resulted in the death of one of his men. Still, most of the indigenous inhabitants of the area were willing to interact peacefully with the Dutch, and trading partnerships were soon established.

As part of their North American empire, the Dutch West India Company built an outpost, called Fort Orange, on the Hudson River at the site of today's Albany, New York. Constructed in 1624, this wooden outpost was about 150 miles (241 km) from the Atlantic. The Dutch held the fort, rebuilt in stone, until 1664, when the English captured it. The Dutch retook the fort in 1672, but they returned it to the English only two years later, and their North American empire was largely finished.

Archaeologists first conducted excavations at the site of Fort Orange in 1970 and 1971. These initial excavations were intended to salvage important information before the site was destroyed by the construction of a highway. The preservation at the site was unexpectedly good, and the archaeologists were able to investigate portions of the fort as well as the remains of four houses located inside its walls. These excavations provided a wealth of information about the material culture of daily Dutch life in the colonies (Figure 12.5).

One curious group of artifacts consisted of over 30 white clay smoking pipe stems with notches cut into them. These stems came from the kind of pipes discussed in Chapter 4 (see Figure 4.6). Paul Huey, the archaeologist who studied the pipes and led the excavation, knew several interpretations might explain their odd appearance. Perhaps the pipes were notched as part of a process of making beads from them. This explanation seemed unlikely because pipe stems are extremely brittle and cutting a notch into them was unnecessary; they could simply be broken without the notch. Another explanation could be that smokers cut the notches to allow more air into the pipe. This practice is unknown and seems unlikely. Another interpretation seems much more plausible. Huey discovered when one blows through these stems they produce a soft, high-pitched whistle. Research indicates that, because Native Americans in New York State commonly used whistles made of reeds and other materials, perhaps they made whistles from white clay smoking pipes. Maybe Dutch settlers, seeing the Indian pipes, decided to fashion their own whistles from pipe stems. A painting dating to the same time as Fort Orange depicts European peasants blowing on flutes looking similar to white clay pipe stems. If the notched pipes were indeed used as whistles, it means Dutch colonists in the New World, who found themselves far from home, may have created the pipe flutes for their own sense of well-being. The sound of a traditional Dutch song may have calmed the homesickness of the colonists. The pipes may also be an example of Dutch settlers learning from the surrounding Native Americans. In

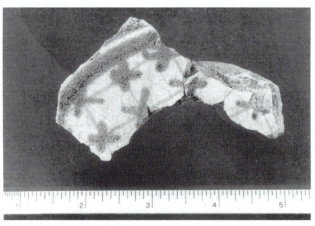

Figure 12.5 Dutch majolica sherds excavated from Fort Orange, ca. 1648–1657
(New York State Office of Parks, Recreation and Historic Preservation, Peebles Island)

any case, their discovery at Fort Orange provides an intriguing view of past life at the frontier fort.

In addition to investigating the remains of Fort Orange itself, historical archaeologists have also conducted excavations at the site of Beverwyck, the town Dutch settlers built around the fort. Others have performed excavations in New Amsterdam, today's New York City, and here and there at other colonial Dutch sites on the Eastern Seaboard.

Archaeologist Meta Janowitz has examined the nature of the colonial Dutch diet in New Amsterdam (New York City). Textual information suggests that the preparation of Dutch food was relatively uncomplicated. Cooks fried pancakes and waffles, and boiled porridge. Common foods like bread, cheese, and smoked meat did not require additional cooking. Other foodstuffs, like fish and meat, required processing before cooking.

Janowitz pointed out that the archaeologist's ability to find evidence of many colonial Dutch foods is unlikely because porridge, waffles, and cheese leave no archaeological traces. As a result, the best routes toward understanding Dutch eating habits is indirectly through their ceramics and animal bone refuse.

The seventeenth-century Dutch commonly used vessels called *grapen* for cooking and food consumption. *Grapen* were bulbous, glazed coarse earthenware pots with three short feet and one or two handles. Dutch households also used a skillet with three squat feet. Janowitz was able to examine archaeological examples of these vessels and, even more intriguing, was able to see them being used in contemporary paintings by Dutch masters.

Records indicate that the residents of New Amsterdam obtained foodstuffs from many sources. They received beef, wheat, pork, and butter from Dutch and English farmers on Long Island; beef, sheep, and cider apples from New England; and beef, pork, and fruit from Virginia. Native American traders also bartered their maize and pumpkins in the city.

The diet of colonial Dutch settlers in New Amsterdam was generally European in character. The colonists may not have had all the foods they had available at home, but they did have the same kinds of food: meats, grains, and fish. Their main concession to North America was the adoption of eating maize, one of the most important staples of the Native American diet. Archaeological evidence from seven sites, dating 1650–1720, indicates that the residents' diets did not change much after the English assumed control of New Amsterdam and renamed it New York in 1664.

In *Unearthing Gotham: The Archaeology of New York City*, archaeologists Anne-Marie Cantwell and Diana diZerega Wall explain how Dutch colonists appropriated the wampum of the Native Americans who lived in the Hudson River region. Native Americans traditionally made tiny beads from shells they found along the coast. The beads were tubular in shape, and white or purplish-black in color (Figure 12.6). They fashioned the white beads from the

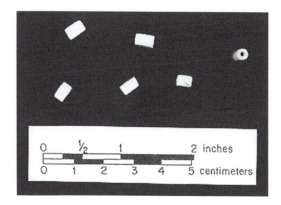

Figure 12.6 Wampum beads
(Courtesy of the New York State Museum, Albany.)

central column of the whelk shell and the dark beads from the purple spots on hard-shell clamshells.

The use of wampum by Native Americans was complex and firmly embedded within their culture. They strung the beads together in long strands or wove them into belts, and gave them away at important times. They considered the beads to be valuable, highly significant objects. They could give the beads away as ceremonial gifts, use them in gambling, or bury them with their dead. Traditional healers could use the beads in their rituals, and entire groups could give wampum belts to Europeans as proof of their commitment to a new treaty. When woven into patterns, wampum belts could also be used as historical records of important events.

The cultural significance of wampum was largely lost on the Dutch. They called it *sewant* and designated it money. Agents from the Dutch West India Company amassed large amounts of wampum and used it in their dealings with Native Americans during the height of the fur trade. Before long, European settlers throughout New York and New England used wampum as their sole currency. Dutch settlers used it to pay rent, make good on a fine, or purchase much-needed foodstuffs. They could even buy property with the tiny shell beads.

Archaeologists excavating in New Amsterdam have discovered evidence of wampum manufacture. At a small outpost called Fort Massapeag, archaeologists discovered a large midden filled with shell beads in various states of manufacture. Unfortunately, this site has suffered from years of thoughtless looting and other forms of destruction, so its evidence is not perfectly reliable. Even so, the discovery of wampum indicates that the manufacture of the shell beads began as an important cultural event that, with the advent of Dutch involvement, became an economic tool of exchange. As the demand for wampum grew, Native Americans and European colonists spent an increasing amount of their time making the beads. Fort Massapeag became a combination Fort Knox and mint, a place where wampum could be made, stored, and collected.

Wampum, though tiny and seemingly insignificant, is central to understanding the interactions between Native Americans and Dutch settlers in one part of colonial North America. Wampum provides an excellent example that the smallest artifacts can have the greatest importance to understanding the past.

The Caribbean and South America

The historical archaeologists working in the Caribbean are making significant contributions to knowledge. Archaeologist Norman Barka conducted several years of excavation on the island of St. Eustatius, where the Dutch settled in 1636 and built Fort Oranje. St. Eustatius is part of the Netherlands Antilles, which includes the islands of Curaçao, Bonaire, Saba, and St. Maarten. Barka and his teams investigated a number of lots in the only town on the island of St. Eustatius, called Oranjestad, also known as Upper Town. Oranjestad was composed of 44 blocks containing dwellings, stores, governmental buildings, and chapels. Barka and his students recorded 397 buildings during an architectural survey of Upper Town. Their excavations in various parts of the settlement retrieved an assortment of Dutch material items, including glazed ceramics and wine and water bottles.

Barka's archaeologists also investigated "Concordia," the country estate of Governor Johannes de Graaff. De Graaff was born on St. Eustatius and served as its commander, or governor, from 1776 to 1781. The island's merchants grew wealthy during these years by supplying arms, ammunition, and other commodities to the rebel forces of the American Continental Army. De Graaff and many of his contemporaries used their newfound riches to purchase land for the cultivation of sugar and enslaved Africans to produce it. Excavations at the estate revealed a number of building foundations, including a sugar boiling house, a section of brick pavement, and a duck pond. The excavations at Concordia thus provided evidence of the lives of the Dutch colonial elite as well as the many enslaved men and women who worked for them.

Historical archaeologists have also researched the Dutch habitation of the islands of Curaçao and St. Maarten. The islands' Dutch settlers followed a pattern established throughout the Caribbean, and in the seventeenth century began growing sugar cane and producing sugar using enslaved African labor.

Dutch explorers and colonists moved into northeast Brazil in 1630 and quickly began to challenge the Portuguese Empire there. They built forts and fortified outposts throughout the territory they controlled. In 1631, they built yet another Fort Orange (Forte Orange), a classic four-bastioned fort in Pernambuco, in northeastern Brazil.

The Dutch colonial forces were intent on keeping their foothold in South America, and they sent regular armed parties to investigate the settlements of both Native South Americans and their Portuguese rivals. The early Portuguese Empire in Brazil was based on the labor of enslaved Africans to cultivate and produce sugar. They stretched their plantations out along the picturesque Brazilian coast, leaving the interior to the indigenous cultures. Enslaved men and women, however, frequently escaped the inhuman slave regime and trekked into the interior in search of freedom. The settlements these fugitive slaves established were called "quilombos" or "maroon communities." One of the largest and most famous quilombos in world history was called Palmares (see Chapter 3).

At its height, Palmares was reported to have as many as 12,000 residents living in ten separate villages. Contemporary reports indicate that the villages were surrounded by stockades and that the houses were made in an African style. The people of Palmares constructed a political system similar to what they had known in Africa, most likely the region of today's Angola. A king ruled the settlements, supported by a number of lesser leaders. Palmares was geographically situated between the towns and plantations of the Portuguese on the coast, the villages of Native South Americans in the interior, and the Dutch outposts to the north (Figure 12.7).

Archaeological research at Palmares found artifacts that may be Dutch in origin. Archaeologists working at the Sierra da Barriga, the site of Macaco, the capital of Palmares, retrieved several coarse earthenware sherds that may be Dutch or Portuguese in origin. Much more research is required before archaeologists will obtain a clear understanding of the history and culture of the great maroon kingdom of Palmares. Research there, however, amply demonstrates the importance of historical archaeology.

Asia

Historical archaeologists have yet to devote intensive interest in the archaeology of Dutch colonialism in Asia, though interest is growing. Some of the reasons for the lack of study are purely practical, but others involve political and economic factors. One important source of information about the Dutch in this region are Dutch East India Company (VOC) shipwrecks. Underwater archaeologists have explored sunken VOC ships in the waters around the Netherlands, southern Africa, India, and Australia. Maritime historians estimate the Company lost somewhere around 250 ships in the 200 years of its existence, many of them in Asian waters.

One of the most famous, and perhaps infamous, VOC wrecks is the *Geldermalsen*. The wreck of the *Geldermalsen* occurred in 1752, when it struck a reef off the Riau Archipelago in Indonesia. The ship broke apart and sank, taking 80 of its men down with it. The cargo of the *Geldermalsen* provided a glimpse at the nature of the trade the VOC carried on between the Netherlands and its numerous Asian outposts.

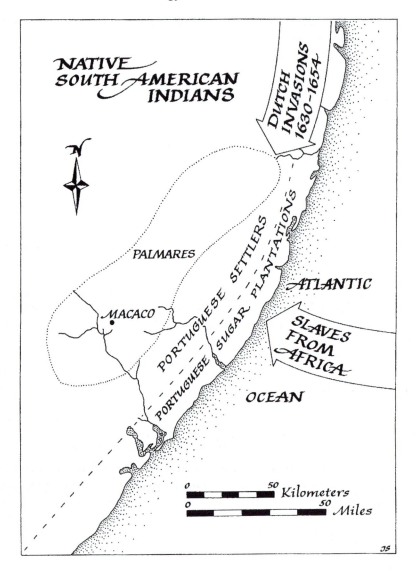

Figure 12.7 Location of Palmares

(C. E. Orser, Toward a Global Historical Archaeology, *Historical Archaeology* 28, 1 [1994]: 17.)

The wreck site contained copper alloy candlesticks, glass stemware, 24 iron cannon, an abundance of German stoneware, and glass bottles of different sizes. The most amazing find by far was 150,000 pieces of fine blue-and-white Chinese porcelain. Originally packed into 203 crates, the collection included complete dinner sets (plates, serving dishes, butter dishes, sauceboats, salad bowls), tea cups and saucers, chocolate cups and saucers, teapots, and milk bowls (Figure 12.8). Also included were soup bowls, cuspidors, and vomit pots. All the pieces were delicately shaped and beautifully decorated. The cargo of the *Geldermalsen* is most definitely a treasure.

Figure 12.8 Colonial-era Chinese porcelain
(Private Collection / Photo © Christie's Images / Bridgeman Images)

Controversy over the *Geldermalsen's* cargo arose precisely because it *was* a treasure. The finds were extremely valuable and the site was not carefully excavated by trained archaeologists. Instead, an English treasure hunter named Michael Hatcher salvaged the collection from the sea bottom in 1985 and realizing its value promptly shipped it to Christie's auction house in Amsterdam. Hatcher had earlier retrieved 23,000 pieces of Chinese porcelain from a sunken Chinese junk dating to around 1640. The auction of these pieces had netted him approximately $2 million. The cargo of the *Geldermalsen* did not disappoint him; he made about $15 million from it.

The mining of archaeological sites, on both land and underwater, raises significant ethical problems for professional archaeologists (see Chapter 13). First, simply removing objects from a wreck site (or a terrestrial site) destroys the archaeological context. As noted earlier, archaeologists obtain information from the soil and an artifact's context. Without this information an artifact is simply a curio. Hatcher's salvors paid no attention to context during their "excavation" of the *Geldermalsen*. In fact, they merely used a vacuum to suck debris from the artifacts. Archaeological contexts were not their concern; they were after valuable artifacts. Second, Hatcher and his crew were only interested in objects they could place on auction. Professional archaeologists know that the most historically important objects can be those with little or no monetary value. Half a Ming dynasty plate, for instance, has as much archaeological importance as a whole plate, but the broken specimen has no resale value. Collectors want whole vessels for their curio cabinets.

Salvaging wrecks like the *Geldermalsen* raises profound, far-reaching questions for archaeologists. The International Congress of Maritime Museums condemned the salvage of the *Geldermalsen* in 1986.

Modern-World Archaeology

In Chapter 1, we remarked that the modern world was shaped by compelling historical forces. The European Age of Discovery, the trade in enslaved Africans, the development of capitalism, and the Industrial Revolution all played major roles in forging nation-states and in mixing and mingling Western and non-Western cultures in every corner of the world. Anthropologist Eric Wolf described this centuries-long process of globalization in *Europe and the People Without History,* published in 1982. He made the point that every human society was affected in one way or another by the expansion of Western civilization into the remotest corners of the globe. The past five centuries have seen the development of what historical sociologist Immanuel Wallerstein has termed the "modern world-system." French historian Fernand Braudel described the "capitalist world-economy" developing after about 1415 C.E. as "a fragment of the world, an economically autonomous section of the planet able to provide for most of its own needs." Braudel felt that the "links and exchanges" between the different parts of the world economy created a kind of global unity.

It would be easy for historical archaeologists to ignore these connections by concentrating only on the minute examination of a single individual, social group, or site. Such research, though extremely important to the maturation of historical archaeology as a discipline and the creation of new historical knowledge, would necessarily miss the wider forces and structures affecting and sometimes even controlling people's lives.

For the purposes of this book, we envision the contacts and associations maintained by Europeans and non-Europeans as a series of interconnected, complex "networks of interaction." Modern-world archaeology was created to focus specifically on the webs of interaction created and maintained throughout the world since about 1500 C.E. One of the inspirations for modern-world archaeology is Eric Wolf, who defined modern world history as composed of "chains of causes and effects at work in the lives of particular populations."

The concept of networks creates the foundation of modern-world archaeology. Network theorists work in many social sciences because networks interlink people, places, and things. Telephone cables, sewer pipelines, and highways can all be described as networks, and we are all familiar with the concept of the computer network. Social network theorists study people and their interrelationships, while geographic network theorists study places and their distributions across landscapes. In social network analysis, individuals and groups are perceived as nodes or points with their relations being represented as lines. A mother and daughter would be represented as two points with a line connecting them. The same can be imagined for places. Two archaeological sites can be represented as dots on a map with a road or path connecting them. Historical archaeologists must understand both social and geographic connections because a social connection between groups may also be geographically expressed. A connection between a mother and her daughter may be geographic as well as social: They may live in different villages but still remain personally "close." The more complex a society, the more frequent and diverse the social and geographic interconnections between people and places. The use of a network model helps archaeologists understand connections in both visual and conceptual ways.

All archaeologists seek to interpret the past using the remains left behind, but a modern-world archaeologist engages in one simple, albeit intensely relevant question: why is today's world the way it is? The basic methodology of all archaeology may be similar (and perhaps even identical), but archaeologists of the recent past have unique opportunities and special burdens. Their research can never be considered irrelevant to present-day life.

Modern-world archaeologists can make substantive contributions to the study of modernity and all its implications. A person can practice historical archaeology, however, and not practice modern-world archaeology, but it is impossible for a person to practice modern-world archaeology and not practice historical archaeology. Modern-world archaeology is historical archaeology but historical archaeology is not necessarily modern-world archaeology. Modern-world archaeology is a specific kind of historical archaeology.

Modern-world archaeology will be forever developing because the very word "modern" is itself constantly being redefined. Scholars and non-scholars variously describe and define modernity, with some definitions being more technical than others. Among the many definitions that have been proposed, perhaps Samuel Johnson's view published in 1760 is the most straightforward: "modern" means "late, recent, not ancient, not antique." Scholars debate the practicality of the term "modernity" and argue that ethnographic research demonstrates the presence of multiple modernities. Rather than shying away from the complexities inherent in the meaning of modernity or to dispute the simultaneous existence of multiple modernities, modern-world archaeologists embrace the confusion and attempt to discern the relevant material manifestations of modernity within specific, local contexts using a perspective employing many scales of analysis.

No need exists to offer a concrete date for the beginning of modernity. It need only be said that modern-world archaeology begins with the union of four forces that, as historian Robert Marks wrote, "come together in ways that interact with one another, creating a unique historical moment." That unique moment is the modern world.

The four forces constitute the "haunts of modernity." The word "haunts" is used for two reasons. First, none of the four forces can be seen or touched, but their effects and impacts have been far-reaching and significant since the late fifteenth century. Second, through coming together in various ways—at different times and in disparate places—the four haunts continue to affect all archaeological practice today. As a result, the four haunt archaeology because they often stay hidden in the background.

The four haunts are colonialism, Eurocentrism, racialization, and capitalism. All four are complicated in their own right, and scholars have written many books about each separately. Each one, however, can be defined in a simple way. Colonialism refers to the spatial movement of people from one culture or region into another culture's territory with the goal of building temporary, intermittent, and permanent settlements. Colonialism differs from colonization because colonialism incorporates unequal relations of power. This means that a more powerful, colonizing culture moves into another culture's region with the intention (or outcome) of dominating them. Eurocentrism is a specialized form of ethnocentrism that elevates to superiority an imagined, common "European" culture and heritage over all other cultures and heritages. Eurocentrism may be nationally based, referring only to one culture, such as the English, or it may be used to lump together all peoples of European background. Racialization is the process of inventing biological and social inferiority using ideology, pseudo-science, administrative power, repressive authority, and other forms of domination and oppression. It is similar to Eurocentrism, but any population can be racialized by a dominant group, including the poor, ethnic groups, and people with certain sexual orientations. Racialization thus concerns more than skin color or physical appearance. Capitalism is an exploitative economic system that creates classes of people and divides them based on their control of production and distribution. In its simplest form, capitalism creates owners who control society and workers who have little control or social power.

These four haunts, as they were envisioned and put into operation in the world after about 1500, are tightly interlinked and coterminous. In fact, the conjunction of the four haunts provides both the uniqueness of the modern era and the rationale for investigating it using the multidisciplinary tools and approaches of historical archaeology.

Modern-world archaeology finds the interwoven character of these haunts especially amenable to archaeological examination and interpretation. While each one might be studied by itself—because of the inherent complexity and changeability of each—modern-world archaeologists understand that they can never be truly separated except artificially. In any particular historical expression, one of the haunts may appear more dominant than the others. This does not mean, however, that the others have disappeared. Equally, the modern-world archaeologist's focus on one of the haunts, such as racialization, does not negate the relevance of the other haunts. For example, the apparent absence of racialization at a site once inhabited by individuals deemed "white" is profoundly meaningful. The perceived absence of race in both the past (with racial invisibility serving as a quiet benefit of white privilege) and the present (the archaeologist's failure to engage whiteness) are equally relevant to modern-world archaeology. A concentrated focus on only one haunt and its implications may simply demonstrate both the realities of research and the significant complexities inherent in the examination of the modern world. To be effective, modern-world archaeology must concentrate on at least two of the haunts simultaneously. Only through this approach will it be possible to demonstrate their true interconnectivity in the post-1500 world.

Modern-world archaeologists overtly reject a biased, Eurocentric perspective even though much of the analytical focus is on the role of Europe in the post-Columbian world. The critique of Eurocentrism and the racialization that often accompanied it constitute two of the central haunts of concern. For example, no reason exists why a scholar cannot conduct research on African chiefdoms as a historical archaeologist using all the tools of the discipline. That the research does not fall within the purview of modern-world archaeology is insignificant because the research intents of the historical archaeologist and the modern-world archaeologist may be quite different. An archaeology that mentions Europe and Europeans and even one that focuses on them is not Eurocentric by definition.

One of the goals of modern-world archaeology is to create an archaeology of recent history that overtly acknowledges and eagerly accepts the linkages between the past and the present. A historical archaeology focused too closely on the particular (e.g., the size and shape of glass beads or the manufacturing techniques of porcelain) or on just one archaeological site has the potential to marginalize the discipline as antiquarianism and thus to reduce its impact on society. At the very least, too narrow a focus may invite attacks from politicians wishing to limit the already-meager funds allocated to archaeological research.

At the same time, particularistic examinations are important to modern-world archaeology, even though they do not constitute modern-world archaeology per se. Detailed studies of Chinese porcelain, glass trade beads, chert gunflints, and whiteware ceramics are immensely important sources for modern-world archaeology even though none can be characterized as modern-world archaeology. Each fits squarely within the purview of historical archaeology.

A concern with the process of modernity, which necessarily encompasses the four haunts, makes the archaeology of recent history relevant to scholars concerned with global emancipation and cultural liberation. To withdraw from a dialogue with modernity because it must necessarily focus on the "West and the rest," ignores a substantial part of global history and does a disservice to our collective understanding of the present world. A confrontation of the four haunts is unavoidable when the subject is post-Columbian world history.

The overarching perspectives of modern-world archaeology should never be considered fixed even though the focus of study remains the process of modernity and the four haunts. Four central characteristics define modern-world archaeology: (1) an explicit appreciation of socio-spatial networks, (2) a trans-regional, transcontinental, and global awareness, (3) an acceptance of multiscalar analysis, and (4) an explicit acknowledgment of the archaeologist's goals.

Modern-world archaeology views social relations as being at the forefront of analysis. For this reason it constitutes a kind of social archaeology. The basic idea between social relations is that humans must interact to survive. For this reason, modern-world archaeology also relies on concepts from network theory. Network theory provides a rigorous set of concepts to examine the power of dominant ideologies and the unequal access to power, knowledge, and opportunity inherent in social relations.

Archaeologists cannot conduct network analysis like sociologists. Archaeologists seldom have the ability to measure the social distances between living individuals, but they can calculate the physical distances between houses, settlements, features, and even artifacts as surrogate indicators of social distance. Modern-world archaeologists have a commitment to relational concepts and processes as an overarching framework and acknowledge that individuals and social groups are inherently interdependent. Also like network analysts, modern-world archaeologists accept that linkages between social entities entail the flow of material and nonmaterial resources, and understand that networks create frameworks of relations between individuals and social groups. Modern-world archaeologists also acknowledge that the webs of interaction constituting the networks were simultaneously linked horizontally through contemporary society (meaning both in history and in the analysts' present) and vertically through time, expressed as tradition, custom, and memory.

The presence of many interlocking, contemporaneous networks means that modern-world archaeologists must adopt a perspective on space and time expanded from what traditional historical archaeologists ordinarily accept. Modern-world archaeologists perceive a site's spatial extent in the broadest possible terms and do not accept that the boundaries of a site end at the edge of the property. Rather, modern-world archaeologists envision a site's social and spatial (or socio-spatial) reach to extend to all those places with which the site's inhabitants had both direct and indirect contact and interaction. Thus, modern-world archaeologists who investigate seventeenth-century settlements in South Africa inhabited by people of Dutch heritage could rightly consider both the Netherlands and New Netherland as within the site inhabitants' actual and cognitive boundaries. Modern-world archaeology eschews the idea that settlements and the people who occupied them were spatially bounded and constrained by what archaeologists causally term a site. Rather, modern-world archaeology embraces the idea of multiple connections with "the outside world," however it might be defined in space and time.

Modern-world archaeologists adopt a trans-regional focus. This means they have global awareness. Modern-world archaeologists appreciate the off-site connections once operating at any specific site. Additionally, the rise of colonialism and the capitalist project, as represented above by the Dutch Empire, meant that the world's peoples increasingly experienced a "time-space compression" serving to connect them in new ways throughout modern history.

Traditional historical archaeologists tend to establish the relevance of their research by linking the past with the present. Their hope is to demonstrate that "we need the past to explain the present." Modern-world archaeologists support this admirable goal but expand it by advocating for dialectical thinking. This means that modern-world archaeologists accept the bidirectionality of history and view the past as influencing the present and the present as influencing the telling of the past. Archaeologists only know the past through the lenses of the present, and their interpretations are influenced, perhaps even unconsciously, by their interests, experiences, and education.

The perspectives encompassed by dialectical thinking and the acceptance of trans-regional awareness means that modern-world archaeologists inherently adopt a multiscalar perspective. At noted in the previous chapter, scale is an important topic in historical archaeology and its understanding provides a necessary foundation for modern-world archaeology. In multiscalar analysis, the analyst examines a sociohistorical moment at one scale (e.g., the household from 1700 to 1750) and, once this setting is reasonably analyzed, moves on to the next scale (perhaps the neighborhood). This process is completed when the analyst is satisfied the research potential has been exhausted. The analyst may then move the investigation to a broader geographical unit (e.g., the region) and perhaps also expand the time frame (e.g., 1680–1800). Frequently, however, the results obtained at one level may conflict with those obtained at another level. This conflict, rather than being problematic, merely reflects the complexities of modern life. Contradictions provide important avenues for further research.

Modern-world archaeologists are also fully committed to self-reflection. This means they constantly evaluate their research goals and intent by asking themselves why they are engaged in certain projects and not others. These questions are seldom easy to answer, but they constitute the heart of research in modern-world archaeology. Some relevant questions an archaeologist may ask himself or herself are: Why have I adopted one theoretical position over others? Why have I cited only certain historical sources? How will my research findings affect descendant communities and ultimately influence how history is written? Modern-world archaeologists also understand their research findings may run counter to what the public expects. The four haunts are significant areas of study because each has effects still being experienced today. In some cases, members of the public may not wish to know about racialization or Eurocentrism in their culture's past. The public's hesitation should not be an impediment to research, but it should cause an archaeologist to pause and consider the practical implications of the research endeavor. In any case, reflexive thinking in archaeology is well established in the archaeological canon of the twenty-first century, and it constitutes a key feature of modern-world archaeology.

Modern-world archaeology seeks to extend the understanding of archaeological ethics at the beginning of the twenty-first century by arguing that archaeologists of post-Columbian history must accept that their research is influenced by the four haunts in ways they may not realize. For example, few professional archaeologists today would consciously conduct overtly racist research. Such research lies strictly within the realm of pseudo-archaeology. But surprisingly, many historical archaeologists—even some investigating the post-Columbian era—refuse to acknowledge the important role capitalism has played and continues to play in the present-day practice of archaeology. Modern-world archaeologists openly acknowledge that professional archaeology is impossible without the capitalist project. The role of capitalism is most obvious in commercial archaeology, where the archaeologists' livelihood is directly influenced by the trajectories of the global economy (see Chapter 9).

Modern-world archaeology represents a complex approach to the examination of the recent past. In what follows, we present a few ideas that outline how the study of globalization—embedded within the haunt of capitalism—might be approached, with the understanding that a full illustration requires a much more in-depth, multiscalar analysis.

Modern-World Archaeology and Globalization

Globalization is a vast subject, and scholars across the academic spectrum have written thousands of articles and books on the subject. That globalization is a topic too big to handle is reinforced by an internet search that yields more than 31 million websites. Globalization, however defined, has had dramatic impacts throughout the world along cultural, historical, political, and economic dimensions through time and across space. It is a topic especially suited to investigation by modern-world archaeologists.

Globalization never encompassed the entire world at one time. Rather, its growth and spread has taken many centuries, beginning in the sixteenth century with the expansion of the Spanish Empire into the New World. Anthropologists have repeatedly demonstrated that the globalization process is never all-pervasive, so a more useful perspective is one that stresses interdependence rather than rapid, wholesale cultural change. Toward this end, a useful definition of globalization is a process with the following characteristics: (1) networks of interdependence at multi-continental distances; (2) connections based on the complex flow of currency, goods, information, ideas, and people; and (3) an overarching structure defined by capitalist social relations.

Modern-world archaeologists can investigate capitalist globalization using diverse sources of information, but most pointedly with excavation and analyses not available to scholars outside archaeology. Much of this research will concentrate on the ways local populations have used, defined, redefined, shaped, and modified newly introduced material objects and ideas within a subprocess called glocalization.

Glocalization is usually defined as the penetration of some globally designed feature into a local area resulting in a transformation of the intro-duced feature. An example is McDonald's who, upon moving into India, had to cease offering beef on its menu. The corporation was still the same, but it was forced to adapt to the local setting to be viable. Glocalization is well known to anthropologists, sociologists, and cultural historians. Studies of glocalization also constitute an important avenue for archaeologists to contribute to the understanding of the historical relations between the global and the local. Archaeologists can use such histories as tools to promote human rights, a goal that has emerged in much contemporary archaeology (see Chapter 13).

Glocalization is only half of the globalization process. A complimentary process is called "grobalization." This process, defined by geographer George Ritzer, refers to the ambitions of nations, corporations, and organizations to impose their desires on various geographic areas. The point of grobalization, and the source of its linguistic root, is that capitalist ventures must grow to be successful. Thus, glocalization and grobalization constitute the two subprocesses of the globalization process.

Glocalization and grobalization are considered in tandem in modern-world archaeology. An explicit focus on the local alone has the tacit appearance of relieving capitalists of their responsibilities, while too strong an emphasis on capitalists erases the power of the indigenous people to reject, refine, and modify. The two subprocesses work dialectically within the globalization process.

Modern-world archaeologists recognize the importance of globalization and are uniquely situated to examine its historical and material roots. The understanding that modern-world archaeology inherently concerns trans-regional history means that modern-world archaeologists must simultaneously think on at least two scales: the local (the smallest) and the global (the largest). Thus, modern-world archaeology is neither simply an archaeological version of world history (using artifacts in the place of texts) nor a one-dimensional examination of a single site at one point in time. The key point of modern-world archaeology is to "dig locally and think globally."

Modern-world archaeology may never supplant traditional historical archaeology as the dominant text-aided archaeology. As archaeologists around the world discover the analytical power and interpretive insights of historical archaeology, they may decide not to examine modernity or to consider the four haunts as part of that historical process. This avoidance is not inherently harmful to historical archaeology because not every historical archaeologist must study the same era or the same historical processes. Studies that openly confront capitalist domination or racialized inferiority may insult the sensibilities of some archaeologists, while others may simply be more interested in material culture. The diversity in approaches, styles, and outlooks represents the vitality of historical archaeology as an exciting field of study.

Other historical archaeologists will be drawn to modern-world archaeology because of its explicit design as an anthropology for liberation. Modern-world archaeology as a special kind of text-aided social archaeology has relevance that extends beyond archaeology because it openly addresses complex topics directly affecting millions of people around the world today. Modern-world archaeology, like all archaeology, can provide tangibility to the past and create unbreakable links between the present and the past. Modern-world archaeology is designed as a critical historical archaeology (see Chapter 10), with the central subject of critique being the modern world. Modern-world archaeologists investigate—with all the tools available to them—the recent, historical antecedents to help us interpret the world in which we live.

Site Visit: Dolly's Creek, Australia, 1860s–1890s

The rush for gold has inspired unbounded hope and depressing madness throughout the world, as eager prospectors have sought their fortunes from the earth. History shows that Europeans have pursued gold both in their settled colonies and in lands fabled for the supposed richness of their untapped deposits. In the 1850s, the Moorabool goldfield of southeastern Australia, located about 38.5 miles (62 km) west of Melbourne, was known as a gold-rich area just waiting to be exploited by eager miners.

Industrial mining involves the studied research of geologists and engineers, with discovered veins being worked by waged miners in the employ of large companies. Such capitalist concerns are usually interested in making a big strike, exhausting it, and then moving on to the next deposit-rich area. This may be the general view of mining today, but many individual prospectors in the mid-nineteenth century were not employed as paid miners; they were subsistence miners who often took their families into the frontier to work "poor man's diggings."

Subsistence miners established communities, often composed of entire families, who mined for precious metals with the goal of providing a sustainable living. Most really did not expect to strike it rich. They would have willingly accepted the "big strike" if it came, but most understood they would never be truly *nouveau riche*; they were simply miners making a living. One community of subsistence miners in Australia was called Dolly's Creek.

In the late 1850s, a group of anonymous miners traveled north up the Moorabool River in search of unexplored gold fields. Near the settlement of a squatter named Morrison, they found, to their excitement, gold-bearing gravels. They decided to establish a camp on the spot, and they promptly named it Dolly's (or Dolly) Creek after a prospecting technique. At the time, a "dolly" was an instrument miners used to divide and mix stiff clay or cement with water in a tub.

At the height of its settlement, more than 600 people lived at Dolly's Creek in more than 200 houses. Most of their homes were of simple construction, with canvas roofs and bark or timber walls. A few houses were more substantial, being made of stone or wood. The canvas houses usually had one room, and measured only about 6.5 by 11.5 feet (2 by 3.5 m) in size. Other houses in the camp could be as large as 11.5 by 16 feet (3.5 by 5 m). The miners equipped their homes with fireplaces built of roughly hewn blocks of quartzite held together with mortar made mostly of mud (Figure 12.9). These fireplaces required almost constant maintenance, because if left untended, they would collapse when the

Figure 12.9 Fireplace at Dolly's Creek, Australia. (Courtesy of Susan Lawrence).

mud washed out. The chimneys above the fireplaces were built of wood, sheets of iron, or even animal hides. Most of the houses had glass windows, and at night people used candles stuck in empty bottles or kerosene lamps for light. At least one house in the village, perhaps used as a store or pub, was built more solidly than the rest. Its walls, composed of a number of layers, made it watertight and relatively secure. Its canvas inner surface was strengthened by several additional layers of newspaper, heavy cardboard, and tin.

The residents of Dolly's Creek had the usual complement of consumer goods available during the period. Many people may envision late-nineteenth-century miners, loggers, and other extractive industry workers using only tin dishes. Tin wares were more durable than ceramics; when dropped they would bend but not break. The men and women at Dolly's Creek may have used tin dishes, but they also used a wide variety of glazed earthenware. The members of individual households owned a number of transfer-printed dinner plates, teacups, saucers, and other vessels decorated in blue, mulberry, green, red, black, and brown. They made no attempt to use matching sets, but they were not immune to adding a few amenities: Some of the houses had wallpaper decorated with floral designs.

The Dolly's Creek villagers probably selected their personal possessions with one eye on their transportability. They undoubtedly realized they might need to relocate to another gold field. It would be a huge inconvenience to carry cartloads of objects along with them. But people in the settlement did have some treasured objects. One notable piece was a brass mantle clock. When the owner of the clock left the village—perhaps hoping to return—he or she took out the working mechanism and left the case behind.

The diet at Dolly's Creek was simple but varied. They drank beer and wine, champagne, gin, whiskey, as well as other drinks. They made stews, soups, and roasts with chicken, beef, pork, mutton, and rabbit, purchasing the meat from butchers who probably lived in the camp. For their health, they relied on patent medicines, just like thousands of other men, women, and children living during the late nineteenth century.

Source: Susan Lawrence, *Dolly's Creek: An Archaeology of a Victorian Goldfields Community.* (Melbourne: Melbourne University Press, 2000).

Chapter 13

Historical Archaeology and the Past Today

Historical archaeology is the archaeology of ourselves, a field of research that spans the most recent centuries of human life on Earth. Historical archaeologists use methods that can be applied with equal facility to sixteenth-century villages in colonial New Spain or in landfills in today's India. Historical archaeology serves as a mirror into our own lives, and of men, women, and children who lived only a few generations ago, or even within living memory. The research of historical archaeologists extends to today.

The innovative research of archaeologist William Rathje attracted wide attention for his examination of modern-day urban landfills and trash dumps. He referred to his research as "garbology." Rathje calculated that the Fresh Kills landfill on Staten Island, New York, is 25 times the size of the Great Pyramid at Giza, Egypt, and 40 times the size of the Temple of the Sun at Teotihuacán, Mexico. Digging into landfills he found fresh hot dogs, guacamole, and other foodstuffs dating to the 1950s. He also discovered that newspaper almost never deteriorates when stuffed into a landfill's air-starved environment. Rathje's excavations have an important bearing on many of today's most serious issues, including recycling and refuse management.

Rathje's research demonstrates that the line between past and present cannot always be easily drawn. When the U.S. Congress enacted legislation establishing the National Register of Historic Places in 1976, it defined "antiquity" as 50 years from the present (see Chapter 9). The 50-year interval is purely arbitrary and effectively meaningless except within a narrow legal context. We all know that the past is a seamless sequence of days, weeks, seasons, and years. But the past and the present intersect. When archaeologist Jane Busch wrote that "The tin can has played a significant role in American history and can play a significant role in archaeology," she was absolutely correct. She envisions tin cans as vehicles of history, easily dated by telltale technological improve-ments in seals and seams. She purposefully incorporated the "modern sanitary can," the kind we all bring home from the grocery store, into her study. Whether we realize it or not, we—and all the things with which we surround ourselves—are actors in history.

In this chapter we explore the role of historical archaeology in today's world. Historical archaeologists are taking the field into diverse directions. Much of the most exciting research involves the place of historical archaeology in highlighting the contributions the discipline offers to today's society, including in the realm of social justice.

Living Museums and Historical Archaeology

Each of us is an actor in the unfolding sweep of history. We are thus repositories of "living history," archives filled with memories of past events and current experiences (see Chapter 6). Our daily comings and goings, the people we meet, and the objects we use all constitute history being lived. It follows from this simple reality that historical archaeologists are part of the history they study. Once an archaeologist excavates a site, he or she is forever part of the history of that place. The line between past and present is blurred in historical archaeology, and archaeologists of modern history cannot truly separate themselves from it. As anthropologist David Pilbeam observed in the *Washington Post* in 1983, "We do not see things as they are, we see things as we are."

Nowhere is this statement truer than at living history exhibits, such as Plimoth Plantation, Massachusetts, which are popular, often international, tourist attractions. Historical archaeologist James Deetz played a leading role at Plimoth by providing accurate plans for the reconstructed buildings. The settlement is today "inhabited" by men and women wearing period costumes. These "residents" shoe horses, card and dye wool, cook over large iron cauldrons, and fashion delicate glass vases and bowls using time-tested methods. Visitors to this "colonial" town experience living history—a modern vision of historical life reconstructed from historical documents and archaeological research.

Scandinavians created the first living museums (also called "open-air" museums), in the 1880s, but today they can be found all over the world. Henry Ford's Greenfield Village (see Chapter 3) is a well-known example in the Midwestern United States. So is the Yorvik Viking Centre in York, England, where the daily life of an Anglo-Scandinavian town dating to 850–1050 C.E. has been recreated so vividly that even voices and smells are piped in. Visitors descend underground in a small car and pass through the centuries until they emerge on a Viking street. The car travels through the excavations that reconstructed the town into a display of important finds. Everything is calculated to entertain and enlighten, to make history come alive. Each of the more than one million individuals who visit Yorvik each year becomes part of the history of the site.

One of the most intriguing living museums in the United States is the slave quarters constructed at Colonial Williamsburg's eighteenth-century Carter's Grove Plantation. The Carter's Grove house, built between 1750 and 1755, is a huge brick mansion with a beautifully restored central stairway and baronial gardens. The cabins of the enslaved tell a story quite different from that of the mansion. They are located about 800 feet (244 m) northwest of the mansion, partially screened by a row of trees. They consist of a cluster of four reconstructed wooden cabins with accompanying yards (Figure 13.1). Their designs are based on archaeological evidence. The largest building belonged to the enslaved foreman and his family. At the quarters today, African American men and women "living" in the cabins explain to modern visitors, in deeply personal terms, what it must have been like to have been enslaved at Carter's Grove. The actors play their parts with passion, and embellish their stories using remembrances collected during the 1930s.

Even as evocative as the cabins are to modern visitors, can we truly say they are *only* about the past? The actors undoubtedly put much of themselves into their historical performances. As actors in our contemporary world, they use history to help us better understand enslavement, racism, and discrimination. Their stories are powerful history lessons that derive much of their power from the reconstructed cabins. When faced with the actual cabins, visitors are unavoidably forced to confront the reality of America's slave past. The cabins are too small and too poorly constructed to have been comfortable in any meaningful way.

Figure 13.1 Reconstruction of the slave quarters at Carter's Grove Plantation, Virginia
(Courtesy of the Colonial Williamsburg Foundation, Williamsburg, VA.)

Another perspective on living history comes from an innovative series of archaeological projects conducted in Annapolis, Maryland, under the general direction of Mark Leone. Using several eighteenth- and nineteenth-century sites as a focus, Leone and his collaborators developed a program using archaeological fieldwork to engage tourists. Leone once even hired a media consultant to help his team create the best site tour possible. Their consultant, Philip Arnoult, the director of a theater project, first queried the archaeologists about what sorts of questions visitors typically ask them. Common queries, actually faced by all archaeologists, are: How do archaeologists know where to look for sites? How do they date objects, and how do they interpret what they find? Armed with these questions, Arnoult worked with Leone and his team on the tour itself. Before long, more than 100 people a day were visiting the Annapolis archaeological project. In the summer and fall of 1982, 7,000 people toured the Victualling Warehouse site alone. This warehouse, built sometime before 1747, housed supplies for the Continental Army during the American Revolution.

The archaeologists at Annapolis learned three important elements of a successful tour. First, the educational aspects of the projects must have as high a priority as the research itself. In other words, research and public education must go hand in hand, with neither dominating or eliminating the other. By educating the public, they could help eliminate two commonly held misconceptions about archaeology: that it is conducted by stuffy old men in pith helmets who are completely oblivious to the world around them, and that archaeologists are determined to stop all construction projects (or "progress") in the name of science. Second, Leone and his team learned that tours had to be structured. Both the visitors' path across the site and the information their guides told them had to be consistent. Archaeological tour guides must be willing to adjust their narratives in light of new finds and to accommodate visitors' questions. Archaeology conducted with these ideas in mind thus becomes an interactive enterprise, with excavators and visitors both engaged in the research, albeit in distinct ways. And finally, the Annapolis archaeologists learned that archaeological research must not be presented as if it is only about the past. In Leone's words, "there must be a convincing tie to the present drawn out of the material from the past." The archaeologists at the Victualling Warehouse told visitors the site's history. They also made certain that visitors understood that many of Annapolis' business owners saw the archaeology as creating a tangible link between them and the city's historic business owners. The warehouse is undeniably an important component of the city's commercial history.

The Annapolis archaeologists used their site-tour approach to draw visitors into the town's history. Each visitor's place in history is as important as was that of Daniel Dulany, the owner of the Victualling Warehouse, whose property was seized in 1781 because of his loyalist sympathies.

Critics have legitimately observed that some open-air museums present static, sanitized versions of history. Living museums consisting only of empty buildings with little interpretation do offer sterile, inaccurate visions of history. The Yorvik Centre attempts to overcome this problem with its multi-sensory approach, just as does Carter's Grove with its engaged storytelling. Even facilities attempting innovative interpretations, however, may be criticized if their explanatory panels and stories never change.

Open-air site creators and managers have an additional problem, one with profound cultural implications. This involves the interpretive material itself, because a central question must be: Whose interpretation is being presented?

Alexander Herrera asked this very question in his investigation of heritage tourism in Peru. Surveys indicate that many tourists visit Peru specifically to experience its archaeological treasures. Machu Picchu and Nasca are two of the places tourists most often mention as desirable destinations.

Herrera discovered that much of what is presented to tourists is a watered-down version of Peruvian history. Being simplified, the stories may present stereotypic images of past life and create false identities and pseudo traditions. He refers to the process as "self-exoticization," meaning that individuals may choose (or be forced because of their economic circumstances) to be regarded as "exotic." An unemployed person, for example, may find a job dancing in an invented "traditional" dance staged just for tourists. Economic need may override historical and cultural accuracy. In such situations, tensions may arise between tour operators, investors, and community members. Additionally, heritage tourism is influenced by global economic forces. A downturn in an economy centralized thousands of miles away may cause a decline in local tourism, which in turn further affects community relations.

Archaeologists have developed a strong interest in the archaeology of tourism, both in the past (at old tourist sites) and in the present (the meaning of tourism at today's archaeological sites and the impact of archaeological tourism, often termed "archaeotourism"). The Archaeological Institute of America (AIA) reports that Americans abroad rank visiting archaeological sites third behind dining and shopping. Hundreds of thousands of "archaeotourists" now visits the world's greatest sites. So important is this industry, and so fragile are the sites, that the AIA has prepared guides both for archaeological tour leaders and tourists. Site managers know very well that too many tourists can spoil an archaeological site. This is just as true for recently inhabited sites as for ancient ones.

Archaeotourism presents major challenges to all archaeologists and almost every issue that arises may have a substantial ethical element. Central questions may be: How many people should be allowed into a tomb, a mansion, or on an archaeological site at one time? Should the interpreters stress national membership, ethnic identity, the common heritage of humankind, or some combination? These are difficult questions to answer. In some cases, archaeologists may find themselves at odds with powerful politicians or business leaders who have a completely different perspective on which interpretation is most important to present. Governmental leaders may hope to sway the world's present-day perception of their nation by presenting false or inflated histories.

The questions raised by archaeotourism highlight a reality of contemporary archaeology: all archaeology is somehow impacted or influenced by politics. Archaeologists conducting excavations outside their home countries may be more aware of the intersection of archaeological research and politics. Their need to acquire visas, excavation permits, and hiring documents highlights national differences. But all archaeologists, wherever they live and work, must understand how political decisions may affect their research.

Politics and Historical Archaeology

The connection between archaeological practice and present-day politics has two dimensions. One is purely practical. Archaeologists, wherever they live, must abide by the laws and regulations passed by governmental organizations. These strictures can either make archaeological research easier or more difficult. As a result, most professional archaeology societies have a governmental liaison committee or dedicated members who stay current with bills and statutes making their way through the legislative process. For example, the Society for Historical Archaeology has a Governmental Affairs Committee that does just this. In the United States and elsewhere, the rapid increase in the number of archaeologists employed by consulting firms rather than educational institutions makes familiarity with the laws essential (see Chapter 9).

The second intersection of politics and archaeology is more theoretical than the first. This dimension involves understanding how political thought and trends affect interpretation. This is the issue archaeologists engaged in archaeotourism most directly confront, but all archaeologists are influenced by political thinking in some way. An unavoidable connection exists between the pasts archaeologists study and the present in which they live. The link between past and present may be especially meaningful for historical archaeologists because they investigate the most recent past.

The situation may be understood by considering the subjects we address in Chapter 10. Historical interpretations of social class, ethnicity, race, gender, and age are all emotional, contemporary issues. Archaeologists who study them must appreciate that they may sometimes tread on potentially slippery political ground in deciding how to address such complicated social identities. That such topics can be controversial amply illustrates the strong connection between past and present.

Governments and emerging states have long used archaeological research for various ends. The Nazis unashamedly used archaeology for political ends in the 1930s and early 1940s. Their program was dramatized in somewhat exaggerated form in the popular Indiana Jones movies. Indiana Jones thwarts evil Nazi archaeologists who are attempting to obtain the Ark of the Covenant, the Holy Grail, and any other powerful objects they can use to dominate the world. The Nazis are fanciful depictions in the movies, but the outline of the story has historical reality.

In 1935, Heinrich Himmler, the head of Hitler's dreaded S.S., created a research organization called *Ahnenerbe*, or "Ancestral Heritage." Much of this organization's "research" was more laughable than dangerous. They really did try to find the Holy Grail (like *Indiana Jones and the Last Crusade*), they searched for Atlantis, they studied the history of German bread, and they believed their early Germanic ancestors had learned to harness the energy of lightning as a weapon. The "scientists" of *Ahnenerbe* also used their often-fudged (or even forged) archaeological findings to support their ideas of ethnic inferiority. They arranged their cultural chronologies of Eastern Europe to fit their theories of Nordic superiority. Archaeology as practiced by the Nazis had a well-defined, horrendous political agenda.

In another overt example of the political use of archaeological knowledge, Hyeong Woo Lee explains the conduct of archaeology in North Korea during the 1950s and 1960s. After World War II, only 20 archaeologists were active in the country. Before the war, Japanese archaeologists performed much of the archaeology in the country, with native Koreans playing only minor roles. Given the modern history of the country, much of the archaeology was nationalist in design and orientation. On one level, archaeology could be used to substantiate the deep history of the Korean people. The division of the country into North and South, however, meant that ethnicity became a major research focus on both sides of the border.

The political history of North Korea in the 1950s and 1960s witnessed different factions struggling for control of the nation. Archaeology was never far from view, as it provided a tangible way to illuminate, and indeed to glorify, Korean identity and cultural history. Professional archaeological journals contained overt political messages, and academic scholars espousing intellectual perspectives not endorsed by the ruling party were purged from academic and museum positions. On September 11, 1961, the party controlling North Korea announced that the nation had finally completed its socialist transformation. Archaeologists in the North were required to adapt and mold their findings to the new reality. During the 1960s, then, North Korean archaeology could be characterized as promoting "socialist patriotism," meaning that people were to be Korean in national identity and Leninist-Marxist in intellect.

In the past, the conquistadors' version of the Conquest of Mexico was the story dominating the history books. The histories and fates of the conquered Aztecs and other Native American peoples were largely ignored or presented in a biased manner. The bias has largely disappeared, as most archaeologists today have accepted a more nuanced, complicated vision of history. Historical archaeology has played a major role in encouraging the transformation. New perspectives are growing in part by an expanding interest in non-Western cultures, and indigenous scholars are actively seeking to reclaim their heritage for themselves and their children. Indigenous peoples are using archaeology to regain control over their histories and to educate their young people about the resilience of their traditional cultures. Australian Aborigine groups are using archaeology to tell their side of the continent's history, and the Maori of New Zealand are aggressively reclaiming their history, both to foster their cultural identity and to support their land claims. Such efforts on the part of indigenous peoples permit archaeologists to develop sophisticated, multifaceted views of history.

Several Native American groups are pursuing active programs of heritage restitution, and many of their projects involve historical archaeology. One such project, sponsored by the Northern Cheyenne of southeastern Montana, was designed to study the Outbreak of 1879.

The Outbreak came about as the result of a series of contacts between the U.S. government and the Northern Cheyenne, who lived in the area of southern Montana and northern

Wyoming. Cheyenne leaders agreed to the Medicine Lodge Treaty of 1867, but they did not understand this meant they would be moved south to "Indian Territory," today's Oklahoma. Several prominent Cheyenne leaders protested the move, and in fact, some of them traveled to Washington in 1872 to plead with President Grant to allow them to stay in their traditional homeland. Grant agreed to let them stay, but with Custer's defeat at the Little Bighorn in 1876, the Northern Cheyenne began to fear reprisals, even though they were not involved in the battle. Under the leadership of Dull Knife and Little Wolf, the Northern Cheyenne sought a safe haven in the Big Horn Mountains. Their peace was short-lived. They were soon discovered and attacked by the U.S. Cavalry. Faced with extreme hardship on the open plains if they fled, the Northern Cheyenne surrendered to the military at Fort Robinson, Nebraska, in April 1877. Tired of trying to feed themselves on a landscape becoming increasingly barren of bison—their main food source—the Northern Cheyenne agreed to try life in Indian Territory. They moved there a couple of months later, but it was not long before more than two-thirds of their people were racked with fever and disease in the unfamiliar environment. Desperate for relief, in September 1878 Dull Knife and Little Wolf led a group of their followers out of Oklahoma and toward their homeland. The 353 Northern Cheyenne who fled, weak from sickness, knew they would be pursued and killed or captured by the cavalry. Splitting into two groups, they maintained a running battle with the soldiers for several days. Little Wolf's band established a camp for the winter in northwestern Nebraska. Dull Knife's people, however, were persuaded to surrender to the cavalry at Fort Robinson. The conditions Dull Knife's band faced at the fort were little better than those in Oklahoma, and on the night of January 9, 1879, he led the famed Outbreak (also called the Northern Cheyenne Exodus) from the fort. Having taken with them only five rifles and several old pistols, Dull Knife's people could not offer much resistance to the cavalry, and 64 of them were killed. The military sent most of the captured male leaders of the Outbreak to Dodge City, Kansas, for trial. They sent the rest of the Cheyenne to the Pine Ridge Agency in southwestern South Dakota. Dull Knife and his family escaped capture by hiding in a cave, but they were eventually also taken to Pine Ridge. Dull Knife's people finally settled on the Tongue River Reservation in Montana, where they remain today.

The Northern Cheyenne have always told a different story of the breakout than that presented by military historians. Official accounts state that the Cheyenne used a northern route to escape. The Cheyenne, relying on oral accounts passed from generation to generation, have always argued for a more southerly route (Figure 13.2). The routes are actually close to one another, and the controversy is seemingly unimportant—unless you are a Northern Cheyenne wanting to reclaim your heritage.

In 1987 Northern Cheyenne individuals from Dull Knife College in Montana teamed up with archaeologist Larry Zimmerman—a leader in promoting relations of understanding between Native Americans and archaeologists—to use archaeology to find evidence of the actual escape route. Native American crewmembers provided geographical guidance and incorporated their traditional prayers and storytelling into the fieldwork. Archaeologists surveyed both routes for lead pistol balls, rifle bullets, and other telltale clues of the pursuit. They found several lead balls and bullets along the southern route, but none along the officially sanctioned northern path. The Cheyenne were vindicated. In the words of project leader, J. Douglas McDonald, they "came to understand that their long-felt mistrust of archaeology might no longer be necessary. Both the archaeologists and the Northern Cheyenne learned that they can be natural allies, sometimes each possessing what the other needs."

Joe Watkins, a member of the Choctaw tribe and the holder of a doctorate degree in archaeology, has asked an important question: "Why don't more American Indians get involved in archaeology?" Some Native American scholars, such as Vine Deloria Jr, author

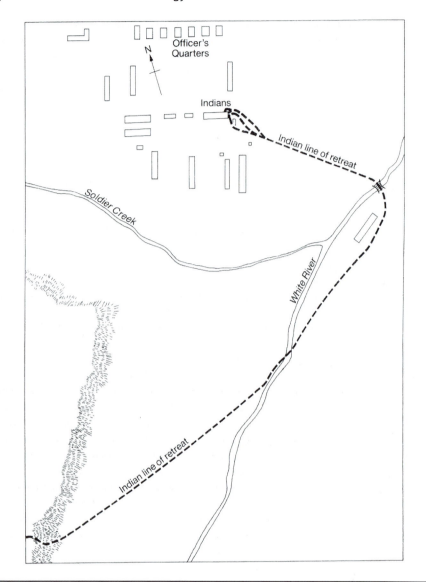

Figure 13.2 The Northern Cheyenne Outbreak according to the U.S. Army Board of Inquiry

(From "The Northern Cheyenne Outbreak of 1879: Using Oral History and Archaeology as Tools of Resistance" by J. Douglas McDonald, Larry J. Zimmerman, A. L. McDonald, William Tall Bull, and Ted Rising Sun in *The Archaeology of Inequality*, Randall H. McGuire and Robert Paynter [Eds.], pp. 64–78. Oxford: Basil Blackwell, 1991.)

of the widely read *Custer Died for Your Sins*, took a strong stand against archaeology, and even espoused pseudo-archaeological interpretations that no professional archaeologist would take seriously. An association with fringe archaeology—dealing with space aliens, lost worlds, and fantastic histories—merely drives a further wedge between archaeologists and indigenous peoples and makes cooperation even more difficult. Watkins has adopted a more measured and sensible approach, and has sought to discover common ground between indigenous peoples and archaeologists. Differences of opinion will arise between indigenous peoples and professional archaeologists, just as individual archaeologists disagree. Such disagreements are inevitable. But archaeologists do not own the past; it is not theirs and theirs alone to interpret. A far more productive perspective is to realize that everyone, regardless of profession, is a steward and guardian of the past.

By the beginning of the twenty-first century, a growing number of archaeologists had acknowledged that their field should not study the past in isolation of the people around them. Traditionally, archaeologists would move into a village or town, establish their housing and laboratory, and have little if anything to do with local residents. These archaeologists saw their research as strictly about "the past" and the people living in the area at the time of excavation were unimportant. The local residents were essentially removed from both the research and the area.

In Chapter 2, we mentioned that a number of archaeological projects are now devised as community-based efforts. In *Archaeology Matters*, Jeremy Sabloff promotes "action archaeology" as archaeological practice engaged with the modern world, meaning it can be used to address problems facing the world today. He explores such timely conundrums as sustainability, warfare, urban life, and heritage preservation and links each to archaeological analysis. The timelessness of these issues reinforces their belonging both to the present and to the past. As such, their understanding should be of paramount concern to the public, individuals making governmental policy, and archaeologists.

Some historical archaeologists are exploring the idea of whether their discipline can be used to change the world. This may seem like an unrealistic goal to many, but it may be possible given the interest the general public typically expresses toward archaeological discovery.

One way to influence the public is through the avenue of "activist archaeology." Activist archaeology goes a step beyond public or community-based archaeology. Public archaeology, as it was designed in the 1970s, was often another name for CRM archaeology (see Chapter 9). Archaeology in this vein was perceived as a public good. If a highway was to be constructed across a rural landscape, archaeology was conducted to identify, study, and if possible, protect archaeological sites for future generations. Community-based archaeology, which developed later (and in fact is still developing), sees archaeologists working hand-in-hand with members of local communities. The goals may vary from project to project, but much of the research is designed, executed, and presented in a collaborative manner. Neither the archaeologists nor members of the descendant community constitute the sole authority. Activist archaeology goes beyond community-based archaeology in that archaeologists become vocal advocates for a community. Archaeologists use all the skills and insights archaeological research offers, but intend to use their knowledge and findings to help a community accomplish something positive.

The archaeological project conducted at Ludlow, Colorado, constitutes an exemplary example of activist archaeology. Ludlow was a tent colony built and inhabited by coal miners striking against the Colorado Fuel and Iron Company. On April 20, 1914, members of the Colorado National Guard attacked the settlement, killing 21 of its inhabitants in what is now called the "Ludlow Massacre." The workers eventually lost the strike, but the national response from the unwarranted armed assault was so widespread it accelerated the cause of better working and living conditions for miners.

The site of the tent city is today owned by the United Mine Workers of America, whose former members led the strike and whose present members consider the site sacred ground. The union has built a monument at the site and they hold an annual commemoration there to honor and remember the strikers and their sacrifices. From 1996 to 2009, archaeologists who excavated at the site attended the ceremonies, and one of the archaeologists, as of this writing, is a member of the commemoration board. The archaeologists also contributed by creating a traveling exhibit about the massacre and the excavations, and writing articles for union publications. They have even spoken at strike rallies.

A similar project in activist archaeology, directed by Paul Shackel, is underway in Pennsylvania at the site of the Lattimer Massacre, a situation remarkably similar to what occurred at Ludlow. In 1897, 400 unarmed miners, on strike against the coal company, were attacked by a force under the authority of the county sheriff. Nineteen miners were killed and 38 were wounded. Just about all of them were immigrants from eastern and central Europe.

Some archaeologists have been in the forefront of expanding the boundaries of activist archaeology. Historical archaeologist Barbara Little has been a leader in challenging her colleagues to think in broad terms about what their discipline can accomplish for the world today.

Little writes about how archaeology might intersect with the Global Justice Movement. The goals of this movement are to create a better world for all humanity in the shortest possible time while fostering cooperation and respect for the environment. The place of historical archaeology in this movement may be difficult to grasp at first, but Little offers suggestions. First, historical archaeologists can contribute by providing an example of inclusion. In archaeological terms, this means studying everyone without exclusion or bias. Whereas in the past, plantation archaeologists, for example, may have been interested only in the planter's family, today archaeologists view everyone—from the highest to the lowest in social position—to be eligible for study. Many historians have been engaged in the same process of historical inclusion, and historical archaeology constitutes a perfect partner, collaborator, and supporter of their effects. Secondly, archaeologists can offer examples of struggle, survival, and hope through time. Specific studies of overcoming poverty, discrimination, segregation, and inequality may help individuals understand that better lives are possible. Third, Little states that archaeology can provide "alternative genealogies" to expose origin myths. She specifically mentions belief in the "blind idolatry" of the free market, and this is one realm where historical archaeology is especially valuable (see Chapter 12). Historical archaeologists, by their excavations at linked economic centers throughout the world, can show how the modern market arose, not through some mysterious force, but through the conscious efforts and activities of real men and women in the past. Archaeological research may also reveal alternative economic strategies that have worked in the past and thus may work in the future.

Activism is an important feature of early twenty-first-century archaeology. Its impact is likely to continue growing. Historical archaeology, because of its focus on the most recent centuries—extending up to the present—has an especially important role to play in promoting and illustrating possible linkages between archeological research and community service.

History Destroyed

Archaeology is under siege all over the world. Deep plowing, industrial development, mining, and runaway urban sprawl, to say nothing of looters and vandals, are decimating the archaeological record everywhere. The past vanishes before our eyes with bewildering and often tragic speed, to the point where one wonders if archaeology will survive the onslaught. As we have emphasized, the archaeological record is a finite source of information. Once disturbed or destroyed, it is gone forever. The battle for the past is serious. At stake is the very survival of humankind's priceless cultural heritage.

In 1989, National Geographic Society archaeologist George E. Stuart gave his assessment of the problem: "To me it is a miracle that any remnant of the human past has survived, for it seems that both nature and man [sic] are constantly engaged in the processes of obliteration." Vandals and looters may destroy what floods and hurricanes have left untouched. Stuart was talking both in general and specific terms. The battle for the past is waged in urban lots, along the rights-of-way of expanding freeways, in lush valleys about to be flooded by hydroelectric dams, and in hundreds of other locales across the globe. Apart from industrial activity, mechanized agriculture, and destruction caused by the population explosion, plain human greed is always at work. Some people have a powerful, illogical urge to collect and own artifacts from the past. They seek to display their finds on their mantles or in cabinets, out of the public eye, available only for their selfish pleasure. Historical archaeology is not immune from looting. Fanatical hobbyists resolutely build their collections of old bottles, beer cans, barbed wire, firearms, and other artifacts made and used during the past 500 years.

Whole sites are especially vulnerable to destruction in the name of "progress." Just south of the traffic-choked city of Dublin, Ireland, sits a castle known as Carrickmines. Anglo-Norman colonists built and used the castle for more than 400 years, from 1200 to 1642, as a base from which to attack Irish chiefdoms living in the Wicklow Mountains. The castle was ruined in 1642 when English soldiers massacred its contingent of Irish rebels.

Archaeologists were familiar with the site for many reasons, including because it yielded one of the largest collections of rural, medieval pottery ever found in Ireland. One important feature of the castle's history stems from its potential to shed new light on the complex social relations existing between Anglo-Norman settlers and indigenous Irish tribes during a period of intense culture contact and change. In late 2001, however, Carrickmines Castle was in danger of being destroyed.

The traffic in Dublin is horrendous and growing worse every year. The number of cars in the city has increased dramatically, and all highways and thoroughfares are clogged most of the day. To solve the burgeoning problem of urban congestion, the Irish National Roads Authority began constructing a large motorway designed to ring the city center. The idea was that drivers could visit the outskirts of the city without first having to travel into the city center. Carrickmines Castle, however, stood directly in the highway's southern path. During the construction of the southern route of the motorway, it was clear that if the road was built, the castle site would be destroyed. Before this could happen, the Irish government spent millions on an archaeological study of the site.

The funds spent on the archaeological research at Carrickmines was indeed vast (in terms of archaeological funds), but a number of committed activists believed it was not adequate. To save the site, they mounted a protest. Some protesters, dubbed "Carrickminders," set up an occupation to block heavy equipment from endangering the site. They said they were not opposed to the highway—its need was obvious—but they did not believe that destroying heritage was a proper way forward. In September 2002, the Irish Minister of Transport stated that 40 percent of the site would be lost to the road, but that construction had to continue. He also noted that archaeologists had worked at the site for two years at a cost of €2 million (about $2.3 million at the time). He said that the government had decided they would move the castle's remaining defensive wall and preserve it for future generations. The protestors condemned this action, stating that it would effectively destroy the integrity of the site. In October 2002, an organization called the Friends of Medieval Dublin, an advocacy group mobilized in the 1970s over the destruction of Wood Quay (the site of Dublin's original Viking town), held the "Carrickmines Forum." A number of Ireland's most important medieval scholars delivered papers on the significance of the site. The Carrickmines case was heard by the Irish High Court, but a final decision may come from the European Union's Court of Justice.

Similar situations are unfortunately being played out across the globe as the presence of important archaeological sites conflict with upgrades and additions to a nation's infrastructure. Wars are especially ruinous to archaeological sites because invading and occupying armies often have little regard for another nation's cultural heritage. Archaeologists, developers, administrators, and politicians must find ways to cooperate for the good of all. One of the goals of cultural resource management archaeology is to discover ways to make collaboration possible, even in the most difficult situations (see Chapter 9).

The Market for History

The conflict over Carrickmines and the looting of the wreck of the *Geldermalsen* (see Chapter 12) raise an important ethical question: Who owns the past? Is the answer humanity as a whole, the owners of a site or collection of artifacts, their descendants, the current landowner, or the government? No easy answers exist, and different nations have devised various solutions. In the United States, for example, people place a high premium on private property, and the destruction of a site on someone's private land generally cannot be stopped. In other countries, such as Ireland, all archaeological artifacts belong to the government as the people's national custodian.

Ancient artifacts can bring big money in the marketplace, often in the millions of dollars. In fact, so many priceless objects of art (including artifacts) have been stolen that an Art Loss Register exists to catalogue the thousands of missing pieces. Art dealers, museum curators, and law enforcement agencies all use the register to help track down stolen objects and return them to their rightful repositories.

Stealing and selling antiquities may seem to involve only the rarest and most valuable works. This is true to some extent, but artifacts from the past 500 years are not immune from theft. A quick search of eBay reveals the huge number of modern-era artifacts available for purchase. For example, the "Pottery and China" category usually has more than 40,000 pieces listed for sale. In all fairness, perhaps most of these of objects derive from personal collections. The problem is, however, that buyers cannot be sure the artifacts have not been stolen from a museum or thoughtlessly dug out of the earth. As a result, the unwary purchaser may be unintentionally contributing to the destruction of archaeological sites by frequenting the website.

Looting is a serious problem at sites of interest to historical archaeologists. Developers seek to build rows of houses on top of old settlements and hobbyists destroy archaeological deposits with their unscientific digging. Many amateur archaeologists might throw up their hands in horror at the destruction of Carrickmines Castle, but they may believe no harm results from running metal detectors over sites in search of coins, buttons, bullets, and other collectibles. After all, historical records, photographs, and even living people have already documented such things. Isn't this enough? Ignoring or being unaware of the information contained in this book, they dismiss or simply do not understand the value of the archaeology of recent history.

Military encampments and battlefields are especially plagued with collectors who have a passionate urge to acquire and sell spent bullets, brass buttons, and other military objects. Bottle hunters tunnel into nineteenth-century trash heaps for patent medicine bottles, old milk and beer bottles, and colorful glass flasks that will fetch money at antique shows or on the internet. Bottle hunters know privies are prime spots for whole specimens, and many avidly seek them. They use long, T-shaped metal probes to locate the soft soils of an abandoned privy, then feverishly dig into it, destroying layer after layer of stratified information in the quest for a discarded, whole bottle. A market that pays hundreds, or even thousands, of dollars for a single specimen fuels their search. These so-called "bottle diggers" know money is to be made in selling archaeological finds. The irony is that many of these diggers are extremely interested in archaeology and often quite knowledgeable about history.

An important program for educating metal detector enthusiasts has been developed at Montpelier, Virginia, the tobacco plantation home of James Madison, the fourth president of the United States. Here, rather than to maintain an adversarial relationship with metal detectorists, archaeologists at the site, led by Matthew Reeves, have created a certification program. This program is designed to explain basic archaeological field methods to metal detector users. The goal is to educate rather than chide, and it works extremely well, as the program is wildly successful. Participants come away with a true understanding of archaeological principles, including understanding the damage they can do to fragile sites by random digging. Students in the program also learn to appreciate archaeology as more than an artifact-based discipline. They learn the significance of context and discover all the information archaeologists can extract from tiny artifacts, microscopic seeds, and cut animal bones. They also learn to appreciate the need for site preservation and protection.

These programs have also illustrated that metal detector surveys are a powerful tool for finding ephemeral sites, places nearly invisible to standard survey techniques. Systematic metal detector surveys (conducted within a standardized grid) have successfully located sites occupied for short periods, such as temporary cabins of the enslaved, barns, and work areas missed by shovel testing (see Chapter 7). An added bonus is that the metal detector surveys do not disturb the sites in any way.

The techniques being used to engage with metal detectorists at Montpelier are at the same time expanding the boundaries of metal detector use as a remote sensing device. The use of metal detectors in serious archaeological research empowers metal detector hobbyists, while instilling in them site preservation ethos and creating new advocates for archaeology.

Many professional historical archaeologists keep large, personal artifact collections, usually acquired by purchase or culled from archaeological site assemblages. They use these collections to train students in artifact identification and for comparative purposes. These "type" or "reference" collections are valuable sources of information when they are composed of non-looted objects. Random collections lacking archaeological context are merely objects with little scientific merit.

The Future of Historical Archaeology

Where does the future of historical archaeology lie? Much depends on the profession's collective success in saving the past for coming generations, on developing working partnerships with landowners, entrepreneurs, history buffs, descendant communities, and local activists, and in learning to respect the views of the world's indigenous peoples. Creative partnerships will undoubtedly become more commonplace in the future as all segments of society find it easier to join hands to protect the environment and the remains of those who inhabited it before us.

Historical archaeology has exploded around the world. The field has the potential to add new theoretical approaches to social science regardless of its period of interest or sociological emphasis. Many new theoretical perspectives will involve issues fundamental to modern society, especially in the realms of cultural interaction, ethnic diversity, social identity, the creation of racial classifications, changing gender roles, and class inequality. Archaeology is unique in its ability to chronicle processes of cultural change over centuries; historical archaeology is unique because its practitioners have opportunities to investigate recent decades and years, social groups and individuals, the local and the global. Archaeologists investigate historical, social, and cultural changes in material terms, in architectural modifications and ever-shifting fashions of style and design, in created landscapes, and technological innovations.

Most history is anonymous, a chronicle of working men and women going about their business day after day, year after year, leaving no record behind except mundane collections of artifacts, food remains, and building foundations. Such finds are the heart and soul of historical archaeology because they open windows on the dark recesses of history. Archaeological evidence allows us to discover the daily lives of the humble folk often left out of written history. Archaeology illuminates the intricate relationships between men and women, conquerors and conquered, oppressors and oppressed.

Historical archaeologists will continue to rewrite important chapters of history. They will document the complex relations that existed between enslaved African Americans and plantation owners, between Spanish friars and Native Americans living in the shadow of Californian mission walls, between Dutch colonists and indigenous peoples across Asia, and between Christianized Native Americans and New England Puritans. Historical archaeology will continue to mature as increasing numbers of archaeologists choose to examine history from the perspective of multiple scales of analysis, as they devise increasingly refined ways to interpret artifacts, and as they invent new field methods.

Unraveling the complexities of the modern world will require multidisciplinary research—conventional archival work and oral histories, as well as linguistic inquiries, ethnographic investigations, and a truly global form of historical archaeology. Historical archaeology is already a multidisciplinary enterprise, but it will become even more so as multicultural perspectives on recent history assume ever-greater importance. Future definitions of history cannot be confined to the narrow universe of documents alone. The study of history must encompass a broad range of disciplines, with each offering its own contributions. Historical archaeology is one of these disciplines.

Most students interested in archaeology and history will never become professional historical archaeologists. Archaeology as a profession is not for everyone, nor should it be. The goal of this book is not to make every reader into a professional archaeologist. Instead, our hope is that it sparks your commitment to the past, that it provides a background making it possible for you to enjoy history and archaeology for the rest of your life. All of us enjoy a magnificent cultural legacy from the remote and not-so-remote past, a past each generation must preserve for their children and grandchildren. So, whatever your level of interest in archaeology and history, please do all you can to save the past for the future. If the archaeological past is lost, generations to come will wonder why more was not done to save it.

Here are some important guidelines to remember:

- Treat every archaeological site and artifact as a finite resource that, once destroyed, can never be replaced.
- Report archaeological discoveries to responsible archaeological authorities (museums, university or college departments, government agencies, historic preservation organizations, local historical societies).
- Obey all laws relating to archaeological sites and heritage centers.
- Never dig at a site without proper training or supervision, even if you think it is a harmless place to find bottles or other artifacts. All excavation destroys something.

- Never collect archaeological finds from any country for your private collection or for profit.
- Respect all burial grounds because most have profound spiritual significance.

Being Educated in Historical Archaeology

How can a person embark on a career in historical archaeology? A growing number of universities around the world now offer training in the subject, and the number grows yearly. Increasing numbers of career opportunities will become available in historical archaeology over the coming years, especially as more multidisciplinary programs are created at institutions of higher education.

To become a professional archaeologist requires at least a master's degree, and a doctorate degree is needed to conduct serious research and teach at the university level. With good grades and high test scores, undergraduate students can usually obtain admission into a good master's or doctoral program even at universities not offering specific training in historical archaeology. Our advice is to declare a major in anthropology or in history, then design your curriculum, as much as you can, around courses in anthropology, archaeology, history, and geography. Enroll in as much cultural anthropology as possible because these courses will give you a solid background in cultural diversity on a global scale and help you to develop an anthropological perspective. In this manner you will also receive knowledge of cultural and social theory, key elements of today's historical archaeology.

In terms of archaeology itself, you should focus on method and theory as much as on the practical aspects of artifact identification. The more you can learn about excavation methods and past archaeologists' theories, the better prepared you will be for future graduate work. Courses in historiography, archival research methods, and oral history, as well as surveys in regional and world history, will stand you in good stead as you develop your skills in historical research methods. Good historical archaeologists must have a strong background in history and historical analysis. Courses in local history will also instill an appreciation for the smallest scale of analysis and interpretation, and illustrate the connections between the global and the local.

Your studies in geography should include courses in cultural geography, landscape design, settlement and spatial analysis, and GIS. Geographers can teach you about vernacular architecture, about analyzing spatial arrangements of people and settlements, and how to read landscapes.

If you are seriously interested in applying to graduate school, you should plan to attend an archaeological field school. An archaeological site is the classroom, and trowels and shovels are the pens and paper. Field schools have been offered since at least the 1930s, and since the late twentieth century, the number of field schools in historical archaeology has grown every year. Both the Society for Historical Archaeology (SHA) and the Archaeological Institute of America (AIA) maintain lists of field schools. *Archaeology* magazine regularly publishes information about archaeological field schools, and numerous websites contain specific information about how to apply to a field school. Today you can find field schools in almost every corner of the world. You can also ask your archaeology or anthropology professors. They may know of local field schools or be able to steer you toward information sent to their departmental office. They may even be offering their own field school.

A field school is the best opportunity to gain practical field experience and also to find out whether you have an aptitude for fieldwork. It is far better to test yourself in the field before you invest in graduate school. Archaeological excavation and survey can be tough, demanding, and dirty work, and it is not for everyone. Many people with a sincere love of history often find the rigors of fieldwork too onerous.

It may also be possible for you to volunteer in your university's archaeological laboratory or in one at a nearby university. Many departments of anthropology also offer courses in archaeological laboratory methods and material culture analysis. These courses, when coupled with a field school, allow students to handle artifacts, conduct preliminary analysis, and use their computer skills.

Anyone seeking to become a professional researcher and university professor must obtain a doctorate degree. This process takes several years and involves completing a major piece of original research. Increasing numbers of people are electing to obtain a master's in archaeology, frequently specializing in conservation, cultural resource management, and other topics with a strong resource management emphasis. Many of these graduates find jobs in government agencies or in the environmental impact assessment industry.

The choice of a graduate program depends upon many variables, including the specialties of the faculty, the kind of historical archaeology you wish to pursue, and your methodological and theoretical interests. You will be best served by studying with a professional engaged in research that interests you. Your archaeology professors will have contacts in the field and will know which departments best suit your interests. If you are not enrolled at a university or college offering archaeology courses, do not be afraid to e-mail or write to nearby professional archaeologists. In most cases, they will be happy to assist you. Remember, they were once aspiring archaeologists, too.

Finally, and most important: Do not contemplate a career in historical archaeology unless you have a passionate interest in the subject and a sincere commitment to the past. Archaeology is not a field for lukewarm enthusiasm or for those seeking undemanding job security. All archaeological jobs require unwavering dedication, a willingness to relocate, abundant physical and intellectual energy, the ability to tolerate discomfort and low salaries, and, above all, passion and a sense of humor. For those who meet these criteria, archaeology is one of the most satisfying jobs on earth.

Professional archaeological societies promote the highest standards of archaeological research. Most of them have created rigid sets of guidelines to judge the qualifications of archaeologists. The guidelines are stringent because archaeological sites are fragile. They deserve nothing but the best professional attention.

Jobs in Historical Archaeology

Archaeologists generally outnumber paying jobs in the field, so the employment picture is always tight, especially at colleges and universities during times of declining resources. Once, archaeologists only worked in universities and colleges, teaching during the academic year, and perhaps conducting field schools or doing research during the summers. Some archaeologists also found positions in museums. The employment picture has changed dramatically since the late 1970s, as more and more professional opportunities for archaeologists have opened up in government, in nonprofit organizations, and in private consulting companies conducting environmental research and cultural resource management (see Chapter 9). Some archaeologists have administrative positions in their country's antiquities bureaus or other agencies charged with protecting cultural history. These bodies find the historical archaeologists' broad, multidisciplinary training in archaeology, historiography, historic preservation, anthropology, and geography extremely useful. Museums and historical societies also offer opportunities to acquire on-the-job training, and sometimes paid internships.

Useful Addresses

A good place to find resources about historical archaeology are the websites of the major societies created specifically for historical archaeology. We have included their addresses below. These sites are all active as of this writing, but should you have difficulties, simply search under the organization's name.

The Society for Historical Archaeology: www.sha.org/
The Society for Post-Medieval Archaeology: www.spma.org.uk/
The Australasian Society for Historical Archaeology: www.asha.org.au/

Other countries may be creating similar societies. For example, Italy has a post-medieval archaeology website: www.archeologiapostmedievale.it. Readers should repeatedly check various websites to find the latest information.

* * *

In this brief introduction to historical archaeology, we have tried to communicate the excitement of this emerging field. We showed in Chapter 2 that historical archaeology is not a discipline with a long and venerable history. Compared with other kinds of archaeology, it is only an infant. Historical archaeology's youth gives it vitality. The field is exciting, and historical archaeologists are pushing current knowledge to the limit, challenging old interpretations and creating bold, new ones. The rapid accumulation of knowledge in a field as new as historical archaeology is inevitable.

We are not troubled that some of what we have written here will be corrected by our colleagues or even replaced with better and more complex examples. On the contrary, we are excited by the prospect. In the social sciences, knowledge is a process of researching, writing, researching anew, and writing again. Change occurs quickly in historical archaeology. New sites are being excavated all the time and increasing numbers of students are being introduced to the field. Historical archaeologists are exploring parts of the globe that only recently were blank territories on the map of archaeological knowledge. If you are fascinated by the archaeology of recent history and are enthused by its promise, then we welcome you to the field with open arms.

Site Visit: John Russell Cutlery Company, Massachusetts, 1833–1933

To many, industrialization appears as a nameless, faceless monolith. Objects are mass-produced in factories and shipped to stores where customers purchase them. Part of the apparent anonymity of industrialism undoubtedly stems from the mass of often poorly documented workers who actually perform the labor. Men and women who stand by machines all day seldom have the time or energy to go home at night and write their memoirs. The urge to produce mass quantities of commodities for sale and profit is generally begun by a single person who perceives an opportunity and who is socially well positioned enough to take advantage of it. Such was the case with the establishment of the John Russell Cutlery Company in northern Massachusetts.

John Russell, born in 1797, was the son of a jeweler and silversmith who lived in Greenfield, Massachusetts, not far from the Vermont border. As a young man, Russell was a speculator in southern cotton, and after making some money in this endeavor, he decided to return to Massachusetts to develop a cutlery industry. His plan was to compete with the highly successful cutlery industry of Sheffield, England, a name synonymous with quality. In partnership with his brother, Russell began producing chisels in the early 1830s. Their firm became widely known for their innovative production methods, and they even won an award for their chisels in 1834. The company branched out into cutlery by the 1840s and began to produce the famous Green River knife. This knife became *the* tool used by fur trappers throughout the American West. A trapper without a Green River knife was not considered much of a frontiersman. The Russell company continued to prosper throughout the late nineteenth century, but by 1900, only about 11 percent of knives produced in the United States came from companies in Massachusetts. In 1933, the Harrington Cutlery Company, in southern Massachusetts, purchased the Russell company, forming Russell-Harrington Cutlery.

The nature of modern industrialism is such that the owners of capitalist industries must constantly strive to stay profitable and efficient. In their drive for profitability, factory administrators must repeatedly upgrade the production process by buying new equipment or inventing innovative, labor-saving techniques. The productive process at the Russell factory changed from simple hammering to mechanical stamping. Stamping was a speedier manufacturing process workers could accomplish with a minimum of skill and training (Figure 13.3).

The transformation of the labor process was accompanied by a modification of the physical structure of the Russell factory. Workers engaged in hammering could be stationed around the factory and conceivably could manufacture an entire knife at their workbench. With increasing mechanization, the arrangement of workers on the shop floor became segmented and ordered. Workers now engaged in monotonous work. Specialized tasks like grinding and polishing knife blades were organized in neat rows. The jobs were as interchangeable as the workers were because skilled labor decreased as industrialization grew. Piece-workers could not even stand up and get a new knife; young boys took the unfinished knives to them. Workers with the most tedious jobs thus labored continuously. Their work was semi-skilled, so if one worker was out for a day, another worker could be slotted into his place without difficulty.

Late-nineteenth-century factories were more than simply places of work; they also included tenements as workers' quarters. These living spaces were usually planned to be as monotonous and interchangeable as the workers themselves. The Russell company tenements were composed of long rows of three-story brick apartments. The company owned both the factory and the tenements, and the loss of a job also meant the loss of a place to live.

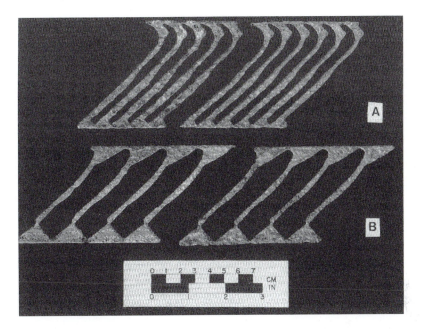

Figure 13.3 Barlow spring and blade cutouts
(From The Social and Political Contexts of Cutlery Production in the Connecticut Valley by Michael S. Nassaney and Marjorie Abel in Dialectical *Anthropology* 18 [1993], fig. 5 © Springer Science.)

The connection between workplace and home had the effect of uniting the processes of living and working. Laboring in the factory for wages under the demands of a foreman was made to seem as natural as living day to day. The link between work and home was made even clearer when families were compelled to take in boarders to make ends meet. Wives of Russell factory workers used the backyards of their apartments for gardening and raising animals for subsistence, and for washing their family's clothes and possibly even the clothes of nearby elite families. Some women even worked in the cutlery factory, but they earned less money than their male counterparts.

Source: Michael S. Nassaney and Marjorie R. Abel, Urban Spaces, Labor Organization, and Social Control: Lessons from New England's Nineteenth-Century Cutlery Industry. In *Lines That Divide: Historical Archaeologies of Race, Class, and Gender,* James A. Delle, Stephen A. Mrozowski, and Robert Paynter (Eds.), pp. 239–275. (Knoxville: University of Tennessee Press, 2000).

Glossary

This glossary gives informal definitions of key words and ideas in the text. It is not a comprehensive dictionary of historical archaeology. Jargon is kept to a minimum, but a few technical expressions are inevitable. Some terms commonly used in archaeology but not specifically described in this book are also included for convenience.

absolute dating: Dating in calendar years before the present; see **chronometric dating**.

action archaeology: Archaeological research directed toward helping to solve some of the problems faced by modern society, such as overcrowding, pollution, and environmental degradation; seeks to help by providing information about problems faced and solved in the past as lessons for today.

activist archaeology: Archaeological research with an overt politically stated message; generally designed to assist local communities to accomplish a goal somehow related to the past.

activity area: A spatial patterning of artifacts and other materials indicating a specific activity, such as bone button making, once took place there.

analogy: A process of reasoning whereby two entities sharing some similarities are assumed to share others.

analysis: A stage of archaeological research involving description, organization, and interpretation of all amassed information.

anthropology: The study of humanity in the widest possible sense, from the earliest times to the present; includes sociocultural and biocultural anthropology, anthropological linguistics, and anthropological archaeology.

anthropological archaeology: A form of anthropology studying extinct human societies or extinct phases of surviving cultures using material remains; its objectives are to construct culture history, reconstruct past lifeways, study cultural process, and understand the social aspects of daily life.

antiquarian: Someone interested in the past who studies, collects, and perhaps even excavates artifacts in an uncontrolled manner; generally nonanthropological in approach; contrasts with today's professional archaeologists.

archaeological context: See **context**.

archaeological culture: A group of assemblages representing the remains of a cultural expression that no longer exists either at all or in the same way today.

archaeological data: Material recognized as significant by an archaeologist and collected and recorded as part of the research process; consists of artifacts, features, structures, and ecofacts.

archaeological reconnaissance: Systematic attempts to locate, identify, and record the distribution of archaeological sites in natural geographic and environmental contexts.

archaeological theory: Philosophical perspectives providing both a framework and a means for archaeologists to look beyond the material objects for explanations and interpretations of the past.

archaeological unit: Arbitrary unit of ordering established by archaeologists to separate one collection of artifacts in time and space from another for the purpose of analysis.

archaeologist: Someone who studies the past using controlled, systematic methods, with the motive of recording and interpreting past cultures; does not collect artifacts for profit or personal display.

archaeomagnetic dating: Chronometric dating using magnetic alignments from buried features, such as ceramic kilns, that can be compared with known fluctuations in the earth's magnetic field; produces a date in years.

area excavation: Excavation of a large, horizontal area, usually intended to expose houses and village settlement patterns.

artifact: Any object manufactured or modified by human beings.

assemblage: The sum of artifacts found at a site, includes subassemblages.

association: The relationship between an artifact and other archaeological finds and features at a site.

attribute: A well-defined feature of an artifact that cannot be further subdivided; archaeologists identify types of attributes, including form, style, and technology, to interpret artifacts.

attribute analysis: Analyzing artifacts using their physical features; the features, or attributes, are studied qualitatively and quantitatively to produce clusters of characteristics used to identity discrete subassemblages of artifacts.

burial site: An archaeological site once used for burying the dead, including cemeteries.

ceramics: Objects of fired clay; historical archaeologists usually use the term to refer to glazed and unglazed pieces of fine earthenware, course earthenware, stoneware, and porcelain; see **pottery**.

chronological types: Artifact forms that serve as time markers.

chronometric dating: Dating in years before the present; absolute dating.

class: Two definitions: in archaeology, the name for an idealized kind of artifact, like "bottles," that can be broken down into specific types, like "wine bottles," "milk bottles," and so on—unlike groups, classes exist independently of specific collections of artifacts; in a wider context, a group of people who have a similar relationship to the structure of social control in a society, and who possess similar amounts of power over the allocation of wealth, privilege, resources, and technology.

classical archaeology: The study of the ancient Greek and Roman civilizations.

classification: The ordering of archaeological data into discrete classes, using various ordering methods.

cognitive archaeology: A theoretical approach concerned with mental patterns existing behind material culture.

colonialism: The movement of people from one place to another with the intention of making lasting settlements; characterized by the domination of a technologically superior culture over less technological cultures.

commodity: An object specifically created for trade.

community: In archaeology, the tangible remains of the activities of the maximum number of people who together occupy a settlement during any one period.

community archaeology: Archaeological research typically completed with local collaboration; involves nonarchaeologists in the entire research process from design to publication.

component: An association of all the artifacts from one occupation level or chronological period of a site.

context: The position of an archaeological find in time and space, established by measuring and assessing its associations, matrix, and provenience; includes the study of what has happened to the find since being buried in the soil.

critical theory: A theoretical approach to archaeology assuming that archaeologists have an active impact on their society; includes the idea that today's interpretations are never truly value-free.

crop marks: Differential growth in crops and other vegetation revealing the outlines of archaeological sites beneath the ground surface; not crop circles!

cross-dating: Dating of sites by objects of known age or with textual records of known age.

cultural evolution: A theory similar to that of biological evolution, arguing that human cultures change gradually throughout time as a result of a number of historical processes.

cultural materialism: A combination of critical theory and materialism in historical archaeology.

cultural process: An approach to archaeological research studying the changes and interactions in cultural systems and the processes by which human cultures change throughout time.

cultural resource management: The study, inventory, and preservation of archaeological sites and historic properties as a means of protecting them from destruction; abbreviated as CRM; also called contract or commercial archaeology.

cultural system: A view that perceives culture and its environment as composed of a number of linked subsystems; change occurs through a series of minor, linked variations in one or more of the subsystems.

culture: A set of designs for living helping to mold a people's response to different situations; culture is the primary means of adapting to an environment; a "culture" in archaeology is a term referring to similar assemblages of artifacts found at several sites, defined in a precise context of time and space; the second meaning is seldom used in historical archaeology.

culture area: A geographic or research area in which general cultural homogeneity is found.

culture contact: The meeting of two cultures never before acquainted with one another; in historical archaeology the term typically refers to the first meeting between Europeans and indigenous peoples.

culture history: An approach assuming artifacts can be used to create a generalized picture of human culture through long temporal periods and across great spatial distances.

DAACS: Digital Archaeological Archives of Comparative Slavery; database cataloguing artifacts discovered at archaeological sites inhabited or associated with the African American enslaved; includes information from sites in the Chesapeake, South Carolina, Tennessee and the Caribbean islands of Jamaica, Nevis, and St. Kitts.

datum point: A location from which all measurements at a site are made; usually tied to an identifiable point, such as an elevation benchmark.

deduction: A process of reasoning involving testing generalizations by generating hypotheses and testing them with data; deductive research is cumulative and involves constant refining of hypotheses; contrasts with inductive approaches where one proceeds from specific observations to general conclusions.

dendrochronology: A dating method using the growth rings of trees.

descriptive type: Category based on the physical, observable properties of an artifact.

direct historical analogy: Analogy using historical records or historical ethnographic data.

direct historical approach: Archaeological technique of working backward in time from historic-period sites of known age to earlier times; usually only used where little migration has occurred, such as the American Southwest.

domestic site: A place where people lived and conducted household activities.

ecofacts: Things modified and used by humans but not exactly created by them; artifacts such as seeds and cut bones.

ethnic group: A collection of people who share enough common physical and cultural characteristics to define themselves as a group; they perceive their group as distinct from all others.

ethnicity: The characteristics a group accepts as pertinent to them.

ethnoarchaeology: A form of ethnography mostly concerning material remains and their uses; archaeologists use it to document the relationships between human behavior and the patterns of artifacts and food remains in the archaeological record; also called living archaeology.

ethnobotany: The study of the cultural use of plants.

ethnography: A descriptive, in-depth examination of a specific culture.

ethnohistory: The study of the past using indigenous oral traditions, textual sources, and often, but not necessarily, archaeological research.

ethnology: The comparative study of several cultures.

Eurocentrism: A belief that Europeans are superior to all other peoples in the world; a potent force during the European Age of Discovery.

European Age of Discovery: The period of Western global expansion, ca. 1415 to about 1800 C.E.

excavation: The digging of archaeological sites, removal of the soil matrix, observance of the proveniences and contexts of the finds therein, and the recording of all information in a three-dimensional manner.

exchange system: A network for trading goods and services between individuals and communities.

experimental archaeology: The use of carefully controlled experiments to provide data to aid in interpreting archaeological finds and procedures.

feature: An artifact, such as a house or storage pit, that can be excavated but not removed from an archaeological site.

form: The physical characteristics—size and shape or composition—of any archaeological find; an essential part of attribute analysis.

form analysis: Analysis of artifacts based on the assumption that shape directly reflects function.

formation processes: Humanly caused or natural processes by which an archaeological site is modified during and after occupation and abandonment; ongoing while an archaeological site exists.

foot (or pedestrian) survey: Archaeological reconnaissance while walking; often with a set interval between members of the survey team.

formula dating: Absolute dating using artifact attributes, especially applied to pipe stems and glazed European ceramics; unique to historical archaeology.

functionalism: The theory that an institution within a society can fulfil all the needs of the people and the entire organization, and that all the institutions work together to ensure the continuation of the culture through time.

functional type: A category based on cultural use or function rather than on outward form or chronological position.

geographic information systems: Computer-generated mapping systems that allow archaeologists to plot and analyze site distributions against environmental and other background data derived from remote sensing, digitized maps, and other sources; abbreviated as GIS.

global historical archaeology: Historical archaeology occurring throughout the world; only possible once the field matured and grew in all parts of the world.

globalization: The process whereby products, ideas, and ways of doing things are transmitted from an origination point to the other places on Earth; never total in its extent and reach.

GPS: Global positioning system; used to pinpoint a location on the surface of the Earth using satellites.

ground-penetrating radar (GPR):   A sophisticated scientific tool that helps archaeologists to locate sites underground without excavation; the radar transmits a pulse into the earth and calculates its findings based on the returned pulse.

HABS/HAER survey: Historic American Buildings Survey/Historic American Engineering Record; detailed, precise surveys of notable buildings in the United States; consists of scale drawings and notes.

Harris matrix: A method of graphically representing the relationships between soil layers and features at an archaeological site; invented by Edward Harris.

historical archaeology: The study of archaeological sites in conjunction with text-based records and other kinds of information; once called "historic sites (or site) archaeology" in Europe, generally called Post-Medieval Archaeology.

historical structuralism: An approach to historical archaeology that tries to discover the hidden themes of a culture.

historiography: The study of how history is written.

history: Two definitions: the study of the past with written records and other sources, often excluding archaeology; what happened in the past.

horizon: A widely distributed set of cultural traits and artifact assemblages whose distribution and chronology allow one to assume they spread rapidly; often indicated by artifacts associated with widespread, distinctive beliefs.

horizontal (area) excavation: Archaeological investigation designed to uncover large areas of a site, especially settlement layouts and entire buildings and yards.

household: A group of people who lived together.

humanistic historical archaeology: Archaeological research intended to complement the humanistic understanding of culture history; heavily reliant on historical rather than anthropological concepts and sources.

ideology: Two definitions: beliefs intended to hide the reality of daily life by using slogans, expressions, and attitudes that appeal to people on a visceral level; a people's knowledge or beliefs developed as part of their culture.

induction: Reasoning by which one proceeds from specific observations to general conclusions.

industrial archaeology: The study of sites showing some evidence of production; sometimes used to refer specifically to the Industrial Revolution and later.

industrial site: In historical archaeology, a location where manufacturing of commodities takes place; any place where some production has occurred.

inorganic materials: Objects that are not part of the animal or vegetable kingdom.

interpretation: The research stage during which the results of archaeological analyses are synthesized and explained.

interpretive archaeology: An approach to archaeological interpretation stressing the commonality of humanity; seeks to transcend boundaries of time to engage present-day individuals with people in the past using shared features of human life, such as childrearing.

kinship: Relationships between people based on real or imagined descent or marriage; imposes mutual obligations on all members of a related group; such ties exist at the core of most societies.

landscape archaeology: Archaeological research directed toward the survey, study, and interpretation of specified pieces of territory; includes houses, yards, fences, outbuildings, roads, and other human-built features.

living museum: A place where the past has been recreated for the sake of modern-day visitors; attempts to increase an awareness of history in tourists and the general public.

magnetometer: A subsurface detection device measuring minor variations in the earth's magnetic field; locates archaeological features without disturbing the soil.

maritime archaeology: Archaeology conducted at locales related to shipping, seaside activities, or coastal settlement; encompasses underwater archaeology.

markers' marks: Manufacturing marks drawn, etched, or stamped onto mass-produced ceramics, glassware, and metals; also called hallmarks.

material culture: All the objects with which people surround themselves; ranging from the kitchen stove to the patterns produced by a marching band on a football field.

materialism: Theoretical perspectives where the reality of physical matter takes precedence over ideas and thought processes.

mean ceramic dating formula: A formula used for assigning the temporal association of a collection of glazed ceramics by the cumulative ranges of their manufacture; abbreviated as MCD.

microhistory: The historical examination of a past person's or community's life in intimate detail; one goal is to use the example as a way to understand a wider historical context.

military site: An archaeological site where military activities took place; campsites, battlefields, and fortifications.

mitigation: In archaeology, measures taken to minimize destruction of archaeological sites.

MNV: Minimum number of vessels; a counting method used by historical archaeologists to determine the fewest number of ceramic vessels present in an assemblage or collection.

model: A theoretical construction of a set of phenomena, devised for better understanding; archaeological examples can be descriptive or explanatory.

modern-world archaeology: A kind of historical archaeology designed to investigate the historical roots of the modern world; concentrates on the union of Eurocentrism, capitalism, colonialism, and racialization.

multipurpose site: An archaeological locale where numerous activities took place.

National Register of Historic Places: In the United States, a federal list of places and properties deemed notable in American history; includes archaeological sites, standing structures, and entire districts of buildings.

neighborhood: A group of households within a well-defined area.

oral history: The collection of personal memories from living individuals with the goal of learning about a time or event.

oral tradition: Beliefs, customs, and ideas passed from generation to generation by word of mouth; can include genealogies.

ordering: In archaeology, the arranging of artifacts in logical categories; often chronological.

organic materials: Materials such as bone, wood, horn, or hide that were once living organisms.

pontil scar: The characteristic mark left on the base of glass vessels by breaking off the glass blower's rod.

Post-Medieval Archaeology: The name of historical archaeology in places like Europe, where a long tradition of literacy exists; the post-medieval period immediately follows the medieval period, however defined.

post-processual archaeology: Theoretical approaches critical of processual archaeology and emphasizing social factors in human societies.

POTS: Potomac Typological System, a system for classifying ceramics used in the Chesapeake Bay area of Virginia and Maryland.

pottery: Generally used by historical archaeologists to refer to unglazed, low-fired clay objects made by indigenous peoples; contrast with ceramics.

primary context: An undisturbed association, matrix, and provenience.

primary source: An original historical source, like a letter written by a direct observer.

privy: A toilet; usually a building outdoors.

probate records: A list of a dead individual's estate; an important source of historical information.

process: In archaeology, the cultural changes occurring over time as people find new ways of doing things and different ways of interacting with their environment.

provenience: The position of an archaeological find in time and space, recorded three-dimensionally.

public archaeology: Archaeology for the "public good"; the original name for cultural resource management archaeology.

racialization: A social process whereby some people are designated as inferior based on physical, cultural, or social variables.

radiocarbon dating: An absolute dating method for measuring the decay rate of the carbon isotope, carbon 14, to stable nitrogen; seldom used in historical archaeology.

region: A geographically defined area in which cultural patterns are basically similar.

relative chronology: Time scale developed by the law of superposition or artifact ordering.

remote sensing: Reconnaissance and site survey methods using such devices as aerial photography to detect subsurface features and sites.

research design: A carefully formulated and systematic plan for executing archaeological research.

resistivity survey: The measurement of differences in electrical conductivity in soils; used in archaeology to detect buried features such as walls and ditches.

Sanborn maps: Maps produced by the D. A. Sanborn National Insurance Diagram Bureau (later, the Sanborn Map and Publishing Company) beginning in the mid-nineteenth century; show the location and construction type of buildings in cities and towns.

scale: In archaeology, referring to the focus of analysis, extending from the very small (local) to the extremely large (global); a major concern of modern-world archaeology.

secondary context: An archaeological find that has been disturbed by subsequent human activity or natural phenomena.

secondary source: A historical source that draws upon primary sources.

settlement archaeology: The investigation of residential, industrial, and other patterns of design and placement of buildings.

settlement pattern: Distribution of human locations on a landscape.

sherd: A fragment of pottery or ceramic; also spelled "shard."

shovel test: A small excavation used to investigate the subsurface character of an archaeological site; in historical archaeology, typically measures about the size of a shovel's width.

significance: In cultural resource management, the assessed importance of an archaeological site or historic property to provide important information about history, people, and events.

site: Any place where objects, features, or other finds manufactured or modified by human beings are found; can range from a house to a quarry.

site plans: Specially prepared maps for recording the horizontal provenience of artifacts, food remains, and features; usually keyed to topographic maps.

site survey: The collection of surface data and the evaluation of a site's archaeological significance.

slip: A fine, wet clay finish applied to the surface of a clay vessel before firing and decoration.

society: A group of people who share the same basic beliefs, attitudes, customs, and traditions and who regularly interact.

sociocultural anthropology: Anthropology focused on the customs and traditions of living societies throughout the world.

soil phosphate analysis: Geochemical tests measuring the phosphate levels in the soil to detect the presence of human settlement beneath the ground; requires minimal disturbance of the soil.

sonar: Underwater detection using sound waves.

stratification: Two definitions: the formation by natural processes of geological layers; the hierarchical formation of social classes in human societies.

stratigraphy: Analysis of the superimposed layers at an archaeological site.

stratum: Two definitions: a single layer of soil; a social level in a hierarchical society.

structuralism: A perspective attempting to discover the hidden themes in a culture.

stylistic analysis: Artifact analysis concentrating not only on form and function, but on the decorative styles used by the makers; a much-used approach in ceramic analysis.

subassemblage: Association of artifacts denoting a particular activity practiced by a society or culture; a division created from an assemblage.

subsurface testing: Any small-scale archaeological excavation.

surface survey: The collection of archaeological finds from sites, with the objective of gathering representative samples of artifacts from the surface; establishes the types of activities at the site, locates major structures, and gathers information on the most densely occupied areas of a site that may be productive for excavation.

synthesis: The assemblage and analysis of data preparatory to interpretation.

taxonomy: An ordered set of operations resulting in the subdividing of objects into ordered categories.

test pit: An excavation unit used to sample a site before large-scale excavation or to check surface surveys; often 1x1 meter size in historical archaeology.

text-aided archaeology: A name for the broad combination of archaeological and historical sources.

topographic maps: Maps showing the features of a natural landscape; extensively used to plot archaeological sites.

total excavation: Complete investigation of an archaeological site; usually confined to small sites such as cellars, cabins, and privies.

type: In archaeology, a collection of artifacts created for comparison with other collections; may not coincide with the actual categories used by the original manufacturers.

UAV: Unmanned aerial vehicle; refers to hobbyists' airplanes and helicopters used to survey and photograph archaeological sites from the air.

underwater archaeology: Study of archaeological sites and shipwrecks beneath the surface of the water.

unit: In archaeology, an artificial grouping used to describe artifacts; also a single archaeological excavation pit.

vertical excavation: Investigation to establish a chronological sequence, normally covering a limited area.

zooarchaeology: The study of animal remains in archaeology providing information about subsistence practices and past environments.

Guide to Further Reading

The references that follow, though selective, will give you access to the more technical literature of historical archaeology. Any one of several comprehensive method and theory texts on the market will provide you with excellent background to the general principles of archaeology. Much of the literature of historical archaeology appears in professional journals or in reports of limited distribution. We recommend you consult an expert before attacking the more specialist literature. For your convenience, however, we include the archaeological works used to prepare each chapter, as well as a few more general background readings.

Students may wish to read works exploring the humorous side of archaeology. Three excellent, fun books are Paul Bahn's *Bluff Your Way in Archaeology* (Partridge Green, Horsham: Ravette, 1989), and Paul Bahn and Bill Tidy's *Disgraceful Archaeology, or Things You Shouldn't Know About the History of Mankind!* (Stroud, Gloucestershire: Tempus, 1999). A classic is David Macaulay's, *Motel of the Mysteries* (Boston, MA: Houghton Mifflin, 1979).

Professional archaeologists are even beginning to write theory-based novels and even comic books. Interested students should see Adrian Praetzellis's *Death by Theory: A Tale of Mystery and Archaeological Theory* (Walnut Creek, CA: AltaMira, 2000), his *Dug to Death: A Tale of Archaeological Method and Mayhem* (Walnut Creek, CA: AltaMira, 2003), and Johannes H.N. Loubser's *Archaeology: The Comic* (Walnut Creek, CA: AltaMira, 2003).

General Works on Historical Archaeology

The best short account of historical archaeology is James Deetz's widely read *In Small Things Forgotten: The Archaeology of Early American Life*, revised and expanded ed., (Garden City, NY: Anchor Press/Doubleday, 1996). Ivor Noël Hume's *Historical Archaeology* (New York: Alfred A. Knopf, 1972) is a somewhat outdated but still elegant work focusing on European American sites in North America. The same author's *The Virginia Adventure* (New York: Alfred A. Knopf, 1994) is a fascinating account of historical archaeology at Roanoke and Jamestown, Virginia. Mark P. Leone's *Critical Historical Archaeology* (Walnut Creek, CA: Left Coast Press, 2010) provides information about one perspective used by many historical archaeologists. Abundant information about the field also appears in Charles E. Orser, Jr. (Ed.), *The Encyclopedia of Historical Archaeology* (London: Routledge, 2002).

More specialized edited volumes include Steven N. Archer and Kevin M. Bartoy (Eds.), *Between Dirt and Discussion: Methods, Methodology, and Interpretation in Historical Archaeology* (New York: Springer, 2006); Geoff Egan and R. L. Michael (Eds.), *Old and New Worlds* (Oxford: Oxbow, 1999); Lisa Falk (Ed.), *Historical Archaeology in Global Perspective* (Washington, DC: Smithsonian Institution Press, 1991); Pedro P. A. Funari, Martin Hall, and Siân Jones (Eds.), *Historical Archaeology: Back from the Edge* (London: Routledge, 1999); Martin Hall and Stephen W. Silliman (Eds.), *Historical Archaeology* (Malden, MA: Blackwell, 2006); Henrik Harnow, David Cranstone, Paul Belford, and Lene Høst-Madsen (Eds.), *Across the North Sea: Later Historical Archaeology in Britain and Denmark, c. 1500–2000 A.D.* (Copenhagen: University Press of Southern Denmark, 2012); Dan Hicks and Mary C. Beaudry (Eds.), *The Cambridge Companion to Historical Archaeology* (Cambridge: Cambridge University Press, 2006); Teresita Majewski and David Gaimster (Eds.), *International Handbook of Historical Archaeology* (New York: Springer, 2009); Mark P. Leone and Parker Potter, Jr. (Eds.), *The Recovery of Meaning: Historical Archaeology in the Eastern United States*, 2nd ed. (Clinton Corners, NY: Percheron Press, 2003); Randall H. McGuire and Robert Paynter (Eds.), *The Archaeology of Inequality* (Oxford: Basil Blackwell, 1991); Robert L. Schuyler (Ed.), *Historical Archaeology: A Guide to Substantive and Theoretical Contributions* (Farmingdale, NY: Baywood, 1978); Stanley South, *Method and Theory in Historical Archaeology* (New York: Academic Press, 1977); and Stanley South (Ed.), *Research Strategies in Historical Archaeology* (New York: Academic Press, 1977).

Students interested in post-medieval archaeology in Great Britain should consult David Crossley, *Post-Medieval Archaeology in Britain* (Leicester: Leicester University Press, 1990) and Richard Newman, *The Historical Archaeology of Britain, c. 1540–1900* (Stroud, Gloucestershire: Sutton, 2001). Increasing numbers of historical archaeologists are writing monographs detailing their research at individual sites. Three excellent studies are: Kenneth L. Feder, *A Village of Outcasts: Historical Archaeology and Documentary Research at the Lighthouse Site* (Mountain View, CA: Mayfield, 1994); Janet D. Spector, *What This Awl Means: Feminist Archaeology at a Wahpeton Dakota Village* (St. Paul, MN: Minnesota Historical Society Press, 1993); and Samuel Sweitz, *On the Periphery of the Periphery: Household Archaeology at Hacienda San Juan Bautista Tabi, Yucatán, Mexico* (New York, Springer, 2012). A workbook for historical archaeology students has been published: Russell J. Barber's *Doing Historical Archaeology: Exercises Using Documentary, Oral, and Material Evidence* (Englewood Cliffs, NJ: Prentice-Hall, 1994).

Major Journals Covering Historical Archaeology

The major English-language journals dealing solely with historical archaeology are *Historical Archaeology* (published in the U.S. by the Society for Historical Archaeology), *Post-Medieval Archaeology* (published in the UK by the Society for Post-Medieval Archaeology), the *International Journal of Historical Archaeology* (published in the United States by Springer), and the *Australasian Journal of Historical Archaeology* (published by the Australasian Society for Historical Archaeology). Articles by historical archaeologists are beginning to appear with more regularity in professional journals once not inclined to accept manuscripts about more recent history. Students should check these journals for articles about historical archaeology: *American Antiquity, Latin American Antiquity, Antiquity, Journal of Social Archaeology,*

Journal of Field Archaeology, Journal of Conflict Archaeology, and *Archaeologies: Journal of the World Archaeological Congress*.

Chapter 1: What Is Historical Archaeology?

The topics explored in this chapter are discussed, usually superficially, in most of the books mentioned above. For the use of written records in historical archaeology, consult Mary C. Beaudry (Ed.), *Documentary Archaeology in the New World* (Cambridge: Cambridge University Press, 1988) and Barbara J. Little (Ed.), *Text-Aided Archaeology* (Boca Raton, FL: CRC Press, 1992).

Historiography has generated an enormous literature, and students should consult their library's database for the most recent titles. Two classics are Marc Bloch, *The Historian's Craft*, trans. Peter Putnam (New York, Vintage, 1953) and Edward H. Carr, *What Is History?* (New York: Alfred A. Knopf, 1961). A similar work, written by a respected archaeologist, is V. Gordon Childe, *History* (London: Cobbett Press, 1947). More recent essays include: R. F. Atkinson, *Knowledge and Explanation in History: An Introduction in the Philosophy of History* (London: Macmillan, 1978); Daniel J. Boorstin, *Hidden History* (New York: Harper and Row, 1987); and David Hackett Fischer, *Historians' Fallacies: Toward a Logic of Historical Thought* (New York: Harper and Row, 1970). A wonderful book by a historian that makes explicit use of historical archaeology is T. H. Breen, *Imagining the Past: East Hampton Histories* (Reading, MA: Addison-Wesley, 1989). Another of the same author's books with relevance to historical archaeology is T. H. Breen, *The Marketplace of Revolution: How Consumer Politics Shaped American Independence* (New York: Oxford University Press, 2005).

Students wishing to learn how the presentation of history can be skewed should begin with Michael Parenti, *History as Mystery* (San Francisco, CA: City Lights Books, 1999) and Michel-Rolph Trouillot, *Silencing the Past: Power and the Production of History* (Boston, MA: Beacon, 1995).

Eric Wolf, *Europe and the People Without History* (Berkeley, CA: University of California Press, 1984) is indispensable on the European Age of Discovery and issues of interconnectedness. Another superb source is Thomas C. Patterson, *Inventing Western Civilization* (New York: Monthly Review Press, 1997).

Specialist Literature

Armstrong, Douglas V., *The Old Village and the Great House: An Archaeological and Historical Examination of Drax Hall Plantation, St. Ann's Bay, Jamaica*. (Urbana: University of Illinois Press, 1990).

Courtney, Paul, Historians and Archaeologists: An English Perspective. *Historical Archaeology* 41, 2 (2007):34–45.

Hagget, Peter, *The Geographer's Art*. (Oxford: Basil Blackwell, 1990).

Hogarth, David G., *Authority and Archaeology: Sacred and Profane*. (London: John Murray, 1899).

Schmidt, Peter R., *Historical Archaeology: A Structural Approach in an African Culture*. (Westport, CT: Greenwood, 1978).

Schuyler, Robert L., Historical Archaeology and Historic Sites Archaeology as Anthropology: Basic Definitions and Relationships. *Historical Archaeology* 4 (1970):83–89.

———, Parallels in the Rise of the Various Subfields of Historical Archaeology. *Conference on Historic Site Archaeology Papers* 10 (1977):2–10.

Chapter 2: A Brief History of Historical Archaeology

Father Martin's excavations at Sainte Marie appear in Kenneth E. Kidd's *The Excavation of Ste. Marie I* (Toronto: University of Toronto Press, 1949), and mention of Hall's excavations can be found in Deetz's Late Man in North America: Archaeology of European Americans, in *Anthropological Archaeology in the Americas* (Washington, DC: Anthropological Society of Washington, 1968) pp. 121–130. In addition to Leone and Potter's *The Recovery of Meaning* and McGuire and Paynter's *The Archaeology of Inequality* already mentioned, case studies in contemporary historical archaeology can be found in the special issue of *Historical Archaeology* "Meanings and Uses of Material Culture," Barbara J. Little and Paul A. Shackel (Eds.), 26 (1992).

Increasing numbers of books and articles are being written about civic engagement in archaeology. Good places to start are Sonya Atalay's *Community-Based Archaeology: Research with, by, and for Indigenous and Local Communities* (Berkeley, CA: University of California Press, 2012); Barbara J. Little and Paul A. Shackel's (Eds.) *Archaeology as a Tool of Civic Engagement* (Lanham, MD: AltaMira Press, 2007); and Michael S. Nassaney and Mary Ann Levine's (Eds.) *Archaeology and Community Service Learning* (Gainesville, FL: University Press of Florida, 2009).

Specialist Literature

Baker, Vernon G., *Historical Archaeology at Black Lucy's Garden, Andover, Massachusetts: Ceramics from the Site of a Nineteenth Century Afro-American.* (Andover, MA: Philips Academy, 1978).

Beaudry, Mary C. and Stephen A. Mrozowski (Eds.), *Interdisciplinary Investigations of the Boott Mills, Lowell, Massachusetts, Volume I: Life at the Boarding Houses, A Preliminary Report.* (Boston: National Park Service, 1987).

Binford, Lewis R., Archaeology as Anthropology. *American Antiquity* 28 (1962):217–225.

Cohn, Bernard S., An Anthropologist among the Historians: A Field Study. *The South Atlantic Quarterly* 61 (1962):13–28.

Deagan, Kathleen, Avenues of Inquiry in Historical Archaeology. In *Advances in Archaeological Method and Theory*, vol. 5, Michael B. Schiffer (Ed.), pp. 151–177. (New York: Academic Press, 1982).

Delle, James A., *An Archaeology of Social Space: Analyzing Coffee Plantations in Jamaica's Blue Mountains.* (New York: Plenum, 1998).

Fish, Carl Russell, Relation of Archaeology and History. *Proceedings of the State Historical Society of Wisconsin at the Fifty-Eighth Annual Meeting Held October 20, 1910*, pp. 146–152. (Madison: State Historical Society of Wisconsin, 1911).

Fontana, Bernard L., On the Meaning of Historic Sites Archaeology. *American Antiquity* 31 (1965):61–65.

Greenman, Emerson F., *Old Birch Island Cemetery and the Early Historic Trade Route, Georgian Bay, Ontario.* (Ann Arbor: University of Michigan Press, 1951).

Hagen, Richard S., Back-Yard Archaeology at Lincoln's Home. *Journal of the Illinois State Historical Society* 44 (1951):340–348.

Hardesty, Donald C., *The Archaeology of Mining and Miners: A View from the Silver State.* (Tucson, AZ: Society for Historical Archaeology, 1988).

Harrington, J.C., Archaeology as an Auxiliary Science of American History. *American Anthropologist* 7 (1955):1121–1130.

———, *New Light on Washington's Fort Necessity.* (Richmond, VA: Eastern National Park and Monument Association, 1957).

Hodder, Ian, *Reading the Past: Current Approaches to Interpretation in Archaeology*. (Cambridge: Cambridge University Press, 1986).

Isaac, Rhys, *The Transformation of Virginia, 1740–1790*. (Chapel Hill: University of North Carolina Press, 1982).

Jelks, Edward B., Archaeological Explorations at Signal Hill, Newfoundland, 1965–1966. *Canadian Historic Sites: Occasional Papers in Archaeology and History*, no. 7. (Ottawa: National Historic Sites Service, 1973).

Kidd, Kenneth E., *The Excavation of Ste: Marie I.* (Toronto: University of Toronto Press, 1949).

Leone, Mark P., Interpreting Ideology in Historical Archaeology: Using the Rules of Perspective in the William Paca Garden in Annapolis, Maryland. In *Ideology, Power, and Prehistory*, Daniel Miller and Christopher Tilley (Eds.), pp. 25–35. (Cambridge: Cambridge University Press, 1984).

Little, Barbara J., Archaeology and Civic Engagement. In *Archaeology as a Tool of Civic Engagement*, Barbara J. Little and Paul A. Shackel (Eds.), pp. 1–22. (Lanham, MD: AltaMira, 2007).

Mouer, L. Daniel, Chesapeake Creoles: The Creation of Folk Culture in Colonial Virginia. In *The Archaeology of 17th-Century Virginia*, T.R. Reinhart and D.J. Pogue (Eds.), pp. 105–166. (Courtland: Archaeological Society of Virginia, 1993.).

Paynter, Robert, Historical and Anthropological Archaeology: Forging Alliances. *Journal of Archaeological Research* 8 (2000):1–37.

———, Historical Archaeology and the Post-Columbian World of North America. *Journal of Archaeological Research* 8 (2000):169–217.

Shackel, Paul A. and Barbara J. Little (Eds.), *Historical Archaeology of the Chesapeake*. (Washington, DC: Smithsonian Institution Press, 1994).

South, Stanley, *Method and Theory in Historical Archaeology*. (New York: Academic Press, 1977).

Wheaton, Thomas R. and Patrick W. Garrow, Acculturation and the Archaeological Record in the Carolina Lowcountry. In *Archaeology of Slavery and Plantation Life*, Theresa A. Singleton (Ed.), pp. 239–259. (Orlando: Academic Press, 1985).

Woolworth, Alan and Raymond Wood, The Archaeology of a Small Trading Post. *River Basin Survey Papers, Bulletin 176*. (Washington, DC: U.S. Government Printing Office, 1960).

Yentsch, Anne, Chesapeake Artifacts and Their Cultural Context: Pottery and the Food Domain. *Post-Medieval Archaeology* 25 (1991):25–72.

Chapter 3: Culture, History, and Archaeological Sites

Anthropologists have written numerous books about the history, nature, and future directions of their discipline. An excellent and very readable history of anthropology is Annemarie de Waal Malefijt, *Images of Man: A History of Anthropological Thought* (New York: Alfred A. Knopf, 1974). For a more complete synthesis, see Fred W. Voget, *A History of Ethnology* (New York: Holt, Rinehart, and Winston, 1975). Good collections of readings in anthropology are Paul Bohannan and Mark Glazer (Eds.), *High Points in Anthropology*, 2nd ed. (New York: Alfred A. Knopf, 1988) and Johnnetta B. Cole (Ed.), *Anthropology for the Nineties: Introductory Readings* (New York: The Free Press, 1988).

For archaeology as anthropology see Guy Gibbon *Anthropological Archaeology* (New York: Columbia University Press, 1984). An older source is Mark P. Leone (Ed.),

Contemporary Archaeology: A Guide to Theory and Contributions (Carbondale, IL: Southern Illinois University Press, 1972).

Classic articles on ethnographic analogy and the direct historical approach include: Robert Ascher, Analogy in Archaeological Interpretation, *Southwestern Journal of Anthropology* 17 (1961):317–325; and Julian H. Steward, The Direct Historical Approach to Archaeology, *American Antiquity* 7 (1942):337–343. The use of analogy in historical archaeology: Charles E. Orser, Jr., Ethnohistory, Analogy, and Historical Archaeology, *Conference on Historic Site Archaeology Papers* 13 (1979):1–24; and Robert L. Schuyler, The Use of Historic Analogs in Archaeology, *American Antiquity* 33 (1968):390–392. For analogical reasoning in archaeology, see P. Nick Kardulias, Estimating Population at Ancient Military Sites: The Use of Historical and Contemporary Analogy, *American Antiquity* 57 (1992): 276–287.

Research designs and sampling are controversial issues. Research designs are discussed in Lewis R. Binford, A Consideration of Archaeological Research Design, *American Antiquity* 29 (1963):425–441. For sampling, see James W. Mueller (Ed.), *Sampling in Archaeology* (Tucson, AZ: University of Arizona Press, 1975). Another good source is Stephen Plog, Fred Plog, and Walter Wait, Decision Making in Modern Surveys, in *Advances in Archaeological Method and Theory, Vol. 1,* Michael B. Schiffer (Ed.), pp. 383–421. (New York: Academic Press, 1976).

Many books and articles discuss historic preservation. Books heavily slanted toward archaeology are Thomas F. King, Patricia Parker Hickman, and Gary Berg (Eds.), *Anthropology in Historic Preservation: Caring for a Culture's Clutter* (New York: Academic Press, 1977), and Thomas F. King, *Cultural Resource Laws and Practice: An Introductory Guide* (Walnut Creek, CA: AltaMira, 1998). Two good books about the preservation of historical buildings, towns, and environments are Antoinette J. Lee (Ed.), *Past Meets Future: Saving America's Historic Environments* (Washington, DC: Preservation Press, 1992); and Arthur P. Ziegler, Jr. and Walter C. Kidney, *Historic Preservation in Small Towns: A Manual of Practice* (Nashville, TN: American Association for State and Local History, 1980).

For microhistory, consult Carlo Ginzburg, *The Cheese and the Worms: The Cosmos of a Sixteenth-Century Miller,* John Tedeschi and Anne C. Tedeschi (Trans.) (Baltimore, MD: Johns Hopkins University Press, 1980), and Donna Merwick, *Death of a Notary: Conquest and Change in Colonial New York* (Ithaca, NY: Cornell University Press, 1999). Microhistories are extremely popular, and any good bookstore should have several, as the number of excellent studies grows every year.

Specialist Literature

Beattie, Owen and John Geiger, *Frozen in Time: Unlocking the Secrets of the Doomed 1845 Arctic Expedition.* (New York: Penguin, 1987).

Binford, Lewis R., Smudge Pits and Hide Smoking: The Use of Analogy in Archaeological Reasoning. *American Antiquity* 32 (1967):1–12.

Blackbeard's Queen Anne's Revenge, 1718. <www.qaronline.org>

Boorstin, Daniel, *Hidden History.* (New York: Harper and Row, 1987).

Breen, Colin and Wes Forsythe, The French Shipwreck *La Surveillante,* Lost in Bantry Bay, Ireland in 1797. *Historical Archaeology* 41, 3 (2007):39–50.

Carman, John, *Archaeologies of Conflict.* (London: Bloomsbury, 2013).

Carr, Gillian, The Archaeology of Occupation and the V-Sign Campaign in the Occupied British Channel Islands. *International Journal of Historical Archaeology* 14 (2010): 575–592.

Casella, Eleanor Conlin, "Social Workers": New Directions in Industrial Archaeology. In *Industrial Archaeology: Future Directions*, E. C. Casella and J. Symonds (Eds.), pp. 3–31. (New York: Springer, 2005).

Cherryson, Annia, Zoë Crossland, and Sarah Tarlow, *A Fine and Private Place: The Archaeology of Death and Burial in Post-Medieval Britain and Ireland*. (Leicester: University of Leicester, 2012).

Davidson, James M., "Resurrection Men" in Dallas: The Illegal Use of Black Bodies as Medical Cadavers (1900–1907). *International Journal of Historical Archaeology* 11 (2007):193–220.

de Barros, P. L., The Effect of the Slave Trade on the Bassar Ironworking Society, Togo. In *West Africa During the Atlantic Slave Trade: Archaeological Perspectives*, C. R. DeCorse (Ed.), pp. 59–80. (London: Leicester University Press, 2001).

Fox, Richard Allan, Jr., *Archaeology, History, and Custer's Last Battle: The Little Bighorn Reexamined*. (Norman: University of Oklahoma Press, 1993).

Gibbs, Martin, The Archaeology of Crisis: Shipwreck Survivor Camps in Australasia. *Historical Archaeology* 37, 1 (2003):128–145.

Graff, Rebecca S., Being Toured While Digging Tourism: Excavating the Familiar at Chicago's 1893 World's Columbian Exposition. *International Journal of Historical Archaeology* 15 (2011):222–235.

Handler, Jerome S. and Frederick W. Lange, *Plantation Slavery in Barbados: An Archaeological and Historical Investigation*. (Cambridge: Harvard University Press, 1978).

Harrington, Spencer P. M., Bones and Bureaucrats: New York's Great Cemetery Imbroglio. *Archaeology* 46, 2 (1993):28–38.

Heite, Edward F., *Archaeological Data Recovery on the Collins, Geddes Cannery Site, Road 356A, Lebanon North Murderkill Hundred, Kent County, Delaware*. (Wilmington: Delaware Department of Transportation, 1990).

Kelly, Roger E. and Marsha C. S. Kelly, Arrastras: Unique Western Historic Milling Sites. *Historical Archaeology* 17, 1 (1983):85–95.

Kidder, A. V., *An Introduction to the Study of Southwestern Archaeology, with a Preliminary Account of the Excavations at Pecos*. (New Haven: Yale University Press, 1924).

Lamb, Teresia A., *Preliminary Archaeological Reconnaissance and Assessment of Destrehan Plantation, St. Charles Parish, Louisiana*. (New Orleans: Archaeological and Cultural Research Program, University of New Orleans, 1983).

Lewis, Kenneth E. and Helen W. Haskell, *The Middleton Place Privy: A Study of Discard Behavior and the Archaeological Record*. Research Manuscript 174. (Columbia: South Carolina Institute for Archaeology and Anthropology, 1981).

Linebaugh, D. W., Forging a Career: Roland W. Robbins and Iron Industry Sites in the Northeastern U.S. *Industrial Archaeology* 26 (2000):5–36.

Moore, David D. and Corey Malcom, Seventeenth-Century Vehicle of the Middle Passage: Archaeological and Historical Investigations on the *Henrietta Marie* Shipwreck Site. *International Journal of Historical Archaeology* 12 (2008):20–38.

Mrozowski, Stephen A., Historical Archaeology as Anthropology. *Historical Archaeology* 22, 1 (1988):18–24.

Munson, Patrick J., Comments on Binford's "Smudge Pits and Hide Smoking: The Use of Analogy in Archaeological Reasoning." *American Antiquity* 34 (1969):83–85.

Murray, Jeffrey S., The Mounties of Cypress Hill. *Archaeology* 41, 1 (1988):32–38.

Pastron, Allen G., William C. Hoff's Gold Rush Emporium: Bonanza from Old San Francisco. *Archaeology* 41, 4 (1988):32–39.

————, On Golden Mountain. *Archaeology* 42, 4 (1989):48–53.

Pearce, J., A Late 18th-Century Inn Clearance Assemblage from Uxbridge, Middlesex. *Post-Medieval Archaeology* 34 (2000):144–186.

Rainbird, Paul, Representing Nation, Dividing Community: The Broken Hill War Memorial, New South Wales, Australia. *World Archaeology* 35 (2003):22–34.

Reinhart, Theodore R. (Ed.), *The Archaeology of Shirley Plantation.* (Charlottesville: University Press of Virginia, 1984).

Rice, Prudence M., *Vintage Moquegua: History, Wine, and Archaeology on a Colonial Peruvian Periphery.* (Austin: University of Texas Press, 2011).

Schofield, John, *Combat Archaeology: Material Culture and Modern Conflict.* (London: Duckworth, 2005).

Scott, Douglas D., Richard A. Fox, Jr., Melissa A. Connor, and Dick Harmon, *Archaeological Perspectives on the Battle of the Little Bighorn.* (Norman: University of Oklahoma Press, 1989).

Smith, Ian, Angela Middleton, Jessie Garland, and Naomi Woods, *Archaeology of the Hohi Mission Station, Volume I: The 2012 Excavations.* (Otago, New Zealand: Department of Archaeology and Anthropology, University of Otago, 2012).

Starbuck, David R., *Massacre at Fort William Henry.* (Hanover: University Press of New England, 2002).

Starbuck, David R. and Mary Bentley Dupré, Production Continuity and Obsolescence of Traditional Red Earthenwares in Concord, New Hampshire. In *Domestic Pottery of the Northeastern United States, 1625–1850*, Sarah Peabody Turnbaugh (Ed.), pp. 133–152. (Orlando: Academic Press, 1985).

Stewart, Tamara, Five Cannon Raised at *Queen Anne's Revenge* Shipwreck. *American Archaeology* 17, 4 (2013):10.

Tuck, James, A Sixteenth-Century Whaling Station at Red Bay, Labrador. In *Early European Settlement and Exploration in Atlantic Canada*, G. M. Story (Ed.), pp. 41–52. (St. John's: Memorial University of Newfoundland, 1982).

Tylor, Edward Burnett, *The Origins of Culture, Part I of "Primitive Culture."* (New York: Harper and Row, 1958).

Upward, Geoffrey C., *A Home for Our Heritage: The Building and Growth of Greenfield Village and Henry Ford Museum, 1929–1979.* (Dearborn, MI: Henry Ford Museum Press, 1979).

Van Tilburg, Hans K., *Chinese Junks on the Pacific: Views from a Different Deck.* (Gainesville: University Press of Florida, 2007).

Chapter 4: Time and Space

Context, time, and space are central concepts discussed by any basic archaeological method and theory textbook. David Lowenthal's *The Past is a Foreign Country* (Cambridge: Cambridge University Press, 1985) offers a fascinating commentary on the meaning of time to modern society.

For information about association, superposition, relative chronology, and dating methods in archaeology, consult any basic text for up-to-date descriptions of the various methods. The basics of site formation processes appears in Michael B. Schiffer's *Formation Processes of the Archaeological Record* (Albuquerque, NM: University of New Mexico Press, 1987).

Space and settlement archaeology continue to be major topics in archaeology. Three older, but still very good, studies are K. C. Chang (Ed.), *Settlement Archaeology* (Palo Alto, CA:

National Press, 1968); David L. Clarke (Ed.), *Spatial Archaeology* (London: Academic Press, 1977); and Ian Hodder and Clive Orton, *Spatial Analysis in Archaeology* (Cambridge: Cambridge University Press, 1976). A good settlement study in historical archaeology is Michael J. O'Brien's *Grassland, Forest, and Historical Settlement: An Analysis of Dynamics in Northeast Missouri* (Lincoln, NE: University of Nebraska Press, 1984).

For proxemics see Edward T. Hall, *The Hidden Dimension* (Garden City, NY: Doubleday, 1966). An archaeological discussion of how humans learn about space is Thomas Wynn, *The Evolution of Spatial Competence* (Urbana, IL: University of Illinois, 1989). An archaeological treatment of proxemics is Ruth Tringham (Ed.), *Territoriality and Proxemics: Archaeological and Ethnographic Evidence for the Use and Organization of Space* (Andover, MA: Warner Modular, 1973).

The literature on GIS applications in archaeology is immense and growing. Three useful general introductions are James Connelly and Mark Lane, *Geographical Information Systems in Archaeology* (Cambridge: Cambridge University Press, 2006); chapter 9 of Shannon P. McPherron and Harold L. Dibble, *Using Computers in Archaeology: A Practical Guide* (Boston, MA: McGraw-Hill Mayfield, 2002); and Kathleen Allen, Stanton Green, and Ezra Zubrow (Eds.), *Interpreting Space: GIS and Archaeology* (London: Taylor and Francis, 1990).

Four GIS books for historians are: Ian N. Gregory, *A Place in History: A Guide to Using GIS in Historical Research* (Oxford: Oxbow, 2003); Ian N. Gregory and Paul S. Ell, *Historical GIS: Technologies, Methodologies, and Scholarship* (Cambridge: Cambridge University Press, 2007); Anne Kelly Knowles (Ed.), *Past Time, Past Place: GIS for History* (Redlands, CA: ESRI Press, 2002); and Anne Kelly Knowles and Amy Hillier (Eds.) *Placing History: How Maps, Spatial Data, and GIS are Changing Historical Scholarship* (Redlands, CA: ESRI Press, 2008). At the time of this writing, the University of Houston is hosting the Digital History Site at http://www.digitalhistory.uh.edu/index.cfm. Other sites created by historians and archaeologists are sure to exist as well.

Specialist Literature

Biddle, Martin, The Rose Revisited: A Comedy (?) of Errors. *Antiquity* 63 (1989):753–760.

Binford, Lewis R., A New Method of Calculating Dates from Kaolin Pipe Stem Fragments. *Southeastern Archaeological Conference Newsletter* 9, 1 (1962):19–21.

Burke, Heather, *Meaning and Ideology in Historical Archaeology: Style, Social Identity, and Capitalism in an Australian Town.* (New York: Kluwer Academic/Plenum, 1999).

Catts, Wade P. and Jay F. Custer, *Tenant Farmers, Stone Masons, and Black Laborers: Final Archaeological Investigations of the Thomas Williams Site, Glasgow, New Castle Country, Delaware.* (Wilmington: Delaware Department of Transportation, 1990).

Cotter, John L., Daniel G. Roberts, and Michael Parrington, *The Buried Past: An Archaeological History of Philadelphia.* (Philadelphia: University of Pennsylvania Press, 1992).

Hamilton, Scott, Over-Hunting and Local Extinctions: Socio-Economic Implications of Fur Trade Subsistence. In *Images of the Recent Past: Readings in Historical Archaeology*, Charles Edward Orser, Jr. (Ed.), pp. 416–436. (Walnut Creek, CA: AltaMira, 1996).

Harrington, J. C., Dating Stem Fragments of Seventeenth and Eighteenth Century Clay Tobacco Pipes. *Quarterly Bulletin of the Archaeological Society of Virginia* 9, 1 (1954):10–14.

Harris, Edward C., *Principles of Archaeological Stratigraphy.* (New York: Academic Press, 1979).

Heighton, Robert F. and Kathleen A. Deagan, A New Formula for Dating Kaolin Clay Pipestems. *Conference on Historic Site Archaeology Papers* 6 (1972):220–229.

Kent, Susan, *Analyzing Activity Areas: An Ethnoarchaeological Study of the Use of Space*. (Albuquerque: University of New Mexico Press, 1984).

Lawrence, Susan, *Dolly's Creek: An Archaeology of a Victorian Goldfields Community*. (Melbourne: Melbourne University Press, 2000).

Madry, Scott, The Integration of Historical Cartographic Data within the GIS Environment. In *Between Dirt and Discussion: Methods, Methodology, and Interpretation in Historical Archaeology*, Steven N. Archer and Kevin M. Bartoy (Eds.), pp. 33–60. (New York: Springer, 2006).

Noël Hume, Ivor, *Martin's Hundred: The Discovery of a Lost Colonial Virginia Settlement*. (New York: Delta, 1983).

Orrell, John and Andrew Gurr, What the Rose Can Tell Us. *Antiquity* 63 (1989):421–429.

Praetzellis, Mary and Adrian Praetzellis, *"For a Good Boy": Victorians on Sacramento's J Street*. (Rohnert Park, CA: Anthropological Studies Center, Sonoma State University, 1990).

———, *The Mary Collins Assemblage: Mass Marketing and the Archaeology of a Sacramento Family*. (Rohnert Park, CA: Anthropological Studies Center, Sonoma State University, 1990).

Robinson, William J., Tree-Ring Studies of the Pueblo de Acoma. *Historical Archaeology* 24, 3 (1990):99–106.

Sampeck, Kathryn, Jonathan Thayn, and Howard H. Earnest, Jr., GIS Modeling of De Soto's Route from Joara to Chiaha: Archaeology and Anthropology of Southeastern Road Networks in the Sixteenth Century. *American Antiquity* 80 (2015):46–66.

Sharp, Warren D., Jennifer G. Kahn, Christine M. Polito, and Patrick V. Kirch, Rapid Evolution of Ritual Architecture in Central Polynesia Indicated by Precise ^{230}Th/U Coral Dating. *Proceedings of the National Academy of Sciences of the United States of America* 107 (2010):13234–13239.

South, Stanley, Evolution and Horizon as Revealed in Ceramic Analysis in Historical Archaeology. *Conference on Historic Site Archaeology Papers* 6 (1972):71–116.

Towner, Ronald H. and Pearce Paul Creasman, Historical Dendrochronology in the El Malpais Area: Lessons from the Savage Homestead. *Historical Archaeology* 44, 4 (2010):8–27.

Wernke, Steven A., Spatial Network Analysis of a Terminal Prehispanic and Early Colonial Settlement in Highland Peru. *Journal of Archaeological Science* 39 (2012):1111–1122.

Chapter 5: Site Survey and Location in Historical Archaeology

Much of the information covered in this chapter can be found in Noël Hume's *Historical Archaeology*. The application of subsurface surveying techniques in archaeology is covered in Don H. Heimmer, *Near-Surface, High Resolution: Geophysical Methods for Cultural Resource Management and Archaeological Investigations* (Denver, CO: Interagency Archaeological Services, National Park Service, 1992). Although much of the presentation is technical, this book has a comprehensive bibliography with many sources directly related to historical archaeology. Other extremely useful sources are E.B. Banning, *Archaeological Survey* (New York: Kluwer Academic/Plenum, 2002), and James Wiseman and Farouk El-Baz's (Eds.) *Remote Sensing in Archaeology* (New York: Springer, 2007).

Classic works on reading the landscape are W.G. Hoskins, *The Making of the English Landscape* (New York: Penguin, 1970); E. Sloane, *Our Vanishing Landscape* (New York:

Ballantine, 1974); and M. T. Watts, *Reading the Landscape of America* (New York: Macmillan, 1957).

General books about subsurface surveying in archaeology include Anthony Clark's *Seeing Beneath the Soil: Prospecting Methods in Archaeology* (London: Batsford, 1990) and Irwin Scollar's *Archaeological Prospecting, Image Processing, and Remote Sensing* (Cambridge: Cambridge University Press, 1989). Also useful is the British journal *Archaeometry*.

Classic sources on the earliest efforts to use aerial surveying in archaeology are both by O. G. S. Crawford: *Air Survey and Archaeology* (Southampton: His Majesty's Stationery Office, 1924) and *Air-Photography for Archaeologists* (London: His Majesty's Stationery Office, 1929).

Specialist Literature

Arnold, J. Barto, III, Marine Magnetometer Survey of Archaeological Materials near Galveston, Texas. *Historical Archaeology* 21, 1 (1987):18–47.

Arnold, J. Barto, III, G. Michael Fleshman, Curtiss E. Peterson, W. Kenneth Stewart, Gordon P. Watts, Jr. and Clark P. Weldon, USS *Monitor:* Results from the 1987 Season. *Historical Archaeology* 26, 4 (1992):47–57.

Bailey, Richard N., Eric Cambridge, and H. Denis Briggs, *Dowsing and Church Archaeology.* (Wimborne, Dorset: Intercept, 1988).

Benn, David W. (Ed.), *Big Sioux River Archaeological and Historical Resources Survey, Lyon County, Iowa: Volume I.* (Springfield: Center for Archaeological Research, Southwest Missouri State University, 1987).

Bevan, Bruce W., David G. Orr, and Brooke S. Blades, The Discovery of the Taylor House at the Petersburg National Battlefield. *Historical Archaeology* 18, 2 (1984):64–74.

Clapp, N., *The Road to Ubar: Finding the Atlantis of the Sands.* (Boston: Houghton Mifflin, 1998).

Connor, Melissa and Douglas D. Scott, Metal Detector Use in Archaeology: An Introduction. *Historical Archaeology* 32, 4 (1998):76–85.

Costello, Julia G. and Phillip L. Walker, Burials from the Santa Barbara Presidio Chapel. *Historical Archaeology* 21, 1 (1987):3–17.

Ellwood, Brooks B., Electrical Resistivity Surveys in Two Historical Cemeteries in Northeast Texas: A Method for Delineating Burial Shafts. *Historical Archaeology* 24, 3 (1990):91–98.

Feversham, Polly and Leo Schmidt, The Berlin Wall: Border, Fragment, World Heritage? In *A Fearsome Heritage: Diverse Legacies of the Cold War*, John Schofield and Wayne Cocroft (Eds.), pp. 193–209. (Walnut Creek, CA: Left Coast Press, 2007).

Fife, Lawrence Raymond, *Bach Mã: History and Archaeology at a French Colonial Hill Station, Central Vietnam, 1930–1991.* Doctoral Dissertation, University of New England, Armidale, Australia, 2009.

Fowler, William R., Jr., Francisco Estrada-Belli, Jennifer R. Bales, Matthew D. Reynolds, and Kenneth L. Kvamme, Landscape Archaeology and Remote Sensing of a Spanish-Conquest Town: Ciudad Vieja, El Salvador. In *Remote Sensing in Archaeology*, James Wiseman and Farouk El-Baz (Eds.), pp. 395–421. (New York: Springer, 2007).

Freund, Richard A., *Digging Through History: Archaeology and Religion from Atlantis to the Holocaust.* (Lanham, MD: Rowman and Littlefield, 2012).

Gasco, Janine, Survey and Excavation of Invisible Sites in the Mesoamerican Lowlands. In *Approaches to the Historical Archaeology of Mexico, Central and South America*, J. Gasco, G. C. Smith, and P. Fournier-Garcia (Eds.), pp. 41–48. (Los Angeles: Institute of Archaeology, 1997).

Hill, Austin Chad, Archaeology and UAVs: Legal, Ethical, and Safe Use of Drones for Archaeological Research. *Anthropology News* 54, May/June (2013):29.

Kenyon, Jeff L. and Bruce Bevan, Ground-Penetrating Radar and Its Application to a Historical Archaeological Site. *Historical Archaeology* 11 (1977):48–55.

Mason, Randall J., An Unorthodox Magnetic Survey of a Large Forested Historic Site. *Historical Archaeology* 18, 2 (1984):54–63.

Noël Hume, Ivor, *Archaeology and Wetherburn's Tavern.* (Williamsburg: Colonial Williamsburg Foundation, 1969).

Randi, James, The Matter of Dowsing. *Skeptic* 6, 4 (1998):6–7.

Sonderman, Robert C., Looking for a Needle in a Haystack: Developing Closer Relationships between Law Enforcement Specialists and Archaeology. *Historical Archaeology* 35, 1 (2001):70–78.

Synenki, Alan T. (Ed.), *Archaeological Investigations of Minute Man National Historical Park, Volume I: Farmers and Artisans of the Historical Period.* (Boston: National Park Service, 1990).

Thakuria, Tilok, Tosabanta Padhan, Rabindra Kumar Mohanty, and Monica L. Smith, Google Earth as an Archaeological Tool in the Developing World: An Example from India. *The SAA Archaeological Record* 13, 1 (2013):20–24.

Ur, Jason, CORONA Satellite Photography and Ancient Road Networks: A Northern Mesopotamian Case Study. *Antiquity* 77 (2003):102–115.

von Frese, Ralph R.B., Archaeomagnetic Anomalies of Midcontinental North American Archaeological Sites. *Historical Archaeology* 18, 2 (1984):4–19.

von Frese, Ralph R.B. and Vergil E. Noble, Magnetometry for Archaeological Exploration of Historical Sites. *Historical Archaeology* 18, 2 (1984):38–53.

Weymouth, John W. and William I. Woods, Combined Magnetic and Chemical Surveys of Forts Kaskaskia and de Chartres Number 1, Illinois. *Historical Archaeology* 18, 2 (1984):20–37.

Whittaker, William E., Testing the Effectiveness of Ground-Penetrating Radar at Three Dragoon Forts in Iowa and Wisconsin. *Historical Archaeology* 43, 4 (2009):56–74.

Chapter 6: Pre-Excavation Fieldwork: Documents, Interviews, Buildings

Several good books on historical methods have been written by trained historians. Older examples include Mary Sheldon Barnes, *Studies in Historical Method* (Boston, MA: D.C. Heath, 1896) and Gilbert J. Garraghan, *A Guide to Historical Method* (New York: Fordham University Press, 1946). A more recent manual is Robert Jones Shafer (Ed.), *A Guide to Historical Method,* 3rd ed. (Homewood, IL: Dorsey, 1974). Also of use is the undergraduate manual, Norman F. Cantor and Richard I. Schneider, *How to Study History* (New York: Thomas J. Crowell, 1967). For general comments, you may wish to consult Jacques Barzun and Henry F. Graff, *The Modern Researcher,* 4th ed. (San Diego, CA: Harcourt Brace Jovanovich, 1985). The journal *Historical Methods* is also a useful source.

For oral history see Willa K. Baum's *Oral History for the Local Historical Society,* 3rd ed. (Nashville, TN: American Association for State and Local History, 1987). This book includes step-by-step instructions by someone who knows a great deal about conducting oral interviews. Transcribing techniques are explained in Willa K. Baum, *Transcribing and Editing Oral History* (Nashville, TN: American Association for State and Local History, 1977) and

Mary Jo Deering, *Transcribing Without Tears: A Guide to Transcribing and Editing Oral History Interviews* (Washington, DC: George Washington University Library, 1976). Louis Gottschalk, Clyde Kluckhohn, and Robert Angell, *The Use of Personal Documents in History, Anthropology, and Sociology* (New York: Social Science Research Council, 1945) and Jan Vansina, *Oral Tradition as History* (Madison, WI: University of Wisconsin Press, 1985) provide important information as well. An oral history text specifically concerning Native Americans is Charles E. Trimble, Barbara W. Sommer, and Mary Kay Quinlan, *The American Indian Oral History Manual: Making Many Voices Heard* (Walnut Creek, CA: Left Coast Press, 2008).

The definitive source on HABS/HAER documentation and surveying is John A. Burns (Ed.), *Recording Historic Structures* (Washington, DC: American Institute of Architects Press, 1989). An excellent source for learning how to assess standing structures as archaeological sites is Richard K. Morriss, *The Archaeology of Buildings* (Stroud, Gloucestershire: Tempus, 2000). Another superb source is Matthew Johnson, *Housing Culture: Traditional Architecture in an English Landscape* (Washington, DC: Smithsonian Institution Press, 1993).

Specialist Literature

Baker, T. Lindsay and Billy R. Harrison, *Adobe Walls: The History and Archaeology of the 1874 Trading Post*. (College Station: Texas A & M University Press, 1986).

Brandon, Jaime C., Reversing the Narrative of Hillbilly History: A Case Study Using Archaeology at Van Winkle's Mill in the Arkansas Ozarks. *Historical Archaeology* 47, 3 (2013):36–51.

Breen, T.H., *Imagining the Past: East Hampton Histories*. (Reading, MA: Addison-Wesley, 1989).

Buscaglia, Silvana, Maria Ximena Senatore, Eugenia Lascano, Victoria Bongiovanni, Matías de la Vega, and Ana Osella, To Protect an Order: Interdisciplinary Perspectives on Spatial Construction in the Spanish Colony of Floridablanca (Patagonia, Eighteenth Century). *Historical Archaeology* 42, 4 (2008):1–20.

Casella, Eleanor Conlin, "That's Just a Family Thing, You Know": Memory, Community Kinship, and Social Belonging in the Hagg Cottages of Cheshire, North-West England. *International Journal of Historical Archaeology* 16 (2013):284–299.

Davidson, James West and Mark Hamilton Lytle, *After the Fact: The Art of Historical Detection*. (New York: Alfred A. Knopf, 1982).

Jurney, David H. and Randall W. Moir (Eds.), *Historic Buildings, Material Culture, and the People of the Prairie Margin*. (Dallas: Archaeology Research Program, Southern Methodist University, 1987).

Landers, Jane, *Fort Mose, Gracia Real de Santa Teresa de Mose: A Free Black Town in Spanish Colonial Florida*. (St. Augustine: St. Augustine Historical Society, 1992).

Shackel, Paul A., Changing the Past for the Present and the Future. *Historical Archaeology* 47, 3 (2013):1–11.

Shew, Dana Ogo and April Elizabeth Kamp-Whittaker, Perseverance and Prejudice: Maintaining Community in Amache, Colorado's World War II Japanese Internment Camp. In *Prisoners of War: Archaeology, Memory, and Heritage of 19th- and 20th-Century Mass Internment*, Harold Mytum and Gilly Carr (Eds.), pp. 303–337. (New York: Springer, 2013).

Smith, Pamela A. and Richard M. Smith, Bricks and Mortar: A Method for Identifying Construction Phases in Multistage Structures. *Historical Archaeology* 43, 2 (2009):40–60.

Sweitz, Sam R., *On the Periphery of the Periphery: Household Archaeology at Hacienda San Juan Bautista Tabi, Yucatán, Mexico*. (New York: Springer, 2012).

Worthy, Linda H., *All That Remains: The Traditional Architecture and Historic Engineering Structures, Richard B. Russell Multiple Resource Area, Georgia and South Carolina*. (Atlanta: National Park Service, 1983).

Chapter 7: Archaeological Fieldwork: Field and Laboratory

Two good sources to begin with are Philip Barker's *Techniques of Archaeological Excavation*, 2nd ed. (New York: Universe, 1982), and Martha Joukowsky's *A Complete Field Manual of Field Archaeology: Tools and Techniques of Field Work for Archaeologists* (Englewood Cliffs, NJ: Prentice-Hall, 1980). Ivor Noël Hume's *Historical Archaeology*, already cited, is a classic, though somewhat outdated, source on fieldwork for historical archaeologists. The field report for Fort Southwest Point: Samuel D. Smith (Ed.), *Fort Southwest Point Archaeological Site, Kingston, Tennessee: A Multidisciplinary Interpretation* (Nashville, TN: Tennessee Department of Environment and Conservation, Division of Archaeology, 1993).

An excellent, easy-to-read book about simple artifact conservation is Per E. Guldbeck's *The Care of Historical Collections: A Conservation Handbook for the Nonspecialist* (Nashville, TN: American Association for State and Local History, 1972). For information about the Wolstenholme Towne helmets see Ivor Noël Hume, First Look at a Lost Virginia Settlement, *National Geographic* 155, 6 (1979):734–767; and his New Clues to an Old Mystery, *National Geographic* 161, 1 (1982):52–77. Wolstenholme Towne is described in the same author's *Martin's Hundred* mentioned above.

For the basics of archaeological typology, you should consult widely available texts. The Potomac Typological System, POTS, appeared in Mary C. Beaudry, Janet Long, Henry M. Miller, Fraser D. Neiman, and Garry Wheeler Stone, A Vessel Typology for Early Chesapeake Ceramics: The Potomac Typological System, *Historical Archaeology* 17, 1 (1983):18–43.

Useful information about the goals of archaeological writing can be found in Graham Connah, *Writing About Archaeology* (Cambridge: Cambridge University Press, 2010). Interested students should also read one or two older works in archaeology, written at a time when archaeological books were widely read. Three classics are V. Gordon Childe, *What Happened in History* (Harmondsworth, England: Penguin, 1942); Jacquetta Hawkes and Christopher Hawkes, *Prehistoric Britain* (Harmondsworth, England: Penguin, 1943); and Leonard Woolley, *Digging Up the Past* (Harmondsworth, England: Penguin, 1930).

Important information about innovations in techniques of analysis appears regularly in the Technical Briefs series published by the Society for Historical Archaeology. The briefs can be downloaded from the Society's website.

Specialist Literature

Caporaso, Alicia L., Carl G. Carlson-Drexler, and Joel Masters, Metallurgical Analysis of Shell and Case Shot Artillery from the Civil War Battles of Pea Ridge and Wilson's Creek. *Technical Briefs in Historical Archaeology* 3 (2008):15–24.

Cassitti, Patrick, Daniel Berger, and Benjamin Fourlas, "St. Peter in Volders" and Related Base Metal Figurines Resembling the Famous Statue in the Vatican Basilica. *Post-Medieval Archaeology* 47 (2013):323–358.

Crader, Diana C., The Zooarchaeology of the Storehouse and the Dry Well at Monticello. *American Antiquity* 49 (1984):542–558.

———, Slave Diet at Monticello. *American Antiquity* 55 (1990):690–717.

Durst, Jeffrey J., Sourcing Gunflints to Their Country of Manufacture. *Historical Archaeology* 43, 2 (2009):18–29.

Felicísimo, Ángel M., María-Eugenia Polo, and Juan A. Peris, Three-Dimensional Models of Archaeological Objects: From Laser Scanners to Interactive PDF Documents. *Technical Briefs in Historical Archaeology* 7 (2013):13–18.

Harmon, James M., Mark P. Leone, Stephen D. Prince, and Marcia Snyder, LiDAR for Archaeological Landscape Analysis: A Case Study of Two Eighteenth-Century Maryland Plantation Sites. *American Antiquity* 71 (2006):649–670.

Harris, Edward C., Archaeology and the Ethics of Scientific Destruction. In *Between Dirt and Discussion: Methods, Methodology, and Interpretation in Historical Archaeology*, Steven N. Archer and Kevin M. Bartoy (Eds.), pp. 141–150. (New York: Springer, 2006).

Hayes, Katherine Howlett, Field Excavations at Sylvester Manor. *Northeast Historical Archaeology* 36 (2007):34–50.

Herskovitz, Robert M., *Fort Bowie Material Culture*. (Tucson: University of Arizona Press, 1978).

Jones, Geoffrey, Geophysical Mapping of Historic Cemeteries. *Technical Briefs in Historical Archaeology* 3 (2008):25–38.

Lang, Janet and Andrew Middleton (Eds.), *Radiography of Cultural Material*. (Amsterdam: Elsevier, 2005).

Means, Bernard K., Ashley McCuistion, and Courtney Bowles, Virtual Artifact Curation of the Historical Past and the NextEngine Desktop 3D Scanner. *Technical Briefs in Historical Archaeology* 6 (2013):1–12.

Noël Hume, Ivor, *If These Pots Could Talk: Collecting 2,000 Years of British Household Pottery*. (Milwaukee: Chipstone Foundation, 2001).

Peacey, Allan and Alan Vince, Chemical Characterization of Clay Pipes and Wig Curlers from Roy's Orchard, Pipe Aston, Herefordshire. *Post-Medieval Archaeology* 37 (2003):207–216.

Ramenofsky, Ann F., C. David Vaughan, and Michael N. Spilde, Seventeenth-Century Metal Production at San Marcos Pueblo, North-Central New Mexico. *Historical Archaeology* 42, 4 (2008):105–131.

Reitz, Elizabeth J. and C. Margaret Scarry, *Reconstructing Historic Subsistence with an Example from Sixteenth-Century Spanish Florida*. (Tucson, AZ: Society for Historical Archaeology, 1985).

Rice, Prudence M., *Vintage Moquegua: History, Wine, and Archaeology on a Colonial Peruvian Periphery*. (Austin: University of Texas Press, 2011).

Schaefer, Richard G., *A Typology of Seventeenth-Century Dutch Ceramics and Its Implications for American Historical Archaeology*. (Oxford: British Archaeological Reports, 1998).

Skowronek, Russell K., M. James Blackman, and Ronald L. Bishop, Locally-Made or Imported? Identifying Ceramic Composition Variation in the San Francisco Presidio Jurisdiction. *Historical Archaeology* 43, 4 (2009):1–21.

Smith, C. Wayne, The Electronic Darkroom: Turning Bad Photography into Useful Line Art. *Technical Briefs in Historical Archaeology* 1 (2006):1–5.

———, Expanded Spectrum Photography and Archaeological Conservation. *Technical Briefs in Historical Archaeology* 5 (2010):16–19.

Souza, Marcos André Torres de and Luís Cláudio Pereira Symanski, Slave Communities and Pottery Variability in Western Brazil: The Plantations of Chapada dos Guimarães. *International Journal of Historical Archaeology* 13 (2009):513–548.

Stone, Lyle M., *Fort Michilimackinac, 1715–1781: An Archaeological Perspective on the Revolutionary Frontier.* (East Lansing: The Museum, Michigan State University, 1974).

Straube, Beverly A., Surprises from the Soil: Archaeological Discoveries from England's First Successful Transatlantic Colony at Jamestown. *Post-Medieval Archaeology* 47 (2013):263–280.

Switzer, R. R., *The Bertrand Bottles: A Study of 19th-Century Glass and Ceramic Containers.* (Washington, DC: National Park Service, 1974).

Vázquez, Cristina, Susana Boeykens, and Dolores Elkin, The Use of Total Reflection X-Ray Fluorescence in an Underwater Archaeology Case Study. *Technical Briefs in Historical Archaeology* 5 (2010):10–15.

Vince, Alan and Allan Peacey, Pipemakers and Their Workshops: The Use of Geochemical Analysis in the Study of the Clay Tobacco Pipe Industry. In *Between Dirt and Discussion: Methods, Methodology, and Interpretation in Historical Archaeology*, Steven N. Archer and Kevin M. Bartoy (Eds.), pp. 11–31. (New York: Springer, 2006).

Voss, Barbara L. and Rebecca Allen, Guide to Ceramic MNV Calculation Qualitative and Quantitative Analysis. *Technical Briefs in Historical Archaeology* 5 (2010):1–9.

Chapter 8: Artifacts in Historical Archaeology

Many authors have discussed material culture. Some relevant studies and essays include: Leland Ferguson (Ed.), *Historical Archaeology and the Importance of Material Things* (California, PA: Society for Historical Archaeology, 1977); Ian M. G. Quimby (Ed.), *Material Culture and the Study of American Life* (New York: W. W. Norton, 1978); and Thomas J. Schlereth (Ed.), *Material Culture Studies in America* (Nashville, TN: American Association for State and Local History, 1982). See also: Arthur Asa Berger, *Reading Matter: Multidisciplinary Perspectives on Material Culture* (New Brunswick, NJ: Transaction, 1992); Mihaly Csikszentmihalyi and Eugene Rochberg-Halton, *The Meaning of Things: Domestic Symbols and the Self* (Cambridge: Cambridge University Press, 1981); Chandra Mukerji, *From Graven Images: Patterns of Modern Materialism* (New York: Columbia University Press, 1983); Robert Blair St. George (Ed.), *Material Life in America, 1600–1860* (Boston, MA: Northeastern University Press, 1988); and Thomas J. Schlereth, *Artifacts and the American Past* (Nashville, TN: American Association for State and Local History, 1980) and *Cultural History and Material Culture: Everyday Life, Landscapes, Museums* (Ann Arbor, MI: UMI Research, 1990). Two wonderful anthropological studies of material objects are Mary Douglas and Baron Isherwood, *The World of Goods* (New York: Basic, 1979) and Nicholas Thomas, *Entangled Objects: Exchange, Material Culture, and Colonialism in the Pacific* (Cambridge: Harvard University Press, 1991).

Interesting books about historical artifacts in Europe, written by nonarchaeologists, include Lisa Jardine, *Worldly Goods: A New History of the Renaissance* (New York: W. W. Norton, 1998); Sarah Richards, *Eighteenth-Century Ceramics: Products for a Civilised Society* (Manchester: Manchester University Press, 1999); Daniel Roche, *A History of Everyday Things: The Birth of Consumption in France, 1600–1800* (Cambridge: Cambridge University Press, 2000); and Raffaella Sarti, *Europe at Home: Family and Material Culture, 1500–1800* (New Haven, CT: Yale University Press, 2002).

The study of artifacts in historical archaeology is a huge topic. A good starting point is Ivor Noël Hume's *A Guide to Artifacts of Colonial America* (New York: Alfred A. Knopf, 1969). The complexities of the subject are well covered in Richard A. Gould and Michael B. Schiffer (Eds.), *Modern Material Culture: The Archaeology of Us* (New York: Academic,

1981); Daniel Miller, *Material Culture and Mass Consumption* (Oxford, England: Basil Blackwell, 1987); and Suzanne Spencer-Wood (Ed.), *Consumer Choice in Historical Archaeology* (New York: Plenum, 1987). Also see Charles R. Ewen's *Artifacts* (Walnut Creek, CA: AltaMira, 2003).

A huge number of books have been written about specific types of artifacts, refined ceramics perhaps leading the list in number. Just four of the available books are Geoffrey A. Godden, *Godden's Guide to Ironstone, Stone, and Granite Wares* (Woodbridge, UK: Antique Collectors' Club, 1999); Jonathan Rickard, *Mocha and Related Dipped Wares, 1770–1939* (Hanover, NH: University Press of New England, 2006); Gaye Blake Roberts (Ed.), *True Blue: Transfer-Printed Earthenware* (East Hagbourne, UK: Friends of Blue, 1998); and Janine E. Skerry and Suzanne Findlen Hood, *Salt-Glazed Stoneware in Early America* (Williamsburg, VA: Colonial Williamsburg Foundation, 2009). Another extremely valuable source is *Ceramics in America*, edited by Robert Hunter and published annually by the Chipstone Foundation and distributed by the University Press of New England, Hanover, NH.

Maker's marks on ceramics and glass: Geoffrey A. Godden, *Encyclopaedia of British Pottery and Porcelain Marks* (New York: Bonanza, 1964) and Julian Harrison Toulouse, *Bottle Makers and Their Marks* (New York: Thomas Nelson, 1971). American pottery marks: William C. Gates and Dana E. Ormerod, The East Liverpool Pottery District: Identification of Manufacturers and Marks, *Historical Archaeology* 16 (1982):1–2; Ralph M. and Terry H. Kovel, *Dictionary of Marks: Pottery and Porcelain* (New York: Crown, 1953); Arnold A. Kowalsky and Dorothy E. Kowalsky, *Encyclopedia of Marks on American, English, and European Earthenware, Ironstone, and Stoneware, 1780–1980* (Atglen, PA: Schiffer, 1999); and Erica Gibson, *Ceramic Makers' Marks* (Walnut Creek, CA: Left Coast Press, 2011). Books on maker's marks exist for many different classes of artifacts, many of them from small presses, often geared to antique collectors. One example is Malcolm A. Rogers, *American Pewterers and Their Marks* (Southampton, NY: Cracker Barrel Press, 1968).

Some popular books about consumption are Thomas Hine, *I Want That! How We All Became Shoppers* (New York: Perennial, 2002); Martin Lindstrom, *Buy-ology: Truth and Lies About Why We Buy* (New York: Broadway, 2010); and Rob Walker, *Buying In: What We Buy and Who We Are* (New York: Random House, 2008). Two good scholarly books are Ben Fine, *The World of Consumption: The Material and Cultural Revisited*, 2nd ed. (London: Routledge, 2002) and Roberta Sassatelli, *Consumer Culture: History, Theory and Politics* (Los Angeles, CA: Sage, 2007).

Specialist Literature

Allen, J. and J. Barber, A Seventeenth-Century Pottery Group from Kitto Institute, Plymouth. In *Everyday and Exotic Pottery from Europe, c. 650–1900: Studies in Honour of John G. Hurst*, D. Gaimster and M. Redknap (Eds.), pp. 225–254. (Oxford: Oxbow, 1992).

Becker, Carl L., What Are Historical Facts? *Western Political Quarterly* 7 (1955):327–340.

Cotter, John, *Archaeological Excavations at Jamestown Colonial National Historical Park*. (Washington, DC: National Park Service, 1958).

Deagan, Kathleen, *Spanish St. Augustine: The Archaeology of a Colonial Creole Community*. (New York: Academic Press, 1983).

Deetz, James F., Scientific Humanism and Humanistic Science: A Plea for Paradigmatic Pluralism in Historical Archaeology. *Geoscience and Man* 23 (1983):27–34.

Gradwohl, David M. and Nancy M. Osborn, *Exploring Buried Buxton: Archaeology of an Abandoned Iowa Coal Mining Town with a Large Black Population*. (Ames: Iowa State University Press, 1984).

Lehmer, Donald J., *Introduction to Middle Missouri Archaeology*. (Washington, DC: National Park Service, 1971).

Lief, Alfred, *A Close-Up of Closures: History and Progress*. (New York: Glass Container Manufacturers Institute, 1965).

Martin, Ann Smart, The Role of Pewter as Missing Artifact: Consumer Attitudes Toward Tablewares in Late 18th Century Virginia. *Historical Archaeology* 23, 2 (1989):1–27.

Monks, Gregory G., Architectural Symbolism and Non-Verbal Communication at Upper Fort Garry. *Historical Archaeology* 26, 2 (1992):37–57.

Orser, Charles E., Jr., *The Material Basis of the Postbellum Tenant Plantation: Historical Archaeology in the South Carolina Piedmont*. (Athens: University of Georgia Press, 1988).

Pendergrast, Mark, *For God, Country, and Coca-Cola: The Unauthorized History of the Great American Soft Drink and the Company that Makes it*. (New York: Scribner's, 1993).

Schlereth, Thomas J., Material Culture Studies in America, 1876–1976. In *Material Culture Studies in America*, Thomas J. Schlereth (Ed.), pp. 1–75. (Nashville: American Association for State and Local History, 1982).

Schulz, Peter D., Bill Lockhart, Carol Serr, and Bill Lindsey, Rim Codes: A Pacific Coast Dating System for Milk Bottles. *Historical Archaeology* 43, 2 (2009):30–39.

Shackel, Paul A., *Personal Discipline and Material Culture: An Archaeology of Annapolis, Maryland, 1695–1870*. (Knoxville: University of Tennessee Press, 1993).

Stewart-Abernathy, Leslie C., *The Moser Farmstead*. (Fayetteville, AR: Arkansas Archaeological Survey, 1986).

Thomas, David Hurst, Saints and Soldiers at Santa Catalina: Hispanic Designs for Colonial America. In *The Recovery of Meaning: Historical Archaeology in the Eastern United States*, Mark P. Leone and Parker B. Potter, Jr. (Eds.), pp. 73–140. (Washington, DC: Smithsonian Institution Press, 1988).

Chapter 9: Historical Archaeology and Cultural Resource Management

United States legislation appears in King, Hickman, and Berg's *Anthropology in Historic Preservation*, already cited, pp. 199–302, and in Philip Speser and Kathleen Reinburg, *Federal Archaeology Legislation: A Compendium, Vol. 4* (Washington, DC: Foresight Science and Technology, 1986).

Other important books about CRM archaeology and ethics are Donald L. Hardesty and Barbara J. Little, *Assessing Site Significance: A Guide for Archaeologists and Historians* (Walnut Creek, CA: AltaMira, 2000); Thomas F. King, Patricia Parker Hickman, and Gary Berg, *Anthropology in Historic Preservation: Caring for Culture's Clutter* (New York: Academic Press, 1977); Thomas F. King, *Thinking about Cultural Resource Management: Essays from the Edge* (Walnut Creek, CA: AltaMira, 2002); Thomas F. King, *Federal Planning and Historic Places: The Section 106 Process* (Walnut Creek, CA: AltaMira, 2000); Robin Skeates, *Debating the Archaeological Heritage* (London: Duckworth, 2000); Karen D. Vitelli (Ed.), *Archaeological Ethics* (Walnut Creek, CA: AltaMira, 1996); Larry J. Zimmerman, Karen D. Vitelli, and Julie Hollowell-Zimmer (Eds.), *Ethical Issues in Archaeology* (Walnut Creek, CA: AltaMira, 2003); and Francis P. McManamon, Andrew Stout, and Jodi A. Barnes, eds., *Managing Archaeological Resources: Global Context, National Program, Local Actions* (Walnut Creek, CA: Left Coast Press, 2008).

Two excellent examples of professional CRM reports, just from lower Manhattan, are: Charles D. Cheek and Daniel G. Roberts, eds., *The Archaeology of 290 Broadway,* 4 vols. (West Chester, PA: John Milner Associates, Inc., 2009), and Rebecca Yamin (Ed.), *Tales of the Five Points: Working-Class Life in Nineteenth-Century New York*, 7 vols. (West Chester, PA: John Milner Associates, 2000). Hundreds of similar reports exist (though not as large in most cases), and in the United States they are usually housed in the individual State Historic Preservation Offices.

Specialist Literature

Cooper, Anwen and Thomas Yarrow, "The Age of Innocence": Personal Histories of the 1960s "Digging Circuit" in Britain. *International Journal of Historical Archaeology* 16 (2012):300–318.

McGimsey, Charles R., III, "This, Too, Will Pass": Moss-Bennett in Perspective. *American Antiquity* 50 (1985):326–331.

McGuire, Randall H., *Archaeology as Political Action.* (Berkeley: University of California Press, 2008).

Information about the American Cultural Resources Association can be found at http://www. acra-crm.org/.

Chapter 10: Theory in Historical Archaeology

Articles dealing with the development of historical archaeology up to 1978 can be found in Schuyler's *Historical Archaeology,* mentioned above. Humanistic studies are Robert Ascher and Charles H. Fairbanks, Excavation of a Slave Cabin: Georgia, U.S.A., *Historical Archaeology* 5 (1971):3–17; William M. Kelso, *Kingsmill Plantations, 1619–1800: Archaeology of Country Life in Colonial Virginia* (Orlando, FL: Academic Press, 1984). More scientific studies include Stanley South, *Method and Theory in Historical Archaeology* (previously cited); Kenneth E. Lewis, *Camden: A Frontier Town in Eighteenth-Century South Carolina* (Columbia, SC: South Carolina Institute of Archaeology and Anthropology, 1976). Studies by Deetz are Material Culture and Worldview in Colonial Anglo-America, in Leone and Potter's *The Recovery of Meaning,* pp. 219–233, and his *In Small Things Forgotten* (both mentioned above). His much less structuralist book is *Flowerdew Hundred: The Archaeology of a Virginia Plantation, 1619–1864* (Charlottesville, VA: University Press of Virginia, 1993). Henry Glassie's book is *Folk Housing in Middle Virginia: A Structural Analysis of Historic Artifacts* (Knoxville, TN: University of Tennessee Press, 1975). Martin Hall's paper on Cape Town, South Africa, appears as Small Things and the Mobile, Conflictual Fusion of Power, Fear, and Desire, in *The Art and Mystery of Historical Archaeology: Essays in Honor of James Deetz,* Anne Elizabeth Yentsch and Mary C. Beaudry (Eds.), pp. 373–399 (Boca Raton, FL: CRC Press, 1992). Mark Leone's principal paper is: The Georgian Order as the Order of Merchant Capitalism in Annapolis, Maryland, in Leone and Potter's *The Recovery of Meaning,* pp. 235–261. His paper on Mormon fences is Archaeology as the Science of Technology: Mormon Town Plans and Fences, in *Research and Theory in Current Archaeology,* Charles Redman (Ed.), pp. 125–150 (New York: John Wiley and Sons, 1973). Also extremely useful is Paul A. Shackel's, *Personal Discipline and Material Culture,* mentioned above.

Specialist Literature

Hayes, Katherine Howlett, *Slavery Before Race: Europeans, Africans, and Indians at Long Island's Sylvester Manor Plantation, 1651–1884*. (New York: New York University Press, 2013).

Hodder, Ian, Interpretive Archaeology and Its Role. *American Antiquity* 56 (1991):7–18.

Leone, Mark P., Parker B. Potter, Jr., and Paul A. Shackel, Toward a Critical Archaeology. *Current Anthropology* 28 (1987):283–302.

Wilkie, Laurie A., Interpretive Historical Archaeologies. In *International Handbook of Historical Archaeology*, Teresita Majewski and David Gaimster (Eds.), pp. 333–345. (New York: Springer, 2009).

Chapter 11: The Historical Archaeology of Individuals and Social Groups

Class, ethnicity, gender, and race have generated a vast literature. The following are useful for our purposes: William C. McCready, *Culture, Ethnicity, and Identity: Current Issues in Research* (New York: Academic Press, 1983); H. Edward Ransford, *Race and Class in American Society: Black, Chicano, Anglo* (Cambridge, MA.: Schenkman, 1977); Peter I. Rose, *They and We: Racial and Ethnic Relations in the United States* (New York: Random House, 1981); and Stephen Steinberg's *The Ethnic Myth: Race, Ethnicity, and Class in America* (Boston, MA: Beacon Press, 1989). These books, and the sources they cite, give an ample introduction to the topic of social groups. Marvin Harris's definition comes from his introductory textbook *Culture, People, and Nature: An Introduction to General Anthropology*, 4th ed., (New York: Harper and Row, 1985).

Archaeological studies of gender can be found in Dale Walde and Noreen D. Willows (Eds.), *The Archaeology of Gender: Proceedings of the Twenty-Second Annual Conference of the Archaeological Association of the University of Calgary* (Calgary: University of Calgary, 1991), and in Cheryl Claasen (Ed.), *Exploring Gender Through Archaeology: Selected Papers from the 1991 Boone Conference* (Madison, WI: Prehistory Press, 1992). Archaeologists examining gender are making great strides, and students are encouraged to search their library databases for the most recent books.

Specialist Literature

Baugher, Sherene and Robert W. Venables, Ceramics as Indicators of Status and Class in Eighteenth-Century New York. In *Consumer Choice in Historical Archaeology*, Suzanne M. Spencer-Wood (Ed.), pp. 31–53. (New York: Plenum Press, 1987).

Baxter, Jane Eva, *The Archaeology of Childhood: Children, Gender, and Material Culture*. (Walnut Creek, CA: AltaMira Press, 2005).

———, The Archaeology of Childhood. *Annual Review of Anthropology* 37 (2008):159–175.

Brashler, Janet G., When Daddy was a Shanty Boy: The Role of Gender in the Organization of the Logging Industry in Highland West Virginia. *Historical Archaeology* 26, 4 (1991):54–68.

Bugarin, Flordeliz T., Constructing an Archaeology of Children: Studying Children and Child Material Culture from the African Past. In *Children in Action: Perspectives on the Archaeology of Childhood*, Jane Eva Baxter (Ed.), pp. 13–26. (Washington, DC: American Anthropological Association, 2006).

Church, Minette C., Jason Yaeger, and Jennifer L. Dornan, The San Pedro Maya and the British Colonial Enterprise in British Honduras. In *Enduring Conquests: Rethinking the Archaeology of Resistance to Spanish Colonialism in the Americas*, Matthew Liebmann and Melissa S. Murphy (Eds.), pp. 173–197. (Santa Fe, NM: School for Advanced Research Press, 2010).

Clark, Lynn, Gravestones: Reflections of Ethnicity or Class? In *Consumer Choice in Historical Archaeology*, Suzanne M. Spencer-Wood (Ed.), pp. 383–395. (New York: Plenum Press, 1987).

De Cunzo, Lu Ann, *Economics and Ethnicity: An Archaeological Perspective on Nineteenth Century Paterson, New Jersey*. PhD Dissertation, University of Pennsylvania, Philadelphia, 1983.

Edwards-Ingram, Y., African American Medicine and the Social Relations of Slavery. In *Race and the Archaeology of Identity*, Charles E. Orser, Jr. (Ed.), pp. 34–53. (Salt Lake City: University of Utah Press, 2001).

Gaulton, Barry C. and Tânia Manuel Casimiro, Custom-Made Ceramics, Transatlantic Business Partnerships, and Entrepreneurial Spirit in Early Modern Newfoundland: An Examination of the SK Vessels from Ferryland. *International Journal of Historical Archaeology* 19 (2015):1–20.

Greenwood, Roberta S., The Chinese on Main Street. In *Archaeological Perspectives on Ethnicity in America: Afro-American and Asian American Culture History*, Robert L. Schuyler (Ed.), pp. 113–123. (Farmingdale, NY: Baywood, 1980).

Hall, Martin and Stephen W. Silliman (Eds.), Introduction: Archaeology of the Modern World. In *Historical Archaeology*, pp. 1–19. (Malden, MA: Blackwell, 2006).

Kruczek-Aaron, H., Choice Flowers and Well-Ordered Tables: Struggling over Gender in a Nineteenth-Century Household. *International Journal of Historical Archaeology* 6 (2002):173–185.

Lima, Tania Andrade, The Dark Side of Toys in Nineteenth-Century Rio de Janeiro, Brazil. *Historical Archaeology* 46, 3 (2012):63–78.

Loren, Diana DiPaolo, *The Archaeology of Clothing and Bodily Adornment in Colonial America*. (Gainesville: University Press of Florida, 2010).

McEwan, Bonnie G., The Archaeology of Women in the Spanish New World. *Historical Archaeology* 26, 4 (1991):33–41.

Mullins, Paul R., *Race and Affluence: An Archaeology of African America and Consumer Culture*. (New York: Kluwer Academic/Plenum, 1999).

Orser, Charles E., Jr., (Ed.), *Race and the Archaeology of Identity*. (Salt Lake City: University of Utah Press, 2001).

———, *Race and Practice in Archaeological Interpretation*. (Philadelphia: University of Pennsylvania Press, 2003).

———, *A Primer on Modern-World Archaeology*. (Clinton Corners, NY: Percheron Press, 2014).

Otto, John Solomon, Race and Class on Antebellum Plantations. In *Archaeological Perspectives on Ethnicity in America: Afro-American and Asian American Culture History*, Robert L. Schuyler (Ed.), pp. 3–13. (Farmingdale, NY: Baywood, 1980).

Paynter, Robert, Steps to an Archaeology of Capitalism: Material Change and Class Analysis. In *The Recovery of Meaning: Historical Archaeology in the Eastern United States*, Mark P. Leone and Parker B. Potter, Jr. (Eds.), pp. 407–433. (Washington, DC: Smithsonian Institution Press, 1988).

Prangnell, Jonathan and Kate Quirk, Children in Paradise: Growing Up on the Australian Goldfields. *Historical Archaeology* 43, 3 (2009):38–49.

Rotman, Deborah, *Historical Archaeology of Gendered Lives*. (New York: Springer, 2009).

Rubertone, Patricia E., *Grave Undertakings: An Archaeology of Roger Williams and the Narragansett Indians*. (Washington, DC: Smithsonian Institution Press, 2001).

Saitta, Dean J., *The Archaeology of Collective Action*. (Gainesville: University Press of Florida, 2007).

Sando, Ruth Ann and David L. Felton, Inventory Records of Ceramics and Opium from a Nineteenth-Century Chinese Store in California. In *Hidden Heritage: Historical Archaeology of the Overseas Chinese*, Priscilla Wegars (Ed.), pp. 151–176. (Amityville, NY: Baywood, 1993).

Seifert, Donna J., Within Sight of the White House: The Archaeology of Working Women. *Historical Archaeology* 26, 4 (1991):82–108.

Shepherd, Steven J., Status Variation in Antebellum Alexandria: An Archaeological Study of Ceramic Tableware. In *Consumer Choice in Historical Archaeology*, Suzanne M. Spencer-Wood (Ed.), pp. 163–198. (New York: Plenum Press, 1987).

Voss, Barbara L., *The Archaeology of Ethnogenesis: Race and Sexuality in Colonial San Francisco*. (Berkeley: University of California Press, 2008).

Wilson, Kristin J. and Melanie A. Cabak, Feminine Voices from Beyond the Grave: What Burials Can Tell Us about Gender Differences among Historic African Americans. In *Engendering African American Archaeology: A Southern Perspective*, Jillian E. Galle and Amy L. Young (Eds.), pp. 263–285. (Knoxville: University of Tennessee Press, 2004).

Wurst, Lu Ann and Robert K. Fitts (Eds.), Confronting Class. *Historical Archaeology* 33, 1 (1999):1–195.

Wylie, Jerry and Richard E. Fike, Chinese Opium Smoking Techniques and Paraphernalia. In *Hidden Heritage: Historical Archaeology of the Oversees Chinese*, Priscilla Wegars (Ed.), pp. 255–303. (Amityville, NY: Baywood, 1993).

Chapter 12: Global Historical Archaeology and Modern-World Archaeology

Europe and the People without History by famed anthropologist Eric Wolf (Berkeley, CA: University of California Press, 1982) is a fundamental source for this chapter. A more popular account focusing on a variety of groups is Brian Fagan, *Clash of Cultures* (New York: W. H. Freeman, 1984). The sources used in preparing this chapter are:

Africa

DeCorse, Christopher R., *An Archaeology of Elmina: Africans and Europeans on the Gold Coast, 1400–1900*. (Washington, DC: Smithsonian Institution Press, 2001).

Hall, Martin, *Archaeology and the Modern World: Colonial Transcripts in South Africa and the Chesapeake*. (London: Routledge, 2000).

Jordan, Stacey C., Coarse Earthenware at the Dutch Colonial Cape of Good Hope, South Africa: A History of Local Production and Typology of Products. *International Journal of Historical Archaeology* 4 (2000):113–143.

Jordan, Stacey C. and Carmel Schrire, Material Culture and the Roots of Colonial Society at the South African Cape of Good Hope. In *The Archaeology of Colonialism*, C. L. Lyons and J. K. Papadopoulos (Eds.), pp. 241–272. (Los Angeles: Getty Research Institute, 2002).

Schrire, Carmel, The Historical Archaeology of the Impact of Colonialism in Seventeenth-Century South Africa. In *Historical Archaeology in Global Perspective*, Lisa Falk (Ed.), pp. 69–96. (Washington, DC: Smithsonian Institution Press, 1991).

———, Digging Archives at Oudepost I, Cape, South Africa. In *The Art and Mystery of Historical Archaeology*, Anne Elizabeth Yentsch and Mary C. Beaudry (Eds.), pp. 361–372. (Boca Raton, FL: CRC Press, 1992).

———, *Digging Through Darkness: Chronicles of an Archaeologist*. (Charlottesville: University Press of Virginia, 1995).

Schrire, Carmel, K. Cruz-Uribe, and J. Klose, The Site History of the Historical Site of Oudepost I, Cape. *South African Archaeological Society Goodwin Series* 7 (1993):21–32.

Schrire, Carmel and D. Merwick, Dutch-Indigenous Relations in New Netherland and the Cape in the Seventeenth Century. In *Historical Archaeology in Global Perspective*, L. Falk (Ed.), pp. 11–20. (Washington, DC: Smithsonian Institution Press, 1991).

Werz, B. E. J. S., Maritime Archaeological Project Table Bay: Aspects of the First Field Season. *South African Archaeological Society Goodwin Series* 7 (1993):33–39.

North America

Cantwell, Ann-Marie and Diana diZerega Wall, *Unearthing Gotham: The Archaeology of New York City*. (New Haven: Yale University Press, 2001).

Gilbert, A. S., G. Harbottle, D. DeNoyelles, A Ceramic Chemistry Archive for New Netherland/New York. *Historical Archaeology* 27, 3 (1993):17–56.

Huey, Paul R., Reworked Pipe Stems: A 17th Century Phenomenon from the Site of Fort Orange, Albany, New York. *Historical Archaeology* 8 (1974):105–111.

———, The Dutch at Fort Orange. In *Historical Archaeology in Global Perspective*, L. Falk (Ed.), pp. 21–67. (Washington, DC: Smithsonian Institution Press, 1991).

Janowitz, Meta F., Indian Corn and Dutch Pots: Seventeenth-Century Foodways in New Amsterdam/New York. *Historical Archaeology* 27, 2 (1993):6–24.

Peña, Elizabeth S., The Role of Wampum Production at the Albany Almshouse. *International Journal of Historical Archaeology* 5 (2001):155–174.

The Caribbean and South America

Huey, Paul R., Dutch Colonialism. In *The Encyclopedia of Historical Archaeology*, Charles E. Orser, Jr. (Ed.), pp. 161–164. (London: Routledge, 2002).

Menezes, J. L. M. and J. R. R. Rodrigues, *Fortificações Portuguesas no Nordeste do Brasil: Séculos XVI, XVII, e XVIII*. (Recife: Pool Editorial, 1986).

Orser, Charles E., Jr., Toward a Global Historical Archaeology: An Example from Brazil. *Historical Archaeology* 28, 1 (1994):5–22.

Orser, Charles E., Jr. and Pedro Paulo A. Funari, Archaeology and Slave Resistance and Rebellion. *World Archaeology* 33 (2001):61–72.

Asia

Gawronski, Jerz, VOC Shipwrecks. In *The Encyclopedia of Historical Archaeology*, Charles E. Orser, Jr. (Ed.), pp. 563–566. (London: Routledge, 2002).

Jörg, C. J. A., *The Geldermalsen: History and Porcelain*. (Groningen: Kemper, 1986).

Kist, J. B., Integrating Archaeological and Historical Records in Dutch East India Company Research. In *Maritime Archaeology: A Reader of Substantive and Theoretical Contributions*, L. E. Babits and H. Van Tilburg (Eds.), pp. 39–45. (New York: Plenum Press, 1998).

Miller, George L., The Second Destruction of the *Geldermalsen*. *Historical Archaeology* 26, 4 (1992):124–131.

Globalization

A huge literature exists, but a few goods sources to get started are:

Edelman, Marc and Angelique Haugerud (Eds.), *The Anthropology of Development and Globalization: From Classical Political Economy to Contemporary Neoliberalism*. (Malden, MA: Blackwell, 2005).

Hopkins, A. G. (Ed.), *Globalization in World History*. (London: Pimlico, 2002).

Inda, Jonathan Xavier and Renato Rosaldo (Eds.), *The Anthropology of Globalization: A Reader*. 2nd ed. (Malden, MA: Blackwell, 2007).

Ritzer, George, *The Globalization of Nothing 2*. (Thousand Oaks, CA: Pine Forge Press, 2007).

Modern-World Archaeology

Orser, Charles E., *An Historical Archaeology of the Modern World*. (New York: Plenum Press, 1996).

———, The Archaeologies of Recent History: Post-Medieval, Historical, and Modern-World. In *The Blackwell Companion to Archaeology*, John Bintliff (Ed.), pp. 272–290. (Oxford: Basil Blackwell, 2002).

———, *A Primer on Modern-World Archaeology*. (Clinton Corners, NY: Percheron Press, 2014).

Chapter 13: Historical Archaeology and the Past Today

Site visitation at Annapolis is covered in Mark Leone, Method as Message: Interpreting the Past with the Public, *Museum News* 62, 1 (1983):34–41, and in Parker B. Potter, Jr., *Public Archaeology in Annapolis: A Critical Approach to History in Maryland's Ancient City* (Washington, DC: Smithsonian Institution Press, 1994). An important statement of the program appears, with the comments of critics and supporters, in Leone, Potter, and Shackel, Toward a Critical Archaeology, mentioned above. A critique of the Carter's Grove slave quarters appears in Terrence W. Epperson's Race and the Disciplines of the Plantation, *Historical Archaeology* 24, 4 (1990):29–36.

An excellent starting point for learning about the political uses of archaeology is Peter Gathercole and David Lowenthal (Eds.), *The Politics of the Past* (London: Unwin Hyman, 1990). This book contains information about the Nazis' program of "archaeology," as well as information about the efforts of several indigenous groups to reclaim their histories. Also see Yannis Hamilakis and Philip Duke (Eds.), *Archaeology and Capitalism: From Ethics to Politics* (Walnut Creek, CA: Left Coast Press, 2007).

Site destruction, vandalism, and looting continue to constitute major problems for archaeology. For a starting point, see Ian Graham, Looters Rob Graves and History, *National Geographic* 169, 4 (1986):452–461; George E. Stuart, The Battle to Save Our Past, *National Geographic* 175, 3 (1989):392–393; Brian Alexander, Archaeology and Looting Make a Volatile Mix, *Science,* 250 (1990): 1074–1075; James Walsh, It's a Steal, *Time* 138, 21 (1991):86–88; Christopher B. Donnan, Archaeology and Looting: Preserving the Record,

Science 251 (1991): 498; Colin Renfrew, *Loot, Legitimacy, and Ownership: The Ethical Crisis in Archaeology* (London: Duckworth, 2000).

For controversies over artifact collecting, see Gillett B. Griffen, In Defense of the Collector, *National Geographic* 169, 4 (1986):462–465; and Colin Renfrew, Collectors are the Real Looters, *Archaeology* 46, 3 (1993):16–17.

For discussions of the relations between archaeologists and indigenous peoples, see Joe Watkins, *Indigenous Archaeology: American Indian Values and Scientific Practice* (Walnut Creek, CA: Altamira, 2000).

For job opportunities and training in historical archaeology, your best source is a professional archaeologist, but the website of the Society for Historical Archaeology is also a good source. A careful check of their website will provide useful information for students wishing to pursue a career in historical archaeology. A number of blogs also address issues related to having a career in archaeology.

The tourism guidelines created by the Archaeological Institute of America can be found at http://www.archaeological.org /tourism_guidelines. The Art Loss Register can be accessed at http://www.artloss.com/en.

Specialist Literature

Busch, Jane, An Introduction to the Tin Can. *Historical Archaeology* 15, 1 (1981):95–104.

Herrera, Alexander, Heritage Tourism, Identity, and Development in Peru. *International Journal of Historical Archaeology* 17 (2013):275–295.

Lee, Hyeong Woo, The Politics of Archaeology in North Korea: Construction and Deterioration of Toh's Knowledge. *International Journal of Historical Archaeology* 17 (2013):401–421.

Little, Barbara J., What Can Archaeology Do for Justice, Peace, Community, and the Earth? *Historical Archaeology* 43, 4 (2009):115–119.

McDonald, J. Douglas, Larry J. Zimmerman, A.L. McDonald, William Tall Bull, and Ted Rising Sun, The Northern Cheyenne Outbreak of 1879: Using Oral History and Archaeology as Tools of Resistance. In *The Archaeology of Inequality*, Randall H. McGuire and Robert Paynter (Eds.), pp. 64–78. (Oxford: Basil Blackwell, 1991).

Orser, Charles E., Jr., *Historical Archaeology at Marsh House (Residence Hill Site, 16IB130), Avery Island, Louisiana.* (Avery Island: Avery Island, Inc., 1987).

Sabloff, Jeremy A., *Archaeology Matters: Action Archaeology in the Modern World.* (Walnut Creek, CA: Left Coast Press, 2008).

Saitta, Dean J., *The Archaeology of Collective Action.* (Gainesville: University Press of Florida, 2007).

Shackel, Paul A. and Michael Roller, The Gilded Age Wasn't so Gilded in the Anthracite Region of Pennsylvania. *International Journal of Historical Archaeology* 16 (2012):761–775.

Stottman, M. Jay (Ed.), *Archaeologists as Activists: Can Archaeologists Change the World?* (Tuscaloosa: University of Alabama Press, 2010).

Index